Immigration
and the
American Tradition

THE AMERICAN HERITAGE SERIES

D1514391

The American Heritage Series

under the general editorship of
LEONARD W. LEVY *and* ALFRED F. YOUNG

Immigration
and the
American Tradition

Edited by

MOSES RISCHIN
San Francisco State University

THE BOBBS-MERRILL COMPANY, INC.

INDIANAPOLIS

For the American people
in the year of the
Bicentennial

The Bobbs-Merrill Company, Inc.
4300 West 62nd Street
Indianapolis, Indiana 46268

First Edition
First Printing 1976

Library of Congress Cataloging in Publication Data

Rischin, Moses
  Immigration and the American tradition.
  (The American heritage series, AHS-79)
  Bibliography: p. xi
  Includes index.
  1. United States—Immigration and emigration—History—Sources. I. Title
JV6450.156   323.73   75-19336
ISBN 0-672-60130-3 (pbk)

Contents

Foreword

Americans have a peculiar method of compartmentalizing history. On the one hand they recognize, sometimes boastfully, that America has been "a nation of many nations," settled by immigrants. But when American history is studied it usually is broken up into segments: political (which frequently comes first), economic, foreign policy, intellectual—in all of which the immigrants get lost. Or a separate study is made (usually in distinct courses) of the frontier, cities, labor, and more frequently nowadays, immigration. In standard textbooks immigrants usually are not considered until they become a national "problem" and an object of hatred and exclusion. More recently, in sympathetic works, they are recognized when they become "famous" and can be studied for their contributions to American life. However presented, the importance of immigration to the American tradition—and the enormity of the fact that more than forty-five million immigrants have come to these shores over three centuries—is lost, buried, or blurred.

This collection of documents will be of special interest to the growing number of Americans who are rediscovering their ethnic identities and are turning to history, either on their own or in formal courses on the ethnic experience. The book should also be of interest to any serious student of the American past. It will be difficult to put it down without an increased awareness of the way in which "immigrants" have shaped the history of American society, politics, reform, foreign policy, and popular culture, including the language. This is a collection in which Thomas Paine, Carl Schurz, Abraham Cahan, Reinhold Niebuhr, Louis Brandeis, Al Smith, and John F. Kennedy "fit" as part of both immigrant history and American history; and that, argues the editor, is the way it should be.

The editor, Moses Rischin, is uniquely equipped for his task. A scholar of American history, he is a specialist in the immigration story, particularly that of the American Jew. His teaching has taken him from Brandeis University in the East to San Francisco State University in the West. His book *The Promised City: New York's Jews, 1870–1914* is the indispensable work in its field, and he has been recognized by fellow scholars who have elected him president of the Immigration History Society. He has selected original sources in this volume not with the impossible goal of "covering" all ethnic groups but with the aim of illuminating what is representative of many.

This book is one of a series created to provide the essential primary sources of the American experience, especially of American thought. The American Heritage Series constitutes a documentary library of United States history, filling a need long felt among scholars, students, libraries, and general readers for authoritative collections of original materials. Some volumes illuminate the thought of significant individuals, such as James Madison or John Marshall; some deal with movements, such as the Antifederalist or the Populist; others are organized around special themes, such as Puritan political thought or American Catholic thought on social questions. Many volumes take up the large number of subjects traditionally studied in American history for which surprisingly there are no documentary anthologies; others pioneer in introducing new subjects of increasing importance to scholars and to the contemporary world. The series aspires to maintain the high standards demanded of contemporary editing, providing authentic texts, intelligently and unobtrusively edited. It also has the distinction of presenting pieces of substantial length which give the full character and flavor of the original. The American Heritage Series is, we believe, the most comprehensive and authoritative of its kind.

Alfred F. Young
Leonard W. Levy

Selected Bibliography

The immigration myth and its relationship to the American tradition has in this generation skyrocketed into an unprecedented full-scale historical reassessment of the ethnic dimensions of American life. "The immigrants *were* American history," as Oscar Handlin has put it so famously. The vitality, wealth, and sweep of the historical literature that has been generated as a result of this new historical self-consciousness can merely be suggested here for at some point virtually every aspect of the American experience intersects with the saga of immigration and its consequences. To begin, it is essential to identify the key bibliographical guides that have become available for the first time in the last few years. Indispensable are the bibliographical essays "Race and Nationality in American History" that significantly comprise the opening section in William H. Cartwright & Richard L. Watson, Jr., eds., *The Reinterpretation of American History and Culture* (Washington, D.C.: National Council for the Social Studies, 1973): Robert F. Berkhofer, Jr., "Native Americans and United States History;" John W. Blassingame, "The Afro-Americans: From Mythology to Reality;" Rudolph J. Vecoli, "European-Americans: From Immigrants to Ethnics;" Rudolfo Acuna, "Freedom in a Cage: The Subjugation of the Chicano in the United States;" and Roger Daniels, "The Asian American Experience." Part 20, "Immigration and Ethnicity," in the revised edition of the monumental *Harvard Guide to American History* (Cambridge: Harvard University Press, 1974), 2 vols., edited by Frank Freidel is especially useful as are many of the related special subject bibliographies. Readily available are the American Historical Association booklets *The Peopling of America: Perspectives on Immigration* (Washington: American Historical Association, 1972) by Franklin D. Scott, *Religion in America: History and Historiography* (Washington: American Historical Association, 1973) by Edwin S. Gaustad as well as Chapter 14, "Encounters with Evidence," in the revised edition of *The Uprooted* (Boston: Little Brown, 1973) by Oscar Handlin and the bibliography in Handlin's *A Pictorial History of Immigration* (New York: Crown Publishers, 1972). An important resource for the more advanced student is *Immigrants and Their Children in the United States: A Bibliography of Doctoral Dissertations, 1892–1973* (Philadelphia: Balch Institute, in press) compiled by William Hoglund who lists nearly 1500 titles in history and thirty other fields.

Some basic works with which every student ought to be familiar are Rowland T. Berthoff, *An Unsettled People: Social Order and Disorder in American History* (New York: Harper and Row, 1971); Wesley F. Craven, *The Legend of the Founding Fathers* (New York: New York University Press, 1956); Marcus Lee Hansen, *The Atlantic Migration* (Cambridge: Harvard University Press, 1940) and *The Immigrant in American History* (Cambridge: Harvard University Press, 1940); Oscar Handlin, *The Uprooted, The American People in the Twentieth Century* (Cambridge: Harvard University Press, 1954), and *Race and Nationality in American Life* (Boston: Little Brown, 1957); John Higham, *Strangers in the Land* (New Brunswick, N.J.: Rutgers University Press, 1955) and *Send These to Me: Jews and Other Immigrants in Urban America* (New York: Athenaeum, 1975); Maldwyn A. Jones, *American Immigration* (Chicago; University of Chicago Press, 1960); Winthrop Jordan, *White over Black: American Attitudes toward the Negro, 1550–1812* (Chapel Hill: University of North Carolina Press, 1968); Philip A. M. Taylor, *The Distant Magnet: European Emigration to the U.S.A.* (New York: Harper & Row; 1971); Brinley Thomas, *Migration and Economic Growth: A Study of Great Britain and the Atlantic Economy.* 2d ed. (Cambridge, Eng.: Cambridge University Press, 1973), and Carl Wittke, *We Who Built America.* Rev. ed. (Cleveland: Western Reserve University Press, 1964).

Stimulating recent works are Josef Barton, *Peasants and*

Strangers: Italians, Rumanians and Slovaks in an American City, 1890–1950 (Cambridge: Harvard University Press, 1975); Carla Bianco, *The Two Rosetos* (Bloomington, Ind.: Indiana University Press, 1975); Robert H. Billigmeier, *Americans from Germany: A Study in Cultural Diversity* (Belmont, Calif.: Wordsworth, 1974); John E. Bodnar, ed., *The Ethnic Experience in Pennsylvania* (Lewisburg: Bucknell University Press, 1973); John D. Buenker, *Urban Liberalism and Progressive Reform* (New York: Charles Scribner's, 1973); Dennis Clark, *The Irish in Philadelphia: Ten Generations of Urban Experience* (Philadelphia: Temple University Press, 1973); John Cogley, *Catholic America* (New York: Dial Press, 1973); Adrian Cook, *The Armies of the Streets* (Lexington: University of Kentucky Press, 1974); George Dargo, *Jefferson's Louisiana: Politics and the Clash of Legal Traditions* (Cambridge: Harvard University Press, 1975); Allen Davis and Mark Haller, eds., *The Peoples of Philadelphia* (Philadelphia: Temple University Press, 1973); David B. Davis, *The Problem of Slavery in the Age of Revolution: 1770–1823* (Ithaca: Cornell University Press, 1975); Lawrence B. Davis, *Immigrants, Baptists, and the Protestant Mind in America* (Urbana, Ill.: University of Illinois Press, 1973); J. L. Dillard, *Black English: Its History and Usage in the United States* (New York: Random House, 1972); Henry L. Feingold, *Zion in America* (New York: Hippocrene Books, 1974); Donald Fleming and Bernard Bailyn, eds., "Dislocation and Emigration: The Social Background of American Immigration," *Perspectives in American History*, vol. 7 (1973), a thematic volume with essays on Britain, Scotland, Wales, Austria-Hungary, Greece, Switzerland, Germany, and Mexico by Maldwyn A. Jones, Malcolm Gray, Alan Conway, Johan Chmelar, Theodore Saloutos, Leo Schelbert, Wolfgang Kollmann, Peter Marschalk, and Arthur F. Corwin, respectively is followed in vol. 9 (1975) with an essay "Immigration of Russian Jews to the United States" by Simon Kuznets, E.R.R. Green, and Rudolph J. Vecoli; Saul S. Friedman, *No Haven for the Oppressed: United States Policy Toward Jewish Refugees, 1938–1945* (Detroit: Wayne State University Press, 1973); Richard Gambino, *Blood of My Blood: The Dilemma of the Italian American* (New York: Doubleday, 1974); Eugene D.

Genovese, *Roll, Jordan, Roll: The World That Slaves Made* (New York: Pantheon Books, 1974); Rudolf Glanz, *Jew and Italian* (New York: Ktav, 1971) and *Studies in Judaica Americana* (New York: Ktav, 1970); Victor Greene, *For God and Country: The Rise of Polish and Lithuanian Ethnic Consciousness in America, 1860–1910* (Madison, Wisc.: State Historical Society of Wisconsin, 1975); John S. Haller, *Outcasts from Evolution: Scientific Attitudes of Racial Inferiority* (Urbana, Ill.: University of Illinois Press, 1971); Abraham Hoffman, *Unwanted Mexican-Americans in the Great Depression: Repatriation Pressures, 1929–1939* (Tucson, Arizona: University of Arizona Press, 1974); H. Stuart Hughes, *The Sea Change: The Migration of Social Thought, 1930–1965* (New York: Harper & Row, 1975); Kristian Hvidt, *Flight to America* (New York: Academic Press, 1975); James B. Lane, *Jacob A. Riis and the American City* (Port Washington, N.Y.: Kennikat Press, 1974); Richard M. Linkh, *American Catholicism and European Immigrants* (Staten Island, N.Y.: Center for Migration Studies, 1975); Harold C. Livesay, *Andrew Carnegie and the Rise of Big Business* (Boston: Little Brown, 1975); James Loewen, *The Mississippi Chinese between Black and White* (Cambridge: Harvard University Press, 1971); Frederick C. Luebke, *Bonds of Loyalty, German-Americans and World War One* (DeKalb, Ill.: Northern Illinois University Press, 1974); Gary B. Nash, *Red, White, and Black: The Peoples of Early America* (Englewood Cliffs, N.J.: Prentice-Hall, 1974); Joseph P. O'Grady, *How the Irish Became Americans* (New York: Twayne Publishers, 1973); Thomas M. Pitkin, *Keepers of the Gate: A History of Ellis Island* (New York: New York University Press, 1975); Diane Ravitch, *The Great School Wars: New York City, 1805–1973* (New York: Basic Books, 1974); Richard Sallett, *Russian-German Settlements in the United States*, tr. by Lavern J. Rippley and Armand Bauer (Fargo: North Dakota Institute for Regional Studies, 1974). Dorothy Burton Skårdall, *The Divided Heart: Scandinavian Immigrant Experience through Literary Sources* (Lincoln: University of Nebraska Press, 1974); Stephan Thernstrom, *The Other Bostonians* (Cambridge: Harvard University Press, 1973); Silvano M. Tomasi, *Piety and Power: The Role of the Italian Parishes in the*

New York Metropolitan Area 1880–1920 (Staten Island, N.Y.: Center for Migration Studies, 1975); David B. Tyack, *The One Big System* (Cambridge: Harvard University Press, 1974); Melvin I. Urofsky, *American Zionism from Herzl to the Holocaust* (New York: Doubleday, 1975); Wilcomb E. Washburn, *The Indian in America* (New York: Harper & Row, 1975); Robert H. Wiebe, *The Segmented Society* (New York: Oxford University Press, 1975); Peter Wood, *Black Majority* (New York: Alfred A. Knopf, 1974).

ORIGINAL SOURCES

Three immigration reprint series include the best of the older historical and sociological literature and serve as derivative accounts, contemporary history and sources for the period in which they were written: *American Immigration Collection* (New York: Arno Press), 72 vols.; *The American Immigration Library* (New York: Jerome S. Ozer), 30 vols.; and *Americanization Studies* (Montclair, N.J.: Patterson Smith), 10 vols. The United States Immigration Commission, *Report* (New York: Arno Press), 42 vols., first published in 1911, provides a detailed record of early twentieth-century attitudes to every phase of immigration. In addition the Arno Press has published a number of special-subject series, making readily accessible scores of out-of-print volumes that shed light on various phases of the immigrant experience. *Black Studies Program, The Irish Americans, The Italian American Experience, The Mexican American, The Modern Jewish Experience, The Puerto Rican Experience* and *Religion in America*, as well as *American Labor* and *The Rise of Urban America* are particularly valuable.

One-volume source collections include the following: John J. Appel, ed., *The New Immigration* (New York: Pitman, 1971); Oscar Handlin, ed., *Immigration as a Factor in American History* (Englewood Cliffs, N.J.: Prentice-Hall, 1959); Oscar Handlin, ed., *The Children of the Uprooted* (New York: George Braziller, 1966); Cecilye S. Neidle, ed., *The New Americans* (New York: Twayne, 1967); and Thomas C. Wheeler, ed., *The Immigrant Experience* (New York: Dial, 1971).

Editor's Note and Acknowledgments

The publication of *Immigration and the American Tradition* on the occasion of the American Bicentennial is especially opportune. After a time of troubles, it is important that we be reminded of the sources of the nation's strength as well as its weaknesses. Appropriately, the American Issues Forum Bicentennial program developed by the National Endowment for the Humanities and cosponsored by the American Revolution Bicentennial Administration has chosen the theme of this text to open its nation-wide discussion of the issues and ideals that have been central to the nation's history.

To include as wide a variety of selections as possible so as to do justice to the all-embracing theme, *Immigration and the American Tradition*, is the challenge of this collection. Clearly, other scholars would have chosen different documents, stressed different themes, and indeed provided perhaps an interpretation of the role of immigration as an ideal and as a reality (in shaping American attitudes and possibilities) at variance with my own.

Aware at all times as I have been of the unique histories of each ethnic and racial group, I have made no deliberate effort to balance the ticket in the selection of documents at the expense of the integrity of common themes. The pan-ethnic scope of the subject has compelled me to select those documents that best exemplify strategic topics central to an understanding of the larger American experience in which all groups have shared. This will satisfy no ethnic group but hopefully will stir and stimulate all to a greater awareness of the epic and often tragic but ever hopeful experiment that has been America.

Immigration to America rooted as idea and reality in Bible and

Reformation, Enlightenment and Revolution, has extended to every feature of American life—to Europe, to Africa, and to Asia in America, to labor and culture conflict, to two world wars, to the vision of a world of free nations and a fear of world cataclysm, to racism and the shaping of a new American culture, to the recasting of Americans as symbols, and to the renewal of the vital sources of the nation's liberal ideals. The problems of culture, of human relations, of the texture and quality of life, of clash and accommodation, are the heritage of the classic nation of immigrants. The documents selected were chosen to illustrate both the triumphs and defeats, the good tensions and the bad.

Throughout original spelling and punctuation have been retained. Brackets indicate a change, addition or explanation. To conform to space limitations, I have had at times to abridge documents drastically, but never at the expense of their integrity or coherence. Ellipses indicate where cuts have been made.

I am thankful to Professor Alfred F. Young for his acute editorial counsel. I am grateful to Helene Whitson of the San Francisco State University Library for her relentless aid in locating documents, to Diane Litchfield, Joan Ovalle, and Lorraine Whitemore and her staff for cheerfully putting their expert typing services at my disposal, and finally to Ruth who has been at my side and to Sarah, Abigail, and Rebecca in the wings.

Introduction

America's most celebrated woman stares out on upper New York Bay. At the east end of Liberty Island (Bedloe's Island until 1956), and southwest of the now-deserted immigration station at Ellis Island, stands Auguste Bartholdi's 151-foot sculpture, perched atop a 142-foot granite and concrete pedestal. Silhouetted by New York's skyline, the figure of *Liberty Enlightening the World* portrays Liberty as a lady stepping forward from the broken shackles of tyranny: in her right hand she holds uplifted a flaming torch, in her left a tablet representing the Declaration of Independence, inscribed "July 4, 1776."

A gift from France, it was originally intended to commemorate the centennial of "the alliance of two nations in achieving the independence of the United States of America," a testimony to "their abiding friendship." But generations of immigrants have since transformed the monument into a symbol for one of the nation's oldest traditions: that of asylum.[1] In the present era of limited immigration and mass air travel, the "Mother of Exiles" no longer welcomes "huddled masses yearning to breathe free." But some ten miles away, at Kennedy International Airport's vast terminal on Jamaica Bay, latter-day newcomers are still greeted by a plaque with the famous lines from Emma Lazarus's sonnet to the New Colossus, a continuing reminder of one of the nation's most inspiring myths.[2]

1. On September 26, 1972, the American Museum of Immigration at the base of the Statue of Liberty National Monument was dedicated.

2. Frederic Auguste Bartholdi, *The Statue of Liberty Enlightening the World* (Philadelphia: F. L. Maule, 1885), *passim*; John Higham, "Emma Lazarus, The New Colossus, 1883," *An American Primer*, ed. Daniel J. Boorstin (Chicago: University of Chicago Press, 1966), vol. I, pp. 458–62; Oscar Handlin, *Statue of Liberty* (New York: *Newsweek*, 1971), pp. 14–29, 50–66.

In the land of immigrants, the freedom to migrate has acquired a transcendence unique in the history of nations. Since 1607 nearly 50 million people have come to the present United States in the largest migration in recorded history. Over 35 million of these immigrants migrated between 1815 and 1920, when the new American republic welcomed more strangers to its shores than did all other nations combined.[3] Indeed, the freedom to migrate was inseparable from the pursuit of liberties that made the nineteenth century the most inspiring in human history for the common men of Europe.

Freedom and nationalism—one and inseparable, expanding across the continent—promised to reach deeply into society and loosen the bonds of tradition, class, and empire. In so many ways, the era of the great migration was both cause and effect of the shaking up of European society, and it was inseparable from the ideological revolutions set in motion by the America of 1776 and the France of 1789. Exploding populations, expanding foreign markets, freer—if not free—trade, international merchant marine competition, internationalized banking and finance, and—above all—a hundred-year peace in the Western world all combined to set ideal terms for an "era of free trade in people"[4] that progressively embraced all of Europe.

The United States became the classic country of immigration. By the mid-nineteenth century, it had expanded from thirteen original states bunched along the Atlantic seaboard into a vast two-ocean transcontinental empire. Its distant unsettled regions and burgeoning agricultural and industrial belts became a lodestone for the peoples of Europe, as well as for its native-born. Out of this magnificent new bounty, its colonial heritage, and the tens of millions of European newcomers and their progeny, a new

---

3. 1,000,000 is the figure usually given for the migrations before 1776; 300,000 is the estimate for the subsequent four decades. Demographers have recently become extremely conservative in their estimates of total net immigration for the nineteenth and twentieth centuries, setting it as low as 35,500,000 for the years 1790 to 1970.

4. Marcus L. Hansen, *The Atlantic Migration 1607–1860* (Cambridge: Harvard University Press, 1940), pp. 3–12; Marcus L. Hansen, *The Immigrant in American History* (Cambridge: Harvard University Press, 1940), p. 5.

United States was created, an experiment in liberty and democracy without precedent in world history.

Almost at every turn, the immigrant's experience seemed to exemplify the inherently problematic relationship between the ways of this new and freer nation—composed of immigrants and former colonials, "conceived in liberty and dedicated to the proposition that all men are created equal"—and those of the old nations, from where the new Americans had originated, and where feudal traditions and habits survived intact. Freedom and order, change and tradition, America and Europe inevitably were juxtaposed, as the old society accorded the new the tribute that mass immigration, of necessity, imposed. Since the eighteenth century, an awareness of the overseas experiment had led enlightened Europeans to view America as the world's future hope. ". . . The vague aspirations of Europeans toward a new society were given solidity by the concrete appearance of the world of tomorrow in the thirteen colonies. The fortunes of the many thousands who sailed from Europe to seek a new homeland, with all their fears and hopes, had become part of the stream of consciousness of those who were left behind. . . ." [5] Only the coerced African immigration (that led Samuel Johnson to charge that the loudest yelps for liberty came from slave drivers) and the expelling of aboriginal Indians to the barren western plains continued to cast a long shadow over the dream of redemption.

But the European parameters of the liberal spirit were also tested, for the American heirs of the Reformation identified liberty with Protestantism and shared an acute hostility to pre-Reformation Europe and its representatives. These attitudes were to condition libertarian ideals during the great migration, when—for the first time—Catholics became numerous in the

5. Michael Kraus, *The Atlantic Civilization: Eighteenth Century Origins* (Ithaca: Cornell University Press, 1949), p. 220; cf. Robert R. Palmer, *The Age of the Democratic Revolution, v. I: The Challenge* (Princeton: Princeton University Press, 1959), 185 ff., 545–46; Jacques Godechot, *France and the Atlantic Revolution of the Eighteenth Century, 1770–1796* (New York: Free Press, 1965), pp. 42 ff. Also see Antonello Gerbi, *The Dispute of the New World: The History of a Polemic, 1750–1900*, revised and enlarged edition trans. by Jeremy Moyle (Pittsburgh: University of Pittsburgh Press, 1973).

United States. Long before the spectre of class struggle and social revolution came to haunt Americans, the phantom of "Papism" loomed in the minds of many and seemed to threaten the sovereignty, identity, and assumptions of the new republic. In the nineteenth century, American exceptionalism—wedded to an evangelical sectarianism that rejected all vestiges of hierarchical Europe and Rome, its historic center—crystallized into a Protestant crusade that jeopardized the nation's libertarian myth. Stirred to fear and hysteria, Americans in the name of liberty yielded to the spirit of repression and intolerance that they so passionately condemned in the older nations. Yet, recurrent nativist crises failed to shut the gates until 1921, when world war and revolution seemed to leave no alternative. Free immigration then came to a close, and the nineteenth-century ethos that had made it possible seemed spent.

The nineteenth-century pattern of unrestricted free immigration was a product of international forces and conditions that had been virtually unknown earlier. Although the English mainland colonies differed radically from those of France, the Netherlands, Portugal, and Spain, not until the American Revolution was the principle of liberty canonized before all the world as peculiarly and pre-eminently American. It was the logical outcome of English tutelage and a mounting sense of independence calling for nationhood; both creed and deed were spelled out with a finality and persuasiveness that left no doubt that the American experiment in freedom would have almost immediate world-wide repercussions.[6] In the great migration era, the great democratic experiment was to be tested repeatedly by all the tensions that continue to be the price of freedom in a complex society.

Exodus

In its mythic thrust, colonial America anticipated the nation of immigrants, as its covenant theology opened a path to later

6. Howard Mumford Jones, *O Strange New World* (New York: Viking Press, 1964), especially Ch. VIII, "The Radical Republic." See John Higham, "Immigration," in *The Comparative Approach to American History*, ed. C. Vann Woodward (New York: Basic Books, 1968), pp. 91–92.

democracy. The ideology of the American Reformation—pervaded by a sense of religious election and an urge to independence—subsequently fused with that of the enlightenment to generate the prime rhetoric and ethos of the new nation. The crossing of the Atlantic by the first immigrants provided the great baptismal; like the fording of the Red Sea by the ancient Israelites, it was the initial step out of European captivity, an experience to be re-enacted continuously and dramatically by subsequent newcomers to American shores.[7] All strangers in the land of promise, they recapitulated in lesser or greater degree William Bradford's venture across "a sea of troubles" and bore witness to the impulse to liberation that was migration (see Document 1). Cotton Mather's latter-day explication of "the *Wonders of Christian Religion*, flying from the depravations of Europe, to the American strand . . . ," proclaimed a more complex continuing bond to the old world for the settlers of Massachusetts Bay than did the Plymouth governor for the Mayflower voyagers (see Document 2). But taken together, Bradford and Mather gave classic utterance to their commitment to the founding of a new, more perfect society uncontaminated by the vices of the old but borne up by its virtues.

If, by later standards, the theology and polity of colonial New England appear narrow and drab, the margin for individual liberty slim, and the immigration policy parochial, the New England utopia—by the religious measure of the seventeenth century—was fraught with a sense of mission that was to contribute profoundly to the psychology of the Yankee nation and to the welcome accorded tens of millions of immigrants. It was to contribute, as well, to a sense of self-righteousness that could easily deteriorate into suspicion and fear and the repression of those who were different and could not or would not conform.

New Men and Old

By the mid-eighteenth century, the outlines of a new nation

7. See Perry Miller, *Nature's Nation* (Cambridge: Harvard University Press, 1967), pp. 6–8.

were discernible on the Atlantic shore. From New Hampshire to Georgia, the American colonies—relatively free of European feudal traditions—were participating vigorously in the American counterpart of the European enlightenment. Of America's originality in the world of nations, a new American who ever remained an old Frenchman could write with romantic admiration and assurance out of his own experience, "The American is a new man, who acts on new principles; he must therefore entertain new ideas, and form new opinions." But as a man of the old world no less than the new, Hector St. John de Crèvecoeur, not unlike Cotton Mather almost a century earlier, affirmed a dual mission for new Americans that committed them to extend the old European civilization westward, as well as to offer a model of new possibilities for Europe to the east. "Americans are the western pilgrims, who are carrying along with them that great mass of arts, sciences, vigour, and industry which began long since in the east; they will finish the great circle" (see Document 3).

Crèvecoeur's romantic vision of mutuality between the old world and the new acquired an unintended intensity as the French Revolution followed on the heels of the American. The heights and depths that the cause of liberty entailed in an era of world conflict were exemplified best in the life and writings of Thomas Paine (1737–1809). The fresh contagion of American citizenship in polyglot Pennsylvania (see Document 4), sparked by a cosmopolitan missionary zeal, spurred this English Quaker immigrant to a dedication to the cause of liberty in America, England, and France unmatched by any other compatriot. Unlike Crèvecoeur, the author of *Common Sense* not only saw America as the unique "asylum for the persecuted lovers of civil and religious liberty from every part of Europe" but acknowledged no limits to the American mission. That premier celebrant and publicist of liberty and revolution was to inspire generations of Americans, both native-born and immigrant, who also aspired to become friends of mankind. But the vicissitudes of politics, an uncompromising pen, imprisonment in Paris during the French Revolution, and an inability to adjust to everyday affairs left the indefatigable pamphleteer isolated and disillusioned. In 1796 in a well-known letter, Paine bitterly assailed the first President of the United States for betraying the ideals of the American Revolution.[8] In despair over the failure of the American promise, Paine made no allowance for his country's urge to self-preservation in a world at war.

In the closing years of the American Revolution, America's emissaries abroad already were receiving countless inquiries from Europeans interested in going to the new United States. Indeed, had peace prevailed, the Treaty of Paris might well have launched the great migration that had appeared imminent despite prevailing European governmental restrictions. In 1782, to discourage the wrong people from migrating, Benjamin Franklin, Minister to France and envoy extraordinary, framed a widely distributed statement succinctly describing both the general conditions of the new country and its social philosophy (see Document 5). Franklin's successor in Paris echoed his sentiments and shared in his cautions to emigrants. "If they come of themselves," wrote Thomas Jefferson in his *Notes on Virginia*, published in 1785, "they are entitled to all the rights of citizenship; but doubt the expediency of inviting them by extraordinary encouragements. . . ."[9]

From the very beginning, the image of America as a sanctuary for Europe's oppressed was a critical element in the shaping of the nation's consciousness, inseparable from its vision of itself if it was to be worthy of the "opinions of mankind." On a number of occasions before becoming president of the new republic, George Washington gave eloquent expression to the idea of the United States as asylum and refuge (see Document 6). American traditions of natural rights assured the eligibility of the foreign-born for all political offices in the republic, except that of president. Even that office, according to Article I, Section Two of the Constitution, was open to a foreigner who was "a citizen of the United

8. Philip Foner, ed., *Complete Writings of Thomas Paine* (New York: Citadel Press, 1945), vol. 2, p. 691.

9. A. A. Lipscomb and A. E. Bergh, eds., *The Writings of Thomas Jefferson: Memorial Edition* (Published under the auspices of Thomas Jefferson Memorial Association, Washington, 1903), II, p. 121.

States, at the time of the adoption of this Constitution," provided that person "shall . . . have attained to the age of thirty-five years and been fourteen years a resident within the United States." In 1790 the nation's first naturalization act stipulated that only a two-year residence would be required for the conferral of citizenship. This law underlined the active commitment of the United States to the right of expatriation, a principle which the leading immigrant-receiving country in the world was the first to formulate and to champion.

With the close of the Napoleonic wars, mass immigration to the United States became a reality for the first time. On the threshold of the great migration that would soon reach flood tide, American immigration policy was given its first formal expression. In an era in which an assertive new nationalism came to overshadow an earlier cosmopolitanism, Secretary of State John Quincy Adams reasserted earlier commitments to free unassisted immigration with equal rights for all but without privileges for any. He insisted as well, however, that immigrants "must cast off the European skin never to resume it" (see Document 17). His categorical statement setting forth the spirit of America's immigration policy and voicing the American consensus neatly complemented the Monroe Doctrine, for which he was in great part responsible. The one welcomed the people of Europe to American shores provided they severed all ties with the old world; the other banned the extension of the European "system" to the Western hemisphere, insisting on a hands-off policy by European governments so that the old world would not threaten the new from without no less than from within. The "errand into the wilderness" undertaken by the first Adams in the first great migration to New England was reflected nearly two centuries later in the policies of Monroe's secretary of state, which reaffirmed the superiority of the new world to the old.

Europe: Specter and Hope

In the generations after 1776, the emulation of the American revolutionary example by the aggrieved peoples of Europe flattered the new nation. Henry Grattan, famed Anglo-Protestant leader of the Irish Volunteers, acclaimed it "the only refuge of the liberties of mankind." But for a quarter of a century following the outbreak of the French Revolution, France succeeded the United States as the new herald of a more compelling revolution that accelerated American libertarian impulses, while at the same time appearing to threaten American sovereignty. The excesses of the French Revolution and international war for a time seemed to jeopardize all liberties, including the liberty to emigrate. But the Alien and Sedition Acts, directed ostensibly against French foreign agents during the war hysteria of 1798 proved an aberration. Upon his election, the new president, Thomas Jefferson, reaffirmed the American tradition of asylum for the oppressed and the repressive laws were allowed to lapse.

No more fitting tribute to the transatlantic tradition of revolution and its ambiguities was the formal invitation by Congress in January, 1824, to the Marquis de Lafayette (1757–1834) to visit the United States, assured by President James Monroe that "the whole Nation . . . ardently desires to see you again among them." Celebrated as a hero of the American Revolution and the apostle of liberty in two hemispheres, Lafayette now became a symbol of unity and reaffirmation in a nation increasingly torn by factionalism and sectionalism, as it approached the fiftieth anniversary of its founding. Indeed, everything about him seemed symbolic. "The Marquis spoke English as readily as French; his children, Virginia and George Washington Lafayette, spoke English and sang American songs; two American Indian boys were part of his household; an engraved copy of the Declaration of Independence hung on the wall of his study in one side of a double frame, the other side empty, 'waiting for the declaration of rights of France.' Washington was his god, the Declaration of Independence his Bible. It was a sacrilege, he said, 'to mention any day as the beginning of the year but the blessed 4th of July'." [10] Accompanied by his son, George Washington Lafayette, he toured every

10. Merrill D. Peterson, *Thomas Jefferson and the New Nation: A Biography* (New York: Oxford University Press, 1970), p. 316; cf. Anne C. Loveland, *Emblem of Liberty: The Image of Lafayette in the American Mind* (Baton Rouge: Louisiana State University Press, 1971).

one of the twenty-four states in the union in the course of his trip
of over a year although he had initially intended to visit only the
original thirteen states. At Monticello, he fell tearfully into the
arms of an aged Jefferson, friend and comrade of two great
revolutions and all their vicissitudes in the course of nearly half a
century (see Document 9).

Throughout the nineteenth century the tide of revolution
continued unabated as the old order recoiled in the face of
demands for constitutional government and individual rights. The
era of repression that followed the Congress of Vienna appeared
but an interlude in the universal acceptance of the promise of
American liberty and equality heralded by Greek independence
and pending revolt. When the heady days of 1848 dawned, all
Europe seemed on the brink of a new era, its problems as
amenable to solution as those of the United States.[11]

Yet the righteous conviction that the American faith would
prevail both at home and abroad was accompanied by anxiety and
distrust. Cultures regarded as hostile to the American impulse
were especially suspect. Most intense was the historic Protestant
fear that the immigration of Catholics might bring, and indeed
had already brought, all the evils and dispositions of Europe's
autocracies that could not be purged in the Atlantic crossing and
that would bring disaster upon America and its institutions.

This historic prejudice was best exemplified in the career and
writings of Samuel F. B. Morse, who became alarmed by New
York's turbulent democracy in the throes of mass migration (see
Document 9). To this extremely self-conscious American, just
returned from a European sojourn, the solution appeared self-evident: Immigration laws ought to be enacted that would curtail the
rights of immigrants to participate in American politics, and thus
the riot and disharmony that appeared to threaten the American

11. Cf. Michael Kraus, "America and the Irish Revolutionary Movement in the
Eighteenth Century," in R. B. Morris, ed., *The Era of the American Revolution*
(New York: Columbia University Press, 1939), p. 346; Owen D. Edwards, "The
American Image of Ireland: A Study of Its Early Phases," *Perspectives in American
History* (Cambridge, Mass.: Harvard University Press, 1970), vol. IV, 199 ff.;
Halvdan Koht, *The American Spirit in Europe* (Philadelphia: University of
Pennsylvania Press, 1949).

experiment would be thwarted at its source. Otherwise, America's first major anti-Catholic pamphleteer warned—citing chapter and verse from Thomas Jefferson's writings, unrestricted European immigration would have dire consequences for the nation. "Voluntary Citizens," however, mustered eloquent defenders (see Document 12) who contested the assumptions of the nativist. On a more primitive anti-Catholic plane, the *Awful Disclosures of Maria Monk* catered to the sex-obsessed fantasies of Protestants who were convinced that international Jesuit conspiracies, both obscene and subversive, lurked behind every convent door and beneath every carnival tent (see Document 10).

But on balance, decadent Europe was always disposed to hope. Revolution appeared ever imminent. At mid-century, American public opinion proved unflaggingly sympathetic to European peoples aspiring to republicanism, national self-determination, and unity, even when not quite modeled on the American pattern. The spirit of '76 still stirred in the hearts of Americans; they were as sensitive to revolts against tyranny then as they had been to revolts in Greece, Poland, and South America earlier. Indeed, the modern world's first democracy seemed pledged to seek out and support potential ideological allies wherever they might be found.

In 1848 the fall of Louis Philippe in France set off paroxysms of rejoicing throughout the United States, marked by meetings, banquets, demonstrations, and torchlight parades. In that year, the American government sent to the quixotic Frankfort Parliament its minister in Berlin, accompanied by a distinguished naval captain who, had things gone differently, might have helped found a strong German fleet. Two years later, Secretary of State Daniel Webster defended the dispatch of an American emissary to the rebelling Hungarians and gratuitously tweaked the Hapsburg nose. "The power of this republic at the present moment, is spread over a region one of the richest and most fertile on the globe, and of an extent in comparison with which the possessions of the house of Hapsburg are as but a patch on the earth's face." In 1851 an American naval vessel brought "the general representative of liberty in Europe," confined in Turkey, to the United States, where tumultuous crowds acclaimed Louis Kossuth as the

personification of the Hungarian revolution. Again, in the final
months of his life, Webster spoke eloquently for the principle of
the self-determination of nations (see Document 12) and, to the
displeasure of the Austrian charge d'affaires, in the famous
Hülsmann letter insisted on the propriety of his revolutionary
address.[12]

The appearance of *Uncle Tom's Cabin* riveted attention on the
slavery question to the virtual exclusion of all else and cooled the
Kossuth excitement. Yet dedicated German and other political
refugees continued to cling to visions of a transatlantic manifest
destiny. "Young Germany" at home and in exile shared a
nationalistic, democratic, and expansionist élan, which readily
erupted into visions of a "United States" of Europe or of the
world. *The New Rome; or The United States of the World*, a
chimerical book outlined in 1852 by a German immigrant in a
speech in Wheeling, Virginia, at a congress of German revolutionary societies, left no doubt that in an era of great German
expectations and heavy German immigration, the United States
loomed forth more than ever as the nation manifestly destined to
free the world. Indeed the transatlantic co-authors of *The New
Rome* also saw in their collaboration a felicitous reversal in
German and American habits of thought, a happy omen that
presaged the coming-together of two worlds.[13]

Although little given to ecumenical visions, Carl Schurz (1829–
1906), more than any other American of the mid-nineteenth
century, was personally implicated in the cause of freedom both
at home and abroad. Despite his meteoric public career, for many
years Schurz held to the hope that his energetic participation in
American politics would permit him in some way to fulfill his

12. Arthur J. May, *Contemporary American Opinion of the Mid-Century-Revo-
lutions in Central Europe* (Philadelphia: University of Pennsylvania Press, 1927), p.
122; *The Writings and Speeches of Daniel Webster*, 18 vols. (Boston: Little,
Brown, 1903), vol. 14, p. 503.
13. Carl Wittke, *Refugees of Revolution: The German Forty-Eighters in
America* (Philadelphia: University of Pennsylvania Press, 1952), pp. 102–05; cf.
Réne Rémond, *Les États-Unis devant L'Opinion Française 1815–1852* (Paris:
Libraire Armand Colin, 1962), II, 853–54; Theodore Poesche and Charles Goepp,
The New Rome; or The United States of the World (New York, 1853).

commitment to liberate his beloved homeland (see Document 13). Indeed, on the eve of his election to the United States Senate from Missouri in 1868, he wrote to his fellow Forty-eighter and beloved teacher, Gottfried Kinkel: "The temptation to return to the old fatherland has this time been particularly enticing. . . ." [14] But this echo from the past proved to be a parting gesture. The triumph of what Schurz called "True Americanism" (see Document 15) over native Americanism in his great speech at Boston's Faneuil Hall left no doubt that this gifted son of two continents had committed his libertarian impulses and political gifts to a nation represented by Abraham Lincoln (see Document 14) and not to one dominated by a Prussian sympathizer to slaveholders. In the age of Bismarck, the sober Schurz could not be tempted down the pathways of Thomas Paine. In postwar America, he would continue to pursue the logic of mid-nineteenth century liberalism. Schurz would become renowned as an advocate of civil service, Indian reform, sound money, conservation, anti-imperialism, and international peace. But the divisive new problems of an industralized America during the latter decades of Schurz's life evaded his grasp.

The "Labor" Question

In the late nineteenth and early twentieth centuries the United States beckoned ever more strongly to potential immigrants as the arc of immigration extended northward, southward, and eastward. But industrialization increasingly created problems unanticipated by the nation's democratic ideology. On the heels of the regional agricultural slavery that had come close to destroying the United States, there arose an industrial neo-feudalism that especially affected the latest immigrants. The increasing polarization between native Americans and immigrants, capital and labor, the privileged and unprivileged, seemed to divest formal politics of relevance. The inability of the American people and their institutions to confront urban and industrial problems in terms of

14. Carl Schurz to Gottfried Kinkel, *Intimate Letters of Carl Schurz*, ed. Joseph Schafer (Madison, Wisc.: Wisconsin Historical Collections, 1928), vol. XXX, p. 425.

their own democratic assumptions weakened confidence in the magical powers of American ideals and institutions to cope with radical economic and cultural change.

Yet the evils of rampant individualism in an industrializing and urbanizing society were slow to gain recognition in a nation which clung to Jeffersonian values and sentiments. Nationalism and individualism had become inseparable and synonymous with Americanism and patriotism.[15] Beyond this national consensus lay the unpalatable "labor question" or "social question" linked inevitably to immigrant and foreign influences that might be best ignored or repressed. If this meant a spiritual and ethical decline from the nation's professed ideals that spelled catastrophe, so be it.

For over half a century, labor would fight an uphill battle to dissociate itself from un-Americanism and to acquire status within the American value system. In the 1930s, the coming of age of American labor signalled the beginning of a new era of acceptance. The cessation of mass immigration and the coalescence of "old" and "new" immigrants as allies of the new welfare state, pre-eminently American in its auspices and mandate, gave status and prestige to immigrant labor traditions that had been slow to gain recognition earlier. Irish, German, and Jewish labor traditions, especially those that had been associated with violence, subversion, anarchism, and socialism, became the naturalized crusaders of the new liberalism. As a matter of course, Samuel Gompers, Terence Powderly, P. J. McGuire, Walter Reuther, Sidney Hillman, David Dubinsky, and George Meany gained a respectability that seemed unimaginable earlier.

For three generations, however, from the 1870s on, the labor movement had appeared to be not an ally of liberty and a generator of social vitality but a perennial threat to the American verities smuggled from abroad in immigrant chests. In the 1870s mayhem in the coal fields sparked by the Molly Maguires had become associated in the popular mind not with economic tyranny and a need for social justice but with labor and Irish

15. Yehoshua Arieli, *Individualism and Nationalism in American Ideology* (Cambridge: Harvard University Press, 1964), p. 332 ff.

conspiracies to undermine the whole social order (see Document 16). "Not until the ominous figure of the foreign-born radical displaced him did the Molly depart the public mind; it took Catholics even longer to forget him. Some he roused to a new social consciousness, but most he compelled to draw back momentarily from a labor movement, one episode of which had reflected so disastrously on the respectability of Catholics." [16]

In the 1880s the Haymarket trial indelibly impressed the image of the foreign anarchist (see Document 17) upon the public mind and raised tragic doubts regarding the viability of democracy in an industrial society. The Haymarket executions, the meteoric rise and fall of the Knights of Labor, and the seeming futility of labor organization encouraged sensitive immigrants to embark on a labor crusade to cure the ills of their adopted land. To Abraham Cahan, a young Russian immigrant just seven years in the country, the centennial of the inauguration of the first president of the United States (1889) seemed not an occasion for celebrating American progress but a time for lamenting the poverty of American democracy (see Document 18). A former Russian revolutionary, Cahan was to devote his long life to the editorship of the *Jewish Daily Forward*, which became the largest and most influential labor and socialist daily in the world (see Document 19). The *Forward* profoundly influenced and reflected the social mind of three generations of America's Jews. In the process it became a mainstay of labor organization and a mainspring for the social reform that culminated in the age of Roosevelt. With the recognition of labor's right to organize and bargain collectively, mass organization of industrial workers, and federal social legislation that became the cornerstone of the welfare state, two successive generations of labor leaders helped impress a new social ethic upon the nation.[17]

16. James E. Roohan, "*American Catholics and the Social Question 1865–1900*" (Doctoral dissertation, Yale University, 1952), pp. 183–84; cf. Wayne G. Broehl, Jr., *The Molly Maguires* (Cambridge: Harvard University Press, 1964).

17. Moses Rischin, "From Gompers to Hillman: Labor Goes Middle Class," *Antioch Review* XIII (Summer, 1953): 191–201; Moses Rischin, "The Jewish Labor Movement in America: A Social Interpretation," *Labor History* IV (Fall, 1963): 227–47.

Yellow Peril and White

The era that saw the rise of labor and class consciousness also saw not only the re-emergence of ethnic and religious tensions but of race tensions as well, particularly in the state of California, where for the first time Pacific immigrants appeared on American soil in significant numbers to compete with American and Atlantic immigrant labor. San Francisco's Angel Island was not destined to rival New York's Castle Garden or its successor, Ellis Island, as a receiving station for immigrants. The first Asians to pass through the Golden Gate were to become victims of the first exclusionist legislation in the nation's history.

The gold rush attracted a myriad of newcomers to California, among them a few Chinese merchants, who were soon followed by thousands of indentured servants employed first in the gold mines, then in the building of railroads and, in time, in manufacturing industries. By 1880 there were over 100,000 Chinese in the United States, the great majority of them in California.

Initially, Chinese immmgrants were welcomed, but as early as 1852, the Foreign Miner's Tax was enacted and applied almost exclusively against the Chinese. For the next quarter of a century, the California legislature repeatedly attempted to exclude the Chinese, only to be frustrated by the federal courts. During the depressed 1870s, however, anti-Chinese sentiment raged. Unemployed laborers were inflamed by the "Chinese Must Go!" exhortations of Dennis Kearney of the Workingmen's Party and other demagogues. Violence resulted, along with a renewed demand for exclusion of the Chinese. Latent anti-Chinese sentiment (see Document 20) coalesced with extreme doubts as to the ability of Americans to accommodate to non-whites of any kind (see Document 21)—American Indians, Blacks, or Chinese. In 1882 Congress responded. "The coming of Chinese laborers to this country," began the Chinese Exclusion Act somewhat disingenuously, "endangers the good order of certain localities." The first piece of federal legislation to debar immigrants from the

United States on the grounds of race or nationality, the law forbade the immigration of Chinese laborers for ten years and explicitly prohibited the naturalization of all Chinese. Renewed in 1892, the law was extended indefinitely thereafter.

Chinese exclusion paved the way for the subsequent debarring of the Japanese and all other Asians and contributed as well to crystallizing the sentiment that would logically lead to general immigration restriction. To fears of labor competition and race mixing now was added a fear of Asia's most rapidly westernizing nation and America's Pacific naval rival. The Gentlemen's Agreement of 1907 that singled out Japanese immigrants for virtual exclusion especially distressed Sidney Gulick, an American Protestant missionary with over three decades of service in Japan. Ironically, despite Gulick's ingenious efforts (see Document 22) to fashion quota immigration legislation that would not separate out Asians for exclusion, the immigration law of 1924 denied even token admission to Japanese and other Asians. The Supreme Court's decision declaring Japanese, as well as Hindus, ineligible for naturalization confirmed the dominant mood.

World War as Civil War

Fear of non-European immigration and its consequences reflected the extreme anxieties that surged through American society in the late nineteenth and early twentieth century when confronted by an increasingly heterogeneous population. Its climax came during the First World War. The "world war of races," in John R. Commons's phrase, divided the nation along ethnic lines as did no other war in its history. In the decades immediately preceding the war, immigration reached its apex, accounting for well over half the newcomers of the nineteenth century. At no time in that century was the proportion of Americans of recent immigrant stock so high, their variety so great, their cultures so baffling as it was in the early twentieth century, when immigration averaged one million a year.

In the face of a European Armageddon, ex-Europeans could not quite be expected to attain neutrality of thought. "Immigration to

America suddenly stopped when the oppressed and the oppressing races of our immigrants began depopulating each other by violence and starvation. . . ." [18] Most severely shocked were Americans of German origin. "For . . . millions of German-Americans, it is the bitterest tragedy. The ground on which they stood trembled and broke: abysses are around them. Their daily companions have turned into their persecutors, their intimate friends into their adversaries . . . ," [19] lamented a famed Harvard psychologist of German birth. With a status and prestige that ranked them ahead of all others, the most numerous non-British ethnic group in America registered confusion and dismay at the cruel turn of events. Prosperous, industrious, varied in their skills, they seemed more suited to America's needs, more fraternal in their aspects and origins than any other group. Americans had long admired German cultural accomplishments and in a world progressively dominated by science and technology looked to German models of excellence (see Document 23). For well over half a century, ambitious young Americans had attended German institutions of higher learning almost exclusively.

World War I shattered confidence in everything German, proving nearly fatal for German cultural life. "German culture, which had given many of the best impulses to American life through half a century, is suddenly nothing but an object of ridicule." [20] All foreign-sounding Americans fell under suspicion, all foreign speakers appeared sinister, all foreign languages appeared subversive (see Document 25). Virtually everything alien became anathema. Symphony and opera, song and dance festivals, hamburgers and frankfurters, all seemed to border on the treasonous. Although German-Americans stoically endured their unpopularity, the price was high, the hurt deep (see Document 24).

World War II, coming nearly a generation after free immigra-

18. John R. Commons, *Races and Immigrants in America*, 2nd ed. (New York: Macmillan, 1920).

19. Hugo Münsterberg, *The Peace and America* (New York: D. Appleton, 1915), pp. 264–65.

20. *Ibid.*, p. 270.

tion had come to a close, affected the nation's ethnics far less intimately than did World War I. German culture and language, newspapers and other institutions had failed to recover from the ravages of the First World War, from the natural attrition that followed, and from the ultra-assimilative urge of Americans of German origin. Furthermore, the American image of Nazi Germany was decisively ideological rather than cultural, its totalitarianism a naked threat to all civilization that could not be blinked and that left little margin for pro-German sentiment or divided loyalties. But as John Hawgood has written, "German America lived through the decade of the 1930s in and out of the shadow of the Swastika, and that decade had therefore, been disturbed and chaotic instead of a calm period of settling down after earlier storms." More so than any other large group of Americans, German America succumbed to isolationism, ever wary of another fratricidal war that would pit them against the Fatherland.[21] Yet no man sensed more deeply the tragedy that had overtaken the homeland of his ancestors and the Nazi threat to mankind than did the distinguished Christian theologian, Reinhold Niebuhr (see Document 26). "Christians in Germany will face the terrible alternative of either willing the defeat of their nation in order that Christian civilization may survive, or willing the victory of their nation, and thereby destroying civilization," [22] wrote the brilliant young German theologian, Dietrich Bonhoeffer, to Niebuhr, his host in New York, in July, 1939, when he refused asylum in the United States to return to Germany to combat absolute evil and to be martyred in the cause of liberty.

By contrast with World War I, World War II incited relatively little provocation for the suppression of civil liberties. Indeed, President Franklin Roosevelt made amply clear the distinction between American and Nazi ideals (see Document 27), while a notable federal judge took the opportunity offered by an "I Am

21. John A. Hawgood, *The Tragedy of German-America* (New York: G. P. Putnam's, 1940), pp. 301–02; Ray Billington, "The Origins of Middle Western Isolationism," *Political Science Quarterly* LX (March, 1945): 44–64.

22. Dietrich Bonhoeffer, *The Years of Decision Letters, Lectures, Notes 1935–1939* (New York: Harper & Row, 1966), p. 246.

An American Day" festival to stress how problematic were all liberties when the spirit of liberty was absent from the hearts of men (see Document 28). The treatment of one group, however, blemished the American record. That group was singled out for an ostracism without precedent in the nation's history. On December 7, 1941, the surprise attack on Pearl Harbor aroused unparalleled hostility against Japanese-Americans, who were hysterically condemned as a collective menace to America's Pacific defense system. Executive Order 9066, issued by President Franklin Roosevelt on February 19, 1942, led to the forcible evacuation of over 100 thousand Japanese-American men, women, and children from the West Coast. Their detention in ten isolated relocation centers made vivid the extreme prejudice against non-European peoples that conditioned the habits and colored the perceptions even of liberal Americans. The plea by Japanese-Americans that they be judged individually as were other Americans coming from enemy lands and not be prejudged on racial grounds gained little sympathy (see Document 29). Despite the nation's later repudiation of this wartime act against Japanese-Americans that betrayed all Americans, it has been difficult for some non-whites to entirely discredit the possibility that the World War II episode may yet become a precedent for action against them in a future crisis.

The Self-Determination of Nations

Yet even as racist thinking reached its logical outcome in law and public opinion, the two world wars seemed to vindicate the liberal promise of national self-determination, the first primarily in Europe and the second around the globe. The peace treaties drawn up after World War I extended the right of nationhood to Europe's minorities, thus fulfilling the American revolutionary tradition. With the break-up of the German, Austro-Hungarian, Turkish, and Russian empires, the rising expectations of Europe's minorities were realized, particularly those minorities strongly represented among America's immigrants of the late nineteenth and early twentieth century. Paradoxically, World War I and its aftermath, so devastating to minority rights in the United States, encouraged immigrants to aid and support their overseas brethren and to undertake, as well, the liberation of their homelands beneath the banner of American democracy.

Initially, President Woodrow Wilson's call for self-determination for Europe's minorities had not anticipated national independence. But his Fourteen Points, more than any other single document, sanctioned a universal sentiment for ethnic and cultural self-determination that logically culminated in political independence. The redrawn map of Europe vividly reflected the new ethnic dimension, most especially in central, eastern, and southeastern Europe and the Middle East. As empires and emperors were toppled, to be replaced by republics and presidents and an occasional constitutional monarch, the American revolutionary prototype seemed everywhere in the ascendant. The American nation of immigrants, especially the latest self-conscious immigrant minorities, in conjunction with their overseas brethren had looked to the American president to transform the old world into a new one and to validate their migration as well as the spirit of '76 (see Document 31). Unlike the Czechs, the Croats, the Poles, the Slovaks and others, two major ethnic groups could not directly effect the restoration of their historic homelands through the peace settlements. The Irish (see Document 32) and the Jews (see Document 30) were forced to pursue their objectives in the war's aftermath. The Irish Free State established in 1924 and the State of Israel founded in 1948 would owe much to American support. Although the Great Crusade fell short of its goals and Europe and America drew apart in the years between the two great wars, the principle of self-determination was not seriously contested, even if the wisdom of its application was often doubted in the years ahead.

Beyond Europe, the logic of self-determination did not attain fulfillment until after World War II. In the 1920s, Marcus Garvey's abortive Universal Negro Improvement Association offered to uprooted blacks in America's great northern cities (see Document 33) the promise of an independent Africa. After World War II, with the triumph of the anti-colonial movements and the dissolution of Europe's great overseas empires, that promise became a reality. By then, the League of Nations, primarily a league of European nations, had been succeeded by the United Nations, a league overwhelmingly of non-European nations with over twice the League's membership. As a result of the recognition of the historic African continent and the creation of new African states, Americans of African origin found themselves the beneficiaries of a growing sense of cultural parity with Americans of European origin. With the restoration of their sense of a pre-American past, American blacks could identify with the immigration tradition and share both personally and vicariously in a larger sense of history that was not limited to the era of American slavery.

World Revolution

A new world of nations arose in Europe in the wake of World War I, inspired in great part by the American model. But the liberal euphoria already had been shattered and the Great Crusade derailed by the scourge of xenophobia, the specter of world revolution, and the rumblings of an abortive peace. A century and a quarter earlier, the French Revolution, followed by a generation of international war, had contributed to the consolidation of the new nation and had set the stage for the great migration. Now, a sense of diminished opportunities in industrial America and the world-wide challenge of the Bolshevik Revolution, especially apparent after the founding of the Communist International in March, 1919, helped polarize a nation less assured of its identity and brought the epic migrations to a close.

The Red Scare, coupled with the most decisive paroxysm of nativism in the nation's history, cast a pall of subversion over non-Anglo-America. The restriction of immigration, with the application of a rigid racist quota system, the rise of the Ku Klux Klan, and the enforcement of the Prohibition amendment were all indictments against immigrant America. As a consequence, national dilemmas of morality, religion, culture, and international relations were ascribed to foreign conspirators and their immigrant agents. Deportation, expulsion, and suppression, whatever the cost to the traditions of the nation, followed as a matter of course.

Those immigrants most conspicuously associated with Europe's upheaval, particularly with the Russian Revolution, were especially suspect. Most vulnerable were immigrants from old Russia —now the Soviet Union—so many of whom were Jews. Where earlier Jewish immigrants had been viewed compassionately as victims of barbaric Tsarist pogroms, or admiringly as heroes of revolution, now they were identified with the Bolsheviks, their excesses, their ideology of world revolution and their potential threat to the American republic. In a time of fear and disenchantment, the myth of a world Jewish conspiracy plotted by "the International Jew" to dominate Christian civilization acquired widespread currency (see Document 34), especially through the agency of the credulous American folk hero, Henry Ford.[23] Equally vulnerable to charges of un-Americanism and radical extremism were Italian immigrants. The most numerous of recent newcomers, they had become identified in the popular mind with criminal and anarchist tendencies inimical to all government. The appearance, associations, ideas, and alleged deeds of Nicola Sacco and Bartolemeo Vanzetti seemed proof enough of their guilt (see Document 35). Clearly the melting pot had not melted. Fomenters of world revolution and anarchy from southern and eastern Europe distinctly came of national stocks congenitally unsuited to an orderly democratic society. Legislation that would limit the entry of their kind into the United States now seemed urgent.

Restriction and Race

Despite recurrent waves of nativism, the idea of America as a refuge for Europe's oppressed and the belief that upon migration Europeans would become new men was sustained throughout most of the nineteenth century. The passage of the Chinese Exclusion Act of 1882, however, had foreshadowed a reversal of the American tradition of free immigration. That law had implications not only for immigration from Asia but, as would soon become apparent, for immigration from Europe as well. The

23. Norman Cohn, *Warrant for Genocide: The Myth of the Jewish World-Conspiracy and the Protocols of the Elders of Zion* (New York: Harper & Row, 1967), pp. 25 ff.

law of 1882 would prove the harbinger of a concerted movement for the restriction of immigration that would stress racial homogeneity as essential for the national unity of the American people and the survival of its democratic ideals and institutions (see Document 36).

Within a decade, immigrants from southern and eastern Europe would be stereotyped as "new" immigrants and contrasted with mythical "old" immigrants from northern and western Europe. Between 1896, when the first literacy test bill was introduced in Congress, and 1924, when permanent immigration restriction became the law of the land, the "new" immigration was subjected to continuous scrutiny by investigators eager to demonstrate the unsuitability of people of inferior race for admission to the United States. Thousands of pages of the *Congressional Record*, the 42-volume *Report of the United States Immigration Commission*, and other special studies emphasized the dire threat that unrestricted immigration presented to the country. Much energy, ingenuity, arrogance, and race theory would be expended to bring free immigration to a close.

The literacy test, the first device selected to restrict immigration from Europe, was introduced in Congress in 1896 and endorsed later that year by the Republican party platform. Henry Cabot Lodge, the bill's chief sponsor, made clear its purpose: "The races most affected by the illiteracy test are those whose emigration to the country has begun in the last twenty years and swelled rapidly to enormous proportions, races with which the English-speaking people have never hitherto assimilated, and who are most alien to the great body of people in the United States." [24] Roundly debated by both houses before being passed, the literacy bill was vetoed by President Cleveland on the grounds that it radically departed from American tradition. Two decades later, just before the United States entered World War I, the literacy test bill became law over the objections of President Woodrow Wilson (see Document 37). Although the law failed to achieve the

24. Quoted in Philip Taylor, *The Distant Magnet* (New York: Harper & Row, 1971), p. 244.

immediate curtailment of immigration that had been anticipated, it proved the wedge and cornerstone for a total reversal of the American tradition of free immigration. Designed to restrict immigration from southern and eastern Europe where the literacy rate was low, the law projected a principle of group selection that was to become the postulate underlying the immigration legislation of the 1920s.

Between May 29, 1921, when President Harding signed the first bill in the nation's history limiting European immigration and July 1, 1929, when the national origins plan went into effect, the new immigration restriction policy of the United States was debated and hammered out. The temporary law of 1921 inaugurating the quota system limited immigration to 3 percent of the number of foreign-born of each European nationality living in the United States in 1910. The permanent law of 1924 reduced the annual quota from 355,000 to 150,000 and changed the base year to 1890, radically reducing the proportion of immigrants from southern and eastern Europe and decisively committing the United States to a policy of racial homogeneity and limited immigration. The 1924 law also provided for the adoption of a national origins quota system, as soon as it was feasible, based on the ethnic composition of the whole population in 1920 that would for the first time include everybody's ancestors. By taking careful account of people of colonial stock in assigning quotas, the proportion of immigrants from southern and Eastern Europe was reduced even further while the proportion of immigrants from England was increased (see Document 38). For the next four decades, the law of the land with its quotas would blatantly reflect the prejudices and fears of important segments of Anglo-Saxon old America—intimidated by urban and industrial change, threatened in its culture and folkways by the felt presence of exotic ethnics, and unnerved by the totalitarian defiance that succeeded the old order and undercut America's basic assumptions regarding its historic role.

The Dilemmas of a New Culture

The confrontation at so many points between an older and a newer America reflected significant change in the composition of the American people. In the early twentieth century, when the United States stood on the threshold of a major cultural upheaval, the nation's population included a higher proportion of immigrants and their children than at any time in the country's history. These latest comers accounted for nearly half of the whole white population and as late as 1930 numbered almost 39 million Americans. Still many millions more in all regions except the South were attuned to the ethos of their immigrant forebears. A myriad of churches, cultural groups, fraternal societies, theaters, and newspapers exposed everyday America to the customs of many lands. Foreign-language dailies, weeklies, and monthlies were circulated in three dozen languages and reached more than ten million readers. More than all other institutions, these journals served as transmitters of culture and information, shoring up old world traditions even as they promoted American ways.

Yet the role of immigrant traditions had always been ambiguous, its viability problematic at best. American public policy did not provide for the integration of a many-sided European culture. John Quincy Adams's dictum—"They must cast off the European skin never to resume it"—made no allowance for cultural complexity and an expansively pluralistic society. The dilemmas of civilization and personality generated in every immigrant heart and home did not lend themselves to resolution or even to formulation (see Document 39). Acculturation proceeded apace. Each group moved at its own rate and according to its own style. Each individual proceeded at his own tempo. Each wave of immigrants was succeeded by another and by their native-born sons and daughters bent on amnesia and eager to comply with American expectations. The repressions of World War I and its aftermath decisively undermined the immigrant cultures, hastened their obsolescence, and intensified their rejection. For a brief time, in reaction to repression, the newer ethnics developed a self-consciousness that enhanced their status, generating among some intellectuals visions of a culturally pluralistic America. This envisioned America was to be the complement and counterpart of an emergent new Europe of new, autonomous, and self-determined small nations. But the disequilibrium among the many immigrant and regional American subcultures only accentuated the passion for conformity. In 1910, over 8 million people spoke German, a proportion of non-English speakers unmatched by any other ethnic group. Yet the German mother tongue so dear to Carl Schurz and his compatriots (see Document 40) was only the most conspicuous casualty among the European languages. The restriction of immigration soon accelerated the erosion of the newer immigrant cultures even as the successes of the immigrant press, as much as their failures, insured their demise.[25]

The sense of cultural malaise that perpetually gripped immigrant America reached its climax in the 1920s. By then cultural revolution, which proved no less devastating to the genteel Anglo-American tradition, had come into full swing. Symptomatic was the popularity of Henry L. Mencken, embattled critic of Anglo-Saxondom, mock-apostle of German culture, and self-appointed celebrant of the polyglot sectors that official America rejected. During the war, Baltimore's most vehement Germanophile had kept silent. But after the Armistice, Mencken persuaded the twenties to embrace him as its most civilized jester, insurgent youth, and literary oracle and guide. Month after month, in infectious prose, he scalped the Puritans, denied Anglo-Americans any claim to culture or civilization, and hailed the coming of age of the true Americans of "alien smell" who would liberate the nation from its barbarisms, shams, and provincialisms. Amidst prohibition, political repression, ethnic and religious prejudice, and racist immigration restriction laws, Mencken, in "a first sketch of the living speech of these States" (see Document 43), celebrated a multi-cultural America. *The American Language*, denounced upon publication as "a work . . . overambitiously designed as a wedge to split asunder the two great English-speaking peoples," soon became an American classic, while Mencken's barbs and sallies in the *Smart Set*, the *American Mercury*, and the *Prejudices* series proved tonic to a generation revolting against the village and the blight of raw materialism and conformity.[26]

25. Albert Parry, "Goodbye to the Immigrant Press," *American Mercury* XXVIII (January, 1933): 56 ff.
26. H. L. Mencken, *The American Language* (New York: Alfred Knopf, 1919),

The simultaneous eclipse of the immigrant and the genteel cultures opened the way for the emergence of a new urban mass culture that had long been in ferment. In the latter decades of the nineteenth century, in the popular press and on theater, music hall, and vaudeville stages, Anglo-America and immigrant America had groped toward a common ground even as continuous massive immigration promoted further fragmentation. With the coercive Americanization of the war years and after, the children of immigrants turned compulsively to the novel cultural modes projected by the motion picture, the radio, and the tabloids for the amalgam that would stamp American approval upon them and dissociate them from their parents without directly demanding the surrender of their cultural identity. Origins, language, religion, and race thus were transcended without quite being erased, resulting in a loose-jointed new cultural idiom. Diverse European folk and American regional styles blended into cultural expressions conditioned by the mass media and the mass society.

More than a generation earlier, a Bohemian composer had commemorated the four-hundredth anniversary of the discovery of America by incorporating Negro plantation melodies into his *Symphony from the New World*. So much the European folklorist, Anton Dvořak had found the most authentic American idiom in Negro spirituals, the American equivalents of the mournful Slavic folksongs of his native land. But the new world symphony was to be anything but pastoral and symphonic, for in the 1920s the jazz contagion seized the great cities and carried everything before it. Everyone was doing it. Harlem reigned supreme as the hub of the Black Renaissance; from New Orleans bordellos, ragtime and the blues had become the new hallmark of urban American artistic culture. After Paul Whiteman's premier jazz concert at New York's Aeolian Hall early in 1924—featuring George Gershwin at the piano in his own *Rhapsody in Blue*—affixed the jazz signature to high culture, there was no curbing the magic of the new craze. Three years later, the film *The Jazz Singer*, with Al Jolson, took the

---

p. ix; Stuart P. Sherman, *The Americans* (New York: Charles C. Scribner's, 1922), p. 10.

nation by storm; the first full-length Hollywood talkie, it charmed audiences as no film had done before (see Document 41). The author of the screenplay, Samson Raphaelson, was adominished not to "be quite satisfied with your singer's ragtime as the full modern equivalent for the old Hebrew chants." But Stuart Sherman's genteel strictures were beside the point (see Document 42). His former protégé's Lower East Side melodrama had anticipated a new idiom.

This acute cultural self-consciousness reflected the coming-of-age of urban-rooted immigrants confronted by a rural-oriented nation with threatened traditions. The revolution in manners, morals, and customs that agitated American society upset the traditional consensus in just those areas of life where the American value system was least secure and most sensitive. Heavy with tension and even venom, attempts were made to arrest the disintegration of old ways, as culture, religion, and personal habits all underwent assault and counter-assault. Most notorious of all was the effort to legislate personal morality and to enforce the "Noble Experiment" that was to provide a bonanza for organized crime until a zealous wet campaign and widespread nullification succeeded in repealing the Eighteenth Amendment. Burdened by the earlier criminal stereotype, Italian immigrants especially became identified with the booming bootlegging industry that the Volstead Act inspired. "Americans reacted to crime among Italian newcomers with a frenzy of emotion aroused by no other immigrant activity." [27] Subsequently, their illegal entanglements locally became associated with international conspiracy and moral subversion. A half century later, *The Godfather*, ironically an all-time box office success, enshrined the Mafia stereotype to which American Italians were so sensitive, as it continued to distort the third generation immigrants' quest for ego identity (see Document 44).

By the second half of the twentieth century, America's immigrant languages virtually had become extinct. Mass migration

27. Humbert S. Nelli, *The Italians in Chicago 1880-1930: A Study in Ethnic Mobility* (New York: Oxford University Press, 1970), p. 125.

had long ceased and the quota immigration of the depression years and World War II proved but incidental. The fading of the immigrant press in the face of age, curtailed income and circulation, and the competition of the high-pressure mass media, left only the Spanish language newspapers in New York, Florida, and the Southwest, and a scattering of older and newer immigrant journals. The latter were energized by the postwar newcomers and by a more favorable climate for the foreign-born and the foreign-speaking.

By then, culture in America had extended its locus to the world. A radical new status in law, public opinion, and international relations had been achieved by the descendants of the nation's only enslaved immigrants. Blacks, especially black writers, were now provided with a perspective, a platform, and a world audience that encouraged them to remind Americans of European antecedents of the promise and shortcomings of their society. Some, like Leroi Jones, opted for a separatist Black identity exclusively rooted in an African past. Others, like Ralph Ellison, insisted that the American black subculture was an integral part of the American cultural amalgam, distinct but inseparable from the total American experience as it broadened out to encircle the globe. Whatever their role, self-conscious Negroes injected a new cosmopolitanism into the relations between the new world and the old. Absent since the Western hemisphere had been opened to settlement, this stage of development reflected the quest for a new cultural synthesis, truly universal in its dimensions (see Document 45).

The national awakening to the identity of non-European ethnics was responsible in part for the white ethnic revival of the late 1960s among the children and grandchildren of immigrants, particularly from southern and eastern Europe (see Document 50). But more likely, the white ethnic revival registered the irreducible pride of origin that the historian Marcus Hansen earlier had described as "the principle of the third generation interest." It also was an outgrowth of strivings for legitimacy and recognition by invisible and much-maligned ethnics. The call for a "cultural bill of rights" [28] by a *contemporary* American historian (see Document 46) reflects the continued hunger for identity that has become perennial in a persistently rootless society. The significance of the nation's immigrant cultures may become progressively more evident only after direct immigrant influences have faded away. The urge for a redefinition of American culture to accommodate these new felt needs is already apparent.

The President: The Symbolic American

In politics no less than in culture, the 1920s was a watershed. After three centuries, an ascendant old America was forced to take heed of new American breeds who, having suffered and resented the stigma of recent immigrant origins, yearned to share places of honor and prestige. World War I had dramatized the intense rivalry among ethnic claimants striving for full American acceptance. The drastic restriction of immigration had guaranteed that, henceforth, rivalry would be focused more energetically into domestic channels. Within the reach of latter-day Americans were the essential and indelible attributes of Americanism and patriotism. More than ever the accessibility of the office of the presidency seemed the crowning expression of that total American consummation that would irrevocably join the native sons and daughters of latter-day immigrants to the charter-day sons and daughters of the American Revolution.

In 1928 the stage was set for political confrontation between new and old America that would reach a delayed climax with the election to the presidency of John F. Kennedy in 1960. The first time the ethnic populace of the cities and tenements had cast up a contender for the presidency who was unmistakably one of them was in the 1920s, when Governor Alfred E. Smith of New York became the first Catholic to bid for the highest office in the land (see Document 47). The gravel-voiced man in the brown derby had personified the first challenge to the unstated assumption that

28. See Marcus L. Hansen, "The Problem of the Third Generation Immigrant" (Rock Island: Augustana Historical Society, 1938), p. 9; U. S., Congress, House, Committee on Education and Labor, General Subcommittee on Education, *Hearings on H. R. 14910* . . . , Feb. 18, 1970, 91st Cong., 2nd sess., p. 74.

American nationalism was synonymous with Protestantism. His candidacy foreshadowed the election in 1960, when the American presidency was first assumed by a non-Protestant son of the nineteenth-century immigration. The inauguration of a new tradition at the nation's symbolic summit reflected the realities of a pluralistic nation and was the culmination of almost two generations of re-Americanizing America and of exorcizing the specter of Europe.

The election campaigns of 1928 and 1960 spotlighted a dimension of American life that had never before dominated a presidential campaign. The candidates of one of the two major parties stirred residual hostilities sown by Reformation Europe, rekindled by evangelical America, and stoked by a century of mass immigration and social and industrial disorder. Well-meaning Cassandras, eager to sidestep the "religious issue," urged the New York governor and the Massachusetts senator to withdraw from the presidential race. In 1927, the popular Indiana novelist, Meredith Nicholson, feared that if a Catholic were nominated "the ensuing campaign would develop a bitterness much like that of a civil war." [29] In 1960, shortly after the Wisconsin primary, Walter Lippmann prescribed a compromise to the "Catholic Question": "It is too much to hope that the tendency to bloc voting, already visible in the Wisconsin primary, would not become much more acute and virulent in the national election itself. . . . The solution of the problem lies in nominating Senator Kennedy for Vice-President." [30]

Superficially alike in their postwar affluence, the 1920s and the 1950s differed radically in every other respect. In the 1920s the closing of the gates by Congressional legislation ratified theories of Anglo-Saxon and Nordic supremacy and labeled millions of Americans inferior genetically and undesirable culturally, religiously, and morally. The flowering of the Ku Klux Klan—anti-Catholic, anti-Semitic, anti-immigrant, and anti-Negro, the wide

29. Edmund A. Moore, *A Catholic Runs For President* (New York: Ronald Press, 1956), p. 58.

30. *New York Herald Tribune*, April 14, 1960; cf. Robert D. Cross, "Changing Image of Catholicism in America," *Yale Review* XLVIII (June, 1959): 562ff.

dissemination of the Protocols of the Elders of Zion by Henry Ford's *Dearborn Independent*, the passage of the Compulsory Education Act in Oregon requiring all children to attend public schools, and the "noble experiment" to legislate drinking habits—even as to wine and beer, proclaimed the Know-Nothing spirit of the era. Thirty years later, the nation that had invented and then spurned the League of Nations was a charter member of the United Nations and a zealous proponent of civil rights for all Americans and self-determination for all the world's peoples. The 300-page McCarran-Walter Immigration and Nationality Act of 1952, codifying and consolidating the racist heritage, proved to be a musty anachronism at a time when the United States was discarding nineteenth- and twentieth-century racism and isolationism and reverting to the mandate enunciated by America's founding fathers. In a nation and in a world where overt racism was on the defensive and in retreat, even the mushrooming White Citizens' Councils in the South contributed but a discordant minor note.

Both in 1928 and in 1960, the unfolding of the "religious question" long antedated the campaign itself (see Documents 48 and 49). But in the 1920s it was inseparable from the Prohibition, immigration, and Tammany issues. "The wet cause led by a New York Catholic magnified Smith's religion, and the cultural complex of which it was a part, into a large menace . . ." [31] At the Democratic Convention in New York's Madison Square Garden in 1924, the defeat of the plank denouncing the Klan had dramatized the chasm between Southern small town Democrats—native, dry, and Protestant—and Northern big city Democrats—immigrant, wet, and Catholic—and had doomed Smith's chance for the nomination. "The Catholics of the country can stand it. The Jews can stand it. But the United States of America cannot stand it," remonstrated the New York governor in disgust. [32] Four years later, Smith was nominated on the first ballot but the decade's ugly mood had not washed off (see Document 50).

31. Moore, *A Catholic Runs*, p. 40.
32. Oscar Handlin, *Al Smith and his America* (Boston: Little, Brown, 1958), p. 120.

Throughout the 1928 presidental campaign, the Catholic hierarchy and laity proved especially sensitive to the mischief inherent in the religious question. The distribution of 400 thousand copies of a virulent anti-Catholic pamphlet, *Is Southern Protestantism More Intolerant Than Romanism?* by Bishop James Cannon of the Southern Methodist Episcopal Church, went unanswered. The visit of Cardinal Sincero to the United States during the campaign was barred by Pope Pius XI, mindful doubtless of the riots that had greeted Monsignor Bedini on his visit seventy-five years earlier. Except for the statements of four Roman Catholic prelates on the separation of church and state, released by the chairman of the Democratic National Commitee —himself a Catholic—and the defense of the Catholic position by Dr. John A. Ryan and a few others, the counsel of silence prevailed.

By contrast in 1960, the "religious issue" was aired openly and continually. By then, the 1928 experience and over a century of revolutionary social change had divested the Catholic Church of its foreignness. In a nation of self-conscious minorities, a candidate's Catholicism had become as much political asset as liability and hardly a "silent issue." In the new America, distinguished Jesuits and prominent Catholic laymen did not hesitate to reply to charges of dual loyalty directed at the Roman Catholic Church and its communicants by liberal, as well as by conservative, Protestant clergymen. In September, as the anti-Catholic campaign mounted in intensity, John Courtney Murray, the leading Catholic philosopher of American pluralism, and his equally distinguished fellow Jesuit, Gustav Weigel, responded in measured terms to the allegations that a Catholic who became president could not uphold the First Amendment. The accusations of James A. Pike, the Episcopal Bishop of California; G. Bromley Oxnam, former chairman of the Methodist Council of Bishops; Eugene Carson Blake, past president of the National Council of Churches; and representatives of Protestants and Other Americans United for Separation of Church and State spurred Catholic spokesmen to lively rebuttal and not to prudential silence.

Ever since taking public office, John F. Kennedy had entertained all comers on the religious question, responding off-handedly, good-naturedly, and indulgently. Indeed, on July 4, 1956, Kennedy's advisors had openly interjected the "Catholic Vote" into politics by releasing a 3,000-word memorandum that attempted to demonstrate "scientifically" that there was a "Catholic vote," that the nomination of their candidate for the vice-presidency would bring millions of Catholic voters back to the Democratic party and that their man's Catholicism was clearly a source of strength rather than weakness. When Kennedy failed to get the nomination, the Jesuit weekly, *America*, insisted that religion played no part in his setback.

In 1960, Kennedy met the "religious issue" head on (see Document 51). Following his nomination on the first ballot, on July 15 in Los Angeles, he declared in his acceptance speech, "I am fully aware of the fact that the Democratic party by nominating someone of my faith, has taken on what many regard as a new and hazardous risk—new, at least, since 1928. . . . My decisions on every public policy will be my own—as an American, a Democrat and a free man." On September 12, the Democratic candidate faced the "religious issue" for the last time, and in a nationally televised interview replied to the questions of the Greater Houston Ministerial Association to the total satisfaction of all concerned.

The election of the first non-Protestant president in one of the closest contests in the nation's history was a milestone along the road to national maturity (see Document 52). To the extent that Catholic voters were drawn to Kennedy, "It was due not to anti-Protestant prejudice but to Catholic pride," [33] concluded a member of the Kennedy campaign entourage. The heavy electoral support that he received from non-white minorities as well as from Americans of southern and eastern European origin registered the longing for total American endorsement that his election symbolized.

Following his election, the President demonstrated the ability

33. John Cogley, "Pride and Prejudice," *Commonweal* LXXIII (December 23, 1960), p. 34.

to enhance his office as a showcase for democracy and as a vehicle for a greater national unity. A breakthrough by a Catholic seemed to clear the way to acceptance for all Americans. It now seemed possible that an American of Jewish, Italian, Polish, African, or Asian origin, or even a woman, might be considered for the presidency on personal merit and public performance, vindicating the dream of a truly free pluralistic America.

Beyond Race: An Ecumenical Law

In the new America of the 1960s, the immigration legislation of the 1920s and its formulas, enshrined in 1952 in the 300-page McCarran-Walter Act passed over a presidential veto, appeared a gross anachronism. On July 23, 1963, President John F. Kennedy, appropriately, transmitted to the Congress legislation to revise and modernize the nation's immigration policy that for four decades had been governed by the national origins quota system. Although national quota allotments had been nullified by permissive administrative exceptions and non-quota loopholes, the need for a democratic and realistic immigration policy remained critical. The Kennedy bill answered that need. In his message to Congress, the President called for the outright repudiation of those provisions in the law that betrayed the American tradition.

"The use of a national origins system is without basis in logic or reason. It neither satisfies a national need nor accomplishes an international purpose. In an age of interdependence among nations, such a system is an anachronism, for it discriminates among applicants for admission into the United States on the basis of accident of birth." [34]

The assassination of the President four months later delayed consideration of the pending legislation until 1965. Then, in the wake of the Civil Rights Act of 1964, the late President's brother, Senator Edward Kennedy of Massachusetts reintroduced the Kennedy bill, endorsed by President Johnson, to amend the Immigration and Nationality Act of 1952. The debate in the

34. John F. Kennedy, *A Nation of Immigrants* (New York: Harper & Row, 1964), p. 103.

House, and particularly in the Senate (see Document 53), bared the emotions of pride, prejudice, compassion, and affection to which the nation of immigrants was heir. The resultant bill (see Document 54) divested American immigration policy of all traces of discrimination but the limit set on the total number of immigrants to be admitted annually remained virtually un- changed. The Immigration Act of 1924 had brought the epic of migration to a close. The legislation of 1965 no more questioned that fact than it did the closing of the frontier. But the new law reasserted the nation's positive commitment to one of its great traditions with an explicitness and cosmopolitanism that was unparalleled in its own history and rare among the nations of the world (see Document 55). For the first time after 1968, represent- atives of all mankind became equally qualified for admission to the United States. Indeed, during the first year in which the new law went into effect, 21 percent of the immigrants were Asians, a proportion that had never before been approached by the classic nation of immigrants.

The ideal of immigration lived on in no uncertain terms. The circumstances of history had contributed to the elaboration of the tradition of asylum, of refuge, and of promised land into a myth honored in law and in sentiment, even as the epic migration itself has become ever more remote. Yet the problems of culture, of human relations, of the texture and quality of life that are the heritage and challenge of the nation of immigrants continue to demand a perennial re-education in sensibility, imagination, and consciousness. Americans have been a newer people and an older people derived from older and newer peoples from all the world's nations. So long as the tradition of immigration inspires in Americans a generosity of spirit and understanding toward others, as well as toward themselves, it will continue to be a fructifying symbol holding aloft its historic promise of human renewal in a world in perennial need.

Immigration
and the
American Tradition

PART ONE
Exodus

1. WILLIAM BRADFORD

Being thus arrived in a good harbor

The most powerful and realistic account of the initial encounter between
the American wilderness and its mythic settlers was written by a
Yorkshire farmer. In 1609, William Bradford (1590–1657) had joined a
group of Separatists who, after living in Holland for eleven years,
embarked on the Mayflower in quest of a more perfect home. Governor
of the Plymouth Colony from 1621 until his death in 1657, except for six
years, Bradford began his *History of the Plymouth Colony* in 1630 but did
not complete it until twenty years later. The resultant account was a
providential history of a proud congregation that had planned to be the
first to land at New York Harbor, the natural center of the fish and fur
trade. Instead, on November 11, 1620, after a sixty-five-day voyage, they
landed at Provincetown Harbor on Cape Cod. Of the 102 passengers
aboard the Mayflower at the Cape landing, four died before reaching
Plymouth. By the following summer only twelve of twenty-six heads of
families, four of twelve single men or boys, and a few women survived.
The drawing up of the Mayflower compact, the landing, and the starving
time are but the highlights of Bradford's great history of the pilgrim
fathers. In the three centuries to come, the immigrant pioneers would
recapitulate in different degrees the experience of the first emigrants.

Of Their Voyage and Safe Arrival at Cape Cod

. . . After some deliberation had amongst themselves and with
the master of the ship, they tacked about and resolved to stand for
the southward (the wind and weather being fair) to find some
place about Hudson's River for their habitation. But after they
had sailed that course about half the day, they fell amongst
dangerous shoals and roaring breakers, and they were so far

From William Bradford, *Of Plymouth Plantation*, ed. Samuel Eliot Morison (New
York: Alfred Knopf, 1952), pp. 60–63, 75–79. Copyright © by Samuel Eliot
Morison. Reprinted by permission of the publisher.

entangled therewith as they conceived themselves in great danger; and the wind shrinking upon them withal, they resolved to bear up again for the Cape and thought themselves happy to get out of those dangers before night overtook them, as by God's good providence they did. And the next day they got into the Cape Harbor where they rid in safety. . . .

Being thus arrived in a good harbor, and brought safe to land, they fell upon their knees and blessed the God of Heaven who had brought them over the vast and furious ocean, and delivered them from all the perils and miseries thereof, again to set their feet on the firm and stable earth, their proper element. And no marvel if they were thus joyful, seeing wise Seneca was so affected with sailing a few miles on the coast of his own Italy, as he affirmed, that he had rather remain twenty years on his way by land than pass by sea to any place in a short time, so tedious and dreadful was the same unto him.

But here I cannot but stay and make a pause, and stand half amazed at this poor people's present condition; and so I think will the reader, too, when he well considers the same. Being thus passed the vast ocean, and a sea of troubles before in their preparation (as may be remembered by that which went before), they had now no friends to welcome them nor inns to entertain or refresh their weatherbeaten bodies; no houses or much less towns to repair to, to seek for succour. It is recorded in Scripture as a mercy to the Apostle and his shipwrecked company, that the barbarians showed them no small kindness in refreshing them, but these savage barbarians, when they met with them (as after will appear) were readier to fill their sides full of arrows than otherwise. And for the season it was winter, and they that know the winters of that country know them to be sharp and violent, and subject to cruel and fierce storms, dangerous to travel to known places, much more to search an unknown coast. Besides, what could they see but a hideous and desolate wilderness, full of wild beasts and wild men—and what multitudes there might be of them they knew not. Neither could they, as it were, go up to the top of Pisgah to view from this wilderness a more goodly country to feed their hopes; for which way soever they turned their eyes (save upward to the heavens) they could have little solace or content in respect of any outward objects. For summer being done, all things stand upon them with a weatherbeaten face, and the whole country, full of woods and thickets, represented a wild and savage hue.

If they looked behind them, there was the mighty ocean which they had passed and was now as a main bar and gulf to separate them from all the civil parts of the world. If it be said they had a ship to succour them, it is true; but what heard they daily from the master and company? But that with speed they should look out a place (with their shallop) where they would be, at some near distance; for the season was such as he would not stir from thence till a safe harbor was discovered by them, where they would be, and he might go without danger; and that victuals consumed apace but he must and would keep sufficient for themselves and their return. Yea, it was muttered by some that if they got not a place in time, they would turn them and their goods ashore and leave them. Let it also be considered what weak hopes of supply and succour they left behind them, that might bear up their minds in this sad condition and trials they were under; and they could not but be very small. It is true, indeed, the affections and love of their brethren at Leyden was cordial and entire towards them, but they had little power to help them or themselves; and how the case stood between them and the merchants at their coming away hath already been declared.

What could now sustain them but the Spirit of God and His grace? May not and ought not the children of these fathers rightly say: "Our fathers were Englishmen which came over this great ocean, and were ready to perish in this wilderness; but they cried unto the Lord, and He heard their voice and looked on their adversity," etc. "Let them therefore praise the Lord, because He is good: and His mercies endure forever." "Yea, let them which have been redeemed of the Lord, shew how He hath delivered them from the hand of the oppressor. When they wandered in the desert wilderness out of the way, and found no city to dwell in, both hungry and thirsty, their soul was overwhelmed in them. Let them confess before the Lord His lovingkindness and His wonderful works before the sons of men."

The Remainder of Anno 1620

THE MAYFLOWER COMPACT

I shall a little return back, and begin with a combination made by them before they came ashore; being the first foundation of their government in this place. Occasioned partly by the discontented and mutinous speeches that some of the strangers amongst them had let fall from them in the ship: That when they came ashore they would use their own liberty, for none had power to command them, the patent they had being for Virginia and not for New England, which belonged to another government, with which the Virginia Company had nothing to do. And partly that such an act by them done, this their condition considered, might be as firm as any patent, and in some respects more sure. The form was as followeth:

IN THE NAME OF GOD, AMEN.

We whose names are underwritten, the loyal subjects of our dread Sovereign Lord King James, by the Grace of God of Great Britain, France, and Ireland King, Defender of the Faith, etc.

Having undertaken, for the Glory of God and advancement of the Christian Faith and Honour of our King and Country, a Voyage to plant the First Colony in the Northern Parts of Virginia, do by these presents solemnly and mutually in the presence of God and one of another, Covenant and Combine ourselves together into a Civil Body Politic, for our better ordering and preservation and furtherance of the ends aforesaid; and by virtue hereof to enact, constitute and frame such just and equal Laws, Ordinances, Acts, Constitutions and Offices, from time to time, as shall be thought most meet and convenient for the general good of the Colony, unto which we promise all due submission and obedience. In witness whereof we have hereunder subscribed our names at Cape Cod, the 11th of November, in the year of the reign of our Sovereign Lord King James, of England, France and Ireland the eighteenth, and of Scotland the fifty-fourth. Anno Domini 1620.

After this they chose, or rather confirmed, Mr. John Carver (a man godly and well approved amongst them) their Governor for that year. And after they had provided a place for their goods, or common store (which were long in unlading for want of boats, foulness of the winter weather and sickness of divers) and begun some small cottages for their habitation; as time would admit, they met and consulted of laws and orders, both for their civil and military government as the necessity of their condition did require, still adding thereunto as urgent occasion in several times, and as cases did require.

In these hard and difficult beginnings they found some discontents and murmurings arise amongst some, and mutinous speeches and carriages in other; but they were soon quelled and overcome by the wisdom, patience, and just and equal carriage of things, by the Governor and better part, which clave faithfully together in the main.

THE STARVING TIME

But that which was most sad and lamentable was, that in two or three months' time half of their company died, especially in January and February, being the depth of winter, and wanting houses and other comforts; being infected with the scurvy and other diseases which this long voyage and their inaccommodate condition had brought upon them. So as there died some times two or three of a day in the foresaid time, that of 100 and odd persons, scarce fifty remained. And of these, in the time of most distress, there was but six or seven sound persons who to their great commendations, be it spoken, spared no pains night nor day, but with abundance of toil and hazard of their own health, fetched them wood, made them fires, dressed them meat, made their beds, washed their loathsome clothes, clothed and unclothed them. In a word, did all the homely and necessary offices for them which dainty and queasy stomachs cannot endure to hear named; and all this willingly and cheerfully, without any grudging in the least, showing herein their true love unto their friends and brethren; a rare example and worthy to be remembered. Two of these seven were Mr. William Brewster, their reverend Elder, and

Myles Standish, their Captain and military commander, unto whom myself and many others were much beholden in our low and sick condition. And yet the Lord so upheld these persons as in this general calamity they were not at all infected either with sickness or lameness. And what I have said of these I may say of many others who died in this general visitation, and others yet living; that whilst they had health, yea, or any strength continuing, they were not wanting to any that had need of them. And I doubt not but their recompense is with the Lord.

But I may not here pass by another remarkable passage not to be forgotten. As this calamity fell among the passengers that were to be left here to plant, and were hasted ashore and made to drink water that the seamen might have the more beer, and one in his sickness desiring but a small can of beer, it was answered that if he were their own father he should have none. The disease began to fall amongst them also, so as almost half of their company died before they went away, and many of their officers and lustiest men, as the boatswain, gunner, three quartermasters, the cook and others. At which the Master was something strucken and sent to the sick ashore and told the Governor he should send for beer for them that had need of it, though he drunk water homeward bound.

But now amongst his company there was far another kind of carriage in this misery than amongst the passengers. For they that before had been boon companions in drinking and jollity in the time of their health and welfare, began now to desert one another in this calamity, saying they would not hazard their lives for them, they should be infected by coming to help them in their cabins; and so, after they came to lie by it, would do little or nothing for them but, "if they died, let them die." But such of the passengers as were yet aboard showed them what mercy they could, which made some of their hearts relent, as the boatswain (and some others) who was a proud young man and would often curse and scoff at the passengers. But when he grew weak, they had compassion on him and helped him; then he confessed he did not deserve it at their hands, he had abused them in word and deed. "Oh!" (saith he) "you, I now see, show your love like Christians indeed one to another, but we let one another lie and die like dogs." Another lay cursing his wife, saying if it had not been for her he had never come this unlucky voyage, and anon cursing his fellows, saying he had done this and that for some of them; he had spent so much and so much amongst them, and they were now weary of him and did not help him, having need. Another gave his companion all he had, if he died, to help him in his weakness; he went and got a little spice and made him a mess of meat once or twice. And because he died not so soon as he expected, he went amongst his fellows and swore the rogue would cozen him, he would see him choked before he made him any more meat; and yet the poor fellow died before morning.

2. COTTON MATHER

They were so mindful of their errand into the wilderness

A half century after Bradford completed his eyewitness account, a third-generation New Englander published his prodigiously researched, comprehensive, ecclesiastical history of the founding of New England.

Cotton Mather (1663–1728) was committed above all to explaining the reasons which drove eminently pious men "to endure so many calamities and to undertake so many hardships." The answer was that these men desired to further the Reformation in England but that opposition and persecution forced them to look abroad to fulfill their mission.

Magnalia Christi Americana ("The Great Achievements of Christ in America") is therefore a history of the migration of the Reformation to New England. It is grand in scope, massive in its empirical detail, avid in its pursuit of design, and didactic in its lessons. If Mather's theology fails to satisfy the modern mind, his sense of high purpose looms forth seductively as a prime ingredient of the immigrant myth.

From Cotton Mather, *Magnalia Christi Americana*, or the *Ecclesiastical History of New England From Its First Planting in the Year 1620, Unto the Year of Our Lord, 1698*, in seven books, first American edition, from the London edition of 1702 (Hartford: Silas Andrus, 1820), vol. 1, pp. 23, 68–73.

A General Introduction

1. I WRITE the *Wonders* of the CHRISTIAN RELIGION, flying from the depravations of *Europe*, to the *American Strand:* and, assisted by the Holy Author of that *Religion*, I do, with all conscience of *Truth*, required therein by Him, who is the *Truth* itself, report the *wonderful displays* of His infinite Power, Wisdom, Goodness, and Faithfulness, wherewith His Divine Providence hath *irradiated* an *Indian Wilderness*.

I relate the *Considerable Matters*, that produced and attended the First Settlement of COLONIES, which have been renowned for the degree of REFORMATION, professed and attained by *Evangelical Churches*, erected in those *ends of the earth:* and a *Field* being thus prepared, I proceed unto a relation of the *Considerable Matters* which have been acted thereupon.

I first introduce the *Actors*, that have, in a more exemplary manner served those *Colonies;* and give *Remarkable Occurrences*, in the exemplary LIVES of many *Magistrates*, and of more *Ministers*, who so *lived*, as to leave unto Posterity, *examples* worthy of *everlasting remembrance*.

I add hereunto, the *Notables* of the only *Protestant University*, that ever *shone* in that hemisphere of the *New World;* with particular instances of *Criolians*, in our *Biography*, provoking the *whole world*, with vertuous objects of emulation.

I introduce then, the *Actions* of a more eminent importance, that have signalized those *Colonies:* whether the *Establishments*, directed by their *Synods;* with a rich variety of *Synodical* and *Ecclesiastical* Determinations; or, the *Disturbances*, with which they have been from all sorts of *temptations* and *enemies* tempestuated; and the *Methods* by which they have still weathered out each *horrible tempest*.

And into the midst of these *Actions*, I interpose an entire *Book*, wherein there is, with all possible veracity, a *Collection* made, of *Memorable Occurrences;* and amazing *Judgments* and *Mercies*, befalling many *particular persons* among the people of *New-England*.

Let my readers expect all that I have promised them, in this *Bill of Fare;* and it may be they will find themselves entertained with yet many other passages, above and beyond their expectation, deserving likewise a room in History: in all which, there will be nothing, but the *Author's* too mean way of preparing so great entertainments, to reproach the Invitation. . . .

Chapter V.

1. THE *Governour* and *Company* of the *Massachuset-Bay* then in *London,* did in the year 1629, after exact and mature debates, conclude, that it was most convenient for the *government,* with the charter of the plantation, to be transferred into the plantation it self; and an *order of court* being drawn up for that end, there was then chosen a new *governour,* and a new *deputy-governour,* that were willing to remove themselves with their families thither on the first occasion. The governour was *John Winthrop,* Esq; a gentleman of that wisdom and virtue, and those manifold accomplishments, that after-generations must reckon him no less a *glory,* than he was a *patriot* of the country. The deputy-governour was *Thomas Dudley,* Esq; a gentleman, whose *natural* and *acquired* abilities, joined with his excellent *moral* qualities, entitled him to all the great respects with which his country on all opportunities treated him. Several most worthy *assistants* were at the same time chosen to be in this *transportation;* moreover, several other *gentlemen* of prime note, and several famous *ministers* of the gospel, now likewise embarked themselves with these honourable *adventurers:* who equipped a *fleet,* consisting of ten or eleven ships, whereof the admiral was, *The Arabella* (so called in honour of the right honourable the lady *Arabella Johnson,* at this time on board) a ship of three hundred and fifty tuns; and in some of the said ships there were two hundred passengers; all of which arrived before the middle of *July,* in the year 1630, safe in the harbours of *New-England.* There was a time when the *British sea* was by *Clements,* and the other ancients, called ᾽ ωχεαυτος ᾽ απεραντος, *the unpassable ocean.* What then was to be thought of the vast *Atlantick sea,* on the westward of *Britain?* but this *ocean* must now be *passed!* An heart of stone must have dissolved into *tears* at the affectionate *farewel* which

the governour and other eminent persons took of their friends, at a *feast* which the governour made for them, a little before their going off; however they were acted by principles that could carry them through *tears* and *oceans;* yea, through *oceans* of *tears:* principles that enabled them to leave, *Dulcia Limina, atq; amabilem Larem, quem & parentum memoria, atq; ipsius* (to use *Stupius'* words) *Infamiæ Rudimenta Confirmant.* Some very late *geographers* do assure us, that the breadth of the *Atlantick sea* is commonly over-reckoned by *six,* by *eight,* by *ten* degrees. But let that sea be as narrow as they please, I can assure the reader the passing of it was no little *trial* unto those worthy people that were now to pass it.

2. But the most notable circumstance in their *farewel,* was their composing and publishing of what they called, *The humble request of his Majesties loyal subjects, the Governour and Company lately gone for* New-England, *to the rest of their brethren in and of the Church of* England; *for the obtaining of their prayers, and the removal of suspicions and misconstructions of their intentions.* In this address of theirs, notwithstanding the trouble they had undergone for desiring to see the Church of *England reformed* of several things, which they thought its *deformities,* yet they now called the Church of *England* their *dear mother;* acknowledging that such *hope* and *part* as they had obtained in the *common salvation* they had *sucked from her breasts;* therewithal entreating their many *reverend fathers and brethren* to recommend them unto the mercies of God, in their constant prayers, as a *church* now springing out of their own bowels. *You are not ignorant* (said they) *that the Spirit of God stirred up the apostle* Paul, *to make a continual mention of the church at* Philippi, *which was a colony from* Rome; *let the same spirit, we beseech you, put you in mind, that are the Lord's remembrancers, to pray for us without ceasing, who are the weak* colony *from your selves.* And after such prayers, they concluded, *What goodness you shall extend unto us, in this or any other Christian kindness, we your brethren in Christ shall labour to repay, in what duty we are or shall be able to perform; promising so far as God shall enable us, to give him no rest on your behalfs;*

wishing our heads and hearts may be fountains of tears for your everlasting welfare, when we shall be in our poor cottages in the wilderness, overshadowed with the spirit of supplication, through the manifold necessities and tribulations, which may not altogether unexpectedly, nor we hope unprofitably, befal us.

3. *Reader,* If ever the *charity* of a right christian, and enlarged soul, were examplarily seen in its proper *expansions,* 'twas in the address which thou hast now been reading: but if it now puzzel the reader to reconcile these passages with the *principles* declared, the *practices* followed, and the *persecutions* undergone, by these *American Reformers,* let him know, that there was more than one *distinction,* whereof these excellent persons were not ignorant. First, they were able to distinguish between the *Church of England,* as it *contained* the whole *body of the faithful,* scatered throughout the kingdoms, though of different perswasions about some *rites* and *modes* in religion; many thousands of whom our *Nor-Angels* knew could comply with many things, to which *our consciences* otherwise enlightened and perswaded could not yield such a compliance: and the *Church of England* as it was *confined* unto a certain constitution by *canons,* which pronounced *Ipso Facto,* excommunicate all those who should affirm that the *worship* contained in the book of *Common-Prayer,* and *administrations of sacraments,* is unlawful, or that any of the *thirty-nine articles* are erroneous, or that any of the *ceremonies* commanded by the authority of the church might not be approved, used and subscribed; and which will have to be *accursed* all those, who maintain that there are in the realm any other meetings, assemblies or congregations of the King's born subjects, then such as by the laws of the land are allowed, which may rightly challenge to themselves the name of *true* and *lawful Churches:* and by which, all those that refuse to *kneel* at the reception of the sacrament, and to be present at publick *prayers,* according to the *orders* of the church, about which there are prescribed many formalities of *responses,* with bowing at the *name* of Jesus, are to be denied the *communion;* and all who dare not submit their children to be *baptized* by the undertaking of *god-fathers,* and receive the *cross* as a dedicating badge of

christianity, must not have *baptism* for their children: besides an *Et-cætera* of how many more *impositions!* Again, they were able to distinguish between the *Church of England,* as it kept the true *doctrine* of the *protestant religion,* with a disposition to pursue the *reformation* begun in the former century, among whom we may reckon such men, as the famous *assembly of divines* at *Westminster,* who all but *eight* or *nine,* and the *Scots,* had before then lived in *conformity;* and *the Church of England,* as limiting that name unto a certain *faction,* who together with a *discipline* very much *unscriptural,* vigorously prosecuted the *tripartite plot* of *Arminianism* and conciliation with *Rome,* in the *church,* and unbounded *prerogative* in the *state;* who set themselves to cripple as fast as they could the more learned, godly, painful *ministers* of the land, and silence and ruin such as could not read a *book for sports on the Lord's days;* or did but use a *prayer* of their own conceiving, before or after sermon; or did but preach in an *afternoon,* as well as in a morning, or on a *lecture,* or on a *market,* or in aniwise discountenance *old* superstitions, or *new* extravagancies; and who at last threw the nation into the lamentable confusions of a *civil war.* . . .

4. Being happily arrived at *New-England,* our new planters found the difficulties of a rough and hard *wilderness* presently assaulting them: of which the worst was the *sickliness* which many of them had contracted by their other difficulties. Of those who soon dyed after their first arrival, not the least considerable was the lady *Arabella,* who left an earthly *paradise* in the family of an *Earldom,* to encounter the sorrows of a *wilderness,* for the entertainments of a *pure worship* in the *house of God;* and then immediately left that *wilderness* for the Heavenly *paradise,* whereto the compassionate *Jesus,* of whom she was a *follower,* called her. We have read concerning a noble woman of *Bohemia,* who forsook her friends, her plate, her house and all; and because the gates of the city were guarded, crept through the common-sewer, that she might enjoy the *institutions* of our Lord at another place where they might be had. The spirit which acted that noble woman, we may suppose carried this blessed lady thus to and

through the hardships of an *American* desart. But as for her virtuous husband, *Isaac Johnson,* Esq;

> ———— ——— ———*He try'd*
> *To live without her, lik'd it not, and dy'd.*

His *mourning* for the death of his honourable consort was too bitter to be extended a *year;* about a month after *her* death *his* ensued, unto the extream loss of the whole plantation. But at the *end* of this *perfect and upright man,* there was not only *peace* but *joy;* and his *joy* particularly expressed it self *that God had kept his eyes open so long as to see* one church *of the Lord Jesus Christ gathered in these ends of the earth, before his own going away to Heaven.* The *mortality* thus threatening of this new Plantation so *enlivened* the devotions of this good people, that they set themselves by *fasting* and *prayer* to obtain from God the removal of it; and their brethren at *Plymouth* also attended the like duties on their behalf: the issue whereof was, that in a little time they not only had *health* restored, but they likewise enjoyed the special directions and assistance of God in the further prosecution of their undertakings.

5. But there were two terrible distresses more, besides that of *sickness,* whereto this people were exposed in the beginning of their settlement: though a most seasonable and almost unexpected *mercy from Heaven* still rescued them out of those distresses. One thing that sometimes extreamly exercised them, was a *scarcity of provisions;* in which 'twas wonderful to see their *dependance* upon God, and God's *mindfulness* of them. When the parching droughts of the *summer* divers times threatned them with an utter and a total consumption to the fruits of the earth, it was their manner, with *heart-melting,* and I may say, *Heaven-melting* devotions, to *fast* and *pray* before God; and on the very days, when they *poured out the water* of their *tears* before him, he would *shower down the water* of his *rain* upon their fields; *while they were yet speaking he would hear them;* insomuch that the salvages themselves would on that occasion admire the *Englishman's God!* But the *Englishmen* themselves would celebrate their

days of *Thanksgiving* to him. When their *stock* was likewise wasted so far, which divers times it was, that they were come to the last meal in the barrel, just then, unlooked for, arrived several ships from other parts of the world loaden with supplies; among which, one was by the *lord deputy of Ireland* sent hither, although he did not know the necessities of the country, to which he sent her; and if he had known them, would have been thought as unlikely as any man living to have helpt them: in these extremities, 'twas marvellous to see how *helpful* these good people were to one another, following the example of their most liberal governour *Winthrop*, who made an equal distribution of what he had in his own stores among the poor, *taking no thought for to-morrow!* And how content they were; when an honest man, as I have heard, inviting his friends to a dish of *clams*, at the table gave thanks to Heaven, who *had given them to suck the abundance of the seas, and of the treasures hid in the sands!* . . .

6. The people in the fleet that arrived at *New-England*, in the year 1630, left the fleet almost, as the *family* of *Noah* did the ark, having a whole world before them to be peopled. *Salem* was already supplied with a competent number of inhabitants; and therefore the governour, with most of the gentlemen that accompanied him in his voyage, took their first opportunity to prosecute further settlements about the bottom of the *Massachuset-Bay:* but where-ever they sat down, they were so mindful of their *errand* into the wilderness, that still one of their *first works* was to gather a church into the *covenant* and *order* of the gospel. First, there was a church thus gathered at *Charles-town*, on the north side of *Charles's* river; where keeping a solemn *fast* on *August* 27, 1630, to implore the conduct and blessing of Heaven on their ecclesiastical proceedings, they chose Mr. *Wilson*, a most holy and zealous man, formerly a minister of *Sudbury*, in the county of *Suffolk*, to be their teacher; and although he now submitted unto an ordination, with an imposition of such hands as were by the church invited so to pronounce the benediction of Heaven upon him; yet it was done with a *protestation* by all, that it should be only as a sign of his *election* to the charge of his new flock, without any intention that he should thereby renounce the

ministry he had received in *England*. After the gathering of the church at *Charles-town*, there quickly followed another at the town of *Dorchester*.

And after *Dorchester* there followed another at the town of *Boston*, which issued out of *Charles-town;* one Mr. *James* took the care of the Church at *Charles-town*, and Mr. *Wilson* went over to *Boston*, where they that formerly belonged unto *Charles-town*, with universal approbation became a *distinct church* of themselves. To *Boston* soon succeeded a church at *Roxbury;* to *Roxbury*, one at *Lyn;* to *Lyn* one at *Watertown;* so that in one or two years' time there were to be seen *seven churches* in this neighbourhood, all of them attending to what the *spirit* in the *scripture said unto them;* all of them *golden candlesticks*, illustrated with a very sensible *presence* of our Lord Jesus Christ among them.

7. It was for a matter of *twelve years* together, that persons of all ranks, well affected unto *church-reformation*, kept sometimes *dropping*, and sometimes *flocking* into *New-England*, though some that were coming into *New-England* were not suffered so to do. The persecutors of those *Puritans*, as they were called, who were now *retiring* into that *cold country* from the *heat* of their persecution, did all that was possible to hinder as many as was possible from enjoying of that *retirement*. There were many *countermands* given to the passage of people that were now steering of this *western course;* and there was a sort of uproar made among no small part of the nation, that this people should not be *let go*. Among those bound for *New-England*, that were so stopt, there were especially three famous persons, whom I suppose their adversaries would not have so studiously detained at home, if they had *foreseen* events; those were *Oliver Cromwell*, and Mr. *Hambden*, and Sir *Arthur Haselrig:* nevertheless, this is not the only instance *of persecuting church-mens* not having the *spirit of prophecy*. But many others were diverted from an intended voyage hither by the pure *providence* of God, which had provided other improvements for them. . . .

PART TWO

New Men and Old

3. J. Hector St. John Crèvecoeur

Welcome to my shores, distressed European

Letters from an American Farmer was the first well-known book to broadcast the allure of America to potential immigrants. Both Franklin and Washington recommended the *Letters* to newcomers as authentic if "highly couloured." First published in part in 1782 in London and Dublin (second English and Irish editions appeared within a year and the book was widely excerpted), it appeared in Paris in 1784 in a two-volume French edition and was followed in 1787 by a much augmented three-volume edition. An American edition appeared in Philadelphia in 1793 and a reprint did not follow until 1904.

The author of the *Letters*, Michael-Guillaume Jean de Crèvecoeur (1735–1813), a Norman nobleman, had served with the French army as an engineer at Quebec. After the defeat of Montcalm and an extensive trip through the British colonies, Crèvecoeur settled in the colony of New York, became naturalized, and assumed the name by which Americans know him, Hector St. John Crèvecoeur. Although a Loyalist during the American Revolution, the Orange County farmer's appraisal of the American scene was in no way colored by his political sentiments. When Crèvecoeur succeeded in leaving the country in 1780, he took in manuscript an account of his experience in America written in English. In 1783, he returned to the United States as French consul, remaining seven years before going back to France permanently. There he experienced all the vicissitudes of the French Revolution, including the loss of his friends by execution.

Appropriately the *Letters* were dedicated to Abbé Raynal, who viewed the North American provinces "in their true light, as the asylum of

J. Hector St. John Crèvecoeur, From Letters from an American Farmer. Describing Certain Provincial Situations, Manners, and Customs, Not Generally Known; and Conveying Some Idea of The Late and Present Interior Circumstances of the British Colonies in North America, written for the information of a friend in England (London, 1782), pp. 39–44, 49–51, 56–61, 67–68.

freedom, as the cradle of future nations, and the refuge of distressed Europeans." No one gave wider currency to the idea of America as the union of virtue and enlightenment than did Raynal's disciple. Rural, virtuous, simple, and tolerant, America offered the promise of unlimited opportunity, moral regeneration, and intellectual and political progress. If slavery rebuked that prospect, Crèvecoeur wrote of it as a foil that only accentuated the main drift.

Letter III: What is an American

I wish I could be acquainted with the feelings and thoughts which must agitate the heart and present themselves to the mind of an enlightened Englishman, when he first lands on this continent. He must greatly rejoice that he lived at a time to see this fair country discovered and settled; he must necessarily feel a share of national pride, when he views the chain of settlements which embellishes these extended shores. When he says to himself, this is the work of my countrymen who, when convulsed by factions, afflicted by a variety of miseries and wants, restless and impatient, took refuge here. They brought along with them their national genius, to which they principally owe what liberty they enjoy, and what substance they possess. Here he sees the industry of his native country displayed in a new manner, and traces in their works the embryos of all the arts, sciences, and ingenuity which flourish in Europe. Here he beholds fair cities, substantial villages, extensive fields, an immense country filled with decent houses, good roads, orchards, meadows, and bridges, where an hundred years ago all was wild, woody, and uncultivated! What a train of pleasing ideas this fair spectacle must suggest; it is a prospect which must inspire a good citizen with the most heartfelt pleasure. The difficulty consists in the manner of viewing so extensive a scene. He is arrived on a new continent; a modern society offers itself to his contemplation, different from what he had hitherto seen. It is not composed, as in Europe, of great lords who possess everything, and of a herd of people who have nothing. Here are no aristocratical families, no courts, no kings, no bishops, no ecclesiastical dominion, no invisible power giving to a few a very visible one; no great manufacturers employing thousands, no great refinements of luxury. The rich and the poor are not so far removed from each other as they are in Europe. Some few towns excepted, we are all tillers of the earth, from Nova Scotia to West Florida. We are a people of cultivators, scattered over an immense territory, communicating with each other by means of good roads and navigable rivers, united by the silken bands of mild government, all respecting the laws, without dreading their power, because they are equitable. We are all animated with the spirit of an industry which is unfettered and unrestrained, because each person works for himself. If he travels through our rural districts he views not the hostile castle, and the haughty mansion, contrasted with the clay-built hut and miserable cabin, where cattle and men help to keep each other warm, and dwell in meanness, smoke, and indigence. A pleasing uniformity of decent competence appears throughout our habitations. The meanest of our log-houses is a dry and comfortable habitation. Lawyer or merchant are the fairest titles our towns afford; that of a farmer is the only appellation of the rural inhabitants of our country. It must take some time ere he can reconcile himself to our dictionary, which is but short in words of dignity, and names of honour. There, on a Sunday, he sees a congregation of respectable farmers and their wives, all clad in neat homespun, well mounted, or riding in their own humble waggons. There is not among them an esquire, saving the unlettered magistrate. There he sees a parson as simple as his flock, a farmer who does not riot on the labour of others. We have no princes, for whom we toil, starve, and bleed: we are the most perfect society now existing in the world. Here man is free as he ought to be; nor is this pleasing equality so transitory as many others are. Many ages will not see the shores of our great lakes replenished with inland nations, nor the unknown bounds of North America entirely peopled. Who can tell how far it extends? Who can tell the millions of men whom it will feed and contain? for no European foot has as yet travelled half the extent of this mighty continent!

The next wish of this traveller will be to know whence came all these people? they are a mixture of English, Scotch, Irish, French, Dutch, Germans, and Swedes. From this promiscuous breed, that race now called Americans have arisen. The eastern provinces must indeed be excepted, as being the unmixed descendants of Englishmen. I have heard many wish that they had been more intermixed also: for my part, I am no wisher, and think it much better as it has happened. They exhibit a most conspicuous figure in this great and variegated picture; they too enter for a great share in the pleasing perspective displayed in these thirteen provinces. I know it is fashionable to reflect on them, but I respect them for what they have done; for the accuracy and wisdom with which they have settled their territory; for the decency of their manners; for their early love of letters; their ancient college, the first in this hemisphere; for their industry; which to me who am but a farmer, is the criterion of everything. There never was a people, situated as they are, who with so ungrateful a soil have done more in so short a time. Do you think that the monarchical ingredients which are more prevalent in other governments, have purged them from all foul stains? Their histories assert the contrary.

In this great American asylum, the poor of Europe have by some means met together, and in consequence of various causes; to what purpose should they ask one another what countrymen they are? Alas, two thirds of them had no country. Can a wretch who wanders about, who works and starves, whose life is a continual scene of sore affliction or pinching penury; can that man call England or any other kingdom his country? A country that had no bread for him, whose fields procured him no harvest, who met with nothing but the frowns of the rich, the severity of the laws, with jails and punishments; who owned not a single foot of the extensive surface of this planet? No! urged by a variety of motives, here they came. Every thing has tended to regenerate them; new laws, a new mode of living, a new social system; here they are become men: in Europe they were as so many useless plants, wanting vegetative mould, and refreshing showers; they withered, and were mowed down by want, hunger, and war; but now by the power of transplantation, like all other plants they have taken root and flourished! Formerly they were not numbered in any civil lists of their country, except in those of the poor; here they rank as citizens. By what invisible power has this surprising metamorphosis been performed? By that of the laws and that of their industry. The laws, the indulgent laws, protect them as they arrive, stamping on them the symbol of adoption; they receive ample rewards for their labours; these accumulated rewards procure them lands; those lands confer on them the title of freemen, and to that title every benefit is affixed which men can possibly require. This is the great operation daily performed by our laws. From whence proceed these laws? From our government. Whence the government? It is derived from the original genius and strong desire of the people ratified and confirmed by the crown. This is the great chain which links us all, this is the picture which every province exhibits, Nova Scotia excepted. There the crown has done all; either there were no people who had genius, or it was not much attended to: the consequence is, that the province is very thinly inhabited indeed; the power of the crown in conjunction with the musketos has prevented men from settling there. Yet some parts of it flourished once, and it contained a mild harmless set of people. But for the fault of a few leaders, the whole were banished. The greatest political error the crown ever committed in America, was to cut off men from a country which wanted nothing but men!

What attachment can a poor European emigrant have for a country where he had nothing? The knowledge of the language, the love of a few kindred as poor as himself, were the only cords that tied him: his country is now that which gives him land, bread, protection, and consequence: *Ubi panis ibi patria*, is the motto of all emigrants. What then is the American, this new man? He is either an European, or the descendant of an European, hence that strange mixture of blood, which you will find in no other country. I could point out to you a family whose grandfather was an Englishman, whose wife was Dutch, whose son married a French woman, and whose present four sons have now four wives of different nations. *He* is an American, who, leaving behind him all his ancient prejudices and manners, receives new ones from the new mode of life he has embraced, the new government he obeys, and the new rank he holds. He becomes an American by being

received in the broad lap of our great *Alma Mater*. Here
individuals of all nations are melted into a new race of men, whose
labours and posterity will one day cause great changes in the
world. Americans are the western pilgrims, who are carrying
along with them the great mass of arts, sciences, vigour, and
industry which began long since in the east; they will finish the
great circle. The Americans were once scattered all over Europe;
here they are incorporated into one of the finest systems of
population which has ever appeared, and which will hereafter
become distinct by the power of the different climates they
inhabit. The American ought therefore to love this country much
better than that wherein either he or his forefathers were born.
Here the rewards of his industry follow with equal steps the
progress of his labour; his labour is founded on the basis of nature,
self-interest; can it want a stronger allurement? Wives and
children, who before in vain demanded of him a morsel of bread,
now, fat and frolicsome, gladly help their father to clear those
fields whence exuberant crops are to arise to feed and to clothe
them all; without any part being claimed, either by a despotic
prince, a rich abbot, or a mighty lord. Here religion demands but
little of him; a small voluntary salary to the minister, and gratitude
to God; can he refuse these? The American is a new man, who
acts upon new principles; he must therefore entertain new ideas,
and form new opinions. From involuntary idleness, servile dependence, penury, and useless labour, he has passed to toils of a
very different nature, rewarded by ample subsistence.—This is an
American. . . .

As I have endeavoured to show you how Europeans become
Americans; it may not be disagreeable to show you likewise how
the various Christian sects introduced, wear out, and how
religious indifference becomes prevalent. When any considerable
number of a particular sect happen to dwell contiguous to each
other, they immediately erect a temple, and there worship the
Divinity agreeably to their own peculiar ideas. Nobody disturbs
them. If any new sect springs up in Europe it may happen that
many of its professors will come and settle in America. As they
bring their zeal with them, they are at liberty to make proselytes if

they can, and to build a meeting and to follow the dictates of their consciences; for neither the government nor any other power interferes. If they are peaceable subjects, and are industrious, what is it to their neighbours how and in what manner they think fit to address their prayers to the Supreme Being? But if the sectaries are not settled close together, if they are mixed with other denominations, their zeal will cool for want of fuel, and will be extinguished in a little time. Then the Americans become as to religion, what they are as to country, allied to all. In them the name of Englishman, Frenchman, and European is lost, and in like manner, the strict modes of Christianity as practised in Europe are lost also. This effect will extend itself still farther hereafter, and though this may appear to you as a strange idea, yet it is a very true one. I shall be able perhaps hereafter to explain myself better; in the meanwhile, let the following example serve as my first justification.

Let us suppose you and I to be travelling; we observe that in this house, to the right, lives a Catholic, who prays to God as he has been taught, and believes in transubstantiation; he works and raises wheat, he has a large family of children, all hale and robust; his belief, his prayers offend nobody. About one mile farther on the same road, his next neighbour may be a good honest plodding German Lutheran, who addresses himself to the same God, the God of all, agreeably to the modes he has been educated in, and believes in consubstantiation; by so doing he scandalises nobody; he also works in his fields, embellishes the earth, clears swamps, etc. What has the world to do with his Lutheran principles? He persecutes nobody, and nobody persecutes him, he visits his neighbours, and his neighbours visit him. Next to him lives a seceder, the most enthusiastic of all sectaries; his zeal is hot and fiery, but separated as he is from others of the same complexion, he has no congregation of his own to resort to, where he might cabal and mingle religious pride with worldly obstinacy. He likewise raises good crops, his house is handsomely painted, his orchard is one of the fairest in the neighbourhood.

How does it concern the welfare of the country, or of the province at large, what this man's religious sentiments are, or really whether he has any at all? He is a good farmer, he is a sober, peaceable, good citizen: William Penn himself would not wish for more. This is the visible character, the invisible one is only guessed at, and is nobody's business. Next again lives a Low Dutchman, who implicitly believes the rules laid down by the synod of Dort. He conceives no other idea of a clergyman than that of an hired man; if he does his work well he will pay him the stipulated sum; if not he will dismiss him, and do without his sermons, and let his church be shut up for years. But notwithstanding this coarse idea, you will find his house and farm to be the neatest in all the country; and you will judge by his waggon and fat horses, that he thinks more of the affairs of this world than of those of the next. He is sober and laborious, therefore he is all he ought to be as to the affairs of this life; as for those of the next, he must trust to the great Creator. Each of these people instruct their children as well as they can, but these instructions are feeble compared to those which are given to the youth of the poorest class in Europe. Their children will therefore grow up less zealous and more indifferent in matters of religion than their parents.

The foolish vanity, or rather the fury of making Proselytes, is unknown here; they have no time, the seasons call for all their attention, and thus in a few years, this mixed neighbourhood will exhibit a strange religious medley, that will be neither pure Catholicism nor pure Calvinism. A very perceptible indifference even in the first generation, will become apparent; and it may happen that the daughter of the Catholic will marry the son of the seceder, and settle by themselves at a distance from their parents. What religious education will they give their children? A very imperfect one. If there happens to be in the neighbourhood any place of worship, we will suppose a Quaker's meeting; rather than not show their fine clothes, they will go to it, and some of them may perhaps attach themselves to that society. Others will remain in a perfect state of indifference; the children of these zealous parents will not be able to tell what their religious principles are, and their grandchildren still less.

The neighbourhood of a place of worship generally leads them to it, and the action of going thither, is the strongest evidence they can give of their attachment to any sect. The Quakers are the only people who retain a fondness for their own mode of worship; for be they ever so far separated from each other, they hold a sort of communion with the society, and seldom depart from its rules, at least in this country. Thus all sects are mixed as well as all nations; thus religious indifference is imperceptibly disseminated from one end of the continent to the other; which is at present one of the strongest characteristics of the Americans. Where this will reach no one can tell, perhaps it may leave a vacuum fit to receive other systems. Persecution, religious pride, the love of contradiction, are the food of what the world commonly calls religion. These motives have ceased here; zeal in Europe is confined; here it evaporates in the great distance it has to travel; there it is a grain of powder inclosed, here it burns away in the open air, and consumes without effect. . . .

There is no wonder that this country has so many charms, and presents to Europeans so many temptations to remain in it. A traveller in Europe becomes a stranger as soon as he quits his own kingdom; but it is otherwise here. We know, properly speaking, no strangers; this is every person's country; the variety of our soils, situations, climates, governments, and produce, hath something which must please everybody. No sooner does an European arrive, no matter of what condition, than his eyes are opened upon the fair prospect; he hears his language spoke, he retraces many of his own country manners, he perpetually hears the names of families and towns with which he is acquainted; he sees happiness and prosperity in all places disseminated; he meets with hospitality, kindness, and plenty everywhere; he beholds hardly any poor, he seldom hears of punishments and executions; and he wonders at the elegance of our towns, those miracles of industry and freedom. He cannot admire enough our rural districts, our convenient roads, good taverns, and our many accommodations; he involuntarily loves a country where everything is so lovely.

When in England, he was a mere Englishman; here he stands on a larger portion of the globe, not less than its fourth part, and may see the productions of the north, in iron and naval stores; the provisions of Ireland, the grain of Egypt, the indigo, the rice of

China. He does not find, as in Europe, a crowded society, where every place is over-stocked; he does not feel that perpetual collision of parties, that difficulty of beginning, that contention which oversets so many. There is room for everybody in America; has he any particular talent, or industry? he exerts it in order to procure a livelihood, and it succeeds. Is he a merchant? the avenues of trade are infinite; is he eminent in any respect? he will be employed and respected. Does he love a country life? pleasant farms present themselves; he may purchase what he wants, and thereby become an American farmer. Is he a labourer, sober and industrious? he need not go many miles, nor receive many informations before he will be hired, well fed at the table of his employer, and paid four or five times more than he can get in Europe. Does he want uncultivated lands? thousands of acres present themselves, which he may purchase cheap.

Whatever be his talents or inclinations, if they are moderate, he may satisfy them. I do not mean that every one who comes will grow rich in a little time; no, but he may procure an easy, decent maintenance, by his industry. Instead of starving he will be fed, instead of being idle he will have employment; and these are riches enough for such men as come over here. The rich stay in Europe, it is only the middling and the poor that emigrate. Would you wish to travel in independent idleness, from north to south, you will find easy access, and the most cheerful reception at every house; society without ostentation, good cheer without pride, and every decent diversion which the country affords, with little expense. It is no wonder that the European who has lived here a few years, is desirous to remain; Europe with all its pomp, is not to be compared to this continent, for men of middle stations, or labourers.

An European, when he first arrives, seems limited in his intentions, as well as in his views; but he very suddenly alters his scale; two hundred miles formerly appeared a very great distance, it is now but a trifle; he no sooner breathes our air than he forms schemes, and embarks in designs he never would have thought of in his own country. There the plenitude of society confines many useful ideas, and often extinguishes the most laudable schemes which here ripen into maturity. Thus Europeans become Americans.

But how is this accomplished in that crowd of low, indigent people, who flock here every year from all parts of Europe? I will tell you; they no sooner arrive than they immediately feel the good effects of that plenty of provisions we possess: they fare on our best food, and they are kindly entertained; their talents, character, and peculiar industry are immediately inquired into; they find countrymen everywhere disseminated, let them come from whatever part of Europe. Let me select one as an epitome of the rest; he is hired, he goes to work, and works moderately; instead of being employed by a haughty person, he finds himself with his equal, placed at the substantial table of the farmer, or else at an inferior one as good; his wages are high, his bed is not like that bed of sorrow on which he used to lie: if he behaves with propriety, and is faithful, he is caressed, and becomes as it were a member of the family. He begins to feel the effects of a sort of resurrection; hitherto he had not lived, but simply vegetated; he now feels himself a man, because he is treated as such; the laws of his own country had overlooked him in his insignificancy; the laws of this cover him with their mantle.

Judge what an alteration there must arise in the mind and thoughts of this man; he begins to forget his former servitude and dependence, his heart involuntarily swells and glows; this first swell inspires him with those new thoughts which constitute an American. What love can he entertain for a country where his existence was a burthen to him; if he is a generous good man, the love of this new adoptive parent will sink deep into his heart. He looks around, and sees many a prosperous person, who but a few years before was as poor as himself. This encourages him much, he begins to form some little scheme, the first, alas, he ever formed in his life. If he is wise he thus spends two or three years, in which time he acquires knowledge, the use of tools, the modes of working the lands, felling trees, etc.

This prepares the foundation of a good name, the most useful acquisition he can make. He is encouraged, he has gained friends; he is advised and directed, he feels bold, he purchases some land;

he gives all the money he has brought over, as well as what he has earned, and trusts to the God of harvests for the discharge of the rest. His good name procures him credit. He is now possessed of the deed, conveying to him and his posterity the fee simple and absolute property of two hundred acres of land, situated on such a river. What an epocha [sic] in this man's life! He is become a freeholder, from perhaps a German boor—he is now an American, a Pennsylvanian, an English subject. He is naturalised, his name is enrolled with those of the other citizens of the province. Instead of being a vagrant, he has a place of residence; he is called the inhabitant of such a county, or of such a district, and for the first time in his life counts for something; for hitherto he has been a cypher. I only repeat what I have heard many say, and no wonder their hearts should glow, and be agitated with a multitude of feelings, not easy to describe. From nothing to start into being; from a servant to the rank of a master; from being the slave of some despotic prince, to become a free man, invested with lands, to which every municipal blessing is annexed! What a change indeed! It is in consequence of that change that he becomes an American.

This great metamorphosis has a double effect, it extinguishes all his European prejudices, he forgets that mechanism of subordination, that servility of disposition which poverty had taught him; and sometimes he is apt to forget too much, often passing from one extreme to the other. If he is a good man, he forms schemes of future prosperity, he proposes to educate his children better than he has been educated himself; he thinks of future modes of conduct, feels an ardour to labour he never felt before. Pride steps in and leads him to everything that the laws do not forbid: he respects them; with a heart-felt gratitude he looks toward the east, toward that insular government from whose wisdom all his new felicity is derived, and under whose wings and protection he now lives. These reflections constitute him the good man and the good subject.

Ye poor Europeans, ye, who sweat, and work for the great—ye, who are obliged to give so many sheaves to the church, so many to your lords, so many to your government, and have hardly any left for yourselves—ye, who are held in less estimation than favourite hunters or useless lap-dogs—ye, who only breathe the air of nature, because it cannot be withheld from you; it is here that ye can conceive the possibility of those feelings I have been describing; it is here the laws of naturalisation invite every one to partake of our great labours and felicity, to till unrented, untaxed lands! . . .

After a foreigner from any part of Europe is arrived, and become a citizen; let him devoutly listen to the voice of our great parent, which says to him, "Welcome to my shores, distressed European; bless the hour in which thou didst see my verdant fields, my fair navigable rivers, and my green mountains!—If thou wilt work, I have bread for thee; if thou wilt be honest, sober, and industrious, I have greater rewards to confer on thee—ease and independence. I will give thee fields to feed and clothe thee; a comfortable fireside to sit by, and tell thy children by what means thou hast prospered; and a decent bed to repose on. I shall endow thee beside with the immunities of a freeman. If thou wilt carefully educate thy children, teach them gratitude to God, and reverence to that government, that philanthropic government, which has collected here so many men and made them happy. I will also provide for thy progeny; and to every good man this ought to be the most holy, the most powerful, the most earnest wish he can possibly form, as well as the most consolatory prospect when he dies. Go thou and work and till; thou shalt prosper, provided thou be just, grateful, and industrious."

4. THOMAS PAINE

Europe is the parent country of America

Hardly in the country two years, an erstwhile English staymaker became the new nation's most ardent and most popular pamphleteer. *Common*

Thomas Paine, from *Common Sense And Other Political Writings*, ed. Nelson F. Adkins (Indianapolis: Bobbs-Merrill, 1953), pp. 21–23.

Sense, published on February 14, 1776, in Philadelphia by Thomas Paine (1737–1809), gained immediate acclaim and wide circulation. Enunciating the spirit of liberty, Paine rejoiced in the cosmopolitanizing effects of emigration upon the American colonies, particularly of Pennsylvania, where he detected a distinctly American social mix of great political import.

. . . But Britain is the parent country, say some. Then the more shame upon her conduct. Even brutes do not devour their young nor savages make war upon their families; wherefore the assertion, if true, turns to her reproach; but it happens not to be true, or only partly so, and the phrase "parent" or "mother country" has been jesuitically adopted by the king and his parasites with a low papistical design of gaining an unfair bias on the credulous weakness of our minds. Europe, and not England, is the parent country of America. This New World has been the asylum for the persecuted lovers of civil and religious liberty from *every part* of Europe. Hither have they fled, not from the tender embraces of the mother, but from the cruelty of the monster; and it is so far true of England that the same tyranny which drove the first emigrants from home pursues their descendants still.

In this extensive quarter of the globe, we forget the narrow limits of three hundred and sixty miles (the extent of England) and carry our friendship on a larger scale; we claim brotherhood with every European Christian, and triumph in the generosity of the sentiment.

It is pleasant to observe by what regular gradations we surmount the force of local prejudices as we enlarge our acquaintance with the world. A man born in any town in England divided into parishes will naturally associate most with his fellow parishioners (because their interests in many cases will be common) and distinguish him by the name of "neighbor"; if he meet him but a few miles from home, he drops the narrow idea of a street and salutes him by the name of "townsman"; if he travel out of the county and meet him in any other, he forgets the minor divisions of street and town, and calls him "countryman," i.e., "countyman"; but if in their foreign excursions they should associate in France, or any other part of *Europe*, their local remembrance would be enlarged into that of "Englishmen." And by a just parity of reasoning, all Europeans meeting in America, or any other quarter of the globe, are "countrymen"; for England, Holland, Germany, or Sweden, when compared with the whole, stand in the same places on the larger scale which the divisions of street, town, and county do on the smaller ones—distinctions too limited for continental minds. Not one third of the inhabitants, even of this province [Pennsylvania], are of English descent. Wherefore I reprobate the phrase of parent or mother country applied to England only as being false, selfish, narrow, and ungenerous.

But, admitting that we were all of English descent, what does it amount to? Nothing. Britain, being now an open enemy, extinguishes every other name and title; and to say that reconciliation is our duty is truly farcical. The first king of England of the present line (William the Conqueror) was a Frenchman, and half the peers of England are descendants from the same country; wherefore, by the same method of reasoning, England ought to be governed by France.

Much has been said of the united strength of Britain and the colonies, that in conjunction they might bid defiance to the world. But this is mere presumption; the fate of war is uncertain, neither do the expressions mean anything; for this continent would never suffer itself to be drained of inhabitants to support the British arms in either Asia, Africa, or Europe.

Besides, what have we to do with setting the world at defiance? Our plan is commerce, and that, well attended to, will secure us the peace and friendship of all Europe; because it is the interest of all Europe to have America a free port. Her trade will always be a protection, and her barrenness of gold and silver secure her from invaders.

I challenge the warmest advocate for reconciliation to show a single advantage that this continent can reap by being connected with Great Britain. I repeat the challenge; not a single advantage is derived. Our corn will fetch its price in any market in Europe, and our imported goods must be paid for, buy them where we will.

But the injuries and disadvantages we sustain by that connection are without number, and our duty to mankind at large, as well as to ourselves, instruct us to renounce the alliance; because any submission to or dependence on Great Britain tends directly to involve this continent in European wars and quarrels and sets us at variance with nations who would otherwise seek our friendship and against whom we have neither anger nor complaint. As Europe is our market for trade, we ought to form no partial connection with any part of it. It is the true interest of America to steer clear of European contentions, which she never can do while, by her dependence on Britain, she is made the makeweight in the scale of British politics.

Europe is too thickly planted with kingdoms to be long at peace; and whenever a war breaks out between England and any foreign power, the trade of America goes to ruin *because of her connection with Britain.* The next war may not turn out like the last; and should it not, the advocates for reconciliation now will be wishing for separation then, because neutrality in that case would be a safer convoy than a man-of-war. Everything that is right or natural pleads for separation. The blood of the slain, the weeping voice of nature cries, " *'Tis time to part."* Even the distance at which the Almighty has placed England and America is a strong and natural proof that the authority of the one over the other was never the design of heaven. The time likewise at which the continent was discovered adds weight to the argument, and the manner in which it was peopled increases the force of it. The Reformation was preceded by the discovery of America—as if the Almighty graciously meant to open a sanctuary to the persecuted in future years, when home should afford neither friendship nor safety. . . .

5. BENJAMIN FRANKLIN
America is the land of labour

Following the drawing up of the Treaty of Paris, probably in September, 1782, the official minister to France and unofficial ambassador to Europe, Benjamin Franklin, prepared a general statement to be mailed out to all those inquiring about the conditions and prospects for emigration to the new nation. By 1786, *Information To Those Who Would Remove To America* had appeared in a series of English editions in London and in Dublin, as well as in French, German, and Italian editions. In this brief prospectus, Franklin spelled out the distinctive virtues of a country with cheap land and a dearth of labor but cautioned those unprepared for toil to remain in Europe.

Many Persons in Europe, having directly or by Letters, express'd to the Writer of this, who is well acquainted with North America, their Desire of transporting and establishing themselves in that Country; but who appear to have formed, thro' Ignorance, mistaken Ideas and Expectations of what is to be obtained there; he thinks it may be useful, and prevent inconvenient, expensive, and fruitless Removals and Voyages of improper Persons, if he gives some clearer and truer Notions of that part of the World, than appear to have hitherto prevailed.

He finds it is imagined by Numbers, that the Inhabitants of North America are rich, capable of rewarding, and dispos'd to reward, all sorts of Ingenuity; that they are at the same time ignorant of all the Sciences, and, consequently, that Strangers, possessing Talents in the Belles-Lettres, fine Arts, &c., must be highly esteemed, and so well paid, as to become easily rich themselves; that there are also abundance of profitable Offices to be disposed of, which the Natives are not qualified to fill; and that, having few Persons of Family among them, Strangers of Birth must be greatly respected, and of course easily obtain the best of those Offices, which will make all their Fortunes; that the

Benjamin Franklin, from *The Works of Benjamin Franklin*, 10 vols., ed. Jared Sparks (Boston: Tappan & Whittemore, 1836), vol. II, pp. 467–77.

Governments too, to encourage Emigrations from Europe, not only pay the Expence of personal Transportation, but give Lands gratis to Strangers, with Negroes to work for them, Utensils of Husbandry, and Stocks of Cattle. These are all wild Imaginations; and those who go to America with Expectations founded upon them will surely find themselves disappointed.

The Truth is, that though there are in that Country few People so miserable as the Poor of Europe, there are also very few that in Europe would be called rich; it is rather a general happy Mediocrity that prevails. There are few great Proprietors of the Soil, and few Tenants; most People cultivate their own Lands, or follow some Handicraft or Merchandise; very few rich enough to live idly upon their Rents or Incomes, or to pay the high Prices given in Europe for Paintings, Statues, Architecture, and the other Works of Art, that are more curious than useful. Hence the natural Geniuses, that have arisen in America with such Talents, have uniformly quitted that Country for Europe, where they can be more suitably rewarded. It is true, that Letters and Mathematical Knowledge are in Esteem there, but they are at the same time more common than is apprehended; there being already existing nine Colleges or Universities, viz. four in New England, and one in each of the Provinces of New York, New Jersey, Pensylvania, Maryland, and Virginia, all furnish'd with learned Professors; besides a number of smaller Academies; these educate many of their Youth in the Languages, and those Sciences that qualify men for the Professions of Divinity, Law, or Physick. Strangers indeed are by no means excluded from exercising those Professions; and the quick Increase of Inhabitants everywhere gives them a Chance of Employ, which they have in common with the Natives. Of civil Offices, or Employments, there are few; no superfluous Ones, as in Europe; and it is a Rule establish'd in some of the States, that no Office should be so profitable as to make it desirable. The 36th Article of the Constitution of Pennsilvania, runs expressly in these Words; "As every Freeman, to preserve his Independence, (if he has not a sufficient Estate) ought to have some Profession, Calling, Trade, or Farm, whereby he may honestly subsist, there can be no Necessity for, nor Use in, establishing Offices of Profit; the usual Effects of which are Dependance and Servility, unbecoming Freemen, in the Possessors and Expectants; Faction, Contention, Corruption, and Disorder among the People. Wherefore, whenever an Office, thro' Increase of Fees or otherwise, becomes so profitable, as to occasion many to apply for it, the Profits ought to be lessened by the Legislature."

These Ideas prevailing more or less in all the United States, it cannot be worth any Man's while, who has a means of Living at home, to expatriate himself, in hopes of obtaining a profitable civil Office in America; and, as to military Offices, they are at an End with the War, the Armies being disbanded. Much less is it adviseable for a Person to go thither, who has no other Quality to recommend him but his Birth. In Europe it has indeed its Value; but it is a Commodity that cannot be carried to a worse Market than that of America, where people do not inquire concerning a Stranger, *What is he?* but, *What can he do?* If he has any useful Art, he is welcome; and if he exercises it, and behaves well, he will be respected by all that know him; but a mere Man of Quality, who, on that Account, wants to live upon the Public, by some Office or Salary, will be despis'd and disregarded. The Husbandman is in honor there, and even the Mechanic, because their Employments are useful. The People have a saying, that God Almighty is himself a Mechanic, the greatest in the Univers; and he is respected and admired more for the Variety, Ingenuity, and Utility of his Handyworks, than for the Antiquity of his Family. They are pleas'd with the Observation of a Negro, and frequently mention it, that *Boccarorra* (meaning the White men) *make de black man workee, make de Horse workee, make de Ox workee, make ebery ting workee; only de Hog. He, de hog, no workee; he eat, he drink, he walk about, he go to sleep when he please, he libb like a Gentleman.* According to these Opinions of the Americans, one of them would think himself more oblig'd to a Genealogist, who could prove for him that his Ancestors and Relations for ten Generations had been Ploughmen, Smiths, Carpenters, Turners, Weavers, Tanners, or even Shoemakers, and consequently that they were useful Members of Society; than if he could only prove that they were Gentlemen, doing nothing of Value, but living idly on the Labour of others . . . and otherwise *good for nothing*, till by their Death their Estates, like the Carcass of the Negro's Gentleman-Hog, come to be *cut up*.

With regard to Encouragements for Strangers from Government, they are really only what are derived from good Laws and Liberty. Strangers are welcome, because there is room enough for them all, and therefore the old Inhabitants are not jealous of them; the Laws protect them sufficiently, so that they have no need of the Patronage of Great Men; and every one will enjoy securely the Profits of his Industry. But, if he does not bring a Fortune with him, he must work and be industrious to live. One or two Years' residence gives him all the Rights of a Citizen; but the government does not at present, whatever it may have done in former times, hire People to become Settlers, by Paying their Passages, giving Land, Negroes, Utensils, Stock, or any other kind of Emolument whatsoever. In short, America is the Land of Labour, and by no means what the English call *Lubberland*, and the French *Pays de Cocagne*, where the streets are said to be pav'd with half-peck Loaves, the Houses til'd with Pancakes, and where the Fowls fly about ready roasted, crying, *Come eat me!*

Who then are the kind of Persons to whom an Emigration to America may be advantageous? And what are the Advantages they may reasonably expect?

Land being cheap in that Country, from the vast Forests still void of Inhabitants, and not likely to be occupied in an Age to come, insomuch that the Propriety of an hundred Acres of fertile Soil full of Wood may be obtained near the Frontiers, in many Places, for Eight or Ten Guineas, hearty young Labouring Men, who understand the Husbandry of Corn and Cattle, which is nearly the same in that Country as in Europe, may easily establish themselves there. A little Money sav'd of the good Wages they receive there, while they work for others, enables them to buy the Land and begin their Plantation, in which they are assisted by the Good-Will of their Neighbours, and some Credit. Multitudes of poor People from England, Ireland, Scotland, and Germany, have by this means in a few years become wealthy Farmers, who, in their own Countries, where all the Lands are fully occupied, and the Wages of Labour low, could never have emerged from the poor Condition wherein they were born.

From the salubrity of the Air, the healthiness of the Climate, the plenty of good Provisions, and the Encouragement to early Marriages by the certainty of Subsistence in cultivating the Earth, the Increase of Inhabitants by natural Generation is very rapid in America, and becomes still more so by the Accession of Strangers; hence there is a continual Demand for more Artisans of all the necessary and useful kinds, to supply those Cultivators of the Earth with Houses, and with Furniture and Utensils of the grosser sorts, which cannot so well be brought from Europe. Tolerably good Workmen in any of those mechanic Arts are sure to find Employ, and to be well paid for their Work, there being no Restraints preventing Strangers from exercising any Art they understand, nor any Permission necessary. If they are poor, they begin first as Servants or Journeymen; and if they are sober, industrious, and frugal, they soon become Masters, establish themselves in Business, marry, raise Families, and become respectable Citizens.

Also, Persons of moderate Fortunes and Capitals, who, having a Number of Children to provide for, are desirous of bringing them up to Industry, and to secure Estates for their Posterity, have Opportunities of doing it in America, which Europe does not afford. There they may be taught and practise profitable mechanic Arts, without incurring Disgrace on that Account, but on the contrary acquiring Respect by such Abilities. There small Capitals laid out in Lands, which daily become more valuable by the Increase of People, afford a solid Prospect of ample Fortunes thereafter for those Children. The Writer of this has known several Instances of large Tracts of Land, bought, on what was then the Frontier of Pennsilvania, for Ten Pounds per hundred Acres, which after 20 years, when the Settlements had been extended far beyond them, sold readily, without any Improvement made upon them, for three Pounds per Acre. . . .

The almost general Mediocrity of Fortune that prevails in America obliging its People to follow some Business for subsistence, those Vices, that arise usually from Idleness, are in a great measure prevented. Industry and constant Employment are great preservatives of the Morals and Virtue of a Nation. Hence bad Examples to Youth are more rare in America, which must be a comfortable Consideration to Parents. To this may be truly added, that serious Religion, under its various Denominations, is not only tolerated, but respected and practised. Atheism is unknown there; Infidelity rare and secret; so that persons may live to a great Age in that Country, without having their Piety shocked by meeting with either an Atheist or an Infidel. And the Divine Being seems to have manifested his Approbation of the mutual Forbearance and Kindness with which the different Sects treat each other, by the remarkable Prosperity with which He has been pleased to favour the whole Country.

6. George Washington

An asylum to the oppressed and needy of the earth

Just before returning his commander-in-chief's commission to Congress and formally relinquishing leadership of the Continental Army, George Washington sounded a popular keynote of the new republic. In a letter of welcome to the "Members of the Volunteer Association and other Inhabitants of the Kingdom of Ireland Who Have Lately Arrived in the City of New York," Washington thanked them for their hospitality to American prisoners of war, blessed the Irish struggle for freedom and proclaimed the idea of the new American nation as an asylum for the oppressed. In 1785 in a letter to an admirer, Lucretia Wilhemina Van Winter, Washington reiterated his commitment to the vision of America as a haven for the oppressed.

George Washington to the Members of the Volunteer Association and Other Inhabitants of the Kingdom of Ireland Who Have Lately Arrived in the city of New York, from *The Writings of George Washington*, ed. John C. Fitzpatrick (Washington: Government Printing Office, 1938), vol. 27, pp. 253–54.

To the Members of the Volunteer Association . . .

GENTLEMEN: The testimony of your satisfaction at the glorious termination of the late contest, and your indulgent opinion of my Agency in it, affords me singular pleasure and merit my warmest acknowledgment.

If the Example of the Americans successfully contending in the Cause of Freedom, can be of any use to other Nations; we shall have an additional Motive for rejoycing at so prosperous an Event.

It was not an uninteresting consideration, to learn, that the Kingdom of Ireland, by a bold and manly conduct had obtained the redress of many of its greivances; and it is much to be wished that the blessings of equal Liberty and unrestrained Commerce may yet prevail more extensively; in the mean time, you may be assured, Gentlemen, that the Hospitality and Benificence of your Countrymen, to our Brethren who have been Prisoners of War, are neither unknown, or unregarded.

The bosom of America is open to receive not only the Opulent and respectable Stranger, but the oppressed and persecuted of all Nations And Religions; whom we shall wellcome to a participation of all our rights and previleges, if by decency and propriety of conduct they appear to merit the enjoyment.

New York, December 2, 1783.

To Lucretia Wilhemina Van Winter

MADAM: The honor which your pen has done me so far exceeds my merits, that I am at a loss for words to express my sense of the compliment it conveys.

The Poem, in celebration of my exertions to establish the rights of my Country, was forwarded to me from Philada. by Mr. Vogels; to whom I should have been happy to have offered civilities, but he did not give me the pleasure to see him.

At best I have only been an instrument in the hands of Providence, to effect, with the aid of France and many virtuous

Washington to Lucretia Wilhemina Van Winter, from *The Writings of George Washington*, ed. John C. Fitzpatrick (Washington: Government Printing Office, 1938), vol. 28, pp. 119–20.

fellow Citizens of America, a revolution which is interesting to the general liberties of mankind, and to the emancipation of a country which may afford an Asylum, if we are wise enough to pursue the paths wch. lead to virtue and happiness, to the oppressed and needy of the Earth. Our region is extensive, our plains are productive, and if they are cultivated with liberallity and good sense, we may be happy ourselves, and diffuse happiness to all who wish to participate.

The Lady of whom you have made such honorable mention, is truly sensible of the obligation, and joins with me in wishing you every happiness which is to be found here, and met with hereafter. I have the honor, etc.
March 30, 1785.

7. JOHN QUINCY ADAMS

They must cast off the European skin never to resume it

No American of his generation had seen Europe so intimately and so comprehensively so early in life as had the son of the second president of the United States and none came to reject it so vehemently. Educated in Paris and London, John Quincy Adams (1767–1848) at the age of fourteen already was serving as personal secretary to the American envoy to Russia. Seven years after graduating from Harvard at the age of twenty, he was appointed minister to the Netherlands by President Washington. Following a similar post in Berlin, a term as Senator from Massachusetts, and an eight-year diplomatic stint in St. Petersburg and London, Adams became James Monroe's secretary of state. Above all, he became dedicated to reasserting America's national interests and ideals in a world cast adrift between reaction and revolution.

After the Napoleonic wars, Freiherr von Gagern, Holland's representative at the Diet of the German Confederation, had been greatly alarmed by the state of the war refugees who had fled to the Dutch ports. Blocked

From *Niles Weekly Register*, April 29, 1820, pp. 157–58.

in his efforts to solve the problem on the European side, he proceeded to charge his brother-in-law, the Baron von Furstenwaerther, to observe the state of the Germans there and to approach the American government with a proposal for securing land for them on attractive terms. In the summer of 1818, von Furstenwaerther conveyed his request personally to Secretary of State John Quincy Adams.

On June 4, 1819 in a little-known letter to Baron von Furstenwaerther, Adams formally enunciated the terms of the nation's immigration policy. A year earlier, the House Committee on Public Lands had recommended against selling a township in Illinois territory on long-term credit, instead of the usual four years, to an Irish colony on the grounds that such a concession would establish a principle favoring foreigners over the native-born. In accord with the letter and spirit of this decision, Adams proceeded to make clear that free, unassisted individual migration without privileges but with equal rights would henceforth govern American policy.

From the National Intelligencer:

The letter, of which the following is a copy, appears to have been published in a German translation at Augsburg; whence, by a re-translation, it has appeared in some of the English Gazettes, and from them been extracted into some of the newspapers in this country. In its double transformation it has suffered variations not supposed to be intentional, nor perhaps important, but which render the publication of it proper, as it was written. It has been incorrectly stated to be an answer in the name of the American government. It was indeed written by the secretary of state, as it purports, in answer to an application from an individual and respectable foreigner, who had previously been employed by the baron de Gagern, to collect information concerning the German emigrants to the United States, and to endeavor to obtain encouragements and favors to them from this government.

Upon that mission he had been particularly recommended to Mr. Adams, to whom a printed copy of his report to the baron de Gagern had afterwards been transmitted. There are several allusions to the report, in this letter, which was an answer to one from Mr. Furstenwaerther, intimating a disposition to become himself an American citizen; but suggesting that he had offers of advantageous employment in his native country, and enquiring whether, in the event of his settling here, he could expect any official situation in the department of state, or any other under the government.

Department of State, Washington, 4th June, 1819

Sir—I had the honor of receiving your letter of the 22nd April, enclosing one from your kinsman the baron de Gagern and a copy of your printed report which I hope and have no doubt will be useful to those of your countrymen in Germany, who may have entertained erroneous ideas, with regard to the results of emigration from Europe to this country.

It was explicitly stated to you, and your report has taken just notice of the statement, that the government of the United States has never adopted any measure to *encourage* or *invite* emigrants from any part of Europe. It has never held out any incitements to induce the subjects of any other sovereign to abandon their own country, to become inhabitants of this. From motives of humanity it has occasionally furnished facilities to emigrants who, having arrived here with views of forming settlements, have specially needed such assistance to carry them into effect.

Neither the general government of the union, nor those of the individual states, are ignorant or unobservant of the additional strength and wealth, which accrues to the nation, by the accession of a mass of healthy, industrious, and frugal laborers, nor are they in any manner insensible to the great benefits which this country has derived, and continues to derive, from the influx of such adoptive children from Germany. But there is one principle which pervades all the institutions of this country, and which must always operate as an obstacle to the granting of favors to new comers. This is a land, not of *privileges*, but of *equal rights*. Privileges are granted by European sovereigns to particular classes of individuals, for purposes of general policy; but the general impression here is that *privileges* granted to one denomination of people, can very seldom be discriminated from erosions of the rights of others.

Emigrants from Germany, therefore, or from elsewhere, coming here, are not to expect favors from the governments. They are to expect, if they choose to become citizens, equal rights with those of the natives of the country. They are to expect, if affluent, to possess the means of making their property productive, with moderation, and with safety—if indigent, but industrious, honest, and frugal, the means of obtaining easy and comfortable subsistence for themselves and their families. They come to a life of independence, but to a life of labor—and, if they cannot accommodate themselves to the character, moral, political, and physical, of this country, with all its compensating balances of good and evil, the Atlantic is always open to them to return to the land of their nativity and their fathers. To one thing they must make up their minds, or, they will be disappointed in every expectation of happiness as Americans. They must cast off the European skin, never to resume it. They must look forward to their posterity rather than backward to their ancestors; they must be sure that whatever their own feelings may be, those of their children will cling to the prejudices of this country, and will partake of that proud spirit, not unmingled with disdain, which you have observed is remarkable in the general character of this people, and as perhaps belonging peculiarly to those of German descent, born in this country.

That feeling of superiority over other nations which you have noticed, and which has been so offensive to other strangers, who have visited these shores, arises from the consciousness of every individual that, as a member of society, no man in the country is above him; and, exulting in this sentiment, he looks down upon those nations where the mass of the people feel themselves the inferiors of privileged classes, and where men are high or low, according to the accidents of their birth. But hence it is that no government in the world possesses so few means of bestowing favors, as the governments of the United States. The governments are the servants of the people, and are so considered by the people, who place and displace them at their pleasure. They are chosen to manage for short periods the common concerns, and when they cease to give satisfaction, they cease to be employed. If the powers, however, of the government to do good are restricted, those of doing harm are still more limited. The dependence, in affairs of government, is the reverse of the practice in Europe, instead of the people depending upon their rulers, the rulers, as such, are always dependent upon the good will of the people.

We understand perfectly, that of the multitude of foreigners who yearly flock to our shores, to take up here their abode, none come from affection or regard to land to which they are total strangers, and with the very language of which those of them who are Germans are generally unacquainted. We know that they come with views, not to our benefit but to their own—not to promote our welfare, but to better their own condition. We expect therefore very few, if any transplanted countrymen from classes of people who enjoy happiness, ease, or even comfort, in their native climes. The happy and contented remain at home, and it requires an impulse, at least as keen as that of urgent want, to drive a man from the soil of his nativity and the land of his fathers' sepulchres.

Of the very few emigrants of more fortunate classes, who ever make the attempt of settling in this country, a principal proportion sicken at the strangeness of our manners, and after a residence, more or less protracted, return to the countries whence they came. There are, doubtless, exceptions, and among the most opulent and the most distinguished of our citizens, we are happy to number individuals who might have enjoyed or acquired wealth and consideration, without resorting to a new country and another hemisphere. We should take great satisfaction in finding you included in this number, if it should suit your own inclinations, and the prospects of your future life, upon your calculations of your own interest.

I regret that it is not in my power to add the inducement which you might perceive in the situation of an officer under the government. All the places in the department to which I belong, allowed by the laws, are filled, nor is there a prospect of an early vacancy in any of them. Whenever such vacancies occur, the applications from natives of the country to fill them, are far more numerous than the offices, and the recommendations in behalf of the candidates so strong and so earnest, that it would seldom be possible, if it would ever be just, to give a preference over them to foreigners. Although, therefore, it would give me sincere pleasure to consider you as one of our future and permanent fellow citizens, I should do neither an act of kindness or of justice to you, in dissuading you from the offers of employment and of honorable services, to which you are called in your native country. With the sincerest wish that you may find them equal and superior to every expectation of advantage that you have formed, or can indulge, in looking to them.

I have the honor to be, sir, your very obedient and humble servant,

Mr. Morris de Furstenwaerther, Philadelphia

John Quincy Adams

PART THREE

Europe
Spectre and Hope

8. Thomas Jefferson and Lafayette

A new imported American doctrine
for the instruction of Europe

When the Marquis de Lafayette volunteered his military services to the new nation during the American Revolution, he became—in the eyes of an absolutist Europe—a personification of liberalism, as well as the embodiment of Franco-American cooperation. His friend Thomas Jefferson, who as minister to France had suggested the British Constitution rather than the American as a model for a new France, had been alarmed by Lafayette's republicanism. Lafayette, the most popular figure in France in 1790, proved unable to control events and in 1792 was imprisoned for five years. Yet this celebrated honorary citizen of the United States never relinquished his dream of establishing a French republic and played a leading role in the July Revolution of 1830.

The letters exchanged over nearly half a lifetime between Lafayette and Jefferson reflect the intimate ties not only between two men dedicated to liberty but between two very different nations dedicated to the liberal tradition.

Jefferson to Lafayette

Behold you, then, my dear friend, at the head of a great army establishing the liberties of your country against a foreign enemy. May heaven favor your cause, and make you the channel through which it may pour its favors. While you are estimating the monster Aristocracy, and pulling out the teeth and fangs of its associate, Monarchy, a contrary tendency is discovered in some here. A sect has shown itself among us, who declare they espoused

Jefferson and Lafayette, from *The Writings of Thomas Jefferson: Memorial Edition*, ed. A. A. Lipscomb and A. E. Bergh (published under the auspices of Thomas Jefferson Memorial Association, Washington, 1903–04), vol. 8, pp. 380–82; vol. 14, pp. 245–48, 253–54; vol. 18, pp. 324–28.

our new Constitution not as a good and sufficient thing in itself, but only as a step to an English constitution, the only thing good and sufficient in itself, in their eye. It is happy for us that these are preachers without followers, and that our people are firm and constant in their republican purity.

You will wonder to be told that it is from the eastward chiefly that these champions for a king, lords, and commons, come. They get some important associates from New York, and are puffed up by a tribe of Agioteurs [stock jobbers] which have been hatched in a bed of corruption made up after the model of their beloved England. Too many of these stock-jobbers and king-jobbers have come into our Legislature, or rather too many of our Legislature have become stock-jobbers and king-jobbers. However, the voice of the people is beginning to make itself heard, and will probably cleanse their seats at the ensuing election. The machinations of our old enemies are such as to keep us still at bay with our Indian neighbors. What are you doing for your colonies? They will be lost, if not more effectually succored. Indeed, no future efforts you can make will ever be able to reduce the blacks.

All that can be done, in my opinion, will be to compound with them, as has been done formerly in Jamaica. We have been less zealous in aiding them, lest your government should feel any jealousy on our account. But, in truth, we as sincerely wish their restoration and their connection with you, as you do yourselves. We are satisfied that neither your justice nor their distresses will ever again permit their being forced to seek at dear and distant markets those first necessaries of life which they may have at cheaper markets, placed by nature at their door, and formed by her for their support. What is become of Madame de Tessy and Madame de Tott? I have not heard of them since they went to Switzerland. I think they would have done better to have come and reposed under the poplars of Virginia. Pour into their bosoms the warmest effusions of my friendship, and tell them they will be warm and constant unto death. Accept of them also for Madame de La Fayette, and your dear children; but I am forgetting that you are in the field of war, and they I hope in those of peace.

Adieu, my dear friend. God bless you all. Yours affectionately. *Philadelphia, June 16, 1792.*

Jefferson to Lafayette

MY DEAR FRIEND,—Your letter of August the 14th has been received, and read again and again, with extraordinary pleasure. It is the first glimpse which has been furnished me of the interior workings of the late unexpected but fortunate revolution of your country. The newspapers told us only that the great beast was fallen; but what part in this the patriots acted, and what the egotists, whether the former slept while the latter were awake to their own interests only, the hireling scribblers of the English press said little and knew less. I see now the mortifying alternative under which the patriot there is placed, of being either silent, or disgraced by an association in opposition with the remains of Bonapartism. A full measure of liberty is not now perhaps to be expected by your nation, nor am I confident they are prepared to preserve it. More than a generation will be requisite, under the administration of reasonable laws favoring the progress of knowledge in the general mass of the people, and their habituation to an independent security of person and property, before they will be capable of estimating the value of freedom, and the necessity of a sacred adherence to the principles on which it rests for preservation.

Instead of that liberty which takes root and growth in the progress of reason, if recovered by mere force or accident, it becomes, with an unprepared people, a tyranny still, of the many, the few, or the one. Possibly you may remember, at the date of the *jeu de paume,* how earnestly I urged yourself and the patriots of my acquaintance, to enter then into a compact with the king, securing freedom of religion, freedom of the press, trial by jury, *habeas corpus,* and a national legislature, all of which it was known he would then yield, to go home, and let these work on the amelioration of the condition of the people, until they should have rendered them capable of more, when occasions would not fail to arise for communicating to them more.

This was as much as I then thought them able to bear, soberly and usefully for themselves. You thought otherwise, and that the dose might still be larger. And I found you were right; for subsequent events proved they were equal to the Constitution of 1791. Unfortunately, some of the most honest and enlightened of our patriotic friends, (but closet politicians merely, unpractised in the knowledge of man,) thought more could still be obtained and borne. They did not weigh the hazards of a transition from one form of government to another, the value of what they had already rescued from those hazards, and might hold in security if they pleased, nor the imprudence of giving up the certainty of such a degree of liberty, under a limited monarch, for the uncertainty of a little more under the form of a republic. You differed from them. You were for stopping there, and for securing the Constitution which the National Assembly had obtained. Here, too, you were right; and from this fatal error of the republicans, from their separation from yourself and the constitutionalists, in their councils, flowed all the subsequent sufferings and crimes of the French nation.

The hazards of a second change fell upon them by the way. The foreigner gained time to anarchise by gold the government he could not overthrow by arms, to crush in their own councils the genuine republicans, by the fraternal embraces of exaggerated and hired pretenders, and to turn the machine of Jacobinism from the change to the destruction of order; and, in the end, the limited monarchy they had secured was exchanged for the unprincipled and bloody tyranny of Robespierre, and the equally unprincipled and maniac tyranny of Bonaparte. You are now rid of him, and I sincerely wish you may continue so. But this may depend on the wisdom and moderation of the restored dynasty. It is for them now to read a lesson in the fatal errors of the republicans; to be contented with a certain portion of power, secured by formal compact with the nation, rather than, grasping at more, hazard all upon uncertainty, and risk meeting the fate of their predecessor, or a renewal of their own exile.

We are just informed, too, of an example which merits, if true, their most profound contemplation. The gazettes say that Ferdinand of Spain is dethroned, and his father re-established on the basis of their new Constitution. This order of magistrates must, therefore, see, that although the attempts at reformation have not succeeded in their whole length, and some secession from the ultimate point has taken place, yet that men have by no means fallen back to their former passiveness, but on the contrary, that a sense of their rights, and a restlessness to obtain them, remain deeply impressed on every mind, and, if not quieted by reasonable relaxations of power, will break out like a volcano on the first occasion, and overwhelm everything again in its way. I always thought the present king an honest and moderate man; and having no issue, he is under a motive the less for yielding to personal considerations. I cannot, therefore, but hope, that the patriots in and out of your legislature, acting in phalanx, but temperately and wisely, pressing unremittingly the principles omitted in the late capitulation of the king, and watching the occasions which the course of events will create, may get those principles engrafted into it, and sanctioned by the solemnity of a national act. . . .

You once gave me a copy of the journal of your campaign in Virginia, in 1781, which I must have lent to some one of the undertakers to write the history of the Revolutionary war, and forgot to reclaim. I conclude this, because it is no longer among my papers, which I have very diligently searched for it, but in vain. An author of real ability is now writing that part of the history of Virginia. He does it in my neighborhood, and I lay open to him all my papers. But I possess none, nor has he any, which can enable him to do justice to your faithful and able services in that campaign. If you could be so good as to send me another copy, by the very first vessel bound to any port in the United States, it might be here in time; for although he expects to begin to print within a month or two, yet you know the delays of these undertakings. At any rate it might be got in as a supplement. The old Count Rochambeau gave me also his *memoire* of the operations at York, which is gone in the same way, and I have no means of applying to his family for it. Perhaps you could render them as well as us, the service of procuring another copy.

I learn, with real sorrow, the deaths of Monsieur and Madame de Tessé. They made an interesting part in the idle reveries in which I have sometimes indulged myself, of seeing all my friends of Paris once more, for a month or two; a thing impossible, which, however, I never permitted myself to despair of. The regrets, however, of seventy-three at the loss of friends, may be the less, as the time is shorter within which we are to meet again, according to the creed of our education.

This letter will be handed you by Mr. [George] Ticknor, a young gentleman of Boston, of great erudition, indefatigable industry, and preparation for a life of distinction in his own country. He passed a few days with me here, brought high recommendations from Mr. Adams and others, and appeared in every respect to merit them. He is well worthy of those attentions which you so kindly bestow on our countrymen, and for those he may receive I shall join him in acknowledging personal obligations.

I salute you with assurances of my constant and affectionate friendship and respect. . . .
Monticello, February 14, 1815.

Lafayette to Jefferson

My Dear Friend,—It is a very long while since my eyes were gratified with a sight of your handwriting; I know that occupation is a fatigue to you, and would not be importunate. But when you indulge the pleasure to converse with absent friends, remember few are as old, and none can be more happy than I am in the testimonies of your welfare and affection.

Every account I receive from the United States is a compensation for European disappointments and disgusts. There our revolutionary hopes have been fulfilled, and although I must admire the observations of such a witness as my friend Jefferson, we may enjoy the happy thought that never a nation has been so completely free, so rapidly prosperous, so generally enlightened. Look, on the contrary, to old Europe. Spain, Portugal, Italy, amidst the patriotic wishes of the less ignorant part of the people and the noble sentiments of a few distinguished characters, have shown themselves unequal to a regeneration, less on account of the criminal attacks of diabolical alliance and the perfidious friendships of Great Britain, than because the great masses are still under the influence of prejudice, superstition, vicious habits, and because intrigue and corruption have found their way among the aristocratical part of their patriots.

German patriotism and philanthropy evaporates in romantic ideology; two nations alone, French and English, or one of them, could take the lead in European emancipation. But in England both Whigs and Tories are tenacious of a double aristocracy, their own with respect to the Commoners, that of their island over all the countries of the earth. There is, I am told, more liberality among their Radicals; but hitherto we must take them at their word, as power is elsewhere, and they do nothing to obtain it. You have been a sharer, my dear friend, in my enthusiastic French hopes; you have seen the people of France truly a great nation, when the rights of mankind, proclaimed, conquered, supported by a whole population, were set up as a new imported American doctrine, for the instruction and example of Europe, when they might have been the sole object and the glorious price of a first irresistible impulsion, which has since been spent into other purposes by the subsequent vicissitudes of government; the triple counter revolution of Jacobinism, Bonapartism, and Bourbonism, in the first of which disguised Aristocracy had also a great part, has worn out the springs of energetic patriotism.

The French people are better informed, less prejudiced, more at their ease on the point of property, industry, habits of social equality in many respects, than before the Revolution. But from the day when the National Constitution, made, sworn, worshiped by themselves, was thrown down on a level with the edicts of arbitrary kings, to the present times, when a *chartre octroyée* is invoked by the more liberal among our publicists, so many political heresies have been professed, so dismal instances of popular tyranny are remembered, so able institutions of despotism have crushed all resistance, that, if you except our young generations, egotism and apathy, not excluding general discontent, are the prevailing disposition. In the meanwhile all adversaries of mankind,—coalesced kings, British aristocrats, Continental nobles, Coblentz emigrants, restored Jesuits, are pushing their plot with as much fury but more cunning than they had hitherto evinced.

Emperor Alexander is now the chief of European counter revolution; what he and his allies will do, either in concert or in competition with England, to spoil the game of Greece, and to annoy the new republics of America, I do not know; but although the policy of the United States has been hitherto very prudent, it seems to me they cannot remain wholly indifferent to the destruction, on the American Continent, of every right proclaimed in the immortal Declaration of Independence.

Among the destitutions which the spirit of counter revolution and priestcraft are every day operating in the French seminaries of learning, there is one victim which cannot but be particularly interesting to you. I mean M. Botta, the author of an Italian history of the war of independence, translated first in French, and since, under your auspices, in English. M. Botta, who has obtained your approbation, fully deserves it, and has a proper sense of the testimonies of your esteem, was a peaceful worthy *principal* of the College of Rouen, where his rectorship has been taken from him, under no plausible pretence, unless it is for the supposed congeniality of his opinion with our American doctrines. He had at first, or rather his friends had for him, the idea of his going to the United States. But age, bad health, a family of children keep him in France. I have been applied to on the subject of an American subscription in his behalf. Don't you think, my dear friend, it might take place; and then who could be better fit to give it proper weight and effect than you who have valued the work and the historian so far as to superintend translation for the benefit of the American youth, and give him personal marks of your regard?

I have been desired to enquire whether you have received from Doctor *Defendente Sacchi* a copy of a moral novel, called *Oriele*. The hero of the tale is made to travel throughout the United States, where he has the pleasure to converse with Mr. Jefferson when due homage is paid to the venerated interlocutor. Another copy has been sent to the American Philosophical Society at Philadelphia. No answer has come to hand. The doctor is a respectable scientific inhabitant of Pavia, chief *redacteur* of an important work, *Collection of the Classical Metaphisicians*. You will easily [see?] by whom of our friends I am in this affair commissioned. He is well, and so are both our families, who request their best respects to be presented to you. Remember me to Mrs. Randolph, and receive the most affectionate good wishes of your old tender friend.

La Grange, December 20, 1823

9. SAMUEL F. B. MORSE

Riot and ignorance in human priest-controlled machines

Samuel F. B. Morse's Calvinist background and upbringing predisposed him to fear immigrants who came from the Catholic countries of Europe. His father had been a militant anti-Catholic. During travels in Europe, the younger Morse also became well acquainted with Lafayette, who was aggressively anti-clerical. Upon his return to the United States after three-years of residence in France and Italy, Morse—a painter, inventor, and first president of the National Academy of Arts and Design—became a pamphleteer.

Imminent Dangers to the Free Institutions of the United States Through Foreign Immigration was published in the *New York Journal of Commerce* as a series of letters in 1835 and promptly reprinted in book form. It was a sequel to a series of twelve letters that Morse wrote under the pen name Brutus, entitled *A Foreign Conspiracy Against the Liberties of the United States* and published the previous year in the New York *Observer*. *Imminent Dangers*, like its predecessor, linked immigration with Catholicism as a twin threat to the free institutions of the United States. Further, it enlarged on the international Catholic plot to subvert

From Samuel F. B. Morse, *Imminent Dangers to the Free Institutions of the United States Through Foreign Immigration and the Present State of the Naturalization Laws*, a series of numbers, originally published in the *New York Journal of Commerce* by an American, revised and corrected, with additions (New York: E. B. Clayton, Printer, 1835), pp. iii–iv, 5–7, 15–16, 26–29.

American democracy while ostensibly promoting democracy. Both series of letters were widely reprinted in sectarian and nativist newspapers and widely read. In 1836, when Morse ran for mayor on the Native American ticket, they served as campaign documents. Although he received only a bit more than five percent of the vote, Morse pursued his marginal political career for the next few years, remaining an ardent nativist to the end. In 1854 during the height of Know-Nothingism, when he was considered as a possible Democratic candidate for Congress, he persisted in his earlier views on immigration and Catholicism.

Preface

It is but too common a remark of late, that the American character has within a short time been sadly degraded by numerous instances of riot and lawless violence in action, and a dangerous spirit of licentiousness in discussion. While these facts are universally acknowledged, the surprise is as universal that this degeneracy should exist, and the attempts to explain the mystery are various and contradictory. There are some who rashly attribute it to the natural tendency of Democracy, which they say is essentially turbulent. This is the most dangerous opinion of any that is advanced, as it must of necessity weaken the attachment of those who advance it, to our form of government, and must produce in them a criminal indifference to its policy, or traitorous desires for its overthrow. . . .

I cannot adopt the opinion, either that Democracies are naturally turbulent, or that the American character has suddenly undergone a radical change from good to bad; from that of habitual reverence for the laws, to that of riot and excess. It is not in the ordinary course of things, that the character of nations, any more than of individuals, change suddenly.

When the activity of benevolence, in every shape, which has been so long at work, through the length and breadth of our land, is considered, we naturally look for a corresponding result upon our society, in a more elevated moral character, and greater intellectual improvement, more love of moral truth, and regard for social order. To a slight observer, however, a result the very reverse seems to have been the consequence. I say it *seems* thus to a *slight observer:* to one who looks more deeply, a solid substratum of sound moral principle will appear to be evidently laid, while the surface alone presents to our view this moral paradox. How can it be explained?

If there is nothing *intrinsic* in our society which is likely to produce so sudden and mysterious an effect, the inquiry is natural, are there not *extrinsic* causes at work which have operated to disturb the harmonious movements of our system?

Here is a field we have not explored. We have not taken into the account all, or even the principal adverse causes which affect our government from without. One great opposing cause that embarrasses the benevolent operations of the country has apparently been wholly left out of the calculation, and yet it is a cause, which, more than all others, one would think, ought first to have attracted attention. This cause is FOREIGN IMMIGRATION. It is impossible in the nature of things that the moral character, and condition of this population, and its immense and alarming increase within a few years, should not have produced a counteracting effect on the benevolent operations of the day. How is it possible that foreign turbulence imported by ship-loads, that riot and ignorance in hundreds of thousands of human priest-controlled machines, should suddenly be thrown into our society, and not produce here turbulence and excess? Can one throw mud into pure water and not disturb its clearness?

There are other causes of a deeply serious nature, giving *support*, and *strength*, and *systematic operation*, to all these *adverse* effects of *foreign immigration*, and to which it is high time every American should seriously turn his thoughts. Some of these causes are exposed in the following numbers.

New York, August, 1835.

An American

No. I. Introductory Remarks

The great question regarding Foreigners, and a change in our Naturalization laws, is a *National question,* and at this time a very serious one. It is therefore with deep regret that I perceive an attempt made by both parties, (however to be expected,) to turn the just National excitement on this subject each to the account of their own party. The question, *Whether Foreigners shall be subjected to a new law of naturalization?* which grave circumstances have recently made it necessary to examine, is one entirely separate at present from *party* politics, as parties are now constituted, and is capable of being decided solely on its own merits. The organs of the two parties, however, are noticing the subject, and both engaged in their usual style of recrimination. Neither of them can see the other, nor any measure however separated from party principle, if proposed or discussed by its opponent, except through the distorted medium of prejudice. So degraded in this particular has the party press become, in the view of the intelligent portion of the community, that no one seems to expect impartiality or independence, when any question is debated that affects, or even but seems to affect, the slightest change in the aspect of the party, or in the standing of the individual, whose cause it advocates. The exclusive party character of a great portion of the daily press, its distortion of facts, its gross vituperative tone and spirit, its defence of dangerous practices and abuses, if any of these but temporarily favour mere party designs, is a serious cause of alarm to the American people. To increase the evil, each party adopts the unlawful weapons of warfare of its antagonist, thinking it an ample justification of its conduct, if it can but show that they have been used by its opponent. I cannot but advert to this crying evil at a moment when a great and pressing danger to the country demands the attention of Americans of all parties, and their cool and dispassionate examination of the evidence in the case.

The danger to which I would call attention is not imaginary. It is a danger arising from *a new position of the social elements in the onward march of the world to liberty.* The great struggle for some years has till now been principally confined to Europe. But we cannot exclude, if we would, the influence of foreign movements upon our own political institutions, in the great contest between liberty and despotism. It is an ignorance unaccountable in the conductors of the press at this moment, not to know, and a neglect of duty unpardonable, not to guard the people against the dangers resulting from this source. To deny the danger, is to shut one's eyes. It stares us in the face. And to seek to allay the salutary alarm arising from a demonstration of its actual presence among us, by attributing this alarm to any but the right cause, is worse than folly, it is madness, it is flinging away our liberties, not only without a struggle, but without the slightest concern, at the first appearance of the enemy.

No. II.

The difference of condition of the alien in Europe and in America.—Brief glance at the great steps of political advancement in Europe.—*Action* of American principles on Europe.—*Reaction*, perfectly natural.—Proofs of its actual existence.—The Combination in Europe to react on America.—The St. Leopold Foundation.

Our country, in the position it has given to foreigners who have made it their home, has pursued a course in relation to them, totally different from that of any other country in the world. This course, while it is liberal without example, subjects our institutions to peculiar dangers. In all other countries the foreigner, to whatever privileges he may be entitled by becoming a subject, can never be placed in a situation to be politically dangerous, for he has no share in the government of the country; even in England, he has no political influence, for even *after naturalization* an alien cannot become a member of the House of Commons, or of the Privy Council, or hold offices or grants under the Crown.

In the other countries of Europe, the right of naturalization in each particular case, belongs to the Executive branch of government. It is so in France, in Bavaria, and all the German States. In France, indeed, a residence of 10 years gives to the alien all the rights of a citizen, even that of becoming a member of the Chamber of Deputies, but the limited *suffrage* in that country operates as a check on any abuse of this privilege.

This country on the contrary opens to the foreigner, without other check than an oath, that he has resided five years in the country, a direct influence on its political affairs.

This country, therefore, stands alone, without guide from the example of any other; and I am to show in the sequel some of the peculiar dangers to which our situation in this respect exposes us. But the better to comprehend these dangers, let me briefly trace the prominent steps in European politics which connect the past with the present.

Europe has been generally at rest from war for some 20 years past. The activity of mind which had so long been engaged in war, in military schemes of offence and defence in the field, was, at the general pacification of the world, to be transferred to the Cabinet, and turned to the cultivation of the arts of peace. It was at this period of a General Peace, that a Holy Alliance of the Monarchs of Europe was formed. The Sovereigns professed to be guided by the maxims of religion, and with holy motives seemed solicitous only for the peace of the world. But they have long since betrayed that their plans of tranquillity were to be intimately connected with the preservation of their own arbitrary power, and the destruction of popular liberty every where. Whatever militated against this power, or favoured this liberty, was to be crushed. To this single end has been directed all the diplomatic talent of Europe for years. The "General Peace" was, and still is, the ever ready plea in excuse for every new act of oppression at home, or of interference abroad. The mental elements, however, set in motion remotely by the *Protestant Reformation*, but more strongly agitated by *the American Revolution*, are yet working among the people of these governments to give the Tyrants of the earth uneasiness. Conspiracies and Revolutions in the more absolute governments, (as in Austria, Russia, and the smaller States, Italy, Holland, Belgium, &c.,) and the alternate changes from more to less arbitrary components in the Cabinets of the more popular governments, (as in England, France, and Switzerland,) indicate to us at various times the vicissitudes of the great contest, and the sharpness of the struggle. This being the political condition of Europe, easily shown to have grown out of the great divisions of *free* and *despotic* principles, made at the Reformation, is it at all likely that the happy fruits of this Reformation, more completely developed in this land of liberty, and exhibited perpetually to the gaze of all the world, can have had no influence upon the despotisms of Europe? Can the example of Democratic liberty which this country shows, produce no uneasiness to monarchs? Does not every day bring fresh intelligence of the influence of American Democracy *directly* in England, France, Spain, Portugal, and Belgium, and *indirectly* in all the other European countries? And is there no danger of a *re-action* from Europe? Have we no interest in these changing aspects of European politics? The writer believes, that since the time of the American Revolution, which gave the principles of Democratic liberty a home, those principles have never been in greater jeopardy than at the present moment. To his reasons for thus believing, he invites the unimpassioned investigation of every American citizen. If there is danger, let it arouse to defence. If it is a false alarm, let such explanations be given of most suspicious appearances as shall safely allay it. It is no *party* question, and the attempt to make it one, should be at once suspected. It concerns all of every party. . . .

No. VI.

Recapitulation of Facts.—The necessity and propriety of discussing the political nature of the Roman Catholic System.

I have set forth in a very brief and imperfect manner the evil, the great and increasing evil, that threatens our free institutions from *foreign interference*. Have I not shown that there is real cause for alarm? Let me recapitulate the facts in the case, and see if any one of them can be denied; and if not, I submit it to the calm decision of every American, whether he can still sleep in fancied security, while incendiaries are at work; and whether he is ready quietly to surrender his liberty, civil and religious, into the hands of foreign powers.

1. It is a fact, that in this age the subject of civil and religious liberty agitates in the most intense manner the various European governments.

2. It is a fact, that the influence of American free institutions in

subverting European despotic institutions is greater now than it has ever been, from the fact of the greater maturity, and long-tried character, of the American form of government.

3. It is a fact, that Popery is opposed in its very nature to Democratic Republicanism; and it is, therefore, as a political system, as well as religious, opposed to civil and religious liberty, and consequently to our form of government.

4. It is a fact, that this truth, respecting the intrinsic character of Popery, has lately been clearly and demonstratively proved in public lectures, by one of the Austrian Cabinet, a devoted Roman Catholic, and with the evident design (as subsequent events show) of exciting the Austrian government to a great enterprise in support of absolute power.

5. It is a fact, that this Member of the Austrian Cabinet, [Frederick Schlegel] in his lectures, designated and proscribed this country by name, as the *"great nursery of destructive principles; as the Revolutionary school for France and the rest of Europe,"* whose contagious example of Democratic liberty had given, and would still give, trouble to the rest of the world, unless the evil were abated.

6. It is a fact, that very shortly after the delivery of these lectures, a Society was organized in the Austrian capital, called the St. Leopold Foundation, for the purpose "of promoting the greater activity of Catholic Missions in America."

7. It is a fact, that this Society is under the patronage of the Emperor of Austria,—has its central direction at Vienna,—is under the supervision of Prince Metternich,—that it is an extensive combination, embodying the civil, as well as ecclesiastical *officers*, not only of the *whole Austrian Empire*, but of the neighbouring Despotic States,—that it is actively at work, collecting moneys, and sending agents to this country, to carry into effect its designs.

8. It is a fact, that the agents of these foreign despots, are, for the most part, *Jesuits*.

9. It is a fact, that the effects of this society are already apparent in the otherwise unaccountable increase of Roman Catholic cathedrals, churches, colleges, convents, nunneries, &c., in every

part of the country; in the sudden increase of Catholic emigration; in the increased clanishness of the Roman Catholics, and the boldness with which their leaders are experimenting on the character of the American people.

10. It is a fact, that an unaccountable disposition to riotous conduct has manifested itself within a few years, when exciting topics are publicly discussed, wholly at variance with the former peaceful, deliberative character of our people.

11. It is a fact, that a species of police, unknown to our laws, has repeatedly been put in requisition to keep the peace among a certain class of foreigners, who are Roman Catholics, viz., Priest-police.

12. It is a fact, that Roman Catholic Priests have interfered to influence our elections.

13. It is a fact, that politicians on both sides have propitiated these priests, to obtain the votes of their people.

14. It is a fact, that numerous Societies of Roman Catholics, particularly among the Irish foreigners, are organized in various parts of the country, under various names, and ostensibly for certain benevolent objects; that these societies are united together by correspondence, all which may be innocent and praiseworthy, but, viewed in connexion with the recent aspect of affairs, are at least suspicious.

15. It is a fact, that an attempt has been made to organize a military corps of Irishmen in New-York, to be called the O'Connel Guards; thus commencing a military organization of foreigners.

16. It is a fact, that the greater part of the foreigners in our population is composed of Roman Catholics.

Facts like these I have enumerated might be multiplied, but these are the most important, and quite sufficient to make every American settle the question with himself, whether there is, or is not, danger to the country from the present state of our Naturalization Laws. I have stated what I believe to be facts. If they are *not* facts, they will easily be disproved, and I most sincerely hope they will be disproved. If they are facts, and my inferences from them are wrong, I can be shown where I have erred, and an inference more rational, and more probable, involving less, or perhaps no, danger to the country, can be deduced from them, which deduction, when I see it, I will most cheerfully accept, as a full explanation of these most suspicious doings of Foreign Powers.

I have spoken in these numbers freely of a particular religious sect, the Roman Catholics, because from the nature of the case it was unavoidable; because the foreign political conspiracy is identified with that creed. With the *religious tenets* properly so called, of the Roman Catholic, I have not meddled. If foreign powers, hostile to the principles of this government, have combined to spread any religious creed, no matter of what denomination, that creed does by that very act become a subject of political interest to all citizens, and must and will be thoroughly scrutinized. We are compelled to examine it. We have no choice about it. If instead of combining to spread with the greatest activity the Catholic Religion throughout our country, the Monarchs of Europe had united to spread Presbyterianism, or Methodism, I presume, there are few who would not see at once the propriety and the necessity of looking most narrowly at the political bearings of the peculiar principles of these Sects, or of any other Protestant Sects; and members of any Protestant Sects too, would be the last to complain of the examination. I know not why the Roman Catholics in this land of scrutiny are to plead exclusive exemption from the same trial.

No. XI.

The imperious necessity of a change in the Naturalization Laws.— The dangers from the alarming increase and present character of foreign immigration.—The political changes in Europe double the dangers to the country from foreign immigration.—The test of the existence and strength of the conspiracy in the country, and the first step in the defence against it.

The propriety, nay, the imperious necessity of a change in the Naturalization Laws, is the point to which it is indispensable to the safety of the country, that the attention of Americans, as a whole people, should at this moment be concentrated. It is a national question, not only separate from, but *superior* to all others. All other questions which divide the nation, are peculiarly of a domestic character; they relate to matters between American and American. Whether the *bank system* is, or is not, adverse to our democratic institutions; whether *internal improvement* is constitutionally intrusted to the management of the general government, or reserved to the states respectively; whether *monopolies* of any kind are just or unjust; whether the *right of instructing* representatives is to be allowed or resisted; whether *the high offices* of the nation are safest administered by these or by those citizens; all these, and many kindred questions, are entirely of a domestic character, to be settled between ourselves, in the just democratic mode, by majority, by the prevailing voice of the American people declared through the *ballot box*. But the question of *naturalization*, the question whether *foreigners, not yet arrived*, shall or shall not be admitted to the American right of balloting, is a matter in which the American people are in a certain sense, on one side as the original and exclusive possessors of the privilege, and foreigners on the other, as petitioners for a participation in that privilege; for the privilege of expressing their opinion upon, and assisting to decide all the other questions I have enumerated. It is, therefore, a question separate and *superior* to all these. It is a fundamental question; it affects the very foundation of our institutions, it bears directly and vitally on the *principle of the ballot* itself, that principle which decides the gravest questions of policy among Americans, nay, which can decide the very existence of the government, or can change its form at any moment. And surely this vital principle is amply protected from injury? To secure this point, every means which a people jealous of their liberties could devise was doubtless gathered about it for its preservation? It is not guarded. Be astonished, Americans, at the oversight! The mere statement of the provisions of the Naturalization Law, is sufficient, one would think, to startle any American who reflects at all. FIVE YEARS' RESIDENCE GIVES THE FOREIGNER, WHATEVER BE HIS CONDITION OR CHARACTER, THIS MOST SACRED PRIVILEGE OF ASSISTING TO CONTROL, AND ACTUALLY OF CONTROLLING *(there is not a guard to prevent,)* ALL THE

DOMESTIC INTERESTS OF AMERICA. A simple *five years' residence*, allows any foreigner, (no matter what his character, whether friend or enemy of freedom, whether an exile from proscription, or a pensioned Jesuit, commissioned to serve the interests of Imperial Despots,) to handle this *"lock of our strength."* How came it to pass? How is it possible that so vital a point as the ballot box was not constitutionally surrounded with double, ay, with treble guards? How is it that this *heart* of Democracy was left so exposed; yes; this very *heart* of the body politic, in which, in periodical pulsations, the opinions of the people meet, to go forth again as law to the extremities of the nation; this *heart* left so absolutely without protection, that the murderous eye of Imperial Despots across the deep, can, not only watch it in all its movements, but they are invited from its very nakedness, to reach out their hands to stab it. The figure is not too strong; their blow is aimed, now, whilst I write, at this very heart of our institutions. How is it that none of our sagacious statesmen foresaw this danger to the republic through the unprotected ballot box? It was foreseen. It did not escape the prophetic eye of Jefferson. He foresaw, and from the beginning foretold the evil, and uttered his warning voice. *Mr. Jefferson denounced the encouragement of emigration.* And, oh! consistency, where is thy blush? he who is now urging Jefferson's own recommendation on this vital point, is condemned by some who call themselves Jeffersonian democrats; by some journalists who in one column profess Jeffersonian principles, while in the next they denounce both the principles and the policy of Jefferson, and (with what semblance of consistency let them show if they can,) defend a great political evil, against which Jefferson left his written protest. It may be convenient, for purposes best known to themselves, for such journalists to desert their democratic principles, while loudly professing still to hold them; but the people, who are neither blind nor deaf, will soon perceive whose course is most consistent with that great apostle of democratic liberty. Do they ask, would you defend Mr. Jefferson's opinions when they are wrong?—I answer, prove them to be wrong, and I will desert them. Truth and justice are superior to all men. I advocate Jefferson's opinions, not because they are Jefferson's, but because his opinions are in accordance with truth and sound policy.—Let me show that Mr. Jefferson's opinions in relation to emigration are proved by experience to be sound.

What were the circumstances of the country when laws so favourable to the foreigner were passed to induce him to emigrate and settle in this country? The answer is obvious. Our early history explains it. In our national infancy we needed the strength of *numbers*. Powerful nations, to whom we were accessible by fleets, and consequently also by armies, threatened us. Our land had been the theatre of contests between French, and English, and Spanish armies, for more than a century. Our numbers were so few and so scattered, that as a people we could not unite to repel aggression. The war of Independence, too, had wasted us. We wanted *numerical strength;* we felt our weakness in numbers. *Safety*, then, national *safety*, was the motive which urged us to use every effort to increase our population, and to induce a foreign emigration. Then foreigners seemed all-important, and the policy of alluring them hither, too palpable to be opposed successfully even by the remonstrances of Jefferson. We could be benefited by the emigrants, and we in return could bestow on them a gift beyond price, by simply making them citizens. Manifest as this advantage seemed in the increase of our numerical strength, Mr. Jefferson looked beyond the advantage of the moment, and saw the distant evil. His reasoning, already quoted in a former number, will bear to be repeated. "I beg leave," says Mr. Jefferson, "to propose a doubt. The present desire of America is to produce rapid population by as great importations of foreigners as possible. But is this founded in good policy? *The advantage proposed, is the multiplication of numbers.* But are there no inconveniences to be thrown into the scale against the advantage expected from a multiplication of numbers by the importation of foreigners? It is for the happiness of those united in society to harmonize as much as possible in matters which they must of necessity transact together."

"Civil government being the sole object of forming societies, its administration must be conducted by common consent. Every species of government has its specific principles. Ours, perhaps, are more peculiar than those of any other in the universe. It is a composition of the freest principles of the English constitution, with others derived from natural right and natural reason. To these nothing can be more opposed than the maxims of absolute monarchies. Yet, from such, we are to expect the greatest number of emigrants. *They will bring with them the principles of the governments they leave, imbibed in their early youth; or, if able to throw them off, it will be in exchange for an unbounded licentiousness,* passing, as is usual, from one extreme to another. It would be a miracle were they to stop precisely at the point of temperate liberty. These principles, with their language, they will transmit to their children. *In proportion to their numbers, they will share with us the legislation. They will infuse into it their spirit, warp and bias its directions, and render it a heterogeneous, incoherent, distracted mass."*

"I may appeal to experience, for a verification of these conjectures. But, if they be not *certain in event,* are they not *possible, are they not probable?* Is it not safer to wait with patience—for the attainment of any degree of population desired or expected? May not our government be more homogeneous, more peaceable, more durable?" He asks, what would be the condition of France if twenty millions of Americans were suddenly imported into that kingdom? and adds—"If it would be *more turbulent,* less happy, less strong, we may believe that the addition of *half a million of foreigners* would produce a *similar effect here.* If they come of themselves, they are entitled to all the rights of citizenship; *but I doubt the expediency of inviting them by extraordinary encouragements."* Now, if under the most favourable circumstances for the country, when it could most be benefited, when numbers were most urgently needed, Mr. Jefferson could discover the evil afar off, and protest against encouraging foreign immigration, how much more is the measure now to be deprecated, when circumstances have so entirely changed, that instead of *adding strength* to the country, immigration *adds weakness,* weakness physical and moral! And what overwhelming force does Mr. Jefferson's reasoning acquire, by the

vast change of circumstances which has taken place both in
Europe and in this country, in our earlier and in our later
condition.—*Then* we were few, feeble, and scattered. *Now* we are
numerous, strong, and concentrated. *Then* our accessions by
immigration were real accessions of strength from the ranks of the
learned and the good, from the enlightened mechanic and artisan,
and intelligent husbandman. *Now* immigration is the accession of
weakness, from the ignorant and the vicious, or the priest-ridden
slaves of Ireland and Germany, or the outcast tenants of the
poorhouses and prisons of Europe. And again. *Then* our beautiful
system of government had not been unfolded to the world to the
terror of tyrants; the rising brightness of American Democracy
was not yet so far above the horizon as to wake their slumbering
anxieties, or more than to gleam faintly, in hope, upon their
enslaved subjects. *Then* emigration was natural, it was an
attraction of affinities, it was an attraction of liberty to liberty.
Emigrants were the proscribed for conscience' sake, and for
opinion's sake, the real lovers of liberty, Europe's loss, and our
gain.

Now American Democracy is denounced by name by foreign
despots, waked with its increasing brilliancy. Its splendour dazzles
them. It alarms them, for it shows their slaves their chains. And it
must be extinguished. *Now* emigration is changed; naturalization
has become the door of entrance not alone to the ever welcome
lovers of liberty, but also for the priest-ridden troops of the Holy
Alliance, with their Jesuit officers well skilled in all the arts of
darkness. Now emigrants are selected for a service to their tyrants,
and by their tyrants; not for their affinity to liberty, but for their
mental servitude, and their docility in obeying the orders of their
priests. They are transported in thousands, nay, in *hundreds of
thousands*, to our shores, to our loss and Europe's gain.

It may be, Americans, that you still doubt the *existence* of a
conspiracy, and the reality of danger from Foreign Combination;
or, if the attempt is made, you yet doubt the *power* of any such
secret intrigue in your society. Do you wish to test its existence
and its power? It is easy to apply the test. *Test it by attempting a
change in the Naturalization Law.* Take the ground that such a

change must be made, that *no foreigner who comes into the country after the law is passed shall ever be allowed the right of suffrage.* Stand firmly to this single point, and you will soon discover where the enemy is, and the tactics he employs. . . .

Look a moment at the proposition. You will perceive that in its very nature there is nothing to excite the opposition of a single citizen, native or naturalized, in the whole country, *provided,* be it distincly borne in mind, *that he is not implicated in the conspiracy.* This prohibition, in the proposed change of the law, it is evident, touches not in any way the *native American,* neither does it touch in the slightest degree the already granted privileges of the *naturalized citizen,* nor the *foreigner now in the country,* who is waiting to be naturalized, nor even *the foreigner on his way hither;* no, *not an individual* in the whole country is unfavourably affected by the provisions of such a law, not an individual *except alone the foreign Jesuit, the Austrian stipendiary with his intriguing myrmidons.* And how is he affected by it? He is deprived of his *passive obedience* forces; he can no longer use his power over his slaves, *to interfere in our political concerns;* he can no longer use them in his Austrian master's service; and he therefore, be assured, will resist with all the desperation of a detected brigand. He will raise an outcry. He will fill the public ear with cries of *intolerance.* He will call the measure religious bigotry, and illiberality, and religious persecution, and other popular catchwords, to deceive the unreflecting ear. But, be not deceived; when you hear him, set your mark upon him. That is the man. Try then this test. Again, I say, let the proposition be that the law of the land be so changed, that NO FOREIGNER WHO COMES INTO THE COUNTRY AFTER THE LAW IS PASSED SHALL EVER BE ENTITLED TO THE RIGHT OF SUFFRAGE. This is just ground; it is practicable ground; it is defensible ground, and it is safe and prudent ground; and I cannot better close than in the words of Mr. Jefferson: "The time to guard against corruption and tyranny is *before* they shall have gotten hold on us; IT IS BETTER TO KEEP THE WOLF OUT OF THE FOLD, THAN TO TRUST TO DRAWING HIS TEETH AND TALONS AFTER HE HAS ENTERED."

10. Maria Monk

Few imaginations can conceive deeds so abominable as they practised

The Awful Disclosures, the best native American seller before the publication of Harriet Beecher Stowe's novel, sold 300,000 copies before the Civil War. Numerous subsequent editions earned it the doubtful distinction of being the *Uncle Tom's Cabin* of Know-Nothingism and the most widely distributed anti-Catholic book in the nation's history.

The Awful Disclosures, reputedly dictated by Maria Monk, was written by the Reverend J. J. Slocum, aided by George Bourne. This fanciful titillating tale was published by Harper Brothers, one of whom, James, was elected mayor of New York City in 1844 on a Native American party ticket. Upon the sensational publication of the *Awful Disclosures*, debate and recrimination focused on the "revelations" of priestly immoralities, featuring lust and murder that catered to a credulous Protestant mind. Fanatical Protestants were kept on edge throughout the year by a sequence of events: a point-by-point rebuttal by the champions of the Hotel Dieu Convent, the appearance of Maria Monk at a public meeting in New York, an inspection of the Hotel Dieu Convent by two impartial Protestant clergymen who were ready under oath to declare that all of Maria Monk's accusations were false, and the sudden appearance of a second "escaped nun" claiming the name, Saint Francis Patrick. But a thorough inspection of the Hotel Dieu Convent by Colonel William L. Stone, a mild anti-Catholic, and his published repudiation of Maria Monk and her cohorts proved conclusive.

In 1838, when Maria Monk gave birth to a second fatherless child, she lost the faithful remnant of her supporters. Over a decade later, she died obscurely in prison shortly after being arrested for pick-pocketing in a Five Points house of ill fame. In the next few years, many of her readers were to find a political home in the Know-Nothing Party culminating two decades of Native American agitation on the state and local levels.

The Preface and Chapters 16 and 17 of *Awful Disclosures* provide examples of religious pornography that appealed to a popular audience distrustful of Catholicism and prone to sexual fantasy.

From J. J. Slocum and G. Bourne, *AWFUL DISCLOSURES OF MARIA MONK As Exhibited in a Narrative of her Sufferings.* . . . (New York: Harper Brothers, 1836), pp. 11–16, 167–83.

Preface

It is hoped that the reader of the ensuing narrative will not suppose that it is a fiction, or that the scenes and persons that I have delineated, had not a real existence. It is also desired, that the author of this volume may be regarded, not as a voluntary participator in the very guilty transactions which are described; but receive sympathy for the trials which she has endured, and the peculiar situation in which her past experience, and escape from the power of the Superior of the Hotel Dieu Nunnery, at Montreal, and the snares of the Roman Priests in Canada, have left her.

My feelings are frequently distressed and agitated, by the recollection of what I have passed through; and by night, and by day, I have little peace of mind, and few periods of calm and pleasing reflection. Futurity also appears uncertain. I know not what reception this little work may meet with; and what will be the effect of its publication here, or in Canada, among strangers, friends, or enemies. I have given the world the truth, so far as I have gone, on subjects of which I am told they are generally ignorant; and I feel perfect confidence, that any facts which may yet be discovered, will confirm my words, whenever they can be obtained. Whoever shall explore the Hotel Dieu Nunnery, at Montreal, will find unquestionable evidence that the descriptions of the interior of that edifice, given in this book, were furnished by one familiar with them; for whatever alterations may be attempted, there are changes which no mason or carpenter can make and effectually conceal; and, therefore, there must be plentiful evidence in that institution of the truth of my description.

There are living witnesses, also, who ought to be made to speak, without fear of penances, tortures, and death; and possibly their testimony, at some future time, may be added to confirm my statements. There are witnesses I should greatly rejoice to see at liberty; or rather there *were*. Are they living now? or will they be permitted to live after the Priests and Superiors have seen this book? Perhaps the wretched nuns in the cells have already suffered for my sake—perhaps Jane Ray has been silenced for ever, or will be murdered, before she has an opportunity to add her most important testimony to mine.

But speedy death, in respect only to this world, can be no great calamity to those who lead the life of a nun. The mere recollection of it always makes me miserable. It would distress the reader, should I repeat the dreams with which I am often terrified at night; for I sometimes fancy myself pursued by my worst enemies; frequently I seem as if shut up again in the Convent; often I imagine myself present at the repetition of the worst scenes that I have hinted at or described. Sometimes I stand by the secret place of interment in the cellar; sometimes I think I can hear the shrieks of helpless females in the hands of atrocious men; and sometimes almost seem actually to look again upon the calm and placid countenance of Saint Francis, as she appeared when surrounded by her murderers.

I cannot banish the scenes and characters of this book from my memory. To me it can never appear like an amusing fable, or lose its interest and importance. The story is one which is continually before me, and must return fresh to my mind, with painful emotions, as long as I live. With time, and Christian instruction, and the sympathy and examples of the wise and good, I hope to learn submissively to bear whatever trials are appointed for me, and to improve under them all.

Impressed as I continually am with the frightful reality of the painful communications that I have made in this volume, I can only offer to all persons who may doubt or disbelieve my statements, these two things:—

Permit me to go through the Hotel Dieu Nunnery, at Montreal, with some impartial ladies and gentlemen, that they may compare my account with the interior parts of that building, into which no persons but the Roman Bishop and the Priests are ever admitted; and if they do not find my description true, then discard me as an impostor. Bring me before a court of justice—there I am willing to meet *Latargue, Dufresne, Phelan, Bonin,* and *Richards,* and their wicked companions, with the Superior and any of the nuns, before ten thousand men.

New York, 11th January, 1836

Maria Monk

Chapter XVI

Frequency of the Priests' Visits to the Nunnery—Their Freedom
and Crimes—Difficulty of learning their Names—Their Holy Retreat—Objections in our Minds—Means used to counteract Conscience—Ingenious Arguments.

Some of the priests from the Seminary were in the nunnery
every day and night, and often several at a time. I have seen
nearly all of them at different times, though there are about one
hundred and fifty in the district of Montreal. There was a
difference in their conduct; though I believe every one of them
was guilty of licentiousness; while not one did I ever see who
maintained a character any way becoming the profession of a
priest. Some were gross and degraded in a degree which few of
my readers can ever have imagined; and I should be unwilling to
offend the eye, and corrupt the heart of any one, by an account of
their words and actions. Few imaginations can conceive deeds so
abominable as they practised, and often required of some of the
poor women, under the fear of severe punishments, and even of
death. I do not hesitate to say with the strongest confidence, that
although some of the nuns became lost to every sentiment of
virtue and honour, especially one from the Congregational
Nunnery whom I have before mentioned, Saint Patrick[,] the
greater part of them loathed the practices to which they were
compelled to submit, by the Superior and priests, who kept them
under so dreadful a bondage.

Some of the priests whom I saw I never knew by name, and the
names of others I did not learn for a time, and at last learnt only
by accident.

They were always called "Mon pere," my father; but sometimes
when they had purchased something in the ornament-room, they
would give their real names, with directions where it should be
sent. Many names, thus learnt and in other ways, were whispered
about from nun to nun, and became pretty generally known.

Several of the priests, some of us had seen before we entered the Convent.

Many things of which I speak, from the nature of the case, must necessarily rest chiefly upon my own word, until further evidence can be obtained: but there are some facts for which I can appeal to the knowledge of others. It is commonly known in Montreal that some of the priests occasionally withdraw from their customary employments, and are not to be seen for some time, it being understood that they have retired for religious study, meditation, and devotion, for the improvement of their hearts. Sometimes they are thus withdrawn from the world for weeks: but there is no fixed period.

This was a fact I knew before I took the veil; for it is a frequent subject of remark, that such or such Father, is on a "holy retreat." This is a term which conveys the idea of a religious seclusion from the world for sacred purposes. On the reappearance of a priest after such a period, in the church or the streets, it is natural to feel a peculiar impression of his devout character—an impression very different from that conveyed to the mind of one who knows matters as they really are. Suspicions have been indulged by some in Canada on this subject, and facts are known by at least a few. I am able to speak from personal knowledge: for I have been a nun of Sœur Bourgeoise.

The priests are liable, by their dissolute habits, to occasional attacks of disease, which render it necessary, or at least prudent, to submit to medical treatment.

In the Black Nunnery they find private accommodations, for they are free to enter one of the private hospitals whenever they please; which is a room set apart on purpose for the accommodation of the priests, and is called a retreat-room. But an excuse is necessary to blind the public, and this they find in the pretence they make of being in a "Holy Retreat." Many such cases have I known; and I can mention the names of priests who have been confined in this Holy Retreat. They are very carefully attended by the Superior and old nuns, and their diet mostly consists of vegetable soups, &c. with but little meat, and that fresh. I have seen an instrument of surgery laying upon the table in that holy room, which is used only for particular purposes.

Father Tombau, a Roman priest, was on one of his holy retreats about the time when I left the nunnery. There are sometimes a number confined there at the same time. The victims of these priests frequently share the same fate.

I have often reflected how grievously I had been deceived in my opinions of a nun's condition! All the holiness of their lives, I now saw, was merely pretended. The appearances of sanctity and heavenly mindedness which they had shown among us novices, I found was only a disguise to conceal such practices as would not be tolerated in any decent society in the world; and as for peace and joy like that of heaven, which I had expected to find among them, I learnt too well that they did not exist there.

The only way in which such thoughts were counteracted, was by the constant instructions given us by the Superior and priests, to regard every doubt as a mortal sin. Other faults we might have, as we were told over and over again, which, though worthy of penances, were far less sinful than these. For a nun to doubt that she was doing her duty in fulfilling her vows and oaths, was a heinous offence, and we were exhorted always to suppress our doubts, to confess them without reserve, and cheerfully to submit to severe penances on account of them, as the only means of mortifying our evil dispositions, and resisting the temptations of the devil. Thus we learnt in a good degree to resist our minds and consciences, when we felt the first rising of a question about the duty of doing any thing required of us.

To enforce this upon us, they employed various means. Some of the most striking stories told us at catechism by the priests, were designed for this end. One of these I will repeat. One day, as a priest assured us who was hearing us say the catechism on Saturday afternoon, as one Monsieur . . . . a well-known citizen of Montreal, was walking near the cathedral, he saw Satan giving orders to numerous evil spirits who had assembled around him. Being afraid of being seen, and yet wishing to observe what was done, he hid himself where he could observe all that passed. Satan despatched his devils to different parts of the city, with directions to do their best for him; and they returned in a short time, bringing in reports of their success in leading persons of different classes to the commission of various sins, which they thought would be agreeable to their master. Satan, however, expressed his dissatisfaction, and ordered them out again; but just then a spirit from the Black Nunnery came, who had not been seen before, and stated that he had been trying for seven years to persuade one of the nuns to doubt, and had just succeeded. Satan received the intelligence with the highest pleasure; and turning to the spirits around him, said: "You have not half done your work—he has done much more than all of you."

In spite, however, of our instructions and warnings, our fears and penances, such doubts would intrude; and I have often indulged them for a time, and at length, yielding to the belief that I was wrong in giving place to them, would confess them, and undergo with cheerfulness such new penances as I was loaded with. Others too would occasionally entertain and privately express such doubts; though we all had been most solemnly warned by the cruel murder of Saint Francis. Occasionally some of the nuns would go further, and resist the restraints or punishments imposed upon them; and it was not uncommon to hear screams, sometimes of a most piercing and terrific kind, from nuns suffering under discipline.

Some of my readers may feel disposed to exclaim against me, for believing things, which will strike them as so monstrous and abominable. To such, I would say, without pretending to justify myself—You know little of the position in which I was placed: in the first place, ignorant of any other religious doctrines, and in the second, met at every moment by some ingenious argument, and the example of a large community, who received all the instructions of the priests as of undoubted truth, and practised upon them. Of the variety and speciousness of the arguments used, you cannot have any correct idea. They were often so ready with replies, examples, anecdotes, and authorities, to enforce their doctrines, that it seemed to me they could never have learnt it all from books, but must have been taught by wicked spirits. Indeed, when I reflect upon their conversations, I am astonished at their art and address, and find it difficult to account for their subtlety and success in influencing my mind, and persuading me to any thing they pleased. It seems to me, that hardly anybody would be safe in their hands. If you were to go to confession twice, I believe you would feel very different from what you do now. They have such a way of avoiding one thing, and speaking of another, of affirming this, and doubting or disputing that, of quoting authorities, and speaking of wonders and miracles recently performed, in confirmation of what they teach, as familiarly known to persons whom they call by name, and whom they pretend to offer as witnesses, though they never give you an opportunity to speak with them—these, and many other means, they use in such a way, that they always blinded my mind, and, I should think, would blind the minds of others.

Chapter XVII

Treatment of young Infants in the Convent—Talking in Sleep—Amusements—Ceremonies at the public interment of deceased Nuns—Sudden disappearance of the Old Superior—Introduction of the new one—Superstition—Alarm of a Nun—Difficulty of Communication with other Nuns.

It will be recollected, that I was informed immediately after receiving the veil, that infants were occasionally murdered in the Convent. I was one day in the nuns' private sick-room, when I had an opportunity, unsought for, of witnessing deeds of such a nature. It was, perhaps, a month after the death of Saint Francis. Two little twin babes, the children of Sainte Catharine, were brought to a priest, who was in the room, for baptism. I was present while the ceremony was performed, with the Superior and several of the old nuns, whose names I never knew, they being called Ma tante, Aunt.

The priests took turns in attending to confession and catechism in the Convent, usually three months at a time, though sometimes longer periods. The priest then on duty was Father Larkin. He is a good-looking European, and has a brother who is a professor in the college. He first put oil upon the heads of the infants, as is the custom before baptism. When he had baptized the children, they were taken, one after the other, by one of the old nuns, in the presence of us all. She pressed her hand upon the mouth and nose of the first, so tight that it could not breathe, and in a few minutes, when the hand was removed, it was dead. She then took the other, and treated it in the same way. No sound was heard, and both the children were corpses. The greatest indifference was shown by all present during this operation; for all, as I well knew, were long accustomed to such scenes. The little bodies were then taken into the cellar, thrown into the pit I have mentioned, and covered with a quantity of lime.

I afterward saw another new-born infant treated in the same manner, in the same place: but the actors in this scene I choose not to name, nor the circumstances, as every thing connected with it is of a peculiarly trying and painful nature to my own feelings.

These were the only instances of infanticide I witnessed; and it seemed to be merely owing to accident that I was then present. So far as I know, there were no pains taken to preserve secrecy on this subject; that is, I saw no attempt made to keep any of the inmates of the Convent in ignorance of the murder of children. On the contrary, others were told, as well as myself, on their first admission as veiled nuns, that all infants born in the place were baptized and killed, without loss of time; and I had been called to witness the murder of the three just mentioned, only because I happened to be in the room at the time.

That others were killed in the same manner during my stay in the nunnery, I am well assured.

How many there were I cannot tell, and having taken no account of those I heard of, I cannot speak with precision; I believe, however, that I learnt through nuns, that at least eighteen or twenty infants were smothered, and secretly buried in the cellar, while I was a nun.

One of the effects of the weariness of our bodies and minds, was our proneness to talk in our sleep. It was both ludicrous and painful to hear the nuns repeat their prayers in the course of the night, as they frequently did in their dreams. Required to keep our minds continually on the stretch, both in watching our conduct, in remembering the rules and our prayers, under the fear of consequences of any neglect, when we closed our eyes in sleep, we often went over again the scenes of the day; and it was no uncommon thing for me to hear a nun repeat one or two of our long exercises in the dead of night. Sometimes, by the time she had finished, another, in a different part of the room, would happen to take a similar turn, and commence a similar recitation, and I have known cases in which several such unconscious exercises were performed, all within an hour or two.

We had now and then a recreation-day, when we were relieved from our customary labour, and from all prayers except those for morning and evening, and the short ones said at every striking of the clock. The greater part of our time was then occupied with different games, particularly backgammon and drafts, and in such conversation as did not relate to our past lives, and the outside of the Convent. Sometimes, however, our sports would be interrupted on such days by the entrance of one of the priests, who would come in and propose that his fête, the birthday of his patron saint, should be kept by "the saints." We saints!

Several nuns died at different times while I was in the Convent, how many I cannot say, but there was a considerable number: I might rather say many in proportion to the number in the nunnery. The proportion of deaths I am sure was very large. There were always some in the nuns' sick-rooms, and several interments took place in the chapel.

When a Black nun is dead, the corpse is dressed as if living, and placed in the chapel in a sitting posture, within the railing round the altar, with a book in the hand, as if reading. Persons are then admitted from the street, and some of them kneel and pray before it. No particular notoriety is given, I believe, to this exhibition out of the Convent, but such a case usually excites some attention.

The living nuns are required to say prayers for the delivery of their deceased sister from purgatory, being informed, as in all other such cases, that if she is not there, and has no need of our intercession, our prayers are in no danger of being thrown away, as they will be set down to the account of some of our departed

friends, or at least to that of the souls which have no acquaintances to pray for them.

It was customary for us occasionally to kneel before a dead nun
thus seated in the chapel, and I have often performed that task. It
was always painful, for the ghastly countenance being seen
whenever I raised my eyes, and the feeling that the position and
dress were entirely opposed to every idea of propriety in such a
case, always made me melancholy.

The Superior sometimes left the Convent, and was absent for
an hour, or several hours, at a time, but we never knew of it until
she had returned, and were not informed where she had been. I
one day had reason to presume that she had recently paid a visit
to the priests' farm, though I had not direct evidence that such
was the fact. The priests' farm is a fine tract of land belonging to
the Seminary, a little distance from the city, near the Lachine
road, with a large old-fashioned edifice upon it. I happened to be
in the Superior's room on the day alluded to, when she made some
remark on the plainness and poverty of her furniture. I replied,
that she was not proud, and could not be dissatisfied on that
account; she answered—

"No, but if I was, how much superior is the furniture at the
priests' farm; the poorest room there is furnished better than the
best of mine."

I was one day mending the fire in the Superior's room, when a
priest was conversing with her on the scarcity of money; and I
heard him say, that very little money was received by the priests
for prayers, but that the principal part came with penances and
absolutions.

One of the most remarkable and unaccountable things that
happened in the Convent, was the disappearance of the old
Superior. She had performed her customary part during the day,
and had acted and appeared just as usual. She had shown no
symptoms of ill health, met with no particular difficulty in
conducting business, and no agitation, anxiety, or gloom, had been
noticed in her conduct. We had no reason to suppose that during
that day she had expected any thing particular to occur, any more
than the rest of us. After the close of our customary labours and

evening lecture, she dismissed us to retire to bed, exactly in her usual manner. The next morning the bell rang, we sprang from our bed, hurried on our clothes as usual, and proceeded to the community-room in double line, to commence the morning exercises. There, to our surprise, we found Bishop Lartigue; but the Superior was no where to be seen. The Bishop soon addressed us, instead of her, and informed us, that a lady near him, whom he presented us, was now the Superior of the Convent, and enjoined upon us the same respect and obedience which we had paid to her predecessor.

The lady he introduced to us was one of our oldest nuns, Saint Du . . . , a very large, fleshy woman, with swelled limbs, which rendered her very slow in walking, and often gave her great distress. Not a word was dropped from which we could conjecture the cause of this change, nor of the fate of the old Superior. I took the first opportunity to inquire of one of the nuns, whom I dared talk to, what had become of her; but I found them as ignorant as myself, though suspicious that she had been murdered by the orders of the Bishop. Never did I obtain any light on her mysterious disappearance. I am confident, however, that if the Bishop wished to get rid of her privately and by foul means, he had ample opportunities and power at his command. Jane Ray, as usual, could not allow such an occurrence to pass by without intimating her own suspicions more plainly than any other of the nuns would have dared to do. She spoke out one day, in the community-room, and said, "I'm going to have a hunt in the cellar for my old Superior."

"Hush, Jane Ray!" exclaimed some of the nuns, "you'll be punished."

"My mother used to tell me," replied Jane, "never to be afraid of the face of man."

It cannot be thought strange that we were superstitious. Some were more easily terrified than others, by unaccountable sights and sounds; but all of us believed in the power and occasional appearance of spirits, and were ready to look for them at almost any time. I have seen several instances of alarm caused by such superstition, and have experienced it myself more than once. I was one day sitting mending aprons, beside one of the old nuns, in a community-room, while the litanies were repeating; as I was very easy to laugh, Saint Ignace, or Agnes, came in, walked up to her with much agitation, and began to whisper in her ear. She usually talked but little, and that made me more curious to know what was the matter with her. I overheard her say to the old nun, in much alarm, that in the cellar from which she had just returned, she had heard the most dreadful groans that ever came from any being. This was enough to give me uneasiness. I could not account for the appearance of an evil spirit in any part of the Convent, for I had been assured that the only one ever known there, was that of a nun who had died with an unconfessed sin, and that others were kept at a distance by the holy water that was rather profusely used in different parts of the nunnery. Still, I presumed that the sounds heard by Saint Ignace must have proceeded from some devil, and I felt great dread at the thought of visiting the cellar again. I determined to seek further information of the terrified nun; but when I addressed her on the subject, at recreation-time, the first opportunity I could find, she replied, that I was always trying to make her break silence, and walked off to another group in the room, so that I could obtain no satisfaction.

It is remarkable that in our nunnery, we were almost entirely cut off from the means of knowing any thing even of each other. There were many nuns whom I know nothing of to this day, after having been in the same rooms with them every day and night for four years. There was a nun, whom I supposed to be in the Convent, and whom I was anxious to learn something about from the time of my entrance as a novice; but I never was able to learn any thing concerning her, not even whether she was in the nunnery or not, whether alive or dead. She was the daughter of a rich family, residing at Point aux Trembles, of whom I had heard my mother speak before I entered the Convent. The name of her family I think was Lafayette, and she was thought to be from Europe. She was known to have taken the black veil; but as I was not acquainted with the name of the Saint she had assumed, and I could not describe her in "the world," all my inquiries and observations proved entirely in vain.

I had heard before my entrance into the Convent, that one of the nuns had made her escape from it during the last war, and once inquired about her of the Superior. She admitted that such was the fact; but I was never able to learn any particulars concerning her name, origin, or manner of escape.

11. HENRY E. RIELL

A contest between the advocates of the largest and the smallest liberty

The demand by nativists that a twenty-year residency be required before immigrants might be granted citizenship and that Catholics and the foreign-born be excluded from holding political office aroused Democratic political leaders to defend their immigrant supporters, to denounce native Americanism, and to appeal to "voluntary citizens" to confound their detractors and to support Democratic candidates.

Henry Riell's pamphlet, published by William Cullen Bryant's Democratic *New York Evening Post* on the eve of the presidential election campaign of 1840, presented evidence connecting Federalist-Whig nativism to the laws of 1798 and vigorously defended the immigrant as American patriot.

FELLOW CITIZENS!

Important events are occuring in this republic which call imperatively and especially upon you, its voluntary citizens— upon you, its citizens by enlightened preference and noble choice—to come forth, in the might of your elective franchise, in defence of those principles of liberty, which you have solemnly

Henry E. Riell, "An Appeal to the Voluntary Citizens of the United States From All Nations, On the Exercise of Their Elective Franchise, at the Approaching Presidential Election," *The New York Evening Post*, 1840, pp. 2–4.

sworn to maintain, and those inestimable rights and privileges which you have thereby acquired and enjoy.

It is probably not unknown to any of you that a narrow souled, ignoble, and most ungenerous faction has existed for some years past in this country, whose avowed object is the abrogation of an essentially republican clause of the Constitution, by effecting an "entire repeal" of those laws of naturalization which that sacred charter of human freedom expressly ordains, and which were enacted in obedience to its requisitions. This parricidal faction, under the bigoted pretext, or the hypocritical pretence, that the Constitution, in some vague and unspecified respect, is in danger from your secret subversion, or open hostility, would madly destroy it themselves, by driving the dagger of a morbid, reckless jealousy into one of its most vital provisions, and without the full and healthful action of which it would shrink into a withered and shrivelled mockery of the expansive design of its founders, and become the scorn of all liberal men.

The spirit which actuates this faction, "Native American" though it is unworthly called, is precisely of that gloomy, contracted and tyrannically suspicious kind which distinguished the monarchists of the old world and the political bigots of the darkest ages, and is most debasing to the republican character and dishonorable to the American name.—You are familiar, fellow citizens, with the fact, that it was a specific charge against the last monarch of this country, and one of the explicit arguments in the Declaration of Independence against his unrighteous authority, that he had "endeavored to prevent the population of these states, by obstructing the laws for the naturalization of foreigners, by refusing to pass others to encourage their migration hither, and by raising the conditions of new appropriations of lands." This is precisely the same mistaken, small-minded policy which is pursued by the Native American faction, and for which attempts have been made in several recent sessions of Congress, with a degree of bold effrontery revolting, if not alarming, to every republican mind. You are doubtless as familiar with that stain upon our early republican history, the notorious "Alien and Sedition Laws," which were enacted by the old Federal party (or

rather *faction*, because the advocates of unconstitutional principles and measures are not entitled to the denomination of a party.)
under the administration of the elder Adams. By these atrocious
laws, the President was empowered to banish from the broad
territory of the United States, without examination, without trial,
and even without accusation, any and every foreign resident
whom he might suspect, or pretend to suspect, of views hostile to
the government; and compel them to leave their property, their
families, and their honest avocations, under the penalty of
imprisonment and perpetual disqualification for citizenship. This
was the despotic power given to the President by the federal
faction under the alien law; and the sedition law, which was
enacted at the same, deprived no aliens merely, but virtually all
citizens, of the liberty of speech and the press, concerning the
affairs of government and the conduct of its officers, by imposing
enormous fines and incarceration in a political dungeon, as the
penalty of every constructive offence against its prohibitions. It is
unnecessary to remind you how cruelly these laws were enforced,
for their effects are memorable in our political annals, and remain as
admonitions to us and to our children to resist the attempts which
are now making to revive them, and which have been repeated
during several of our recent sessions of Congress by a faction which
inherits the illiberal spirit from which they originally sprung.

If these attempts were made only by that small and scattered
association of "Native Americans," professedly formed "without
distinction of party," which has heretofore occasionally bur-
lesqued our general elections by an exhibition of numbers as
limited as its principles are contracted, it would be less an object
of apprehension than of ridicule. But that faction can now no
longer be deemed a small one, nor be safely treated with
indifference. Finding that its motives and objects were utterly
repugnant to the opinions and the pride of every high minded
American who appreciated the constitutional standard and magnanimity of this republic, it sought and received the powerful
alliance of that great party which has ever displayed a natural
affinity to the illiberal men and measures of every other, and
which, in fact, has renovated and perpetuated its existence by the

apostates and cast-offs which it has thus acquired. The central association of this body, which exists at Washington, under the title of "the Native American Association of the United States," together with its various branches, which extend to every state and principal town in the Union, subtly penetrating and poisoning every social and political relation of life, and secretly operating with more than jesuitical cunning and pertinacity of purpose through the whole community, constitute in reality, the grand organization of the fraudulently styled "Whig" party, throughout the country. The prostrate and meagre skeleton has thus become endowed with life and vigor, and stands forth with the iron rod of proscription against every refugee from tyranny and oppression who may seek that asylum in our boundless land, and that participation in its freedom, which our institutions guarantee and proclaim.

Fellow citizens: As a native American, and the son of a native American, taught from infancy to revere and love the exalted maxims of equal justice, and the heart expanding breadth of political benevolence upon which our proud system of freedom is founded, I blush with shame at the dishonor which is done to it by those who, from the boasted rights and privileges of their birth, should be the first to do justice to its character, and to protect it from the degrading stigma of inhospitality. I disclaim all fraternity of feeling and connection with such men, and regard them as the worst and the most unnatural of aliens—"aliens in their native land"—aliens in spirit to the institutions which they should proudly cherish as the noblest inheritance of their birthright.

As a native American, I exult in the triumphant truth that the country which gave me birth, is destined, both politically and physically, to be the free asylum for the oppressed and the distressed of the universal world. As an American, with far more than a million millions of the square acres of my native soil around me, I cannot so far crush my feelings of philanthropy and honest pride as to tell mankind that this wide world affords no asylum for suffering humanity—no refuge for the oppressed. On the contrary I would tell them that it is here without money and without price, and that we lay claim to but an humble meed of beneficence, even for this gratuity; for never had a people so much to give at so slight a sacrifice. Sacrifice!—the boasted gratuity is a loan at interest, and the whole commonwealth becomes enriched by the labor, the skill, the industry, which it thus procures. Partial evils there may be—local pauperism, and therefore unequal burdens—but these evils, like those in the economy of a bounteous providence, tends to redress themselves, and are but the concomitants of universal good.

As a native American republican, too, I would protest against that erroneously assumed superiority of hereditary to inherent and natural right; of fortuitous and involuntary to chosen and voluntary citizenship, upon which the false pride, the haughty prejudices, and the arrogant usurpations of the "Native American" faction and its allies are founded.—To attach merit or demerit to fortuitous events over which we have no control, is identically the falacious principle upon which hereditary monarchies, the inequitable laws of primogeniture, and all the aristocratic distinctions which exist from birth are founded; but they are utterly exploded and repudiated in our system of government which is based alone upon the natural rights of man. Every feature of our republican constitution harmonises with the fundamental doctrine previously promulgated in the declaration of independence as a self-evident truth, namely, "that all men are created equal, and endowed by their Creator with certain unalienable rights, among which are life, liberty and the pursuit of happiness."

If this be the prerogative of human nature by birth, then has no man, nor nation of men, any prerogative that contravenes or invalidates it. No nation can righteously deny these natural and equal rights to those who seek them, and, accordingly, our equitable form of government offers them freely to all, upon the reasonable condition that the recipients of them shall solemnly promise to uphold and preserve, for the benefit of others, that constitution which has conferred these blessings upon themselves, and abjure allegiance to every other authority. Nor does the constitution permit the government to make any laws of naturalization that would operate partially and unequally—favoring foreigners of one nation more than those of another, or one class of foreigners from the same nation, more than another. In strict accordance with the doctrine of equal rights, it requires equal laws of naturalization, without which, those rights would be invaded. Every naturalized citizen, therefore, owes it to himself and to the cause of liberty in general, to remember and duly appreciate the truth, that his political position in the United States is in nowise inferior to that of a citizen by birth, except in his disqualification for the two highest offices of the government; and even this exception establishes the general rule of his equality. If the native citizen claims any other superiority from the adventitious circumstance of birth, and would attach any disparagement to the title "adopted," or "naturalized" citizen, he proves himself unworthy of the privileges which accident, rather than choice, has conferred upon him; and he might well be asked for the same pledge of fealty to the institutions of his country that you, its voluntary citizens, have given.

The presidential and congressional election which approaches, is a contest between the advocates of the largest and the smallest liberty, for the ascendancy of their respective systems and the legislation which would flow from them. It is into these two classes that the two great political parties of the republic are and ever have been divided. The friends of the largest liberty are those who advocate equal rights and advantages, and equal laws to obtain and ensure them. The friends of the smallest liberty, are the advocates of partial rights and advantages, and of those partial laws which would produce and perpetuate them.—The latter are the friends not only of those special privileges in pecuniary credit and financial operations which cause undue extremes in the conditions of men, creating aristocratical distinctions, and making the rich man more rich by the very process which makes the poor more poor—placing the workingman's daily wages upon the uncertain tenure of a credit capital which is perpetually liable and eventually sure to explode, and leave its dependants either destitute of all employment for long periods, or reduced to wages by which they can scarcely procure the mere necessaries of life—but the friends also of special privileges in the elective franchise. They would not only make laws which must eventually deprive the great mass of the people of all property, but accumulating it in comparatively few hands; but also deprive them of their elective franchise, by requiring a property qualification, which it would thus be impossible for the mass to obtain. Nor is this all. Their theory of the smallest liberty, includes "that entire repeal of the naturalization laws," which would leave a large and constantly increasing portion of our population without the rights of citizenship, and thus expose the country to those intestine animosities and commotions which would inevitably arise from such an inequality of privilege, instead of binding all classes together in the happy bonds of equal advantage, interest and regard.

These parties, fellow citizens, need no other distinctive designations than those which are stamped upon their characters by their own acts, attempted schemes, and avowed intentions. To remind you of these, and more particularly of such as relate to the rights of aliens, is the object of the following extracts and remarks, which will afford you an unequivocal rule of judgment in deciding which of these parties is entitled to your suffrages and support.— In the recent attempts of the modern "whigs," in reality tories, to substantially revive the alien and sedition laws of the old federal party, and in the insolent arrogance, slander and misrepresentation with which these attempts are accompanied and enforced, you will see that party sailing under its original colors, tolerating only the smallest conceivable amount of human freedom, and composed of the most anti-republican of men that can pretend to the republican name. In the steady and intrepid resistance to these schemes, and in the bold and generous advocacy of liberal principles, feelings and measures, which are exhibited by the democratic party, you will see the republicanism of the Declaration of Independence and the Constitution, and that magnanimous championship of the rights of men which becomes our character as American freemen. From the comparative view which you will thus take of the opposite conduct of the two parties, you will perceive that the memorable contest of '98, which resulted in the triumph of democratic principles, and the election of Thomas Jefferson, is again at hand, with the same principles at stake, and equally important objects of our republican regard, to be lost or won.

That *you*, fellow citizens, will be found wanting at *such* a crisis—that *you*, over whose rights the great political battle of '98 was fought and won,—that *you*, who have ever been among the foremost in the ranks of high-minded freemen, faithfully contending for the purest and loftiest doctrines of our republican creed, and the most vigilant in detecting the insidious designs of our opponents—that *you* will side with the enemy on *this* occasion, can be supposed only by those who basely accuse you of insincerity in your past professions and conduct, and with a secret antipathy to the institutions of our country. On the contrary, I, who know you well, and have never hesitated to incur the obloquy of defending you from these slanders, am convinced that, while the noble and righteous cause of the democracy of this land will receive from you that spontaneous and ardent support which the great majority of naturalized citizens have heretofore given to it; there are few, very few, even of those who may have acted with our opponents, on occasions and measures of inferior moment, who will not unite with us *now*, under one common impulse. The revived questions which are now again at issue, appeal directly and specially to the self-respect, the honest pride, the social dignity, the parental duty, the republican professions, and the sworn obligations of *every* naturalized citizen in the country, whatever may be his opinions upon other questions, or the exercise of his suffrage in other times.

Henry E. Riell

12. DANIEL WEBSTER

A distinct nationality
is essential to human happiness

Doubtless, no emissary of national independence was ever feted as generously and as enthusiastically by Americans as was Louis Kossuth.

Daniel Webster, Speech at the Kossuth Banquet, Washington, January 7, 1852, from *The Writings and Speeches of Daniel Webster*, 18 vols. (Boston: Little,

On December 5, 1851, he, his wife, children, fellow Hungarians, and a few Italian refugees—fifty-eight persons in all—arrived in New York. As the ship entered Lower New York Bay, shore batteries on Staten Island fired salutes, bands played, and a crowd of 200,000 persons crammed the Battery to roar its welcome to the Hungarian liberator. The "Kossuth craze" had been launched.

A parade into the city was followed by speeches of welcome to Kossuth in German, Spanish, Italian, and English and a mass meeting of twenty thousand persons. At Henry Ward Beecher's Plymouth Church on Brooklyn Heights, an admission charge brought in $20,000 for a Hungarian refugee fund. Surrounded by his retinue of liveried servants, secretaries, and guards, Kossuth stormed the country. Everywhere he was greeted by freedom-loving societies, including Little Rock's "Central Southern Association to Promote the Cause of Liberty in Europe."

In Washington, after receptions in the White House and in Congress, the international hero and symbol of all the oppressed of Europe who were yearning for liberty was the honored guest at a Congressional banquet. There Secretary of State Daniel Webster paid impassioned tribute to the cause of Hungarian independence and to the principle of national self-determination, holding out the hope that some day Hungary would adopt the American republican model.

I have great pleasure in participating in this festival. It is a remarkable occasion. He who is your honored guest to-night has led thus far a life of events that are viewed as highly important here, and still more important to his own country. Educated, spirited, full of a feeling of liberty and independence, he entered early into the public councils of his native country, and he is here to-day fresh from acting his part in the great struggle for Hungarian national independence. That is not all his distinction. He was brought to these shores by the authorities of Congress. He has been welcomed to the capital of the United States by the votes of the two Houses of Congress. I agree, as I am not connected with either branch of the Legislature, in joining, and I do join, in my loudest tone, in the welcome pronounced by them

Brown, 1903), vol. 13, pp. 452–57, 461–62. The text of this speech appeared in the *Boston Daily Advertiser*, January 12, 1852.

to him. The House of Representatives,—the immediate representatives of the people,—full themselves of an ardent love of liberty,
have joined in that welcome; the wisdom and sobriety of the
Senate have joined in it; and the head of the Republic, with the
utmost cordiality, has approved of whatsoever official act was
necessary to bid him welcome to these shores. And he stands here
to-night, in the midst of an assembly of both Houses of Congress,
and others of us met here in our individual capacity, to join the
general acclaim, and to signify to him with what pleasure we
welcome him to the shores of this free land—this asylum of
oppressed humanity. Gentlemen, the effect of the reception thus
given him cannot but be felt. It cannot but have its influence
beyond the ocean, and among countries where our principles and
our sentiments are either generally unknown or generally disliked.
Let them go forth—let it be borne on all the winds of
heaven—that the sympathies of the Government of the United
States, and all the people of the United States, have been
attracted toward a nation struggling for national independence,
and toward those of her sons who have most distinguished
themselves in that struggle.

I have said that this cannot be without its effect. We are too
much inclined to underrate the power of moral influence, and the
influence of public opinion, and the influence of principles, to
which great men, the lights of the world and of the age, have
given their sanction. Who doubts that, in our own struggle for
liberty and independence, the majestic eloquence of Chatham,
the profound reasoning of Burke, the burning satire and irony of
Colonel Barré, had influences upon our fortunes here in America?
They had influences both ways. They tended, in the first place,
somewhat to diminish the confidence of the British ministry in
their hopes of success in attempting to subjugate an injured
people. They had influence another way, because, all along the
coasts of the country,—and all our people in that day lived upon
the coast,—there was not a reading man who did not feel
stronger, bolder, and more determined in the assertion of his
rights when these exhilarating accounts from the two Houses of
Parliament reached him from beyond the seas. He felt that those

who held and controlled public opinion elsewhere were with us; that their words of eloquence might produce an effect in the region where they were uttered; and, above all, they assured him that, in the judgment of the just, and the wise, and the impartial, his cause was just, and he was right; and, therefore, he said, "We will fight it out to the last."

Now, gentlemen, another great mistake is sometimes made. We think that nothing is powerful enough to stand before autocratic, monarchical, or despotic power. There is something strong enough, quite strong enough, and, if properly exerted, will prove itself so, and that is the power of intelligent public opinion in all the nations of the earth. There is not a monarch on earth whose throne is not liable to be shaken by the progress of opinion, and the sentiment of the just and intelligent part of the people. It becomes us, in the station which we hold, to let that public opinion, so far as we form it, have a free course. Let it go out; let it be pronounced in thunder-tones; let it open the ears of the deaf; let it open the eyes of the blind; and let it be everywhere proclaimed what we of this great republic think of the general principle of human liberty, and of that oppression which all abhor. Depend upon it, gentlemen, that between these two rival powers,—the autocratic power, maintained by arms and force, and the popular power, maintained by opinion,—the former is constantly decreasing, and, thank God, the latter is constantly increasing. Real human liberty and human rights are gaining the ascendant; and the part which we have to act in all this great drama is to show ourselves in favor of those rights, to uphold our ascendancy, and to carry it on until we shall see it culminate in the highest heaven over our heads.

On the topics, gentlemen, which this occasion seems to invite, I have nothing to say, because, in the course of my political life—not now a short one—I have said all that I wish to say, and all that I wish to transmit to posterity, connected with my own name and history. What I said of Greece twenty-five years ago, when our friend was too young to be in political life, I repeat to-night, *verbum post verbum*, exactly what I said then. What I said of Spain at a later period, when the power of the restored

Bourbons was exerted to impose upon Spain a dynasty not wished by the people of Spain, that I repeat in English, and Spanish, and French, and in every other language, if they choose to translate it.

May I be so egotistical as to say that I have nothing now to say upon the subject of Hungary? Gentlemen, in the autumn of the year before last, out of health, and retired to my parental home among the mountains of New Hampshire, I was, by reason of my physical condition, confined to my house; but I was among the mountains whose native air I was born to inspire. Nothing saluted my senses, nothing saluted my mind or my sentiments but freedom, full and entire; and there, gentlemen, near the grave of my ancestors, I wrote a letter which most of you may have seen, addressed to the Austrian *chargé d'affaires*. I can say nothing of the ability displayed in that letter; but, as to its principles, while the sun and moon endure, and while I can see the light of the sun and the moon, I stand by them. In a letter, dated February last, moved by these considerations, which have influenced all the Christian world, making no particular merit of it, I addressed a letter to the American minister, at Constantinople, at the court of the Sublime Porte, for the relief of Louis Kossuth and his companions in exile; and I happen to know that that letter was not without some effect. At any rate, it is proper for me here to say that this letter, and that one to which I have before alluded, were despatched with the cordial approbation of the President of the United States. It was, therefore, so far the act of the Government of the United States in its executive capacity. Now, I shall not further advert to these topics to-night, nor shall I go back to ancient times, and discuss the provisions of the Holy Alliance; but I say that, in the sentiments avowed by me, I think, in the years 1823 and 1824, in the cause of Greece, and in the more subsequent declarations of opinion, there is that which I can never depart from without departing from myself. I should cease to be what I am if I were to retract a single sentiment which has been expressed on these several occasions.

Now, gentlemen, I do not propose, at this hour of the night, to entertain you, or attempt to entertain you, by any general disquisition upon the value of human freedom, upon the inalienable rights of man, or upon any general topics of that kind; but I wish to say a few words upon the precise question, as I understand it, that exists before the civilized world, between Hungary and the Austrian Government. I wish to arrange the thoughts, to which I desire to give utterance, under two or three general heads.

And, in the first place, I say that wherever there is, in the Christian and civilized world, a nationality of character—wherever there exists a nation of sufficient knowledge and wealth and population to constitute a government, then a national government is a necessary and proper result of nationality of character. We may talk of it as we please, but there is nothing that satisfies the human mind in an enlightened age, unless man is governed by his own country and the institutions of his own government. No matter how easy be the yoke of a foreign power, no matter how lightly it sits upon the shoulders, if it is not imposed by the voice of his own nation and of his own country, he will not, he cannot, and he *means* not to be happy under its burden.

There is, gentlemen, one great element of human happiness mixed up with others. We have our social affections, our family affections; but, then, we have this sentiment of country which imbues all our hearts, and enters into all our other feelings; and that sentiment of country is an affection not only for the soil on which we are born, it not only appertains to our parents and sisters and brothers and friends, but to our habits and institutions, and to the government of that country in all respects. There is not a civilized and intelligent man on earth that enjoys entire satisfaction in his condition if he does not live under the government of his own nation, his own country, whose volitions and sentiments and sympathies are like his own. Hence he cannot say: "This is not my country; it is the country of another power; it is a country belonging to somebody else." Therefore, I say that wherever there is a nation of sufficient intelligence and numbers and wealth to maintain a government, distinguished in its character and its history and its institutions, that nation cannot be happy but under a government of its own choice.

Then, sir, the next question is, Whether Hungary, as she exists in our ideas, as we see her, and as we know her, is distinct in her nationality, is competent in her population, is also competent in her knowledge and devotion to correct sentiment, is competent in her national capacity for liberty and independence, to maintain a government that shall be Hungarian out and out? Upon that subject, gentlemen, I have no manner of doubt. Let us look a little at the position in which this matter stands. What is Hungary? I am not, gentlemen, about to fatigue you with a long statistical statement; but I wish to say that, as I understand the matter, and I have taken some pains to look at it, Hungary contains a sufficient population to constitute a nation. . . .

Hungary is about the size of Great Britain, and comprehends nearly half of the territory of Austria.

It is stated by another authority that the population of Hungary is nearly 14,000,000; that of England (in 1841) nearly 15,000,000; that of Prussia about 16,000,000.

Thus it is evident that, in point of power, so far as power depends upon population, Hungary possesses as much power as England proper, or even as the kingdom of Prussia. Well, then, there is population enough, there are people enough. Who, then, are they? They are distinct from the nations that surround them. They are distinct from the Austrians on the west, and the Turks on the east; and I will say, in the next place, that they are an *enlightened* nation. They have their history, they have their traditions, they are attached to their own institutions—institutions which have existed for more than a thousand years.

Gentlemen, it is remarkable that on the western coast of Europe political light exists. There is a sun in the political firmament, and that sun sheds his light on those who are able to enjoy it. But in Eastern Europe, generally speaking, and on the confines between Eastern Europe and Asia, there is no political sun in the heavens. It is all an arctic zone of political life. The luminary that enlightens the world in general seldom rises there above the horizon. The light which they possess is, at best, crepuscular,—a kind of twilight; and they are under the necessity of groping about to catch, as they may, any stray gleams of the light of day. Gentlemen, the country of which your guest to-night is a native is a remarkable exception. She has shown through her whole history, for many hundreds of years, an attachment to the principles of civil liberty, and of law and of order, and obedience to the Constitution which the will of the great majority has established. That is the fact; and it ought to be known wherever the question of the practicability of Hungarian liberty and independence is discussed. It ought to be known that Hungary stands out from it above her neighbors in all that respects free institutions, constitutional government, and an hereditary love of liberty. . . .

Gentlemen, I have said that a national government, where there is a distinct nationality, is essential to human happiness. I have said that, in my opinion, Hungary is thus capable of human happiness. I have said that she possesses that distinct nationality, that power of population and that wealth which entitle her to have a government of her own, and I have now to add, what I am sure will not sound well upon the Upper Danube, and that is that, in my humble judgment, the imposition of a foreign yoke upon a people capable of self-government, while it oppresses and depresses that people, adds nothing to the strength of those who impose that yoke. In my opinion, Austria would be a better and a stronger government to-morrow if she confined the limits of her power to her hereditary and German domains, especially if she saw in Hungary a strong, sensible, independent neighboring nation; because I think that the cost of keeping Hungary quiet is not repaid by any benefit derived from Hungarian levies or tributes. And then again, good neighborhood, and the good-will and generous sympathies of mankind, and the generosity of character that ought to pervade the minds of governments, as well as those of individuals, is vastly more promoted by living in a state of friendship and amity with those who differ from us in modes of government, than by any attempt to consolidate power in the hands of one over the rest.

Gentlemen, the progress of things is unquestionably onward. It is onward with respect to Hungary; it is onward everywhere. Public opinion, in my estimation at least, is making great progress. It will penetrate all resources; it will come more or less to animate all minds; and in respect to that country for which our sympathies to-night have been so strongly invoked, I cannot but say that I think the people of Hungary are an enlightened, industrious, sober, well-inclined community; and I wish only to add, that I do not now enter into any discussion of the form of government that may be proper for Hungary. Of course, all of you, like myself, would be glad to see her, when she becomes independent, embrace that system of government which is most acceptable to ourselves. We shall rejoice to see our American model upon the Lower Danube and on the mountains of Hungary. But this is not the first step. It is not that which will be our first prayer for Hungary. That first prayer shall be that Hungary may become independent of all foreign power—that her destinies may be intrusted to her own hands, and to her own discretion. I do not profess to understand the social relations and connections of races, and of twenty other things that may affect the public institutions of Hungary. All I say is, that Hungary can regulate these matters for herself infinitely better than they can be regulated for her by Austria; and, therefore, I limit my aspirations for Hungary, for the present, to that single and simple point,—Hungarian independence, Hungarian self-government, Hungarian control of Hungarian destinies. These are the aspirations which I entertain, and I give them to you, therefore, gentlemen, as a toast: *"Hungarian Independence*—Hungarian control of her own destinies; and Hungary as a distinct nationality among the nations of Europe."

13. Carl Schurz

The United States and the freedom of the people of the world

Early in 1855 a gifted Forty-eighter and his family settled in Watertown, Wisconsin, where he soon became the leader of the Germans of the

Schurz to Gottfried Kinkel, from *Speeches, Correspondence and Political Papers of Carl Schurz*, ed. Frederic Bancroft (New York: G. P. Putnam's, 1913), vol. 1, pp. 14–20. Reprinted by permission of G. P. Putnam, original American publisher.

Northwest. In April of that year, however, Carl Schurz returned to Europe with his wife and child primarily so that Mrs. Schurz might recover her health. In London he found an old and depressed Louis Kossuth. There he also was a guest of Gottfried Kinkel, whom he had rescued from Spandau prison and who had visited America five months before the famed Hungarian revolutionary had embarked on a similar mission. His visit with his most influential teacher at Bonn and with other exiled Forty-eighters convinced Schurz that the revolutionary ardor had cooled and that he had made the right decision in choosing to become an American citizen.

Before sailing for Europe, Schurz, in a series of letters to Professor Kinkel, had assured the "German Kossuth" that "I am no less attached to Germany in America than I was in Europe." But by then Schurz, already able to speak and write English, had visited Washington with the vague intent of influencing Franklin Pierce's foreign policy and had come away apparently quite convinced that America offered a more promising arena for his political ambitions and talents than did his native Germany. "When I come in touch with the atmosphere of political activity," he wrote Mrs. Schurz, "I feel the old fire of 1848 coursing in my veins as fresh and young as ever."

In 1856, hardly in the United States four years, the heroic Forty-eighter helped organize the new Republican party in Wisconsin as the vehicle for the liberal impulses which he represented. In 1857, not yet a citizen but already "a phenomenon to the Americans," Schurz was almost elected Lieutenant-Governor of Wisconsin. Defeat, he was convinced, had occurred only by a defection of envious fellow Germans. The following year, he supported Lincoln against Douglas in the Illinois senate race and in 1860 served as chairman of the Wisconsin delegation to the Republican Convention that nominated Lincoln for the presidency. Schurz was to become the only immigrant in the nation's history to serve as diplomat, general, United States senator, cabinet officer, and elder statesman.

Schurz's letters to Kinkel reveal an extraordinary congruence between his own libertarian bent and the crisis issues of the 1850s, which contributed to his remarkable assimilation into the American mainstream even while he protested his loyalty to German liberation.

To Gottfried Kinkel

I quite understand your criticism of America. The present Administration, which took the helm under the most promising auspices, is what is called a total failure. The old parties are in a state of dissolution and the political atmosphere is impregnated with the odor of decay. Until this dissolution shall be accomplished and until there has been time for new developments to become fixed, there can be no thought of a decided policy. At this moment all is at loose ends. Confusion and intrigue reign. The Nebraska question, the tariff question, the homestead question, the naturalization question, the Pacific Railroad question, the Cuban question, the Sandwich Island question, the Nicaragua expedition—all these things are mixed up in a wild jumble and public opinion is unable to arrive at a sane conclusion. When Pierce went into office, public opinion forced him into the making of a new, strong program of foreign policy. He took a few steps in that direction. But hardly had the Cabinet been formed and the other offices filled, before the corruption of the old parties involved him in a lot of petty yet exhausting fights, which a character like Jackson would have crushed with prompt energy, but with which the weak Pierce was wholly unable to cope.

He saw no other course than to seek refuge in the Nebraska bill, which was the product of the unscrupulous ambition of Douglas; and immediately the entire attention of the nation was diverted from foreign politics and concentrated upon the slavery question. Accordingly the Administration lost its natural program and was at the mercy of all the evil influences which the compromise of 1850 has cast about all the political parties. The Nebraska bill burst the moral bonds, and the struggle started again from the beginning. Minds became agitated and responsive to these influences. This condition of public sentiment was utilized by the native Americans for the purpose of advancing their political interests. This essentially weak, nativistic faction joined the majority which has its strongest basis in the Nebraska question. Thus the Know-Nothings suddenly attained enormous influence, which was all the more powerful because of the fact that they conceal their true power beneath the veil of a secret society.

While the anti-Nebraska movement has carried away the entire

North, and the admixture of the nativistic spirit is perceptible in all these victories, and is clouding the triumph of freedom, the slavery question and the foreign elements are the two points of view from which all political matters are regarded at present—and herein lies the confusion of the situation. What is favorable to the rights of the foreigners, is unfavorable to slavery; and yet, not only are the rights of slavery to be limited, but the influence of the foreigners is to be destroyed as well. That is the problem through which the free-soil Know-Nothing must work his way. It is certain that the nativistic movement will be wrecked on this rock of inconsistency. But there is danger that the anti-slavery movement will be weakened by it. Only the South can be consistent in both questions, and unite the strength of two formidable agitations. It will not be long before the slave States become the headquarters of the nativistic movement and there it will remain. This will suffice to secure the rights of the foreign elements in the North. I am convinced, moreover, that we have nothing further to fear from the Know-Nothings, except a weakening of the anti-slavery movement; this would be all the more deplorable because that movement is already so well under way.

The slavery question reveals itself in so many different aspects to him who has recently come to America, that he finds it difficult to work his way through the confusion of considerations and interests, especially where the existence of the Union is involved. After studying all the arguments I could find, with the exception of those in the Bible, I have at length come to the final conclusion that, whatever may be the considerations that demand compromise, there can be but one question of freedom, and the faithful adherence to that principle is, on the whole, more practical than it sometimes seems. It is not the philanthropic side of the question which has brought me to this conclusion, but the direct and indirect effect of the system upon the whole Government of the United States, the aristocratic character of Southern society, the demoralising influence of the slave-power upon the politicians of the North; the consequent partisanship of all political ideas of justice and especially the influence upon our foreign policy. When you ask me, "When will the United States interfere practically in the interest of the freedom of the peoples of the world?" I answer without hesitation and with unquestioning conviction, "As soon as the slaveholders have ceased to be a political power." The slaveholder fears the propaganda of freedom, because he does not know how far it may go. Even the mere word of freedom has to him a dangerous and ambiguous sound. For these reasons, I am decidedly opposed to any extension of the domain of slavery, inclusive of the annexation of Cuba. It is true that this annexation would make the Creoles independent of Spain; but at the same time, it would so much increase the menace to freedom in the United States that the purchase would not be worth the price. It would be splendid if the Spanish Government were to avail itself of the favorable moment and establish the emancipation of the negro in Cuba; then, Cuba would be welcome. It is deplorable that although the anti-slavery party has many talented adherents, but few understand practical politics. They do not know that it is unwise to agitate violently unless there is an immediate object in view. They forget that, at the crucial moment, he predominates who has the reputation of practising calm moderation. They usually consume their best ammunition before the battle begins. Yet, great things were won in the last campaign. Perhaps in the year 1856 we shall completely succeed in breaking up the country-gentry party. I can think of no happier event for the politics of this country.

We have received news of peace in Europe to-day, which will, I trust, not be corroborated. To conclude the war by accepting the four points at issue would certainly be a most disgraceful result. . . .

My wife and I send our greetings with unchanged cordiality. *Philadelphia, January 23, 1855.*

To Gottfried Kinkel

You seem to surmise that my visit to Europe means that I am returning there for good, and I see that many of my friends have the same idea. It is my intention that this visit shall be a mere interlude in my American life. As long as there is no upheaval of affairs in Europe it is my firm resolve to regard this country not as a transient or accidental abode, but as the field for my usefulness. I love America and I am vitally interested in the things about me—they no longer seem strange. I find that the question of liberty is in its essence the same everywhere, however different its form. Although I do not regard the public affairs of this country with the same devotion as those of our old home, it is not mere ambition nor eagerness for distinction that impels me to activity. My interest in the political contests of this country is so strong, so spontaneous, that I am profoundly stirred. More self-control is required for me to keep aloof than to participate in them. These are the years of my best strength. Shall I devote myself wholly to the struggle for existence while I have hopes that I may soon be independent in that respect? I venture to say that I am neither avaricious nor self-indulgent.

If I now seek material prosperity, it is only that I may be free to follow my natural aspirations. Or shall I again subject myself to that dreary condition of waiting, which must undermine the strongest constitution when it is the only occupation? We have both tasted its bitterness; and I am burning with the desire to be employed with visible, tangible things and no longer to be bound to dreams and theories. I have a holy horror of the illusory fussiness which characterizes the life of the professional refugees. My devotion to the cause of the old Fatherland has not abated but my expectations have somewhat cooled; I have only faint hopes for the next few years. Even if the revolution should come sooner than I expect, I do not see why I should not utilize the intervening time. I feel that here I can accomplish something. I am convinced of it when I consider the qualities of the men who are now conspicuous. This inspires me, and even if the prospects of success did not correspond with my natural impulses, I should suddenly find that I had involuntarily entered into the thick of the fight. In these circumstances, why should I wish to return to Europe? I am happy that I have a firm foothold and good opportunities.

After my return from Europe I expect to go to Wisconsin. I

transferred some of my business interests there when on my last trip to the West. The German element is powerful in that State, the immigrants being so numerous, and they are striving for political recognition. They only lack leaders that are not bound by the restraints of money-getting. There is the place where I can find a sure, gradually expanding field for my work without truckling to the nativistic elements, and there, I hope, in time, to gain influence that may also become useful to our cause. It is my belief that the future interests of America and Germany are closely interwoven. The two countries will be natural allies as soon as a European upheaval takes place. However different the two nations may be in character, they will have the same opponents, and that will compel them to have a corresponding foreign policy. American influence in Europe will be based on Germany, and Germany's world-position will depend essentially on the success of America. Germany is the only power in Europe whose interests will not conflict with those of America, and America is the only power in the civilized world that would not be jealous of a strong, united Germany. They can both grow without being rivals, and it will be to the interest of each to keep the adversaries of the other in check. Americans will realize this as soon as the Emperor of Austria and the King of Prussia need no longer be considered, and the Germans will become convinced of it as soon as they consider a national foreign policy.

Philadelphia, March 25, 1855.

14. ABRAHAM LINCOLN

I am not a Know-Nothing

In 1855 in many states, including Illinois, the Know-Nothing party appeared to hold the balance of power. Although Lincoln's nomination

Abraham Lincoln to Joshua Speed, Aug. 24, 1855, from *The Collected Works of Abraham Lincoln*, ed. Roy P. Basler (New Brunswick, N.J.: Rutgers University Press, 1953), II, pp. 320–23.

and election to the presidency in 1860 has been linked to his acceptability among former Know-Nothings, who were committed to barring immigrants and Catholics from American politics, there is no doubt that he loathed nativist demands no less than pro-slavery pretensions. It is true that in 1855, when Owen Lovejoy, the abolitionist Illinois congressman, urged him to fuse his Whig following to the Republican party, Lincoln begged off, mindful that Know-Nothings, still powerful around Springfield, were essential to the success of any political combination.

"About us here are mostly my old political and personal friends," he wrote Lovejoy. "I had hoped their organization would die without the painful necessity of my taking an open stand against them."

A few months later, in a letter to his fellow Kentuckian, Joshua F. Speed, Lincoln left no doubt of his abhorrence of both nativism and slavery.

To Joshua F. Speed

DEAR SPEED:

You know what a poor correspondent I am. Ever since I received your very agreeable letter of the 22nd. of May I have been intending to write you in answer to it. You suggest that in political action now, you and I would differ. I suppose we would; not quite as much, however, as you may think. You know I dislike slavery; and you fully admit the abstract wrong of it. So far there is no cause of difference. But you say that sooner than yield your legal right to the slave—especially at the bidding of those who are not themselves interested, you would see the Union dissolved. I am not aware that *any one* is bidding you to yield that right; very certainly *I* am not. I leave that matter entirely to yourself. I also acknowledge *your* rights and *my* obligations, under the constitution, in regard to your slaves. I confess I hate to see the poor creatures hunted down, and caught, and carried back to their stripes, and unrewarded toils; but I bite my lip and keep quiet. In 1841 you and I had together a tedious low-water trip, on a Steam Boat from Louisville to St. Louis. You may remember, as I well do, that from Louisville to the mouth of the Ohio there were, on board, ten or a dozen slaves, shackled together with irons. That sight was a continual torment to me; and I see something like it every time I touch the Ohio, or any other slave-border. It is hardly fair for you to assume, that I have no interest in a thing which has, and continually exercises, the power of making me miserable. You ought rather to appreciate how much the great body of the Northern people do crucify their feelings, in order to maintain their loyalty to the constitution and the Union. . . .

I do oppose the extension of slavery, because my judgment and feelings so prompt me; and I am under no obligation to the contrary. If for this you and I must differ, differ we must. You say if you were President, you would send an army and hang the leaders of the Missouri outrages upon the Kansas elections; still, if Kansas fairly votes herself a slave state, she must be admitted, or the Union must be dissolved. But how if she votes herself a slave state *unfairly*—that is, by the very means for which you say you would hang men? Must she still be admitted, or the Union be dissolved? That will be the phase of the question when it first becomes a practical one. In your assumption that there may be a *fair* decision of the slavery question in Kansas, I plainly see you and I would differ about the Nebraska-law. I look upon that enactment not as a *law*, but as *violence* from the beginning. It was conceived in violence, passed in violence, is maintained in violence, and is being executed in violence. I say it was *conceived* in violence, because the destruction of the Missouri Compromise, under the circumstances, was nothing less than violence. It was *passed* in violence, because it could not have passed at all but for the votes of many members, in violent disregard of the known will of their constituents. It is *maintained* in violence because the elections since, clearly demand its repeal, and this demand is openly disregarded. *You* say men ought to be hung for the way they are executing that law; and *I* say the way it is being executed is quite as good as any of its antecedents. It is being executed in the precise way which was intended from the first; else why does no Nebraska man express astonishment or condemnation? . . .

That Kansas will form a Slave constitution, and, with it, will ask to be admitted into the Union, I take to be an already settled question; and so settled by the very means you so pointedly condemn. By every principle of law, ever held by any court,

North or South, every negro taken to Kansas is free; yet in utter disregard of this—in the spirit of violence merely—that beautiful Legislature gravely passes a law to hang men who shall venture to inform a negro of his legal rights. This is the substance, and real object of the law. If, like Haman, they should hang upon the gallows of their own building, I shall not be among the mourners for their fate.

In my humble sphere, I shall advocate the restoration of the Missouri Compromise, so long as Kansas remains a territory; and when, by all these foul means, it seeks to come into the Union as a Slave-state, I shall oppose it. I am very loth, in any case, to withhold my assent to the enjoyment of property *acquired*, or *located*, in good faith; but I do not admit that *good faith*, in taking a negro to Kansas, to be held in slavery, is a *possibility* with any man. Any man who has sense enough to be the controller of his own property, has too much sense to misunderstand the outrageous character of this whole Nebraska business. But I digress. In my opposition to the admission of Kansas I shall have some company; but we may be beaten. If we are, I shall not, on that account, attempt to dissolve the Union. On the contrary, if we succeed, there will be enough of us to take care of the Union. I think it probable, however, we shall be beaten. Standing as a unit among yourselves, you can, directly, and indirectly, bribe enough of our men to carry the day—as you could on an open proposition to establish monarchy. Get hold of some man in the North, whose position and ability is such, that he can make the support of your measure—whatever it may be—a *democratic party necessity*, and the thing is done. *Appropos* of this, let me tell you an anecdote. Douglas introduced the Nebraska bill in January. In February afterwards, there was a call session of the Illinois Legislature. Of the one hundred members composing the two branches of that body, about seventy were democrats. These latter held a caucus, in which the Nebraska bill was talked of, if not formally discussed. It was thereby discovered that just three, and no more, were in favor of the measure. In a day or two Douglas' orders came on to have resolutions passed approving the bill; and they were passed by large majorities!!! The truth of this is vouched for by a bolting democratic member. The masses too, democratic as well as whig, were even, nearer unanimous against it; but as soon as the party necessity of supporting it, became apparent, the way the democracy began to see the *wisdom* and *justice* of it, was perfectly astonishing.

You say if Kansas fairly votes herself a free state, as a christian you will rather rejoice at it. All decent slave-holders *talk* that way; and I do not doubt their candor. But they never *vote* that way. Although in a private letter, or conversation, you will express your preference that Kansas shall be free, you would vote for no man for Congress who would say the same thing publicly. No such man could be elected from any district in any slave-state. You think Stringfellow & Co. ought to be hung, and yet, at the next presidential election you will vote for the exact type and representative of Stringfellow. The slave-breeders and slave-traders, are a small, odious and detested class, among you; and yet in politics, they dictate the course of all of you, and are as completely your masters, as you are the masters of your own negroes.

You enquire where I now stand. That is a disputed point. I think I am a whig; but others say there are no whigs, and that I am an abolitionist. When I was at Washington I voted for the Wilmot Proviso as good as forty times, and I never heard of any one attempting to unwhig me for that. I now do no more than oppose the *extension* of slavery.

I am not a Know-Nothing. That is certain. How could I be? How can any one who abhors the oppression of negroes, be in favor of degrading classes of white people? Our progress in degeneracy appears to me to be pretty rapid. As a nation, we began by declaring that *"all men are created equal."* We now practically read it "all men are created equal, *except negroes."* When the Know-Nothings get control, it will read "all men are created equal, except negroes, *and foreigners, and catholics."* When it comes to this I should prefer emigrating to some country where they make no pretence of loving liberty—to Russia, for

instance, where despotism can be taken pure, and without the
base alloy of hypocracy. . . .
Springfield, August 24, 1855.

A. LINCOLN

15. CARL SCHURZ

The noblest idea which ever swelled
a human heart with noble pride

Carl Schurz delivered the most important speech of his career in Boston
at the invitation of local political leaders who recognized him as the
ablest representative of the immigrants. Liberal Massachusetts Republicans were anxious to counter the taint of Know-Nothingism that afflicted
their party after the Massachusetts legislature had passed a "two year
amendment" to the State Constitution, depriving naturalized citizens of
the right to vote or hold office. Although directed at the Irish, the
amendment aroused the ire of German immigrants who also felt
threatened by Republican Know-Nothingism. On April 8, 1859, the
spokesman of "True Americanism" addressed an audience of two
thousand demonstrators against Know-Nothingism, leaving no doubt that
Americanism was not the monopoly of the native-born. The newspapers
responded jubilantly, debating the proper spelling of the Wisconsin
Republican's name. Was it "Shurts," "Schoorts," or "Schurz"? In the
Liberator, William Lloyd Garrison hailed "True Americanism" as "with
one or two exceptions, the most eloquent address that has ever been
made in Faneuil Hall for fifty years." Elated, Schurz wrote to his wife
with great pride, "I spoke like a god and today I cannot get away from
the praises of my speech."

MR. PRESIDENT AND GENTLEMEN:—A few days ago I stood on the
cupola of your statehouse, and overlooked for the first time this
venerable city and the country surrounding it. Then the streets,
and hills, and waters around me began to teem with the life of

Carl Schurz, "True Americanism," Speech delivered in Faneuil Hall, Boston, April
18, 1859, from *Speeches, Correspondence and Political Papers of Carl Schurz*, ed.
Frederick Bancroft (New York: G. P. Putnam's, 1913), vol. 1, pp. 48–57, 62–68,
71–72. Reprinted by permission of G. P. Putnam, original American publisher.

historical recollections, recollections dear to all mankind, and a feeling of pride arose in my heart, and I said to myself, I, too, am an American citizen. There was Bunker Hill; there Charlestown, Lexington and Dorchester Heights not far off; there the harbor into which the British tea was sunk; there the place where the old liberty-tree stood; there John Hancock's house; there Benjamin Franklin's birthplace;—and now I stand in this grand old hall, which so often resounded with the noblest appeals that ever thrilled American hearts, and where I am almost afraid to hear the echo of my own feeble voice;—oh, sir, no man that loves liberty, wherever he may have first seen the light of day, can fail on this sacred spot to pay his tribute to Americanism. And here, with all these glorious memories crowding upon my heart, I will offer mine. I, born in a foreign land, pay my tribute to Americanism? Yes, for to me the word Americanism, *true* Americanism, comprehends the noblest ideas which ever swelled a human heart with noble pride.

It is one of the earliest recollections of my boyhood, that one summer night our whole village was stirred up by an uncommon occurrence. I say our village, for I was born not far from that beautiful spot where the Rhine rolls his green waters out of the wonderful gate of the Seven Mountains, and then meanders with majestic tranquillity through one of the most glorious valleys of the world. That night our neighbors were pressing around a few wagons covered with linen sheets and loaded with household utensils and boxes and trunks to their utmost capacity. One of our neighboring families was moving far away across a great water, and it was said that they would never again return. And I saw silent tears trickling down weather-beaten cheeks, and the hands of rough peasants firmly pressing each other, and some of the men and women hardly able to speak when they nodded to one another a last farewell. At last the train started into motion, they gave three cheers for *America*, and then in the first gray dawn of the morning I saw them wending their way over the hill until they disappeared in the shadow of the forest. And I heard many a man say, how happy he would be if he could go with them to that great and free country, where a man could be himself.

That was the first time that I heard of America, and my childish imagination took possession of a land covered partly with majestic trees, partly with flowery prairies, immeasurable to the eye, and intersected with large rivers and broad lakes—a land where everybody could do what he thought best, and where nobody need be poor, because everybody was free.

And later, when I was old enough to read, and descriptions of this country and books on American history fell into my hands, the offspring of my imagination acquired the colors of reality, and I began to exercise my brain with the thought of what man might be and become when left perfectly free to himself. And still later, when ripening into manhood, I looked up from my school-books into the stir and bustle of the world, and the trumpet-tones of struggling humanity struck my ear and thrilled my heart, and I saw my nation shake her chains in order to burst them, and I heard a gigantic, universal shout for Liberty rising up to the skies; and at last, after having struggled manfully and drenched the earth of Fatherland with the blood of thousands of noble beings, I saw that nation crushed down again, not only by overwhelming armies, but by the dead weight of customs and institutions and notions and prejudices which past centuries had heaped upon them, and which a moment of enthusiasm, however sublime, could not destroy; then I consoled an almost despondent heart with the idea of a youthful people and of original institutions clearing the way for an untrammeled development of the ideal nature of man. Then I turned my eyes instinctively across the Atlantic Ocean, and America and Americanism, as I fancied them, appeared to me as the last depositories of the hopes of all true friends of humanity.

I say all this, not as though I indulged in the presumptuous delusion that my personal feelings and experience would be of any interest to you, but in order to show you what America is to the thousands of thinking men in the old world, who, disappointed in their fondest hopes and depressed by the saddest experience, cling with their last remnant of confidence in human nature, to the last spot on earth where man is free to follow the road to attainable perfection, and where, unbiased by the disastrous influence of traditional notions, customs and institutions, he acts on his own responsibility. They ask themselves: Was it but a wild delusion when we thought that man has the faculty to be free and to govern himself? Have we been fighting, were we ready to die, for a mere phantom, for a mere product of a morbid imagination? This question downtrodden humanity cries out into the world, and from this country it expects an answer.

As its advocate I speak to you. I will speak of Americanism as the great representative of the reformatory age, as the great champion of the dignity of human nature, as the great repository of the last hopes of suffering mankind. I will speak of the ideal mission of this country and of this people.

You may tell me that these views are visionary, that the destiny of this country is less exalted, that the American people are less great than I think they are or ought to be. I answer, ideals are like stars; you will not succeed in touching them with your hands. But like the sea-faring man on the desert of waters, you choose them as your guides, and following them you will reach your destiny. I invite you to ascend with me the watchtower of history, overlooking the grand panorama of the development of human affairs, in which the American Republic stands in so bold and prominent relief.

He who reviews the past of this country in connection with the history of the world besides, cannot fail to discover a wonderful coincidence of great events and fortunate circumstances, which were destined to produce everlasting results, unless recklessly thrown away by imbecile generations.

Look back with me four or five centuries. The dark period of the middle ages is drawing near its close. The accidental explosion of that mysterious black powder, discovered by an obscure German monk, is the first flash of lightning preluding that gigantic thunderstorm which is to shatter the edifice of feudal society to pieces. The invention of gunpowder strips the feudal lord of his prestige as a *warrior;* another discovery is to strip him of his prestige as a *man!* Gutenberg, another obscure German, invents the printing-press, and as gunpowder blows the castles of the small feudal tyrants into the air, so the formidable artillery of printed letters batters down the citadels of ignorance and superstition. Soul and body take up arms and prepare themselves for the great battle of the Reformation. Now the mighty volcano of the German mind bursts the crust of indolence which has covered it. Luther's triumphant thunder rattles against the holy see of Rome. The world is ablaze, all the elements of society are rising up in boiling commotion—two ages are battling against each other.

This is the time when the regeneration of the old world is to take place. But the old order of things, fortified in customs and prejudices and deeply-rooted institutions, does not surrender at the first blast of trumpets. The grand but fearful struggle of the reformatory movement plunges all Europe into endless confusion. The very wheel of progress seems to grind and crush one generation after another. The ideas which concerned the highest and most sacred relations of humanity seem at the same time to call into their service the basest and most violent passions of the human heart, and in all Europe the wars of great principles degenerate into wars of general devastation.

But, meanwhile, a new country has opened its boundless fields to those great ideas, for the realization of which the old world seems no longer to be wide enough. It is as though the earth herself had taken part in the general revolution, and had thrown up from her sea-covered womb a new battle-ground for the spirit of the new era. That is America. Not only the invention of gunpowder and of the printing-press, but also the discovery of America, inaugurates the modern age.

There is the new and immense continent. The most restless and enterprising elements of European society direct their looks towards it. First, the greediness of the gold-hunting adventurer pounces upon the new conquest; but, his inordinate appetites being disappointed, he gradually abandons the field to men in whose hearts the future of the new world is sleeping, unborn.

While the coast of Virginia is settled by a motley immigration, led and ruled by men of ideas and enterprise, the sturdiest champions of principle descend upon the stony shores of New England. While the Southern colonies are settled under the auspices of lordly merchants and proprietaries, original democracy plants its stern banner upon Plymouth Rock. Mercantile speculation, aristocratic ambition and stern virtue that seeks freedom and nothing but freedom, lead the most different classes of people, different in origin, habits and persuasion, upon the virgin soil, and entrust to them the task of realizing the great principles of the age. Nor is this privilege confined to one nationality alone. While the Anglo-Saxon takes possession of New England, Virginia and Pennsylvania, the Frenchman plants his colonies on the soil of French Florida and the interior of the continent; the Hollander locates New Netherlands on the banks of the Hudson; the Swede, led there by the great mind of Oxenstiern, occupies the banks of the Delaware; the Spaniard maintains himself in peninsular Florida, and a numerous immigration of Germans, who follow the call of religious freedom, and of Irishmen, gradually flowing in, scatters itself all over this vast extent of country. Soon all the social and national elements of the civilized world are represented in the new land. Every people, every creed, every class of society has contributed its share to that wonderful mixture out of which is to grow the great nation of the new world. It is true, the Anglo-Saxon establishes and maintains his ascendancy, but without absolutely absorbing the other national elements. They modify each other, and their peculiar characteristics are to be blended together by the all-assimilating power of freedom. This is the origin of the American nationality, which did not spring from one family, one tribe, one country, but incorporates the vigorous elements of all civilized nations on earth.

This fact is not without great importance. It is an essential link in the chain of historical development. The student of history cannot fail to notice that when new periods of civilization break upon humanity, the people of the earth cannot maintain their national relations. New ideas are to be carried out by young nations. From time to time, violent, irresistible hurricanes sweep over the world, blowing the most different elements of the human family together, which by mingling reinvigorate each other, and the general confusion then becomes the starting-point of a new period of progress. Nations which have long subsisted exclusively on their own resources will gradually lose their original vigor, and die the death of decrepitude. But mankind becomes young again by its different elements being shaken together, by race crossing race and mind penetrating mind.

The oldest traditions of history speak of such great revulsions and general migrations, and if we could but lift the veil, which covers the remotest history of Asiatic tribes, we should discover the first scenes and acts of the drama, of which the downfall of the Roman Empire is a portion. When that empire had exhausted its natural vitality, the dark forests of the North poured forth a barbarous but vigorous multitude, who trampled into ruins the decrepit civilization of the Roman world, but infused new blood into the veins of old Europe, grasping the great ideas of Christianity with a bloody but firm hand—and a new period of original progress sprang out of the seeming devastation. The German element took the helm of history. But, in the course of time, the development of things arrived at a new turning-point. The spirit of individualism took possession of the heart of civilized humanity, and the reformatory movement of the sixteenth century was its expression. But continental Europe appeared unable to incorporate the new and progressive ideas growing out of that spirit, in organic political institutions.

While the heart of Europe was ravaged by a series of religious wars, the Anglo-Saxons of England attempted what other nations seemed unable to accomplish. But they also clung too fast to the traditions of past centuries; they failed in separating the Church from the State, and did not realize the cosmopolitan tendency of the new principle. Then the time of a new migration was at hand, and that migration rolled its waves towards America. The old process repeated itself under new forms, milder and more congenial to the humane ideas it represented. It is now not a barbarous multitude pouncing upon old and decrepit empires; not a violent concussion of tribes accompanied by all the horrors of general destruction; but we see the vigorous elements of all nations, we see the Anglo-Saxon, the leader in the practical movement, with his spirit of independence, of daring enterprise and of indomitable perseverance; the German, the original leader in the movement of ideas, with his spirit of inquiry and his quiet and thoughtful application; the Celt, with the impulsive vivacity of his race; the Frenchman, the Scandinavian, the Scot, the Hollander, the Spaniard and the Italian—all these peaceably congregating and mingling together on virgin soil, where the backwoodsman's hatchet is the only battle-axe of civilization; led together by the irresistible attraction of free and broad principles; undertaking to commence a new era in the history of the world, without first destroying the results of the progress of past periods; undertaking to found a new cosmopolitan nation without marching over the dead bodies of slain millions. Thus was founded the *great colony of free humanity*, which has not old England alone, but the *world*, for its mother-country.

This idea is, perhaps, not palatable to those who pride themselves on their unadulterated Anglo-Saxondom. To them I have to say that the destinies of men are often greater than men themselves, and that a good many are swerving from the path of glory by not obeying the true instincts of their nature, and by sacrificing their mission to one-sided pride.

The Anglo-Saxon may justly be proud of the growth and development of this country, and if he ascribes most of it to the undaunted spirit of his race, we may not accuse him of overweening self-glorification. He possesses, in an eminent degree, the enviable talent of acting when others only think; of promptly executing his own ideas, and of appropriating the ideas of other people to his own use. There is, perhaps, no other race that, at so early a day, would have founded the stern democracy of the Plymouth settlement; no other race that would have defied the trials and hardships of the original settler's life so victoriously. No other race, perhaps, possesses in so high a degree not only the daring spirit of independent enterprise, but at the same time the stubborn steadfastness necessary to the final execution of great designs. The Anglo-Saxon spirit has been the locomotive of progress; but do not forget, that this locomotive would be of little use to the world if it refused to draw its train over the iron highway and carry its valuable freight towards its destination; that train consists of the vigorous elements of all nations; that freight is the vital ideas of our age; that destination is universal freedom and the ideal development of man. That is the true greatness of the Anglo-Saxon race; that ought to be the source of Anglo-Saxon pride. I esteem the son who is proud of his father, if, at the same time, he is worthy of him. . . .

Whoever reads the history of this country calmly and thoroughly, cannot but discover that religious liberty is slowly but steadily rooting out the elements of superstition, and even of prejudice. It has dissolved the war of sects, of which persecution was characteristic, into a contest of abstract opinions, which creates convictions without oppressing men. By recognizing perfect freedom of inquiry, it will engender among men of different belief that mutual respect of true convictions which makes inquiry earnest and discussion fair. It will recognize as supremely inviolable, what Roger Williams, one of the most luminous stars of the American sky, called the sanctity of conscience. Read your history, and add the thousands and thousands of Romanists and their offspring together, who, from the first establishment of the colonies, gradually came to this country, and the sum will amount to many millions; compare that number with the number of Romanists who are now here, and you will find that millions are missing. Where are they? You did not kill them; you did not drive them away; they did not perish as the victims of persecution. But where are they? The peaceable working of the great principles which called this Republic into existence, has gradually and silently absorbed them. True Americanism, toleration, the equality of rights, has absorbed their prejudices, and will peaceably absorb everything that is not consistent with the victorious spirit of our institutions.

Oh, sir, there is a wonderful vitality in true democracy founded upon the equality of rights. There is an inexhaustible power of resistance in that system of government, which makes the protection of individual rights a matter of common interest. If preserved in its purity, there is no warfare of opinions which can endanger it—there is no conspiracy of despotic aspirations that can destroy it. But if not preserved in its purity! There are dangers which only blindness can not see, and which only stubborn party prejudice will not see.

I have already called your attention to the despotic tendency of the slaveholding system. I need not enlarge upon it; I need not describe how the existence of slavery in the South affected and demoralized even the political life of the free States; how they attempted to press us, you and me, into the posse of the slave-catcher by that abominable act which, worse than the "alien and sedition laws," still disgraces our statute-book; how the ruling party, which has devoted itself to the service of that despotic interest, shrinks from no violation of good faith, from no adulteration of the constitutional compact, from no encroachment upon natural right, from no treacherous abandonment of fundamental principles. And I do not hesitate to prophesy that, if the theories engendered by the institution of slavery be suffered to outgrow the equalizing tendency of true democracy, the American Republic will, at no distant day, crumble down under the burden of the laws and measures which the ruling interest will demand for its protection, and its name will be added to the sad catalogue of the broken hopes of humanity.

But the mischief does not come from that side alone; it is in things of small beginnings, but fearful in their growth. One of these is the propensity of men *to lose sight of fundamental principles, when passing abuses are to be corrected.*

Is it not wonderful how nations who have won their liberty by the severest struggles become so easily impatient of the small inconveniences and passing difficulties which are almost inseparably connected with the practical working of general self-government? How they so easily forget that rights may be abused, and yet remain inalienable rights? Europe has witnessed many an attempt for the establishment of democratic institutions; some of them were at first successful, and the people were free, but the abuses and inconveniences connected with liberty became at once apparent. Then the ruling classes of society, in order to get rid of the abuses, restricted liberty; they did, indeed, get rid of the abuses, but they got rid of liberty at the same time. You heard liberal governments there speak of protecting and regulating the liberty of the press; and, in order to prevent that liberty from being abused, they adopted measures, apparently harmless at first, which ultimately resulted in an absolute censorship. Would it be much better if we, recognizing the right of man to the exercise of self-government, should, in order to protect the purity of the ballot-box, restrict the right of suffrage?

Liberty, sir, is like a spirited housewife; she will have her whims, she will be somewhat unruly sometimes, and, like so many husbands, you cannot always have it all your own way. She may spoil your favorite dish sometimes; but will you, therefore, at once smash her china, break her kettles and shut her out from the kitchen? Let her practise, let her try again and again, and even when she makes a mistake, encourage her with a benignant smile, and your broth will be right after a while. But meddle with her concerns, tease her, bore her, and your little squabbles, spirited as she is, will ultimately result in a divorce. What then? It is one of Jefferson's wisest words that "he would much rather be exposed to the inconveniences arising from too much liberty, than to those arising from too small a degree of it." It is a matter of historical experience, that nothing that is wrong in principle can be right in practice. People are apt to delude themselves on that point; but the ultimate result will always prove the truth of the maxim. A violation of equal rights can never serve to maintain institutions which are founded upon equal rights. A contrary policy is not only pusillanimous and small, but it is senseless. It reminds me of the soldier who, for fear of being shot in battle, committed suicide on the march; or of the man who would cut off his foot, because he had a corn on his toe. It is that ridiculous policy of premature despair, which commences to throw the freight overboard when there is a suspicious cloud in the sky.

Another danger for the safety of our institutions, and perhaps the most formidable one, arises from the general propensity of political parties and public men to act on a policy of mere expediency, and to sacrifice principle to local and temporary success. And here, sir, let me address a solemn appeal to the consciences of those with whom I am proud to struggle side by side against human thraldom.

You hate kingcraft, and you would sacrifice your fortunes and your lives in order to prevent its establishment on the soil of this Republic. But let me tell you that the rule of political parties which sacrifice principle to expediency, is no less dangerous, no less disastrous, no less aggressive, of no less despotic a nature, than the rule of monarchs. Do not indulge in the delusion, that in order to make a government fair and liberal, the only thing necessary is to make it elective. When a political party in power, however liberal their principles may be, have once adopted the policy of knocking down their opponents instead of voting them down, there is an end of justice and equal rights. The history of the world shows no example of a more arbitrary despotism, than that exercised by the party which ruled the National Assembly of France in the bloodiest days of the great French Revolution. I will not discuss here what might have been done, and what not, in those times of a fearful crisis; but I will say that they tried to establish liberty by means of despotism, and that in her gigantic struggle against the united monarchs of Europe, revolutionary France won the victory, but lost her liberty.

Remember the shout of indignation that went all over the Northern States when we heard that the border ruffians of Kansas had crowded the free-State men away from the polls and had not allowed them to vote. That indignation was just, not only because the men thus terrorized were free-State men and friends of liberty, but because they were deprived of their right of suffrage, and because the government of that territory was placed on the basis of force, instead of equal rights. Sir, if ever the party of liberty should use their local predominance for the purpose of disarming their opponents instead of convincing them, they will but follow the example set by the ruffians of Kansas, although legislative enactments may be a genteeler weapon than the revolver and bowie knife. They may perhaps achieve some petty local success, they may gain some small temporary advantage, but they will help to introduce a system of action into our politics which will gradually undermine the very foundations upon which our republican edifice rests. Of all the dangers and difficulties that beset us, there is none more horrible than the hideous monster, whose name is "Proscription for opinion's sake." I am an anti-slavery man, and I have a right to my opinion in South Carolina just as well as in Massachusetts. My neighbor is a pro-slavery man; I may be sorry for it, but I solemnly acknowledge his right to his opinion in Massachusetts as well as in South Carolina. You tell me, that for my opinion they would mob me in South Carolina? Sir, there is the difference between South Carolina and Massachusetts. There is the difference between an anti-slavery man, who is a freeman, and a slaveholder, who is himself a slave.

Our present issues will pass away. The slavery question will be settled, liberty will be triumphant and other matters of difference will divide the political parties of this country. What if we, in our struggle against slavery, had removed the solid basis of equal rights, on which such new matters of difference may be peaceably settled? What if we had based the institutions of this country upon a difference of rights between different classes of people? What if, in destroying the generality of natural rights, we had resolved them into privileges? There is a thing which stands above the command of the most ingenious of politicians: *it is the logic of things and events.* It cannot be turned and twisted by artificial arrangements and delusive settlements; it will go its own way with the steady step of fate. It will force you, with uncompromising severity, to choose between two social organizations, one of which is founded upon privilege, and the other upon the doctrine of equal rights.

Force instead of right, privilege instead of equality, expediency instead of principle, being once the leading motives of your policy, you will have no power to stem the current. There will be new abuses to be corrected, new inconveniences to be remedied, new supposed dangers to be obviated, new equally exacting ends to be subserved, and your encroachments upon the natural rights of your opponents now, will be used as welcome precedents for the mutual oppression of parties then. Having once knowingly disregarded the doctrine of equal rights, the ruling parties will soon accustom themselves to consult only their interests where fundamental principles are at stake. Those who lead us into this channel will be like the sorcerer who knew the art of making a giant snake. And when he had made it, he forgot the charmword that would destroy it again. And the giant snake threw its horrid coils around him, and the unfortunate man was choked by the monster of his own creation. . . .

Sir, I was to speak on Republicanism at the West, and so I did. This *is* Western Republicanism. These are its principles, and I am proud to say its principles are its policy. These are the ideas which have rallied around the banner of liberty not only the natives of the soil, but an innumerable host of Germans, Scandinavians, Scotchmen, Frenchmen and a goodly number of Irishmen, also. And here I tell you, those are mistaken who believe that the Irish heart is devoid of those noble impulses which will lead him to the side of justice, where he sees his own rights respected and unendangered. Under this banner, all the languages of civilized mankind are spoken, every creed is protected, every right is sacred. There stands every element of Western society, with enthusiasm for a great cause, with confidence in each other, with honor to themselves. This is the banner floating over the glorious valley which stretches from the western slope of the Alleghanies to the Rocky Mountains—that Valley of Jehoshaphat where the nations of the world assemble to celebrate the resurrection of human freedom. The inscription on that banner is not "Opposition to the Democratic party for the sake of placing a new set of men into office"; for this battle-cry of speculators our hearts have no response. Nor is it "Restriction of slavery and restriction of the right of suffrage," for this—believe my words, I entreat you—this would be the signal of deserved, inevitable and disgraceful defeat. But the inscription is "Liberty and equal rights, common to all as the air of Heaven—Liberty and equal rights, one and inseparable!"

With this banner we stand before the world. In this sign—in this sign alone, and no other—there is victory. And thus, sir, we mean to realize the great cosmopolitan idea, upon which the existence of the American nation rests. Thus we mean to fulfill the great mission of true Americanism—thus we mean to answer the anxious question of down-trodden humanity—"Has *man* the faculty to be free and to govern himself?" The answer is a triumphant "Aye," thundering into the ears of the despots of the old world that "a man is a man for all that"; proclaiming to the oppressed that they are held in subjection on false pretences; cheering the hearts of the despondent friends of man with consolation and renewed confidence.

This is true Americanism, clasping mankind to its great heart. Under its banner we march; let the world follow.

PART FOUR

The Labor Question

16. Franklin B. Gowen

The "Molly Maguires" have been denounced by their church and excommunicated

The anthracite region of eastern Pennsylvania bore all the earmarks of a mining frontier—occupational hazards, violence, economic exploitation, and acute ethnic and religious rivalries. In 1877 and 1878 twenty "Molly Maguires," all Irish Catholics, were tried and hanged for the murders of various police and mining officials. Though an aura of conspiracy surrounded the trials, no such allegation was made.

The account of the "Molly Maguires" by Franklin B. Gowen, instigator of the prosecution, president of the Philadelphia and Reading Railroad, and czar of the coal fields, implies an intimate relationship between Ireland's agrarian crime and the pattern of violence in the anthracite fields of Pennsylvania. Gowen, relentlessly opposed to labor unions, more than anyone else, was responsible for creating the Molly Maguire legend. Contemporary witnesses with a different point of view were too ambivalent or too cowed to serve as historical witnesses. The chief witness for the prosecution was the Pinkerton detective, James McParlan, an Irish Catholic who put special stress on just these aspects of the case. Although the terror was real, the exact character of the "Molly Maguires" remains obscure. But the Irish ties of the Mollies, their exaggerated criminality, their affiliation with the Ancient Order of Hibernians, and their similarities to the Ribbonmen all combined to further the stereotype of the brawling Irishman. Behind the scenes much more was happening: ethnic and religious tensions were being exacerbated, social and economic inequities were being camouflaged, and the Roman Catholic Church was being driven farther from the labor movement.

Franklin B. Gowen, *The Lives and Crimes of the Molly Maguires, with an Account of the Organization of the Terrible Society* (Philadelphia, 1877), pp. 65–66, 69–70, 73–79, 87–88.

Mr. Gowen addressed the jury on behalf of the Commonwealth as follows:

With submission to your Honors; gentlemen of the jury: It is frequently customary for lawyers, in opening a cause, to refer to it as one of great importance. I am sure that you will bear with me, when I say that I do not exaggerate the merits of this case in stating that it is perhaps one of the most momentous trials that has ever been submitted to a jury in this country. It is one of that class of cases, which, for so many years, has disgraced the criminal annals of this county. For the first time, after struggling under a reign of terror that has extended over twenty years, we are placed front to front with the inner workings of a secret association, whose members, acting under oaths, have perpetrated crime in this county with impunity.

I desire to say, at the outset of my argument, that when a man is on trial for his life, no matter what may be the gravity of his offence, and no matter what may be the circumstances connected with his participation in it, it is due to the administration of justice that he should have a fair and an impartial trial. . . .

We ask nothing here but an impartial trial. We ask no sympathy, and invoke no prejudice. We try this man according to law; and according to that law which you have sworn to administer, we ask you to convict him. What is this case? On the 1st of September last, Thomas Sanger, a young English boss miner, a man between thirty and forty years of age, who, so far as we know, may not have had an enemy in the world, left his house in the morning to go to his daily work. If there is anything which should be accorded to a member of a free government, if there is any right which the humblest man in this country should possess, it is the right to labor for the support of his family, without hindrance or molestation from any one. Going forward and onward in the performance of his duty, and the prosecution of his daily work, this man was confronted by one of an armed band of five assassins. He was shot in the arm. He turned to run around a house in the neighborhood, and he was there confronted by another of these miscreants who had been sent to intercept him. He again turned and stumbled upon the ground; and then, when the foremost of this band of assassins came up to him, as he lay upon the ground, he discharged his revolver into him, and another turned him, as he lay upon his face, over upon his back, so that he could expose a deadly part for his aim, and then, with calm deliberation, selected a vital spot and shot him as he lay prostrate upon the ground. His wife, from whom he had just parted, hearing his cries, rushed out and reached her husband only in time to hear his last faltering accents: "Kiss me, Sarah, for I am dying."

That is this case. It is not isolated or alone. God knows I wish it was! It is not one case singled out in this great community, but it is one of a number that we have been called upon to confront during the last twenty years. Who were these persons who were guilty of this murder? That is for you to determine, according to the evidence, and I now propose, very concisely and as succinctly as I can, to call your attention to the evidence in this case; and I ask you to find your verdict of guilty solely in accordance with that evidence and acting under the solemnity of your oaths. . . .

We have . . . in this case, positive identification. We need go no further. We show a murder committed, and we need not show the motive. We show the murder committed, and that it was perpetrated by five men; and we identify the prisoner Thomas Munley, the man whom we are trying, as one of the five who committed that murder. We identify him positively by three witnesses as being there, and, upon that evidence alone, leaving out the testimony of McParlan, and leaving out all the subsequent testimony corroborative of McParlan, it would be your duty to convict this defendant if we had introduced no other evidence but that given by Mr. Heaton, by Mrs. Williams, and by Melinda Bickelman. There can be no doubt of this, for what is the defence? An alibi, which I will refer to hereafter, as being composed of such mere webs of gossamer that it needs but a breath to dissolve it into the thinnest air.

I could rest this case here, to-day, as counsel for the Commonwealth, solely upon the testimony of Robert Heaton, Mrs. Williams, and Melinda Bickelman. But I dare not stop without going further, because, in addition to that testimony, which alone is sufficient to convict, we have the positive declarations of the prisoner himself. And how do we show this? By the detective James McParlan, of whom I shall speak hereafter; for, at this stage of the case, I simply desire to call your attention to the fact that on the morning of the 31st of August, McParlan, who had slept the night before with Michael Doyle, was informed by him that he with some others were going to shoot a boss at Raven Run. Doyle wanted one of his (McParlan's) coats, and got it; and Thomas Hurley then came in and instructed Doyle how he should perform his murderous work. After that, this man Hurley remained with McParlan the whole of the day, so as to prevent him communicating with any one; and on the next morning at 8 o'clock, immediately after the perpetration of the crime, panting with the speed of the flight and reeking with the blood of their victims, the five assassins rushed into the house of Michael Lawlor, at Shenandoah, and into the presence of Hurley and McParlan himself.

These men announced, at once, that they had killed a man, that they had killed a boss, that they had intended to kill only one, but that they had to kill another. They said that they did not intend to kill more than one, but the other man interfered and they killed him, too; and then each recounted the share which he had taken in the exploit—Munley, as I shall show you hereafter, specifically detailed the position which he occupied and the part which he had taken in the murder. Here is our case, and were it not for what the defence has offered in evidence, and more particularly for what their counsel have said, it would be unnecessary for me to add a single word to that which I have already uttered; but as my friends, Mr. Bartholomew and Mr. L'Velle, have pleaded before you for the acquittal of this prisoner, and as they have endeavored to attack the credibility of our witnesses, and to blacken the character of James McParlan, it becomes my duty not to stop with the testimony of the Commonwealth, but to go over, in more laborious detail, the evidence for the defence, and to answer the arguments which have been made to secure an acquittal for this prisoner.

What is the first defence? An alibi. That which comes most readily at the beck and call of every criminal who knows himself to be guilty; for, when every other defence fails, the ever ready alibi is always on hand to be proved by a crowd of relatives and retainers, who come forward to say that the man charged with the commission of a particular offence, at a particular time, and in a particular place, was, on that very day, engaged in some lawful and legitimate calling many miles away. When established to the satisfaction of a jury, an alibi is the very best defence that can be offered, but, as it is always the defence that is resorted to by the guilty, and as it is the defence that is most easily manufactured, it becomes the duty of a jury most carefully to scrutinize and examine its truth; and in this case I am glad to say that I think you will have no trouble in disposing of it. . . .

I may say, however, before leaving this branch of the case, that now that the light of day is thrown upon the secret workings of this association, human life is as safe in Schuylkill county as it is in any other part of this Commonwealth; that as this association is broken down and trampled into the dust, its leaders either in jail or fugitives from the just vengeance of the law, the administration of justice in this Court will be as certain as human life is safe throughout the whole length and breadth of the county. The time has gone by when the murderer, the incendiary, and the assassin can go home reeking from the commission of crimes, confident in the fact that he can appear before a jury and have an alibi proved for him to allow him to escape punishment. There will be no more false alibis in this county; the time for them has gone forever. No more false alibis. No more confident reliance upon the perjury of relatives and friends to prove an alibi for him who was seen in the commission of the act. No more dust thrown in the eyes of juries to blind them from looking directly at the facts of a case; and I do say that if there ever was anything to be proud of, to be glad of, after the fact that we are enfranchised and disenthralled from this despotism and this tyranny that has been hanging over us, it is that the administration of justice will no longer be polluted, and disgraced by perjury and false swearing, for the purpose of rescuing a criminal from the just vengeance of the law.

I now come to the testimony of McParlan. Many of you know that some years ago I was the District Attorney of this county. I am, therefore, not very much out of my old paths, and not very much away from my old moorings when I am standing, on behalf of the Commonwealth, in the Court of Pottsville, demanding the conviction of a guilty man. It was when I was District Attorney of this county, a young man, charged with the prosecution of the pleas of the Commonwealth, that for the first time I made up my mind from what I had seen, in innumerable instances, that there then existed in this county a secret organization, banded together for the commission of crime, and for the purpose of securing the escape or acquittal of any · of its members charged with the commission of an offence.

That conviction forced itself indelibly upon my mind. A man who for two years acts as District Attorney in this county prosecuting criminals who are brought before the Court, must be either very obtuse or wilfully blind, if he could close his eyes to the existence of a fact as perceptible as this was then to me. I left this county with that settled conviction, and circumstances that occurred time and again long after I withdrew from the prosecution of criminals, still more deeply fastened this conviction in my mind. Murder, violence and arson, committed without detection, and apparently without motive, attested the correctness of that belief, and when the time came that I became so much interested in the prosperity of this county, and in the development of its mineral wealth, that I saw that it was a struggle between the good citizen and the bad citizen as to which should obtain the supremacy, I made up my mind that if human ingenuity, if long suffering and patient care, and toil that stopped at no obstacle, and would confront every danger, could succeed in exposing this secret organization to light of day, and bringing to well-earned justice the perpetrators of these awful crimes, I would undertake the task.

I knew that it could only be done by secret detectives, and I had had enough experience, both as a lawyer, and as the head of a very large corporation, to know that the public municipal detectives, employed by the police authorities of the cities, who operate only for rewards, are the last persons to whom you could trust a mission and an enterprise such as this. It was as important for us to know who was innocent as it was to know who was guilty.

The detective who operates for rewards, who is only paid upon the conviction of the offender, has a motive to incite him to action which I would be the last man in the world to arouse. I knew, for I had had experience before, of the National Detective Agency of Allan Pinkerton, of Chicago, which was established by an intelligent and broad-minded Scotchman, established upon the only basis on which a successful detective agency can be established, and I applied to Mr. Pinkerton. His plan was simply this: "I will secure an agent, or an officer," said he "to ferret out the existence of this society. Whoever I get is to be paid so much a week, no matter if he finds out nothing. He is bound to me, never, under any circumstances, to take a reward for his services, from anybody, and, if he spends five years and obtains nothing in the way of information, he must have every month or every week exactly the same compensation as if every week he had traced a new murder and every month had discovered a new conspiracy. He is never to gain pecuniarily by the success of his undertaking; but, as a man who goes into this organization, as a detective, takes his life in his own hands, I will send no man on this mission of yours, Mr. Gowen, unless it be agreed, beforehand, and I can tell him so, that he never is to be known in connection with the enterprise." Upon these terms this man James McParlan was selected. A young Irishman and a Catholic, but six or seven years in this country, eminently qualified by his peculiar Irish accomplishments to ingratiate himself with those to whom he was sent, he came here in the fall of 1873, and within six months he had so far won the confidence of the class of people who constituted this order that he was admitted as a member. Remember, now, here, and I advert to it lest I might forget it, that he came here pledged that he should not be used as a witness. Therefore the only object of his coming was to put us upon the track, so that we could discover the crime when it was being perpetrated, and this is the best answer that can possibly be made to the charge that he wilfully withheld his knowledge when he might have saved human life. His only object here was to get knowledge. He never was to be used as a witness. His only object was to find out when a murder was to be committed, to be with the perpetrators if he could, and to give notice to Captain Linden, who had an armed police force ready, so that they might be waiting at the very spot, and not only save the life of the intended victim, but arrest every man engaged in the perpetration of the offence, in order that there could be abundant evidence of their guilt. That was his whole object. Almost every night he made his report; and how well he has performed his duty, the security of human life and property in this county, to-day, as compared with what it was six months ago, is the best commentary I can make upon the subject. . . .

And now some words about this secret organization of Mollie Maguires. . . . If, after this case is over and when you are permitted to read, you will get a little book called "Trench's Realities of Irish Life," written by a relative of that celebrated Dean Trench whose name is well known wherever English literature is read, you will find the history of this organization. It was known as the Ribbonmen of Ireland. It sprang up at a time when there was an organized resistance in Ireland to the payment of rents. The malcontents became known as Ribbonmen, and they generally made their attacks upon the agents of the non-resident landowners, or upon the constables or bailiffs who attempted to collect the rents. Their object was to intimidate and hold in terror all those to whom they owed money, or who were employed in its collection. As a branch of this society, and growing out of it, sprang the men known as Mollie Maguires, and the name of their society simply arose from this circumstance, that in the perpetration of their offences, they dressed as women, and generally ducked or beat their victims, or inflicted some such punishment as infuriated women would be likely to administer. Hence originated the name of the Mollie Maguires, which has been handed down to us at the present day; and the organization of the Mollie Maguires, therefore, is identical with that of the Ribbonmen in Ireland, who have terrorized over the Irish people to so great an extent.

How this association came into this county we do not know. We had suspected for many years, and we know now, that it is criminal in its character. That is proved beyond peradventure. It will not do now to say that it was only in particular localities in this county that it was a criminal organization, because the highest officer in the society in this county, the county delegate, Jack Kehoe, the man who attended the State Convention, and was the representative of the whole order in this county, is to-day as you hear from the testimony, in prison awaiting his trial for murder. Whether this society, known as the Ancient Order of Hibernians, is, beyond the limits of this county, a good society or not, I cannot tell; but I have believed at sometimes that it was, and I am willing to be satisfied of that fact now, if there is any evidence of it. But there has been an attack made upon this organization, and up to this time we have not had furnished to us any evidence that in any place its objects were laudable or commendable. Criminal in its character, criminal in its purpose, it had frequently a political object. You will find the leaders of this society the prominent men in the townships. Through the instrumentality of their order and by its power, they were able to secure offices for themselves. You see here, and now know that one of the commissioners of this county is a member of this order. You know that a previous commissioner of this county was a member of this order, convicted of a high offence and pardoned by the governor. You know that another county commissioner, before that, was a member of this order, convicted of an offence and pardoned by the governor. High constables, chiefs of police, candidates for associate judges, men who were trusted by their fellow-men, were all the time guilty of murder.

But in addition to the criminal and the political motives, these people claim national characteristics. They claim that they were par excellence the representatives of the Irish of this country. They claim more than that, that they represent the Irish Catholics of this country. I shall say but little about the Irish except that I am myself the son of an Irishman, proud of my ancestry, and proud of my race, and never ashamed of it except when I see that Ireland has given birth to wretches such as these. These men call themselves Irishmen! These men parade on St. Patrick's day, and claim to be good Catholics! Where are the honest Irishmen of this county? Why do they not rise up and strike down these wretches that usurp the name of Irishmen? If a German commits an offence, and engages in murder, do all the other Germans take his part and establish a false alibi to defeat the ends of justice? If an American becomes a criminal, do the Americans protect him? Do they not say, "Away with you! You have disgraced the country that bore you?" If an Englishman becomes an offender, do the English nation take him to their arms and make him a hero? Why, then, do not the honest Irishmen of this county come together in public meeting, and separate themselves widely from and denounce this organization? Upon what principle do these men, outcasts from society, the dregs of the earth, murderers and assassins, claim to be Irishmen and arrogate to themselves the national characteristics of the Irish people? It is a disgrace to Ireland that the honest Irish of this county, probably five or ten thousand in number, should permit a few hundred wretches like these to say that they are the true representatives of the Irishmen of Schuylkill county.

Does an Irishman wonder why it is sometimes difficult to get a job in this county? Does he wonder why the boss at a colliery hesitates to employ him, when these people have been permitted to arrogate to themselves the Irish character, and have been permitted to represent themselves to the people of this county as the proper representatives of Ireland? The time has come when there must be a line of demarcation drawn. The time has come when every honest Irishman in this county must separate himself from any suspicion of sympathy with this association. He must denounce its members as outcasts from the land that gave them birth. He must denounce them as covered with infamy and blackened with crime. He must say that they are not true Irishmen and that they are not representatives of Ireland.

But far beyond this attempt to invoke your sympathy on account of their nationality is the attempt to invoke that sympathy on the ground that they belong to a persecuted religion. Was there ever such sublime, such tremendous impudence in the world, as that a member of this secret society, a society which has been denounced by its own Church, and each member of which has been excommunicated by the Archbishop of Philadelphia, and by the Pope himself, outcasts from society, and from the communion of their own religion, the door of the Church shut in their faces and the gates of heaven closed against them by the excommunication of their priests—these men, infidels and atheists, caring for no church, and worshipping no God, set themselves up in this community as the representatives of the Catholic faith.

> Just Allah! what must be thy look?
>   When such a wretch before thee stands,
> Unblushing, with thy sacred book,
>   Turning its leaves with blood-stained hands,
> And wresting from its page sublime
> His creed of lust, and hate, and crime

A few words more upon this subject of Irish Catholics. I was born and am a Protestant; but I was partially educated among the Catholics, and I have always had a kindly feeling for them, and when these assassins, through their counsel, speak of being Catholics, I desire to say to you here, in the first place, that they have been denounced by their Church and excommunicated by their prelates, and that I have the direct personal authority of Archbishop Wood himself to say that he denounces them all, and that he was fully cognizant of and approved of the means I took to bring them to justice. And, for myself, I can say that for many months before any other man in this world except those connected with the detective agency, knew what was being done, Archbishop Wood, of Philadelphia, was the only confidant I had and fully knew of the mission of McParlan in this whole matter. So much then for the assumption of Mr. L'Velle that these men claim sympathy on account of their being Catholics. I can hardly reply calmly to such an argument. I believe that there must be different sects in this country as there are in all countries, and I am one of those who believe that a good Catholic is better than a bad Protestant. . . .

I have been taught to believe that the eyes of justice are closed

not only against individuals and corporations, but against nationalities and sects. I have been taught to believe that he is the good
citizen who is truthful and honest, who is kind-hearted and
affectionate; who lives in charity with all men, who gives freely of
his means to the poor; and, whether he kneels before an altar or
worships God in his own chamber, he is entitled to the favorable
consideration of his fellow-men. And I do know, oh! so well, that
when our lives draw toward their close, and the opening portals of
the tomb reveal to our eyes some glimpses of the boundless waters
of that vast eternity upon which we will all embark, that then, at
that dread moment, it will be to the recollection of the possession
of these simple virtues, this pure morality, this unostentatious
charity that I have named, that we will all cling, in the sublime
confidence that it will avail us most, when the time shall come
that each one of us, Catholic and Protestant, Lutheran and
Calvinist, Gentile and Jew shall be stripped of the thin garb of the
sectarian, and stand in equal favor before the great white throne
of God.

And now one word more upon this subject, and I dismiss it.
Whenever you hear a complaint made against a man because he is
an Irishman, or because he is a Catholic; whenever you hear any
one, no matter who he may be, say that the outrages of this county
are due to the Irishmen, or due to the Catholics, do not, I beg of
you, forget, in your secret hearts, that the highest prelates of that
church have cursed and excommunicated this order. Do not forget
that whatever little credit may be due to him who has conceived
the plan of exposing this association, is due to one who is the son
of an Irishman; and do not forget that a greater honor and a
greater meed of praise than is due to any other, is due to
Detective McParlan, who is an Irishman by birth, and a Catholic
by religion; and if those who profess to be Irish Catholics in this
county have brought their nationality and their religion into
disrepute, I beg of you to remember that both have been
gloriously and successfully vindicated by an Irishman and a
Catholic, in the person of James McParlan. . . .

And now the duty which I owe to this case is almost performed,
and I commit it to your hands. For three years I have been

engaged in an investigation, the result of which has now become known to the community. Two or three days after the commission of this offence, I believed from the information which came to me, that Thomas Munley was one of the assassins of Sanger. I had no evidence that I could use, for it was not until McParlan consented to become a witness that I could furnish the information that led to the arrest of this prisoner. I believe I have done my duty; for God's sake, let me beg of you not to shrink from doing yours. Solemn judges of the law and of the facts—august ministers in the temple of justice—robed for sacrifice, I bring before you this prisoner and lay him upon your altar, bound and fastened by such cords of testimony as all the ingenuity of counsel cannot unloosen, and trembling at the momentous issues involved in your answer, I ask you, Will you let him go? If you perform your duty without favor and without affection, if, in the pursuit of what appears to me to be your plain and bounden duty, you will say almost without leaving the box that this man is guilty of murder in the first degree, you will do that which I believe to be just, and you will do that which will protect society and save the lives of hundreds and thousands of your fellow-men. But if you should falter, if from any false sympathy you should unbind this prisoner and let him go, I tremble for the consequences to society. Who, then, would be safe? For you to do this would be to hold up this prisoner's hands and the hands of all his fellows and associates, to place the dagger and the pistol in their grasp, and with the torch of the incendiary, to send them again throughout this land to play their part of murder, of arson, and of crime.

I have done all that I could to expose the criminal character of this organization; laying aside all other duties, giving up everything else that I had to do, I have tried to devote myself to this cause, for I believe it to be the highest duty that I could be called upon to perform. I am glad, at the conclusion of this case, to return my thanks to the able gentlemen who have been associated with me, and especially to the District Attorney, under whose administration these crimes have come to light. He was an old student of mine when I was in this county, and I was glad to know that it was he who filled the office when this conspiracy was first brought to light. He has done his duty faithfully and nobly, in the face of danger, without fear, or favor, or affection. I know that we have a Court that will not shrink from whatever duty may be imposed upon it, and I believe, from what I have seen of you, that you will walk unshrinkingly in the plain paths of duty that are opened before you. Do this, gentlemen, and I am sure that linked together with that of McParlan and of others who have aided in this *glorious crusade,* your names will be enshrined for long-coming years in the grateful recollections of an enfranchised and redeemed people.

17. Augustus Spies

We would not be socialists if we were beasts

In 1886 a single event climaxing labor's "great upheaval" deeply impressed itself on a whole generation of Americans. On May 4 at a meeting in Chicago protesting the police slaying of two striking unionists, a bomb was thrown that killed seven policemen. The Haymarket trial that followed left no doubt that "law and order" took precedence over justice and human life. Of the eight defendants, six were of German birth or origins, one was an English Chartist, and the last, the editor of the *Alarm,* was an American descendant of Mayflower pioneers and was married to an Indian. They were condemned summarily by beleaguered Americans who had lost confidence in their own credo and who demanded retribution for an unsolved crime. The hanging of Albert Parsons, August Spies, Adolph Fischer, and George Engel, and the suicide of Louis Lingg earned these advocates of an eight-hour day a martyrdom and an immortality that was to haunt the national conscience for years to come. The pardon in 1893 of Samuel Fielden, Michael Schwab, and Oscar Neebe by Governor Altgeld, a German-American with a keen sense of justice, came too late.

"Address of August Spies," *Chicago Martyrs: The Famous Speeches of the Eight Anarchists in Judge Gary's Court* (San Francisco: Free Society, 1889), pp. 1–8, 15–16.

On October 7, 8, and 9, 1886, each of the eight anarchists accused of the Haymarket bomb-throwing delivered a final plea to the court while awaiting sentence to the gallows. The first speaker, August Spies, editor of the anarchist *Arbeiter Zeitung*, denounced the court for martyring innocent men charged, totally without proof, with advocacy and conspiracy to murder.

YOUR HONOR: In addressing this court I speak as the representative of one class to the representative of another. I will begin with the words uttered five hundred years ago on a similar occasion, by the Venetian Doge Faheri, who, addressing the court, said: *"My defense is your accusation; the causes of my alleged crime your history!"* I have been indicted on a charge of murder, as an accomplice or accessory. Upon this indictment I have been convicted. There was no evidence produced by the State to show or even indicate that I had any knowledge of the man who threw the bomb, or that I myself had anything to do with the throwing of the missile, unless, of course, you weigh the testimony of the accomplices of the State's attorney and Bonfield, the testimony of Thompson and Gilmer, by the price they were paid for it. If there was no evidence to show that I was legally responsible for the deed, then my conviction and the execution of the sentence is nothing less than willful, malicious, and deliberate murder, as foul a murder as may be found in the annals of religious, political, or any other sort of persecution. There have been many judicial murders committed where the representatives of the State were acting in good faith, believing their victims to be guilty of the charge accused of. In this case the representatives of the State cannot shield themselves with a similar excuse. For they themselves have fabricated most of the testimony which was used as a pretense to convict us; to convict us by a jury picked out to convict! Before this court, and before the public, which is supposed to be the State, I charge the State's attorney and Bonfield with the heinous conspiracy to commit murder.

I will state a little incident which may throw light upon this charge. On the evening on which the Prætorian Guards of the Citizens' Association, the Bankers' Association, the Association of the Board of Trade men, and the railroad princes, attacked the meeting of workingmen on the Haymarket, with murderous intent—on that evening, about 8 o'clock, I met a young man, Legner by name, who is a member of the Aurora Turn-Verein. He accompanied me, and never left me on that evening until I jumped from the wagon, a few seconds before the explosion occurred. He knew that I had not seen Schwab that evening. He knew that I had no such conversation with anybody as Mr. Marshal Field's protege, Thompson, testified to. He knew that I did not jump from the wagon to strike the match and hand it to the man who threw the bomb. He is not a Socialist. Why did we not bring him on the stand? Because the honorable representatives of the State, Grinnell and Bonfield, spirited him away. These honorable gentlemen knew everything about Legner. They knew that his testimony would prove the perjury of Thompson and Gilmer beyond any reasonable doubt. Legner's name was on the list of witnesses for the State. He was not called, however, for obvious reasons. Aye, he stated to a number of friends that he had been offered $500 if he would leave the city, and threatened with direful things if he remained here and appeared as a witness for the defense. He replied that he could neither be bought nor bulldozed to serve such a damnable and dastardly plot. When we wanted Legner, he could not be found; Mr. Grinnell said—and Mr. Grinnell is an honorable man!—that he had himself been searching for the young man, but had not been able to find him. About three weeks later I learned that the very same young man had been kidnapped and taken to Buffalo, N. Y., by two of the illustrious guardians of "law and order," two Chicago detectives. Let Mr. Grinnell, let the Citizens' Association, his employer, let them answer for this! And let the public sit in judgment upon the would-be assassins!

No, I repeat, the prosecution has not established our legal guilt, notwithstanding the purchased and perjured testimony of some, and notwithstanding the originality of the proceedings of this trial. And as long as this has not been done, and you pronounce upon us the sentence of an appointed vigilance committee, acting as a jury, I say, you, the alleged representatives and high priests of "law and order," are the real and only law breakers, and in this case to the extent of murder. It is well that the people know this. And when I speak of the people I don't mean the few co-conspirators of Grinnell, the noble politicians who thrive upon the misery of the multitudes. These drones may constitute the State, they may control the State, they may have their Grinnells, their Bonfields and other hirelings! No, when I speak of the people I speak of the great mass of human bees, the working people, who unfortunately are not yet conscious of the rascalities that are perpetrated in the "name of the people,"—in their name.

The contemplated murder of eight men, whose only crime is that they have dared to speak the truth, may open the eyes of these suffering millions; may wake them up. Indeed, I have noticed that our conviction has worked miracles in this direction already. The class that clamors for our lives, the good, devout Christians, have attempted in every way, through their newspapers and otherwise, to conceal the true and only issue in this case. By simply designating the defendants as Anarchists, and picturing them as a newly discovered tribe or species of cannibals, and by inventing shocking and horrifying stories of dark conspiracies said to be planned by them—these good Christians zealously sought to keep the naked fact from the working people and other righteous parties, namely: That on the evening of May 4, 200 armed men, under the command of a notorious ruffian, attacked a meeting of peaceable citizens! With what intention? With the intention of murdering them, or as many of them as they could. I refer to the testimony given by two of our witnesses. The wage workers of this city began to object to being fleeced too much—they began to say some very true things, but they were highly disagreeable to our Patrician class; they put forth—well, some very modest demands. They thought eight hours hard toil a day for scarcely two hours' pay was enough. This "lawless rabble" had to be silenced! The only way to silence them was to frighten them, and murder those whom they looked up to as their leaders. Yes, these "foreign dogs" had to be taught a lesson, so that they might never again interfere with the high-handed exploitation of their benevolent and Christian masters. Bonfield, the man who would bring a blush of shame to the managers of the St. Bartholomew night—Bonfield, the illustrious gentleman with a visage that would have done excellent service to Dore in portraying Dante's fiends of hell—Bonfield was the man best fitted to consummate the conspiracy of the Citizens' Association, of our Patricians. If I had thrown that bomb, or had caused it to be thrown, or had known of it, I would not hesitate a moment to say so. It is true that a number of lives were lost—many were wounded. But hundreds of lives were thereby saved! But for that bomb, there would have been a hundred widows and hundreds of orphans where now there are a few. These facts have been carefully suppressed, and we were accused and convicted of conspiracy by the real conspirators and their agents. This, your honor, is one reason why sentence should not be passed by a court of justice—if that name has any significance at all.

"But," says the State, "you have published articles on the manufacture of dynamite and bombs." Show me a daily paper in this city that has not published similar articles! I remember very distinctly a long article in the Chicago *Tribune* of February 23, 1885. The paper contained a description and drawings of different kinds of infernal machines and bombs. I remember this one especially, because I bought the paper on a railroad train, and had ample time to read it. But since that time the *Times* has often published similar articles on the subject, and some of the dynamite articles found in the *Arbeiter-Zeitung* were translated articles from the *Times*, written by Generals Molineux and Fitz John Porter, in which the use of dynamite bombs against striking workingmen is advocated as the most effective weapon against them. May I learn why the editors of these papers have not been indicted and convicted for murder? Is it because they have advocated the use of this destructive agent only against the "common rabble"? I seek information. Why was Mr. Stone of the *News* not made a defendant in this case? In his possession was found a bomb. Besides that Mr. Stone published an article in January which gave full information regarding the manufacture of bombs. Upon this information any man could prepare a bomb ready for use at the expense of not more than ten cents. The *News* probably has ten times the circulation of the *Arbeiter-Zeitung*. Is it not likely that the bomb used on May 4 was one made after the *News'* pattern? As long as these men are not charged with murder and convicted, I insist, your honor, that such discrimination in favor of capital is incompatible with justice, and sentence should therefore not be passed.

Grinnell's main argument against the defendants was—"They were foreigners; they were not citizens." I cannot speak for the others. I will only speak for myself. I have been a resident of this State fully as long as Grinnell, and probably have been as good a citizen—at least, I should not wish to be compared with him. Grinnell has incessantly appealed to the patriotism of the jury. To that I reply in the language of Johnson, the English literateur, "an appeal to patriotism is the last resort of a scoundrel."

My efforts in behalf of the disinherited and disfranchised millions, my agitation in this direction, the popularization of economic teachings—in short, the education of the wage workers, is declared "a conspiracy against society." The word "society" is here wisely substituted for "the State," as represented by the Patricians of today. It has always been the opinion of the ruling classes that the people must be kept in ignorance, for they lose their servility, their modesty and their obedience to the powers that be, as their intelligence increases. The education of a black slave a quarter of a century ago was a criminal offense. Why? Because the intelligent slave would throw off his shackles at whatever cost. Why is the education of the working people of today looked upon by a certain class as an offense against the State? For the same reason! The State, however, wisely avoided this point in the prosecution of this case. From their testimony one is forced to conclude that we had, in our speeches and publications, preached nothing else but destruction and dynamite. The court has this morning stated that there is no case in history like this. I have noticed, during this trial, that the gentlemen of the legal profession are not well versed in history. In all historical cases of this kind truth had to be perverted by the priests of the established power that was nearing its end.

What have we said in our speeches and publications?

We have interpreted to the people their conditions and relations in society. We have explained to them the different social phenomena and the social laws and circumstances under which they occur. We have, by way of scientific investigation, incontrovertibly proved and brought to their knowledge that the system of wages is the root of the present social iniquities—iniquities so monstrous that they cry to heaven. We have further said that the wage system, as a specific form of social development, would, by the necessity of logic, have to give way to higher forms of civilization; that the wage system must furnish the foundation for a social system of co-operation—that is, Socialism. That whether this or that theory, this or that scheme regarding future arrangements were accepted was not a matter of choice, but one of historical necessity, and that to us the tendency of progress seemed to be Anarchism—that is, a free society without kings or classes—a society of sovereigns in which liberty and economic equality of all would furnish an unshakable equilibrium as a foundation for natural order.

It is not likely that the honorable Bonfield and Grinnell can conceive of a social order not held intact by the policeman's club and pistol, nor of a free society without prisons, gallows, and State's attorneys. In such a society they probably fail to find a place for themselves. And is this the reason why Anarchism is such a "pernicious and damnable doctrine?"

Grinnell has intimated to us that Anarchism was on trial. The theory of Anarchism belongs to the realm of speculative philosophy. There was not a syllable said about Anarchism at the Haymarket meeting. At that meeting the very popular theme of reducing the hours of toil was discussed. But, "Anarchism is on trial!" foams Mr. Grinnell. If that is the case, your honor, very well; you may sentence me, for I am an Anarchist. I believe with Buckle, with Paine, Jefferson, Emerson, and Spencer, and many other great thinkers of this century, that the state of castes and classes—the state where one class dominates over and lives upon the labor of another class, and calls this order—yes, I believe that this barbaric form of social organization, with its legalized plunder and murder, is doomed to die, and make room for a free society, voluntary association, or universal brotherhood, if you like. You may pronounce the sentence upon me, honorable judge, but let the world know that in A. D. 1886, in the State of Illinois, eight men were sentenced to death, because they believed in a better future; because they had not lost their faith in the ultimate victory of liberty and justice!

"You have taught the destruction of society and civilization," says the tool and agent of the Bankers' and Citizens' Association, Grinnell. That man has yet to learn what civilization is. It is the old, old argument against human progress. Read the history of Greece, of Rome; read that of Venice; look over the dark pages of the church, and follow the thorny path of science. "No change! No change! You would destroy society and civilization!" has ever been the cry of the ruling classes. They are so comfortably situated under the prevailing system that they naturally abhor and fear even the slightest change. Their privileges are as dear to them as life itself, and every change threatens these privileges. But civilization is a ladder whose steps are monuments of such changes! Without these social changes—all brought about against the will and the force of the ruling classes—there would be no civilization. As to the destruction of society which we have been accused of seeking, sounds this not like one of Æsop's fables—like the cunning of the fox? We, who have jeopardized our lives to save society from the fiend—the fiend who has grasped her by the throat; who sucks her life-blood, who devours her children—we, who would heal her bleeding wounds, who would free her from the fetters you have wrought around her; from the misery you have brought upon her—we her enemies!! Honorable judge, the demons of hell will join in the laughter this irony provokes!

"We have preached dynamite!" Yes, we have predicted from the lessons history teaches, that the ruling classes of today would no more listen to the voice of reason than their predecessors; that they would attempt by brute force to stay the wheel of progress. Is it a lie, or was it the truth we told? Are not the large industries of this once free country already conducted under the surveillance of the police, the detectives, the military and the sheriffs—and is this return to militancy not developing from day to day? American sovereigns—think of it—working like galley convicts under military guards! We have predicted this, and predict that soon these conditions will grow unbearable. What then? The mandate of the feudal lords of our time is slavery, starvation, and death! This has been their program for years. We have said to the toilers, that science had penetrated the mystery of nature—that from Jove's head once more has sprung a Minerva—dynamite! If this declaration is synonymous with murder, why not charge those with the crime to whom we owe the invention?

To charge us with an attempt to overthrow the present system on or about May 4. by force, and then establish Anarchy, is too absurd a statement, I think, even for a political office holder to make. If Grinnell believed that we attempted such a thing, why did he not have Dr. Bluthardt make an inquiry as to our sanity? Only mad men could have planned such a brilliant scheme, and mad people cannot be indicted or convicted of murder. If there had existed anything like a conspiracy or a pre-arrangement, does your honor believe that events would not have taken a different course than they did on that evening and later? This "conspiracy" nonsense is based upon an oration I delivered on the anniversary of Washington's birthday at Grand Rapids, Mich., more than a year and a half ago. I had been invited by the Knights of Labor for that purpose. I dwelt upon the fact that our country was far from being what the great revolutionists of the last century intended it to be. I said that those men, if they lived today, would clean the Augean stables with iron brooms, and that they, too, would undoubtedly be characterized as "wild Socialists." It is not unlikely that I said Washington would have been hanged for treason if the revolution had failed. Grinnell made this "sacrilegious remark" his main arrow against me. Why? Because he intended to inveigh the know-nothing spirit against us. But who will deny the correctness of the statement? That I should have compared myself with Washington, is a base lie. But if I had, would that be murder? I may have told that individual who appeared here as a witness that the workingmen should procure arms, as force would in all probability be the *ultima ratio;* and that in Chicago there were so and so many armed, but I certainly did not say that we proposed to "inaugurate the social revolution." And let me say here: Revolutions are no more made than earthquakes and cyclones. Revolutions are the effect of certain causes and conditions. I have made social philosophy a specific study for more than ten years, and I could not have given vent to such nonsense! I do believe, however, that the revolution is near at hand—in fact, that it is upon us. But is the physician responsible for the death of the patient because he foretold that death? If any one is to be blamed for the coming revolution it is the ruling class who steadily refuses to make concessions as reforms become necessary; who maintain that they can call a halt to progress, and dictate a standstill to the eternal forces of which they themselves are but the whimsical creation.

The position generally taken in this case is that we are morally responsible for the police riot on May 4. Four or five years ago I sat in this very court room as a witness. The workingmen had been trying to obtain redress in a lawful manner. They had voted and, among others, had elected their aldermanic candidate from the fourteenth ward. But the street car company did not like the man. And two of the three election judges of one precinct, knowing this, took the ballot box to their home and "corrected" the election returns, so as to cheat the constituents of the elected candidate of their rightful representative and give the representation to the benevolent street car monopoly. The workingmen spent $1,500 in the prosecution of the perpetrators of this crime. The proof against them was so overwhelming that they confessed to having falsified the returns and forged the official documents. Judge Gardner, who was presiding in this court, acquitted them, stating that "that act had apparently not been prompted by criminal intent." I will make no comment. But when we approach the field of moral responsibility, it has an immense scope! Every man who has in the past assisted in thwarting the efforts of those seeking reform is responsible for the existence of the revolutionists in this city today! Those, however, who have sought to bring about reforms must be exempted from the responsibility—and to these I belong.

If the verdict is based upon the assumption of moral responsibility, your honor, I give this as a reason why sentence should not be passed.

If the opinion of the court given this morning is good law, then there is no person in this country who could not lawfully be hanged. I vouch that, upon the very laws you have read, there is no person in this court room now who could not be "fairly, impartially and lawfully" hanged! Fouche, Napoleon's right bower, once said to his master; "Give me a line that any one man has ever written, and I will bring him to the scaffold." And this court has done essentially the same. Upon that law every person in this country can be indicted for conspiracy, and, as the case may be, for murder. Every member of a trade union, of the Knights of Labor, or any other labor organization, can be convicted of conspiracy, and in cases of violence, for which they may not be responsible at all, of murder, as we have been. This precedent once established, and you force the masses who are now agitating in a peaceable way into open rebellion! You thereby shut off the last safety valve—and the blood which will be shed, the blood of the innocent—it will come upon your heads!

"Seven policemen have died," said Grinnell, suggestively winking at the jury. You want a life for a life, and have convicted an equal number of men, of whom it cannot be truthfully said that they had anything whatever to do with the killing of Bonfield's victims. The very same principle of jurisprudence we find among various savage tribes. Injuries among them are equalized, so to speak. The Chinooks and the Arabs, for instance, would demand the life of an enemy for every death that they had suffered at their enemy's hands. They were not particular in regard to the persons, just so long as they had a life for a life. This principle also prevails today among the natives of the Sandwich Islands. If we are to be hanged on this principle, then let us know it, and let the world know what a civilized and Christian country it is in which the Goulds, the Vanderbilts, the Stanfords, the Fields, Armours, and other local money *hamsters* have come to the rescue of liberty and justice!

Grinnell has repeatedly stated that our country is an enlightened country. The verdict fully corroborates the assertion! This verdict against us is the anathema of the wealthy classes over their despoiled victims—the vast army of wage workers and farmers. If your honor would not have these people believe this; if you would not have them believe that we have once more arrived at the Spartan Senate, the Athenian Areopagus, the Venetian Council of Ten, etc., then sentence should not be pronounced. But, if you think that by hanging us you can stamp out the labor movement— the movement from which the downtrodden millions, the millions who toil and live in want and misery, the wage slaves, expect salvation—if this is your opinion, then hang us! Here you will tread upon a spark, but here, and there, and behind you, and in front of you, and everywhere, flames will blaze up. It is a subterranean fire. You cannot put it out. The ground is on fire upon which you stand. You can't understand it. You don't believe in magical arts, as your grandfathers did, who burned witches at the stake, but you do believe in conspiracies; you believe that all these occurrences of late are the work of conspirators! You resemble the child that is looking for his picture behind the mirror. What you see, and what you try to grasp is nothing but the deceptive reflex of the stings of your bad conscience. You want to "stamp out the conspirators"—the "agitators?" Ah, stamp out every factory lord who has grown wealthy upon the unpaid labor of his employes. Stamp out every landlord who has amassed fortunes from the rent of overburdened workingmen and farmers. Stamp out every machine that is revolutionizing industry and agriculture, that intensifies the production, ruins the producer, that increases the national wealth, while the creator of all these things stands amidst them, tantalized with hunger! Stamp out the railroads, the telegraph, the telephone, steam and yourselves—for everything breathes the revolutionary spirit.

You, gentlemen, are the revolutionists! You rebel against the effects of social conditions which have tossed you, by the fair hand of Fortune, into a magnificent paradise. Without inquiring, you imagine that no one else has a right in that place. You insist that you are the chosen ones, the sole proprietors. The forces that tossed you into the paradise, the industrial forces, are still at work. They are growing more active and intense from day to day. Their tendency is to elevate all mankind to the same level, to have all humanity share in the paradise you now monopolize. You, in your blindness, think you can stop the tidal wave of civilization and human emancipation by placing a few policemen, a few gatling guns, and some regiments of militia on the shore—you think you can frighten the rising waves back into the unfathomable depths, whence they have arisen, by erecting a few gallows in the perspective. You, who oppose the natural course of things, you are the real revolutionists. You and you alone are the conspirators and destructionists! . . .

Now, if I had as much power as the court, and were a law abiding citizen, I would certainly have the court indicted for some remarks made during this trial. I will say that if I had not been an Anarchist at the beginning of this trial I would be one now. I quote the exact language of the court on one occasion. "It does not necessarily follow that all laws are foolish and bad because a good many of them are so." That is treason, sir! if we are to believe the court and the State's attorney. But, aside from that, I cannot see how we shall distinguish the good from the bad laws. Am I to judge of that? No; I am not. But if I disobey a bad law, and am brought before a bad judge, I undoubtedly would be convicted.

In regard to a report in the *Arbeiter-Zeitung,* also read this morning, the report of the Board of Trade demonstration, I would say (and this is the only defense, the only word I have to say in my own defense) that I did not know of that article until I saw it in the paper, and the man who wrote it, wrote it rather as a reply to some slurs in the morning papers. He was discharged. The language used in that article would never have been tolerated if I had seen it.

Now, if we cannot be directly implicated with this affair, connected with the throwing of the bomb, where is the law that says, these men shall be picked out to suffer? Show me that law if you have it! If the position of the court is correct, then half of the population of this city ought to be hanged, because they are responsible the same as we are for that act on May 4. And if half of the population of Chicago is not hanged, then show me the law that says, "eight men shall be picked out and hanged as scapegoats!" You have no good law. Your decision, your verdict, our conviction is nothing but an arbitrary will of this lawless court. It is true there is no precedent in jurisprudence in this case! It is true we have called upon the people to arm themselves. It is true that we told them time and again that the great day of change was coming. It was not our desire to have bloodshed. We are not beasts. We would not be Socialists if we were beasts. It is because of our sensitiveness that we have gone into this movement for the emancipation of the oppressed and suffering. It is true we have called upon the people to arm and prepare for the stormy times before us.

This seems to be the ground upon which the verdict is to be sustained. "But when a long train of abuses and usurpations pursuing invariably the same object evinces a design to reduce the people under absolute despotism, it is their right, it is their duty to throw off such government and provide new guards for their future safety." This is a quotation from the Declaration of Independence. Have we broken any laws by showing to the people how these abuses, that have occurred for the last twenty years, are invariably pursuing one object, viz: to establish an oligarchy in this country so strong and powerful and monstrous as never before has existed in any country? I can well understand why that man Grinnell did not urge upon the grand jury to charge us with treason. I can well understand it. You cannot try and convict a man for treason who has upheld the constitution against those who trample it under their feet. It would not have been as easy a job to do that, Mr. Grinnell, as to charge these men with murder.

Now, these are my ideas. They constitute a part of myself. I cannot divest myself of them, nor would I, if I could. And if you think that you can crush out these ideas that are gaining ground more and more every day; if you think you can crush them out by sending us to the gallows; if you would once more have people suffer the penalty of death because they have dared to tell the truth—and I defy you to show us where we have told a lie—I say, if death is the penalty for proclaiming the truth, then I will proudly and defiantly pay the costly price! Call your hangman! Truth crucified in Socrates, in Christ, in Giordano Bruno, in Huss, Gallileo, still lives—they and others whose number is legion have preceded us on this path. We are ready to follow!

18. ABRAHAM CAHAN

Let us join hands in our war upon the rest of nature

The centennial celebration of Washington's inaugural closed the strife-torn eighties. To a sensitive young Russian revolutionary only seven years in America, Chauncey DePew's commemorative address from the steps of the Sub-Treasury building on Wall Street seemed less a tribute to a century of American progress than a requiem signalling its decline.

Unlike Carl Schurz, so completely attuned to mid-century American political liberalism, Abraham Cahan (1860–1951) found himself totally estranged from the relentless economic individualism of the late nineteenth century. As a consequence he became neither an architect of a major new political party nor the holder even of minor political office. Instead, in 1897 Cahan founded the *Jewish Daily Forward*. For the rest of his life, except for a four-year interlude as a crack reporter for Lincoln Steffens's *Commerical Advertiser*, he shaped the nation's greatest labor and socialist newspaper and came to be regarded as one of the country's great editors.

Cahan's first major article in English, "Social Remedies and Socialism," appeared in two successive issues of the *Workman's Advocate*. In a Marxist critique of capitalism, economic individualism, and reform, the former revolutionary advocated a socialist solution to the dilemmas of democracy in an industrial society.

A century has passed since, having shaken off the yoke of the English crown and rescued their industries from under the foot of English capital, the people of the United States set out in

Abraham Cahan, "Social Remedies and Socialism," *Workmen's Advocate*, May 25 and June 1, 1889.

unhampered, unremitting "pursuit of happiness." A century has passed and "The infant industries, which the first act of our first administration sought to encourage, now give remunerative employment to more people than inhabited the republic at the beginning of Washington's presidency. The grand total of their annual output of $7,000,000,000 in value places the United States first among the manufacturing countries of the earth. One-half the total mileage of all the railroads and one-quarter of all the telegraph lines of the world within our borders, testify to the volume, variety and value of an internal commerce which makes these States, if need be, independent and self-supporting. These hundred years of development under favoring political conditions have brought the sum of our national wealth to a figure which has passed the results of a thousand years for the motherland herself, otherwise the richest of modern empires. . . . Twelve million children in the common schools, 345 universities and colleges for the higher education of men and 200 for women, 450 institutions of learning for science, law, medicine and theology, are the despair of the scoffer and the demagogue, and the firm support of civilization and liberty."

Imagine the delight it would have given the fathers of this republic to hear this statement from the lips of the Hon. Chauncey M. DePew, from the steps of the Sub-Treasury building, Wall Street, in his capacity of orator of the centennial celebration of April 30th, 1889. Imagine the exultation of Washington or Jefferson at the sight of the dazzling pageant of which New York was the scene on the same day—at the sight of the marching hosts of the peaceful militia men, governors and their staffs on the one hand, and the sublime towering edifices of the Broadway warehouses and the imposing castles of Fifth Avenue which the great centennial procession passed, on the other. Could there be, in view of all this over-whelming splendor, any doubt that the search of happiness in which the nation has been engaged was crowned with success?

Unfortunately, however, there was another side to the medal, which Mr. DePew and his "Hon." centennial comrades carefully concealed from view. In collecting his material the orator of the great day shut his eyes to the statistics of unemployed labor; to the odd million of homeless, abandoned, sunken American citizens, who roam along the highways and byways of this happy land; to the cases of suicide in the laboring districts. What if, in eulogizing our schools, colleges and institutions of learning, the president of Vanderbilt's railroads had paused to touch upon the number of illiterate, weazen-faced, over-worked factory workmen and children? What if the procession had turned from the princely palaces of Fifth Avenue farther east or west, into the regions of the "lower classes?" If, instead of glittering diamonds and self-satisfied, rosy-cheeked faces, the marching columns had been greeted from the windows by the inmates of the tenement cells? What would have been the despair of George Washington at the picture of squalor, penury and helplessness! How shocked would he have been to compare the country as it is to-day with what it was when he had first set her free to pursue her happiness!

There were no Vanderbilts in his time, but then there were hardly any cases of starvation. There was no "national wealth," neither was there anything like the national misery of the United States of to-day. Women and children eagerly digging in ash-barrels for coal, and not unfrequently for food, which nowadays attracts no notice, as a matter of common occurrence, was a spectacle utterly unheard of in the United States which George Washington had snatched away from the iron hand of George III.

Every step on the path of development has widened the breach between the successful pursuers of happiness and their beaten rivals; every onward move of the liberated industries has added to the misery of the vanquished, while it increased the luxury and pomp of their victorious fellow citizens; every year has swelled the ranks of the "lower classes," and proportionately narrowed down the number of "good society," until to-day, after a lapse of over one hundred years, we see the people who, having abolished all rank and title, signed a contract guaranteeing to each other the equal right of life, liberty and happiness, divided into millions of starving, abject slaves on one hand, and a handful of railroad kings, coal barons, factory magnates, etc., on the other.

It is not, of course, for "scoffers and demagogues" like the centennial orator to despair at the thought of this result of free pursuit of happiness. These presidential, gubernatorial, senatorial, or aldermanic "possibilities" cannot afford to "despair of the republic." There are plenty of honest citizens who are alive to the growing wretchedness of the masses. Those of them, however, who, not being accustomed to the task of thinking, would be scared by the very idea of any innovation in the life of the society in which they were born and bred, and content themselves with a deep sigh of condolence for their inferior brethren. "The world has always been such, and such it will remain. We have not created it, neither can we change it," with which the venerable conservative recovers his peace of mind and relapses into an admiration of our national wealth, the number of colleges, and all sorts of progress and changes for the better. . . .

After what has been said of the nature of free competition and wages it would be superfluous to dwell much upon the remedies offered by the other gentlemen of the plastering fraternity. Let us imagine all banks and stock exchanges a thing of the past; that the fleecing of the people which is now effected through a control over the money market is done away with; that the income of the manufacturer is shared neither by the money-lender nor by the stock gambler; or suppose that every landlord is ostracized, and that every one is furnished with a free dwelling and with as much vacant land as he knows what to do with (which, by the way, no single-land-tax scheme will bring about), nay, combine all the mentioned remedies together: no bankers, no liquor dealers, no landlords, plenty of charity. Will the laborer, as such, be benefited? Will no machinery be invented? Will no workingmen be thrown out of employment? Will peace reign among the employers? Why, that would mean the death of industry, of civilization, and of progress, wouldn't it?

Well then, so long as competition—that prime mover of the advancement of the nineteenth century—flourishes, the evils connected with it cannot help thriving alongside of it: first, THE WAGES OF THE EMPLOYED MUST REST ON THE MINIMUM LEVEL OF THE NECESSARIES OF LIFE: and second, THE NUMBER OF THE UNEMPLOYED MUST INCREASE. You can no more remove these evils without interfering with free competition than you can wipe away the shadow of a tree without hewing down the tree itself.

And so while the tree of the right to pursue one's own happiness, which was planted by the fathers of this great republic, has grown to sublime dimensions and given us the fruit of a mighty civilization, it casts as it grows a longer and longer shadow of penury, illiteracy, vice and degradation. Strange as it may appear, the present pursuit of happiness is incompatible with life and liberty but for a few chosen favorites of fortune.

What, then, is to be done? Shall the right to pursue happiness be taken away from the people? Shall we return to the days of the never-to-be-forgotten George III?

Nothing of the kind. On the contrary, let us rationalize and intensify our pursuit of happiness. Let us waste as little energy as possible. INSTEAD OF FIGHTING EACH OTHER, LET US JOIN HANDS IN OUR WAR UPON THE REST OF NATURE. LET US TURN OUT IN A BODY, IF WE DESIRE TO BE VICTORIOUS.

This is socialism.

Social pursuit of happiness for individual enjoyment of it, this is the motto of every thinker who is familiar with the physiology of the social organism and to whom the various evils which attract the attention of the afore-mentioned patchwork social reformers are but so many different eruptions on the social body attending the transitional periods in the growth of the organism. The socialist seeks no remedies; it is to the acceleration of the great change which he sees approaching that he devotes his educational activity. To him the competition between man and man contains the germs of the grand competition between the united, organized humanity and the rest of creation.

We have seen that competition carries along with it the concentration of capital. Since the widening of the scale of production is connected with economy in labor, a capitalist investing $2,000 in raw material will be able to undersell a rival who has only $1,000 to invest in the same material. The natural upshot of this is that the smaller capital is swallowed up by the larger, and that small capitalists will join to form "combines," partnerships, syndicates, corporations and trusts. These institutions—the natural offspring of competitive production—will continue the war among themselves, whereupon, as in the case of individual enterprise, the more powerful firm will grow fatter at the expense of the smaller, or, to use a commercial phrase, will buy them out. This rapidly growing socialization of industry, the narrowing of the field of individual enterprise, the consolidation of capital, the multiplication of "trusts" etc., is to the socialist the forerunner of an all-embracing system under which all the resources of production and distribution will be the property of the entire, organized nation as one grand corporation, with each citizen in the double character of shareholder and worker, unrestrainedly enjoying the full result of his exertion according to his individual taste and desire.

Under such an order of things the survival of the naturally unfit, which is the feature of competitive society, would be impossible. With opportunities not only open but insured to all, with no power to take them away, a blockhead will not find his way to the chair of political economy; neither will natural genius wither away in the dungeon of the modern factory, as is so frequently the case under the present struggle between man and man.

Competition has served its term. Its time is up. The SOCIALISTIC nature of modern production cannot much longer endure the INDIVIDUAL control of those who do not produce. Nature cannot continue to be the monopoly of a few men, and the means of applying human energy to nature—capital, which is the result of human energy—will not remain the property of those who have spent no productive energy.

19.   B. CHARNEY VLADECK

The *Jewish Daily Forward*— leader and forerunner in the American labor movement

In the second and third decades of the twentieth century, the *Jewish Daily Forward* became not only the most successful and widely-known immigrant newspaper but a beacon of social and industrial democracy and a leader of the semi-industrial needle trade unions, as well. In its peak years, this Yiddish newspaper attained a circulation of a quarter of a million and appeared in eleven local and regional editions. Hailed by Oswald Garrison Villard as "America's Most Interesting Daily," it catered to the highest aspirations of its readers, and the fact that it was edited by Abraham Cahan was indicative of its social aims.

B. Charney Vladeck (1886–1938), managing editor of the *Forward* from 1918 until his death, sums up the special virtues of his newspaper. A gifted speaker and perennial Socialist candidate for political office, Vladeck was elected to the New York Board of Aldermen in 1917 and again in 1919. In 1937 he was elected to the new City Council in New York City. Supported by the fusion coalition and Mayor Fiorello La Guardia, he became majority leader but died suddenly after only ten months in office.

The *Jewish Daily Forward* today is the largest labor and Socialist daily in the world. Started twenty-five years ago by a group of Socialists who disapproved of the tactics of the Socialist Labor Party and the leadership of Daniel De Leon, it grew in pace with the influx of Jewish immigration into the United States, and has become the largest public influence in the life of the Jewish masses in this country. Of Jews who get their daily information from newspapers in their native tongue, one in every two reads the *Forward*; and the Forward Building on the Lower East Side is the very center of Jewish labor activities in New York.

B. Charney Vladeck, "The Largest Labor Paper in the World," *Labor Age* XII (August, 1922): vol. 6–7. Reprinted by permission of Stephen C. Vladeck and Mary Bromberg.

Two influences may explain the phenomenal growth of the *Forward*. The more important undoubtedly is the personality of its editor, Abraham Cahan. He came to this country at the age of 22, a graduate of one of the best known Teachers' Seminaries in Russia. He was full of idealism and the life experience of every intelligent Russian Jew, with an unexcelled sense for reality and with a deep understanding of human nature, yet he was young enough to adapt himself to the new environment and to be imbued with the dynamic spirit of a new country. Before he could obtain his citizenship papers he knew enough English to become a teacher. Before long he was getting American newspaper experience on the *Commercial Advertiser*, in company with, and under the tutelage of, Lincoln Stephens [sic], Norman and Hutchins Hapgood and others.

Cahan was with the *Forward* when it originally started; but he had to quit later because of a difference of opinion between him and the *Forward* Association as to the general policy of the paper. He insisted that the *Forward* be a real newspaper, living the life of the people, full of "pep" and humor and sprightliness. He opposed its becoming a cut-and-dried affair, loaded down with "learned" and tedious contributions, which the mass of the workers would not understand or find of interest. He believed in getting the latest news, rivaling any other paper in that respect, and giving this news in the most interesting and striking form. It took the association only a short time to find that he was right. When he rejoined the *Forward*, several years later, he was enriched by his experience on the *Commercial Advertiser*, and began immediately to apply the fundamental principles of American journalism to the *Forward*.

He did not print anything in the paper that the least intelligent reader could not understand. He refused manuscripts from his most celebrated contributors if they did not deal with things realistically. He introduced features pregnant with human interest and refused to be bothered by the criticism of the supercilious and intellectual snobs. The *Forward* became a source of news, amusement and education; and its circulation began to grow by leaps and bounds. Mr. Cahan's editorial policy proved so successful that every other Jewish paper has done nothing since but try to imitate his methods, so that the *Forward* practically edits a number of papers in the Yiddish tongue which are antagonistic to its policy and purpose.

With the growth of its circulation the *Forward* steadily grew to be a great leader of the Jewish masses. Conditions in New York shops fifteen and twenty years ago were appalling—long hours, unsanitary lofts, brutal treatment on the part of employers and foremen and utter lack of self-respect and self-confidence. Under the leadership of the *Forward* the scattered and demoralized masses of Jewish immigrants in New York and elsewhere began to acquire spirit and to organize for the purpose of bettering their economic condition. The large needle trade unions which have of late become the subject of investigation and wonderment by sociologists and professors of economics are the children of the *Forward*.

The *Forward* led every strike. It served the purpose of a huge trumpet which warned of danger and summoned help. It was with the working immigrant in his shop, on the picket line, at his home. It collected money for strikers, and it created for them a favorable public opinion. It lifted the Jewish immigrant from the position of a slave and competitor to the American working man, to the position of leader and forerunner in the American Labor Movement.

At no time did the mutual confidence of the *Forward* and the Jewish immigrant weaken in the least. They both grew in mutual strength, so that today the extremists in the labor movement who are endeavoring to acquire power and all that goes with it in the ranks of labor, center their attacks directly on the *Forward*, knowing well that by weakening the *Forward* they would weaken the very heart of the Jewish labor movement as today it is constituted.

Having been Americanized himself in the better sense of the word, he encouraged the study of the English language and of American institutions and ideals. He began to write an eight-volume history of the United States, and he published a book by the managing editor of the *Forward* on American Civics. He also initiated a series of lessons in the English language which has run in the *Forward*. These are now being sold to its reader-family in the form of a book, at cost price. The *Forward* Publishing Co. has published some of the finest works of the best Jewish writers, and translations from Tolstoi, Zola, Shakespeare, etc. The *Forward* is also publishing a monthly magazine which has the largest monthly Yiddish circulation of any in the country.

The *Forward* is published by the *Forward* Association, a membership association. No member of the *Forward* Association is permitted to share in the profits of the daily, and whatever is left, is distributed to help other institutions, or necessarily goes back into improving and enlarging the paper. This is why the *Forward* has become popular not only with the working class but with all Jews. The fact that no owner can pocket the profits automatically keeps the *Forward* on a higher level, technically and editorially, than any other paper. Three years ago the *Forward*, in order to accommodate its Western readers, established a plant in Chicago in which the *Forward* is published for all the territory West of Cleveland. The combined circulation of the New York and Chicago *Forward* is now about 200,000 daily. Since the *Forward* began to make profits, it has distributed, as a rule, from 30 percent to 40 percent of its profits to labor, civic, and cultural institutions. The total of these contributions for the last eleven or twelve years has amounted to upwards of $300,000.

Out of its 25 years of service to Labor has come, therefore, not only inspiration to the Jewish workers, leading them to victory after victory, but also substantial help to other labor causes in their fight against Capitalism. It is a record of achievement that Labor everywhere can look upon with pride.

PART FIVE

Yellow Peril
and White

20. BRET HARTE

"The Heathen Chinee"

Ironically, the first writer to achieve fame as a California local colorist attained notoriety for a sixty-line poem which he had intended as a spoof of the popular prejudice against the Chinese. Deeply troubled by the mistreatment of these immigrants, Bret Harte (1836–1902) had written indignant satire condemning their brutal white oppressors. But "Plain Language from Truthful James"—for which the author had little respect and ultimately came to hate—was taken literally by the popular mind. In the poem, better known as "The Heathen Chinee," both James and the Chinee clearly are knaves, but the reader's sympathy is drawn to Ah Sin because of James's hollow moral posture. Published first in the September 1870 issue of the *Overland Monthly*, the words of Truthful James quickly received wide distribution. Circulating like a popular joke or street song throughout the English-speaking world, they buttressed the popular preconception of the sinfulness of the Chinese.

PLAIN LANGUAGE FROM TRUTHFUL JAMES

Which I wish to remark—
　And my language is plain—
That for ways that are dark
　And for tricks that are vain
The Heathen Chinee is peculiar;
　Which the same I would rise to explain.

Ah Sin was his name;
　And I shall not deny,
In regard to the same,
　What that name might imply.
But his smile it was pensive and childlike,
　As I frequent remarked to Bill Nye.

Bret Harte, "Plain Language from Truthful James," *Overland Monthly* V (September, 1870): pp. 287–88.

It was August the third,
   And quite soft was the skies,
Which it might be inferred
   That Ah Sin was likewise;
Yet he played it that day upon William
   And me in a way I despise.

Which we had a small game,
   And Ah Sin took a hand.
It was Euchre. The same
   He did not understand;
But he smiled as he sat by the table
   With the smile that was childlike and bland.

Yet the cards they were stocked
   In a way that I grieve,
And my feelings were shocked
   At the state of Nye's sleeve,
Which was stuffed full of aces and bowers
   And the same with intent to deceive.

But the hands that were played
   By that Heathen Chinee
And the points that he made
   Were quite frightful to see,
Till at last he put down a right bower
   Which the same Nye had dealt unto me.

Then I looked up at Nye,
   And he gazed upon me.
And he rose with a sigh
   And said, *"Can this be?*
We are ruined by Chinese cheap labor."
   And he went for that Heathen Chinee.

In the scene that ensued
   I did not take a hand.
But the floor it was strewed,
   Like the leaves on the strand,
With the cards that Ah Sin had been hiding
   In the game "he did not understand."

In his sleeves, which were long,

He had twenty-four jacks;
    Which was coming it strong;
        Yet I state but the facts.
And we found on his nails, which were taper,
    What is frequent in tapers—that's wax.

Which is why I remark,
    And my language is plain,
That for ways that are dark
    And for tricks that are vain
The Heathen Chinee is peculiar;
    Which the same I am free to maintain.

21. JAMES G. BLAINE

Legislation for the free
or the servile laborer

The most popular political leader of the post–Civil War era, Senator James G. Blaine (1830–1893), gravely warned his colleagues of the re-emergence of a new slavery, not in the South, but in the West, if Chinese immigration was not terminated. Blaine insisted that to the problem of unfree labor was added the ingredient of race in a country that had yet to resolve its historic racial dilemma. Indeed, Blaine argued that the position of the Chinese had become truly anomalous. In 1870, when the privilege of naturalization had been extended to "Aliens of African nativity and to persons of African descent," Senator Charles Sumner of Massachusetts proposed a bill to delete the word "white" with the intent of including the Chinese in all Congressional legislation pertaining to naturalization. That bill was defeated, as was an amendment to the act, drafted by Lincoln's friend, Lyman Trumbull, which specifically extended naturalization rights to the Chinese. Thereafter, Blaine insisted, the exclusion of the Chinese was inevitable and consistent with the logic of events.

From U.S. Congress, Senate, *Congressional Record*, vol. 8, pt. 2, February 14, 1879, pp. 1299–1303 passim.

. . . The Senate, as in Committee of the Whole, resumed the consideration of the bill (H. R. No. 2423) to restrict the immigration of Chinese to the United States.

Mr. BLAINE.   . . . The . . . question is whether it is desirable to exclude Chinese immigration from this country. . . . I will repeat . . . [the treaty]:

> The United States of America and the Emperor of China cordially recognize the inherent and inalienable right of man to change his home and allegiance, and also the mutual advantage of the free migration and emigration of their citizens and subjects, respectively, from the one country to the other, for purposes of curiosity, of trade, or as permanent residents.
>
> The high contracting parties, therefore, join in reprobating any other than an entirely voluntary emigration for these purposes. They consequently agree to pass laws making it a penal offense for a citizen of the United States or Chinese subjects to take Chinese subjects either to the United States or to any other foreign country, or for a Chinese subject or citizen of the United States to take citizens of the United States to China or to any other foreign country without their free and voluntary consent respectively.

. . . The words are worth emphasizing; not merely "voluntary," it must be "entirely voluntary," and then each nation was to make laws to secure this end. Now, I am told by those who are much more familiar with this subject than I am that there is no notice at the State Department that China ever complied with that provision to make a law; and I suppose that when a nation in a treaty agrees to make a law it agrees to enforce it. The mere making of a law and then not enforcing it, would be no compliance. They agree, in other words, to enforce the provision that there should be nothing else than voluntary emigration, and entirely voluntary emigration. They have never done it, and have been absolutely false and faithless on that point.

The treaty stands broken and defied by China from the hour it was made to this time. It never has been complied with. We had to legislate against it. We legislated against it in the cooly law. The Chinese were so flagrantly and so palpably violating it that statutes of the United States were enacted to contravene the evil they were doing, and it has gone on, probably not so grossly since those laws were passed as before, but in effect the same. So that all the point the Senator makes about our Punic faith in attempting to break this treaty, is answered by the fact that the treaty has been broken by the other power continuously.

The Senator from Ohio asked what we should do in a similar case if the other contracting party were Great Britain or Germany or France or any power that was able to make war. I ask the honorable Senator what he would advise us to do if Great Britain or France or Germany should locate six commercial companies in New York, whose business it should be to bring hither to this country the worst class and the lowest class of the population of those three kingdoms? What would the honorable Senator from Ohio say to that, or does he hesitate to believe what we would say to it? . . .

Mr. [STANLEY] MATTHEWS [Ohio]. . . . Mr. President, I would say this, that instead of inaugurating an arbitrary and *ex parte* act of legislation on our own part, giving our own construction to the treaty and the conduct of the other party under it, I would, through the usual diplomatic representative of this country, make representations to that government making complaints of the alleged breach of the treaty, and ask what answer could be made to that; and only in the event, as a last resort, of a contumacious refusal to obey the plain requisitions of the treaty obligation, would I resort to a repudiation of our own obligations under it.

Mr. BLAINE. Ah! but the Senator does not answer the question I asked him, what he would do in case they had themselves broken it, and we were the victims of the breach? He answers me that he would take hat in hand and bow politely before them, and ask them if they would not do better! What are we to do as a measure of self-defense when they have broken it, and taken the initiative? I say that this country and this Senate would not hesitate to defy any European power. The argument the Senator meant to employ was that we were doing toward a helpless power, not able to make war with us, that which we would not do if a cannon were pointed toward us. Does the Senator doubt that if any one of these countries should locate six commercial companies here to import the worst portion of their population and put it upon our shores, (and you cannot even find so bad a population as this in Europe,) that we would hesitate in our course towards the offending power? . . .

. . . The Chinese question is not new; we have had it here very often; and . . . I lay down this principle, that so far as my vote is concerned I will not admit a man to immigration to this country that I am not willing to place on the basis of a citizen. Let me repeat that. We ought not to admit in this country of universal suffrage the immigration of a great people, great in numbers, whom we ourselves declare are utterly unfit to become citizens.

What do we say on that point? In the Senate of the United States on the 4th day of July, 1870, a patriotic day, we were amending the naturalization laws. We had made all the negroes of the United States voters practically; at least we had said they should not be deprived of suffrage by reason of race or color. We had admitted them all, and we then amended the naturalization laws so that the gentleman from Africa himself could become a citizen of the United States; and an immigrant from Africa to-morrow, from the coast of Guinea or Senegambia, can be naturalized and made an American citizen. Then Senator Trumbull moved to add:

Or persons born in the Chinese empire.

He said:

I have offered this amendment so as to bring the distinct question before the Senate whether they will vote to naturalize persons from Africa and vote to refuse to naturalize those who come from China. I ask for the yeas and nays on my amendment.

. . . There was a vote of 31 against 9 in a Senate three-fourths republican declaring that the Chinaman never ought to be made a citizen. I think that settles the whole question if that was a correct vote, because you cannot in our system of government as it is to-day, with safety to all, permit a large immigration of people who are not to be made citizens and take part in the Government. The Senator from California tells us that already the male adult Chinese in California are more numerous than the white voters. I take him as an authority for his own State, and I should expect him to take my statement about my own State. . . .

Mr. [HENRY] DAWES [Mass.]. I should like to be certain about this matter of the naturalization of Chinamen. They naturalize Chinamen in my State.

Mr. BLAINE. Then they do it by what law?

Mr. DAWES. United States laws, of course.

Mr. BLAINE. The United States laws are directly in the teeth of that.

Mr. DAWES. I cannot help that.

Mr. BLAINE. Then if you choose to disobey the United States laws you can do it, but the United States laws say that those naturalized shall be white persons or natives of Africa.

Mr. [JOHN] MITCHELL [Oregon]. Or of African descent.

Mr. DAWES. I state the fact of my personal knowledge. I have seen Chinamen naturalized in our courts.

Mr. [AARON] SARGENT [Calif.]. The United States circuit court in San Francisco on a test case and in a very able opinion delivered by Judge Sawyer, held that under the laws of the United States Chinamen cannot be naturalized. . . .

Mr. SARGENT. . . . I understood [Mr. HAMLIN] to say that the average importation of Chinese during the last twenty years had been four thousand a year.

Mr. HAMLIN. Between four and five thousand.

Mr. SARGENT. Now, sir, Rev. Otis Gibson, a missionary laborer among the Chinese of San Francisco, as much their friend as the Senator from Maine, [Mr. HAMLIN,] has written a work upon this subject; he had access to the books of the six companies in San Francisco; and in his book he gives the following table of Chinese importation down to April 1, 1876, over two years ago, and the number has increased since that time. The Ning Yung Company has imported 75,000 during the time the Senator referred to; and an average of 4,000 for twenty years is 80,000. He says the Hop

Wo Company imported 34,000; the Kong Chow Company 15,000; the Yung Wo Company 13,000; the Sam Yup Company 11,000; the Yan Wo Company 4,300, making in all 151,300 against 80,000 the Senator would calculate upon, and at the port of San Francisco alone, saying nothing of those who come into Oregon and those that come into Washington Territory who crowd out the men at the Colville mines, a continual stream of them coming all the time.

Mr. [JUSTIN S.] MORRILL [Vt.].   May I ask my friend from California if it is not true that a much larger number have returned to China in the last year than have come here.

Mr. SARGENT.   I think on account of the excitement existing in California, on account of the danger of trouble there—and you will have to reconstruct those States by and by if you do not take care of this question soon—the Chinese have been deterred to a considerable extent in coming. There has been called a halt on account of the great public meetings held there, on account of the people I might say showing their teeth. That has repressed it somewhat.

Mr. MORRILL.   I merely desire to say that I have understood there were now three or four times more going back to China than were coming this way. . . .

Mr. BLAINE.   I do not justify the brutality of the treatment of those Chinese who are here; it is greatly to be regretted; it is greatly to be condemned; but you must deal with things as you find them. If you foresee a conflict upon that coast by reason of an immigration that calls for the interposition of the military, I think it is a good deal cheaper and more direct way to avoid the trouble by preventing the immigration.

I have heard a good deal about their cheap labor. I do not myself believe in cheap labor. I do not believe cheap labor should be an object of legislation, and it will not be in a republic. You cannot have the wealthy classes in a republic where suffrage is universal, legislate for cheap labor. I undertake to repeat that. I say that you cannot have the wealthy classes in a republic where suffrage is universal legislate in what is called the interest of cheap labor. Labor should not be cheap and it should not be dear; it should have its share and it will have its share. There is not a laborer on the Pacific coast to-day, I say that to my honorable colleague—whose whole life has been consistent and uniform in defense and advocacy of the interests of the laboring classes— there is not a laboring-man on the Pacific coast to-day who does not feel wounded and grieved and crushed by the competition that comes from this source. Then the answer is, "Well, are not American laborers equal to Chinese laborers?" I answer that question by asking another. Were not free white laborers equal to African slaves in the South? When you tell me that the Chinaman driving out the free American laborer only proves the superiority of the Chinaman, I ask you, did the African slave labor driving out the free white labor from the South prove the superiority of slave labor? The conditions are not unlike; the parallel is not complete, and yet it is a parallel. It is servile labor; it is not free labor such as we intend to develop and encourage and build up in this country. It is labor that comes here under a mortgage. It is labor that comes here to subsist on what the American laborer cannot subsist on. You cannot work a man who must have beef and bread, and would prefer beer, alongside of a man who can live on rice. It cannot be done. In all such conflicts and in all such struggles the result is not to bring up the man who lives on rice to the beef and bread standard, but it is to bring down the beef and bread man to the rice standard. . . . Slave labor degraded free labor; it took out its respectability; it put an odious caste upon it. It throttled the prosperity of a fine and fair portion of the United States; and a worse than slave labor will throttle and impair the prosperity of a still finer and fairer section of the United States. We can choose here to-day whether our legislation shall be in the interest of the American free laborer or for the servile laborer from China. . . .

22.   SIDNEY L. GULICK

The benefits that would
come through the presence of Asiatics

The exclusion of the Chinese left the issue of Oriental immigration
dormant for awhile. But Japanese immigration, mounting to more than
30,000 in 1907, reactivated anti-Oriental prejudice and bigotry. Again
anti-Oriental sentiment crystallized, particularly in California. The effort
to exclude the Japanese from the San Francisco public schools, the
subsequent "Gentlemen's Agreement" by which the Japanese government ceased granting passports to all laborers, and the California Alien
Land Act directed against the Japanese without actually mentioning
them by name, stirred and reflected hostilities that were to lead to total
exclusion.

Long before World War I, the Japanese had found a dedicated
advocate and publicist in a Congregational missionary committed to
Asian-American amity. In the course of two decades, Sidney L. Gulick
wrote more than fifty books, articles, and pamphlets and he delivered
hundreds of lectures and sermons urging Americans to transcend their
Caucasian prejudices and to accept the Japanese and other Asians as their
peers. On the eve of the first world war, the growing immigration
restriction sentiment led Gulick, Secretary of the National Committee for
Constructive Immigration Legislation, to formulate a scheme to salvage
Japanese pride by fixing annual quotas, however small, based on the
proportion of each nationality already residing in the United States so
that no nation would be excluded outright. *The American Japanese
Problem*, Gulick's major book, candidly stated his case and launched his
fruitless campaign.

The writer heartily agrees with the fundamental postulate of
California's general oriental policy. An immigration from Asia
swamping the white man, overturning the democratic institutions
of the Pacific coast, and bringing wide economic disaster to
Caucasian laborers and farmers is not for a moment to be

tolerated. The writer advocates nothing of the kind. Nor does Japan ask for rights of unlimited immigration. Her statesmen see very well that large influx of Japanese and Chinese laborers into the United States would soon produce intolerable conditions and inevitably lead to serious race conflict. All are agreed in regard to this point. I have talked with many Japanese gentlemen on this matter and not one have I found who dissents.

The present chapter, therefore, is not concerned with this fundamental postulate but rather with what may be regarded as the secondary aspects of the policy—the spirit and the method with which many Californians have urged it. These latter seem to the writer psychologically and strategically mistaken.

For sixty years the treaties between Japan and the United States have emphasized the friendship of the two peoples. Not the Japanese Government alone but the people also have taken these assurances seriously and have acted, for decades, in harmony with them. Hundreds of Japanese attending our colleges and universities have received ideal treatment from our people and on going back to their land have reported their experiences to their astonished kindred and acquaintances and to public audiences. These reports have contributed to that amazing change of the Japanese national attitude to the white man which has been characteristic of Japan during the past forty years.

Japan on her side has effected changes in her national life, laws, and political organization, unheard of till modern times, granting protection and large opportunity to foreigners in her midst.

Responding to the solicitation of planters in the nineties, many thousand Japanese laborers went to the Hawaiian Islands for work on the sugar plantations, and thus began Japan's first experience of emigration. To facilitate this enterprise there sprang up and flourished in Japan a number of emigration societies. Not until the annexation of Hawaii, in 1899, however, did any considerable emigration arise of Japanese laborers to California. At first they were generally welcomed, but as soon as they came in numbers large enough to form local groups and to assert race distinction then difficulties began to arise. The first conspicuous instance of anti-Japanese feeling was the so-called school question when the

School Board of San Francisco adopted the principle of race segregation. This the Japanese resented as contrary to the treaty, invidious, and humiliating. Shortly thereafter came the "gentlemen's agreement," which from 1908 put a complete stop to Japanese labor immigration, the Japanese Government preferring the prevention of immigration undesired by us to the enactment of legislation humiliating to her. In carrying out this arrangement the emigration companies were abolished, causing much hardship.

Japan has earnestly desired to maintain relations with America on the basis of the historic friendship. The entire history of America's helpfulness to Japan, from the days of Commodore Perry and Minister Harris to the time of the war with Russia and the Portsmouth Treaty of Peace, justified Japan's admiration. Rather than sacrifice America's friendship, she was willing to do almost anything. She voluntarily undertook to keep back from our shores all undesired immigration. And when the treaty of unlimited arbitration was negotiated between the United States and England, in 1911, which seemed to conflict with England's obligations to Japan on account of the Treaty of 1905, Japan, expressing her friendship for and confidence in both countries, voluntarily made the change in the clause of the Alliance Treaty which would, under certain conditions, have required England to fight with her against the United States. . . .

In connection with the anti-Japanese agitation many things have been said highly insulting to the Japanese and intended to be so. But the Japanese should not take these utterances too much to heart, for they do not represent, I feel confident, the thought of the real majority, even of Californians.

Months of study of this question in California have convinced the writer that the popular approval of the anti-Japanese agitation and legislation does not concern the details of the proposed bills nor the insulting language used by a few, but rests entirely on the conviction that there should be no swamping immigration from Japan. Their universal and unqualified approval of this position, which is fundamental, has led the good people to keep silence in regard to details which they consider are but incidental.

The objectionable features, however, of this anti-Japanese legislation are many and serious.

It is needless; for under the effective operation of the "gentlemen's agreement" Japanese immigration has ceased, and the number of Japanese in America is diminishing. There is, therefore, no danger whatever of a swamping Japanese invasion nor of any considerable purchase by Japanese of agricultural or other land. The number of acres bought by Japanese during the two years preceding the passage of the law was less than two thousand.

It is misleading; for it implies an issue which does not in fact exist.

The policy is *humiliating to Japan;* for it misrepresents her attitude and conduct, treats her as though she could not be trusted, and ignores her friendship, which, however, has been consistently maintained for sixty years.

It disgraces the United States by presenting us in a wrong attitude to a friendly nation and also by making it appear that we cannot distinguish between solid facts and palpable illusions. We seem to be ruled by hallucinations.

This agitation is *positively injurious;* for it antagonizes Japanese landowners and thus interferes with the process of their assimilation. It thus tends to keep them as a permanently alien element in the midst of our people, helping to create the very difficulty it fears.

It is based on ignorance of the Japanese. It exaggerates their defects and overlooks their virtues.

The whole agitation is *unscientific.* It does not seek accurate and verified facts; being highly suspicious, it accepts as true every maligning story. Moreover, it defends and justifies itself by discredited theories of race psychology and sociology. It confuses biological and sociological assimilation, regarding the two as inseparable.

It is *unjust and unkind.* The spirit which prompted the fifty-one bills in the last two sessions of the legislature is not one that seeks to deal justly or kindly with the stranger in our land. We criticise the Japanese for lack of the spirit of fair play and for failure to keep an open door for us in Manchuria. Are Americans in

California carrying out the spirit of fair play and an open door?

It ignores the new Orient. . . . The world has irrevocably entered on a new era of human development. All the nations of the Orient are awakening to a new life and a new self-consciousness; they are increasingly sensitive to their plight, their needs, and their rights. They are also developing military power. All this is ignored. It is willing to create international difficulty and promote increasing alienation of Asiatic good-will. It pays no attention to the Yellow Peril which it is evoking. As Mr. Rowell well says, "ninety-nine percent of the whole Japanese question is National and International." It ignores the large relations and seeks to settle the problem exclusively from the standpoint of local interests.

It is *short-sighted.* Even from the standpoint of selfish interests, it is calculated to bring disaster. Our international commerce depends in no small degree on the good-will of the purchasing nations. The Chinese boycott of 1905–6 shows what possibilities lie in that direction. Germany and England are competing in the Orient for commercial supremacy. Should wide-spread and strong anti-American feeling in Japan and China be put into the commercial scales, who can foretell the results to our commerce?

Moreover, this anti-Japanese agitation little notes how important for the promotion of a higher standard of living and of wages in the Orient is the movement back and forth of considerable populations belonging to the industrial and agricultural classes. In proportion as the standard of living advances in Asia will the coming economic and industrial competition of those lands with ours be lessened in severity.

Nor does this agitation recognize the benefits, direct and indirect, that would come to our land through the presence here of Asiatics. Those who despise and dislike them cannot apparently see these benefits. Nevertheless, there are such, not only in the manual work done by them, but also in the realm of culture, of religious feeling, and of art. Of these latter benefits little, it is true, has yet been received; the time has been too short, and our attitude to them has been too unfavorable. We have lacked the teachable spirit. Moreover, those who have come to us from Asia have encountered severe economic struggles. Should Asiatics assimilated to our civilization acquire financial prosperity comparable with that of our own middle classes, it is altogether probable that they would make valuable contributions to our life. In all these respects California's anti-Japanese agitation is short-sighted.

It is contrary to the spirit of all American treaties with Japan. Japan opened her doors at our earnest request. We led her out among the nations, much against her will. We pledged mutual friendship. Japan has carried out her side of the compact more faithfully than we have carried out ours. She allows Americans to become citizens of Japan. We refuse to naturalize Japanese, whatever their character or qualifications. Japan allows American residents in Japan, though alien, whether as individuals or as regular corporations, to own land. California and several other States refuse this privilege to Japanese in this country.

The agitation is *hysterical.* Those who advocate it invariably talk of the threatened swamping Asiatic invasion, the Japanization of our entire Pacific coast, the ease and even the likelihood of a Japanese military invasion, and the horrors of intermarriage. These are all the creations of ignorance and fear. That there is no danger whatever of war with Japan is conclusively shown by the facts presented in a later chapter. The very talk of it is absurd. There is, in truth, nothing whatever in the situation in California to call for anti-Japanese legislation.

It is well to ponder the following statements from the eminently sane article by Mr. Rowell: "It may be asserted unconditionally that the menace of Japanese land ownership in California is not a present fact, but is a fear of the future. . . . The intense interest aroused in the whole proposal is based upon this imaginative picture of what some day might happen, rather than upon any present facts of what has happened. . . . Practically all the berries, most of the vegetables, more than half of the grapes, and one-third of the citrus and deciduous fruits of California are produced by Japanese labor. If there is any invasion, this is where it is, but there seems to be no agitation against this real displacement of our own race from an important industry. . . . In the case of land holding the situation is exactly the reverse. Here, instead of dominating anything, the Japanese are practically a negligible quantity. . . . These figures . . . are relatively insignificant in a state which has single holdings of millions of acres. All the Japanese farms in California owned or leased, could be located on the Miller and Lux ranches and be lost in the shuffle."

To one looking calmly at the facts, the present anti-Japanese agitation of Californian politicians appears like a case of hysteria.

And finally, the anti-Japanese policy is *unchristian.* There is no more important teaching of the Old and New Testaments than that of dealing justly and kindly with the stranger in the land. The peculiar new insight of the Apostolic church was the fact that Gentiles are co-heirs with the Jews in the Kingdom of God, who is the Father of all men, and that all men of all races are brothers.

A policy open to so many and such serious criticisms surely cannot be the only one. Californians seem to assume that there are only two alternatives—one, this policy of complete exclusion, hampering legislation, and social ostracism; the other, that of complete surrender to an overwhelming Japanese invasion, resulting in the economic ruin of white laborers and the establishment on the Pacific coast of an Asiatic civilization.

There is, however, a third alternative, a policy calculated to conserve all real interests, on the side both of America and of Japan, dignified, courteous, honorable, and mutually advantageous. . . .

PART SIX

World War
as Civil War

23. Hugo Münsterberg

So many American
and German flags intertwined

During the twenty-odd years in which Hugo Münsterberg (1863–1916)
lived in the United States, he devoted a good part of his energies to
promoting cultural harmony between his adopted country and his native
Germany. In 1892, at the invitation of William James, he resigned from
his teaching post at the University of Freiburg and came to Harvard,
where he was put in charge of the psychological laboratory. A tireless
lecturer and prolific author on experimental psychology, in 1898 he
became president of the American Psychological Association. In 1910
Münsterberg served as an exchange professor at the University of Berlin's
Amerika-Institute.

At the outbreak of war in 1914, the Harvard professor felt impelled to
defend the German position in a series of articles for the press. Published
as *The War in America*, it was to be the first book in a trilogy that
enunciated Münsterberg's views. *The Peace in America* mirrored his
agony in the face of the personal attacks upon him for being a German
propagandist. "Since the slaves were freed, no people in this land have
struggled against their chains with such bitter tears as the German-Americans in the last seven months . . ." (*The Peace in America*, New York:
Appleton, 1915, p. 266). His last book, *Tomorrow* (1916), looked ahead to
peace and the restoration of international relations.

In 1916, a month after aiding in Wilson's reelection, Münsterberg
collapsed just after reaching the lecture platform at Radcliffe. He died

immediately, heartsick and exhausted by his strenuous efforts. Four
months later, the United States and Germany were at war.

I never before saw so many American and German flags
intertwined as to-day in the gaily decorated streets of Utica. It
was a splendid procession of American troops, German-American
societies with their banners and picturesque floats with scenes
from the War of Independence, and from German and German-
American history. We were to unveil the statue of General von
Steuben. Hundreds of thousands had streamed to the town; every
house was gay with waving flags and with black, white and red
decorations; every window crowded with cheering throngs: truly
it was German day.

When through the long avenue of elms we reached the
monument, the sight from the speaker's stand was overwhelming.
The German-American population had streamed out and ten
thousand men and women surrounded the spot. The German
songs rolled through the air; the New York state regiments passed
the bronze statue of the great soldier. It is a fine work of art. You
can really imagine that this was the stature and the gesture and
the look of that great warrior who served through the Seven Years'
War of Prussia, was adjutant of Frederick the Great and who then
gave up everything which he had in his fatherland to serve the
cause of American independence. . . .

I spoke about the threefold meaning of this monument. My
favorite topic came first; the need of discipline in our modern life.
Steuben found men full of dash and courage, and yet they did not
count until he taught them the greatest lesson in war as in peace,
the lesson of subordination, of self-control, of obedience. . . .

The second aspect which I emphasized was suggested by the
fact that German-Americans had erected this monument. I said
that it showed that the Germans in America were finally conscious
of their position, of their rights in this country, and of their duties
to it. Too long they had lived under the illusion that America was
an Anglo-Saxon country and that all the other racial stocks were
only tolerated as more or less welcome guests. . . .

Not long ago the German-Americans were not aware of how

strong they were, or rather they were not strong because they were not aware of their strength. They served faithfully, but did not dare to insist on respect and did not venture to ask for thanks. The last twenty years have changed their place in the world. While the German immigration decreased and the new incoming masses were recruited more and more from Italy and Turkey and Russia, the German-American spirit has steadily become stronger. The German-Americans have become conscious of their duties in the highest historic sense of their mission, and they demand their rights in the shaping of the country's fate.

Their cause had only one element of weakness. The one great binding force was the memory of the past, and not a forceful, positive programme. They sympathized with the Republican party as much as with the Democratic party; their interests were divided on almost every economic question; religiously they were scattered; their common love of German literature and music naturally became weaker with the second and third generation; and so it happened most unfortunately that only the pitiful stein of beer appeared the one object of common wishes. The fight against prohibition, upon which the opinions of Germans might be just as divided as upon any practical question before the nation, was artificially made the center of German-American public activity; it was bolstered up with great words of personal liberty. Nothing has hurt the German-Americans in their struggle for the place which belongs to them so much as the illusion that the negative side of the prohibition question can be in our present time a great vital issue.

It was as if the German-American masses had only waited for a really convincing goal common to all in order to be filled with that enthusiasm which secures strength. The lightning of the European thunderstorm has suddenly shown them their true duty. The policy of this country which they love with their whole hearts must be one of sincere friendship not only with England but also with Germany. They will break down this anti-German agitation; they will punish every effort to inject hatred of Germany into the veins of the American political body. Their National German-American Alliance with two and a half million voters as members,

their intellectual leaders and their economic captains of commerce and industry, their farmers and their workingmen, old and
young, men and women, first generation and second and third,
every religious sect, North Germans and South Germans, Austrians and Swiss—they will be united and will show a crushing
power of which the reckless torchbearers of German hatred did
not dream.

This European war will not reach its end without being deeply
influenced by American public opinion. At an early or at a late
stage, American sentiment will play its rôle. Since I heard the
Watch on the Rhine thundering in the Mohawk Valley I know
that twenty-five millions will take care that this national sentiment
is ultimately not misled as it has been in the first hour of
confusion. They will take care that this powerful American
influence cannot be prostituted to a breach of neutrality in order
to back the allies of Russia who are trying to throw into the dust
America's staunchest friend, the German nation. Never until
to-day have I seen so many American and German flags intertwined.

24. HERMANN HAGEDORN

A renegade American
I certainly was not

The son of a Brooklyn household as German as Bingen on the Rhine,
Hermann Hagedorn (1882–1964) never forgot World War I. Shortly
before his death nearly half a century later, this grandson of a German
Forty-eighter and former executive director of the Theodore Roosevelt
Memorial Association, completed the last of his many books, this one
apparently long postponed, commemorating his war experience. *The
Hyphenated Family* is a unique account of the break-up of a family in the

From Hermann Hagedorn, *The Hyphenated Family: An American Saga* (New
York: Macmillan, 1960), pp. 233–35, 242, 244–49, 261–64. Copyright © 1960 by
Hermann Hagedorn. Reprinted by permission of McIntosh and Otis, Inc.

time of the breaking of nations. In the preface to this, his last testament, which failed even of mention in an extended *New York Times* obituary, the author leaves no doubt of the anguish that had never quite departed:

> This is a true story. I wish it weren't. I wish it were somebody's book of fiction. . . . It is a story of a family that tried to live in two countries at once; a story of a strong man betrayed at the height of his success by a strain of sentimentalism that brought his triumphs tumbling down around him; a story, finally, of one member of the family, its youngest, who tried to make himself what his German-born mother, rich in sentiment but without a grain of sentimentality, wanted him to be, an unhyphenated American. [*The Hyphenated Family*, p. vii.]

After war was declared against Germany in April 1917, the recent Harvard graduate and former student at the University of Berlin volunteered to serve the American government as head of the Vigilantes, a group dedicated to countering German propaganda in the United States, particularly among German-Americans.

I did not have to look about for "war work." I had it. I was running the Vigilantes, an organization of writers whose aim was to bring the issues confronting the nation clearly before the public through articles, poems and stories syndicated to newspapers all over the country. We had cherished the dream of awakening the public, especially in the schools and colleges, to the need of education for citizenship, but America's participation in the war had narrowed our original purpose. The war held our whole attention, its causes, its aims, the uncertain German-Americans, the pro-German periodicals of the prewar period converted to a poisonous pseudo patriotism; racial prejudice, class antagonism; all the foes of our own household, open and covert; all the forces working against national unity.

Before the war was three months old, four hundred writers aligned with us were fighting the German propaganda in America by bringing to the presentation of pedestrian themes the touch of the imagination which gave them wings. Editors all over the country recognized it, and printed what we sent. By the end of the war fifteen thousand newspapers were publishing our material. . . .

A pro-German periodical, in the course of an attack on the

Vigilantes, took a sideswipe at me as a "renegade German-American." The term itself was absurd. A renegade German I could not be since I had never been a German. A renegade American I certainly was not, for if I were, the periodical in question would be praising me. Was it possible that there were people in the United States who regarded German-Americanism as a definite entity?

To my astonishment, I found that my father's old friends, in what my sisters and I had always called, not too respectfully, "the German crowd," took the renegade idea seriously. I began to hear from them and, when I met any of them downtown, they told me sharply what they thought of me. For me to do what I was doing—that is, utilizing the talent and the machinery of the Vigilantes to call attention to the insidious nature of the German propaganda, was treason to my German heritage and a disgrace to my father's name.

An old friend of the family stated the case against me with no malice but with deep conviction. He himself was entirely loyal to America, in a negative fashion, and he expected me to be loyal. I should buy Liberty Bonds, of course. If I were drafted, I must, of course, serve. (It happened that I was well over draft age, and he knew it.) But voluntary, open and active espousal of the American cause, No; by all that was absolute, No. Any other course was disloyal to my father and to the rest of the family now living in Germany and, in one way or another, fighting for Germany.

I could not accept his well meant plea, or the pleas of other family friends who were sincerely concerned for me personally and for my family's good name. In any such crisis as the nation was confronting, family ties, I pointed out, could not be allowed to interfere with the individual's freedom of action, or fetter his hands, brain or spirit.

The very heart of the American experiment in free government was involved. As no other nation in the world, America depended for the unity of her people, even for her existence, on the speedy amalgamation of the aliens who came from the four corners of the earth to claim her welcome. The melting pot had done its work; and it had done it because, by and large, the men and women who had claimed the liberty and the opportunity that America offered had recognized and sought to fulfill the dream that motivated her—the dream of a people united on the basis not of soil, tradition, blood, race or ethnic solidarity, but of an idea, the idea of freedom for the individual to fashion his own life, and, in cooperation with others, a new society, freer and politically more disciplined than any the world had known. To let sentiment, even the sentiment of family love, paralyze the capacity for action, even the willingness to act—at a moment in history when that idea, that dream were in deadly peril—would, in my eyes, be a betrayal of everything that the words "America" and "American" implied.

This, or something like it, was my answer to my father's friends. . . .

The attitude of these people, these basically honest, loyal people, made me aware, for the first time, of the depth and scope of the problem that the divided hearts of the German-Americans presented. The great majority, I was certain, were normally for America first, last and always, having no sympathy for the German government and no more than the normal sentiment, shading off into indifference, of any naturalized American for the country of his birth. But the Wilson administration had given them no leadership. America's voice, during the years of her neutrality, had been ambiguous, tortured and self-questioning. The German voices, speaking to the German-Americans, had, on the other hand, been clear, definite and assured: Germany had been flagrantly attacked by Britain, Russia, France and Belgium, for no reason except jealousy, envy and general malice. Britain controlled the American press, so the news America was getting was false. Germany was winning the war and would show this British "vassal," America, who was master. Germany was the greatest nation in the world; republics were hopelessly corrupt and inefficient, democracy was a delusion, and so forth and so on, straight from the shoulder, and beyond debate.

Millions of the German-Americans, hearing the two voices— one timid, hesitant and uncertain; the other, masterful, clear-cut and assured—followed the leadership that seemed to them to know where it was going and that definitely intended getting there.

I determined to do what I could to show these misguided people where, I believed, their hearts' home really was, and where, I knew, their true destiny lay. I would frame an appeal to them to stand forth and say where they stood. . . .

In Germany, meanwhile, the activities of mine which had so enraged some of the family's old New York friends, as well as other pro-Germans, were receiving occasional scurrilous attention. The Cologne *Gazette* paid me the compliment of declaring me a *Schweinehund*, a mythical animal supposed to combine the most reprehensible characteristics of bitch and swine. Another paper labeled me a *Schmutzfink*, a creature wallowing in the mire for sheer delight in filth.

Someone apparently sent my brother Fred, now Under Secretary of State in the ministry of Food Supply in Berlin, the reference to my "unholy activities," as the Cologne paper described them, for he wrote me—and how the letter got through the American lines I have no idea—that if I had any feeling at all for Father I should stop at once what I was doing. So far, he wrote, he had managed to keep the press reports about me from Father's eyes. If ever Father found out about them, he said, it would put an unbearable burden on his unhappy spirit. . . .

I don't believe that Father would have been as distressed as Fred imagined if he had known the form that my "unholy activities" had taken. The appeal to the confused and double-minded among the German-Americans that I had set out to write had grown into a little book, whose challenge was epitomized in its title, *Where Do You Stand?* To my delight, it brought almost immediately a break in the lines of that "German crowd" in New York that had been so sure I was a traitor to all they held most dear. Addie, who himself thoroughly approved of my "appeal" and had actually, I suspect, felt more acutely than I the abuse poured on me by the German irreconcilables in New York, jubilantly brought me reports of one family after another in our acquaintance reading the book and finding it "a real comfort." I was, they declared, "decidedly on the right track."

The book traveled fast and I began to get letters from German-Americans in other parts of the country, including many editors of German-language newspapers and periodicals who admitted that the way I pointed out to them was the way they wanted to go. They knew that America was their home, and they actually wanted no other; knew, too, that they had been running on the wrong track, and wanted to get back on the main line. But they were not to be won by the persuasion of the sledge hammer, or drawn into the American community with the lasso. With so many emotions, memories, urges, longings involved, I knew what caring and tact would be needed to bring these people back into the American fold. . . .

I enlisted the interest of German-American leaders in New York and in the West in the possibility of an organization that should testify to the American people the single-minded loyalty of the Americans of German origin to the United States and her free institutions. Here, it happened, we crossed wires with a government-sponsored society, The Friends of German Democracy, which had been created by the federal government's propaganda arm, the Committee on Public Information.

So far as my associates and myself were concerned, any effort to develop among German-Americans an interest in German democracy was beside the point. Let the Germans have any form of government they wanted. Our aim was simply to make German-Americans into straight Americans, looking forward, not back.

We determined to organize what we called a "National Patriotic Council of Loyal Americans of German Origin." Influential support was promised us in Washington by such men as Franklin K. Lane, Secretary of the Interior, and Senator Henry Cabot Lodge. The principal German-language papers across the country agreed to back us, and leading papers in New York City indicated that we might count on them. What, in our political inexperience, we failed to reckon with was the possibility that the Committee on Public Information might not look kindly on our effort to supplant its own German-American "baby," the Friends of German Democracy. . . .

It seemed a far-reaching piece of good fortune when, on the

recommendation of Frances Kellor, special adviser on race relations, the federal Commissioner of Education, P. C. Claxton, invited me to serve as a dollar-a-year "racial adviser on Americans of German origin."

My job was to promote "mutual understanding and unity" between the German-Americans and their fellow citizens, to develop "an understanding of American ideals, principles and action" among them, and "to stimulate the understanding and prosecution of the war."

I rounded up the German-American leaders in New York—in the main newspaper publishers, editors, or presidents of social, singing or athletic societies with large memberships—but had barely got started on a series of conferences with them when Miss Kellor was told that I must hold no more talks in the Interior Department offices in New York with German-American leaders. The Committee on Public Information, it seemed, had got wind of my approach to the German-American question. Its chairman, an able journalist, named George Creel, was inclined, like government propagandists the world over, to paint in blacks and whites, and to see the German-American issue in terms of the bludgeon. To such a mind my efforts to deal with the German-Americans on the basis of compassion, reason and faith, were darkly suspect. . . .

A distorted account of the most recent of the conferences I had held took me to the office of the New York *Tribune*, the morning that my associates and I had selected for the release of our story on the organization of the "Patriotic Council."

By a happy accident, the *Tribune*'s managing editor was a Harvard classmate of mine, Ernest H. Gruening. "I'm so glad you came," he said. "I've had quite a battle over you." An editorial based on the story to which I was objecting had been put on his desk for publication that morning. "On the strength of a wire from Washington, it denounced you as a fraud, and actually a stockholder in disloyal German-language papers. I told the people upstairs that the editorial would be printed only over my dead body, not alone out of justice to you but because it would bring the *Tribune* a libel suit which I knew the paper would be bound to lose."

I thanked my friend as well as I could in the dazed and breathless state into which the interview had plunged me, and went on to my office in the Interior Department's New York headquarters.

That afternoon one of Creel's top assistants called me from Washington. He had seen the story about the formation of the Patriotic Council, he said. "I think you ought to know," he went on, "that if this Council becomes active it will gravely interfere with certain work which the Committee on Public Information has in hand." He was referring, I gathered, to the Friends of German Democracy. "I hope," he went on, "that you will decide not to go ahead with it. I hope it, I might add, for your own good." A sinister note crept into his voice. "For if you go ahead, we shall expose you as an impostor who has falsely represented himself to be an official of the United States government."

I pointed out hotly that I had been appointed by the Commissioner of Education.

"Dr. Claxton will deny your appointment. Moreover, if you persist, you will be exposed as the tool and cat's-paw of the German-language press."

The pleasant places in which my lines had hitherto fallen, the intercourse I had had with decent people in Europe and in my own country and the standards of conduct I had been taught to respect, had not prepared me for this kind of intimidation by an official of the United States government.

I don't know what I said to him. I might have told him, and I assume that I did, of Secretary Lane's approval of our Patriotic Council as "highly important and absolutely practical." But his approval had been verbal, and he was away on government business in Hawaii. I might have told Creel's man to ask the German-language editors and publishers I had enlisted in the struggle for a sound solution of the German-American problem, how pliable a "cat's-paw" they had found me. But that would have done no good; he would not have listened to them.

I was actually too dazed to say much of anything, but I made no promises.

I had barely pulled myself together from this second shock when Dr. Claxton himself called me from Washington, denying categorically that he had given me any appointment.

Miss Kellor had no light to shed on the Commissioner's repudiation, not of me only but of herself.

For hours, that afternoon and evening, I walked the streets of New York in humiliation and misery. I had plenty of documentation to prove that I was no impostor. No government sleuth, moreover, would find any record of my owning a single share of stock in any German-language newspaper, loyal or disloyal. I could make a clear case for myself in the press, but what chances would I have against the official propaganda machine of the United States government, or its ruthless engineers?

No, my part was to "take it," keep my mouth shut, and beware in the future of playing marbles with boys who were tougher than I was.

The wisdom of my decision was proved next day. Most of the men in Washington whom we had listed in our press release as supporting our "Patriotic Council" had apparently been tipped off that we were "phony." One after another—happily, for my faith in man, not all!—they disclaimed any sympathy with us.

I was afraid that Colonel Roosevelt would think me a "molly-coddle" for not standing up to the arm-twisters. But the "fightingest man in America" shared Solomon's philosophy of "seasons," and said nothing of fighting. All the advice he gave me was, "Get the record down."

I did it in a letter to the President, asking his counsel in the "dilemma" in which I found myself "because of unwarranted charges brought against me," on the one hand, and my reluctance, on the other, to make a public issue of a case that might "serve to shake the confidence of the public in the sense of responsibility of the heads of important government departments." Might I count on his support?*

* H.H. to the President of the United States, June 14, 1918.

The President's secretary acknowledged the letter. That was all. No one in the White House could be bothered even to the extent of a perfunctory promise to make inquiries.

Under pressure from Miss Kellor, the falsity of the "impostor" charges was admitted by Dr. Claxton within forty-eight hours and acknowledged by him to the Creel office.

But neither he nor anyone in the Creel office offered any apology. . . .

Recognizing that I might be needing a touch of solace and a word of defense in the New York *Tribune* and the other newspapers that were publishing his syndicated articles, Mr. Roosevelt used my little book, *Where Do You Stand?* as a springboard for his own appeal to his fellow citizens of German descent. With characteristic munificence, he described its author as "an American of the best and bravest and most loyal type," and made that American thereby reach up and out toward the dream of becoming, some day, by God's grace, the kind of American Mr. Roosevelt described him as being. . . .

Here then is the story of the family that tried to live in two countries at once. I have called it a tragedy, and it was such for Father and Mother and, in varying degrees, for us all.

For myself, thanks to Mother, it was something else, also: a challenge to seek the meaning of this high dream that we call America, and, so far as in me lay, to interpret it and to live it.

America, I have learned in the course of the years, is more than these beloved stretches of natural beauty, washed by two great oceans; these multitudes in seething cities and friendly towns on highways leading everywhere or nowhere; more than the free political institutions that dedicated minds and spirits created, and brave and temperate men have maintained; more than the flag which symbolizes both the body of a nation and the soul which gives it meaning.

America is man's highest vision, to this hour, of human society based on the realities of human nature as it is, and the hope of human nature as it might become.

America is an idea, a dream, a perpetual act of faith that man is the child of God and that the forces in him that aspire will ever in the end be victorious over the forces in him that destroy.

America is the many-made-one, the children of feuding races, creeds and nations, united by a conception that shrivels in its glow all lesser loyalties. America is the free association of people, recognizing and basing their lives upon those absolute standards of human conduct that are the pure metal smelted from the experience and dedicated thinking of the most profound and socially-minded spirits on the five continents, through ten thousand years of human history.

To America has been given both the vision of what human society might be and the awful responsibility, as a nation and as individuals, of translating that vision into day-by-day individual, social, national and international conduct.

America today is the fulfillment of the dream of the prophets and seers of a hundred generations, or it is the cynical toss of that dream into the ashcan of history. America is the creative response to the hunger of mankind for hope, self-respect and brotherhood, or it is earth's final disillusionment, its ultimate object of derision and hate, standing, black and alone, against the blaze of thermonuclear fire.

Is it conceivable that the Mind that sets the stars in their cycles, and has given to man the capacity to set stars of his own in orbit, should give a people so compelling a dream, lay upon them so heavy a responsibility, and not give them also the faith, the vision, the courage, the will and the stamina—in a word, the greatness—triumphantly to carry the burden and make the dream come true? . . .

If the forty years since Father's death have given me an ever-deepening sense of the meaning of America, the last decade of those four has given me an admiration for the German people far transcending my boyhood's sentimental attachment to German landscape and German song, German friends and German *Gemütlichkeit*.

In the depths of Father's agony over his country's collapse, the reader will recall, he recognized that the German people—and he identified himself with them—had been "weighed in the balance and found wanting." Somehow they had lost their way, but he never doubted that God would set them on the highroad once more. "When our people shall have found themselves again," he added, "He will lead us out of this valley of humiliation."

His faith has been triumphantly justified. His people's further years in the wilderness were tragic for themselves and for the world, beyond anything which the darkest forebodings of his sleepless nights might have tortured him with. But the redemption, the moral and economic recovery of that portion of his people that was free to be itself, have been, also, beyond the boldest dreams that he might have dared permit himself. A defeated, abject people, facing, fifteen years ago, what seemed to themselves and to their neighbors final annihilation as a great nation; today one of the most respected and prosperous countries in Europe! Once an aggressive, self-centered, bellicose government, the object of universal fear and distrust; today, the protagonist in the struggle for a united European family of nations! Day before yesterday, the glittering symbol of authority and the discipline of power; yesterday the black example of inhuman despotism; today, one of the world's strongest bulwarks in the battle for a free world!

If, on his off-Sundays from Elysium, Father revisits his beloved Fatherland, he has deeper and more genuine reasons for devotion than any he knew in life. . . .

The history of the "hyphenated family" does not end with the final chapter of this book. The next generation has a different and more inspiring story that must some day be told, of a human family losing and finding itself in a world family; of nationalism transcended, not in any blueprint of a supernational government but in the individual's identification, in action, with the peoples of all nations—their problems, their sins, and their hunger to achieve the inner unity, the freedom and the power of the God-centered life; the story of an American prophet's world-encompassing vision that came to palpitating reality for one of Charlotte Hagedorn's great-granddaughters and her husband in Berkeley Square, London, and on Rio de Janeiro's riot-ridden waterfront, in American labor conflict and in African villages and throne rooms;

a story of unity in place of division, of a common purpose in men and women of many nations; and of fellowship and growth, instead of sorrow, in the face of racial, cultural and national divergencies; a story, finally, of self-will resolved in the course of common, everyday living under the challenge of absolute moral standards and the guidance of that Spirit which, Dante assures us in the concluding words of his *Paradiso*, "moves the sun and the other stars."

25.   W. L. HARDING

Use of a language other than that of this country

The laconic proclamation issued by Iowa's Governor W. L. Harding revealed the extent to which World War I divided the nation of immigrants irrespective of their national origins. A nation of many cultures and languages demanded conformity of all foreign-speaking peoples, native American and foreign-born, citizen and alien. The effort to snuff out all traces of foreign background, especially language, for so many the very breath of life, underlined the tragedy of a war that extended to all Americans.

To the People of Iowa:

WHEREAS, our country is engaged in war with foreign powers; and

WHEREAS, controversy has arisen in parts of this State concerning the use of foreign languages;

Therefore, for the purpose of ending such controversy and to bring about peace, quiet and harmony among our people, attention is directed to the following, and all are requested to govern themselves accordingly.

W. L. Harding, "Language Proclamation," from Iowa War Proclamations in *Iowa and War*, ed. B. F. Shambaugh (Iowa: State Historical Society, 1919), pp. 43–47.

The official language of the United States and the State of Iowa is the English language. Freedom of speech is guaranteed by federal and State Constitutions, but this is not a guaranty of the right to use a language other than the language of this country— the English language. Both federal and State Constitutions also provide that "no laws shall be made respecting an establishment of religion or prohibiting the free exercise thereof." Each person is guaranteed freedom to worship God according to the dictates of his own conscience, but this guaranty does not protect him in the use of a foreign language when he can as well express his thought in English, nor entitle the person who cannot speak or understand the English language to employ a foreign language, when to do so tends in time of national peril, to create discord among neighbors and citizens, or to disturb the peace and quiet of the community.

Every person should appreciate and observe his duty to refrain from all acts or conversation which may excite suspicion or produce strife among the people, but in his relation to the public should so demean himself that every word and act will manifest his loyalty to his country and his solemn purpose to aid in achieving victory for our army and navy and the permanent peace of the world.

If there must be disagreement, let adjustment be made by those in official authority rather than by the participants in the disagreement. Voluntary or self-constituted committees or associations undertaking the settlement of such disputes, instead of promoting peace and harmony, are a menace to society and a fruitful cause of violence. The great aim and object of all should be unity of purpose and a solidarity of all the people under the flag for victory. This much we owe to ourselves, to posterity, to our country and to the world.

Therefore, the following rules should obtain in Iowa during the war:

First. English should and must be the only medium of instruction in public, private, denominational or other similar schools.

Second. Conversation in public places, on trains and over the telephone should be in the English language.

Third. All public addresses should be in the English language.

Fourth. Let those who cannot speak or understand the English language conduct their religious worship in their homes.

This course carried out in the spirit of patriotism, though inconvenient to some, will not interfere with their guaranteed constitutional rights and will result in peace and tranquillity at home and greatly strengthen the country in battle. The blessings of the United States are so great that any inconvenience or sacrifice should willingly be made for their perpetuity.

Therefore, by virtue of authority in me vested, I, W. L. Harding, Governor of the State of Iowa, commend the spirit of tolerance and urge that henceforward the within outlined rules be adhered to by all, that petty differences be avoided and forgotten, and that, united as one people with one purpose and one language, we fight shoulder to shoulder for the good of mankind.

> *In Testimony Whereof, I have hereunto*
> *set my hand and caused to be affixed*
> *the Great Seal of the State.*
>
> *Done at Des Moines, this twenty-third*
> *day of May, 1918.*
>
> *W. L. Harding*

26. Reinhold Niebuhr

I am an American
of pure German stock

Americans of German origin during World War II were spared the ordeal of World War I. But the rise of Hitler to power in 1933 and the threat of a holocaust that again would pit the great powers, including the United States, against one another along earlier lines confirmed many of them in their isolationism. Reinhold Niebuhr (1892–1970) had never wavered in his keen sense of the tragedy of Europe and of Germany after World War I. Even before 1933, he had warned against Hitler's rise. Thereafter, he not only helped settle refugees in the United States, beginning in 1933 with the distinguished theologian, Paul Tillich, but maintained contact with anti-Nazis—on both religious and secular sides—who remained behind and with the German Underground.

Only briefly, in 1934, did he endorse neutrality. But as the U.S. position of neutrality hardened into isolationism and the need for intervention became more and more apparent, Niebuhr drove himself to the point of nervous collapse, as inner conflict and outer catastrophe sapped his energies and tortured his spirit. After Hitler marched on Poland in September, 1939, Niebuhr joined the William Allen White Committee to Defend America by Aiding the Allies, hoping that outright war might be avoided. "I do wish that they'd hate Hitler more and me less," said Niebuhr to a friend as pacifists and isolationists attacked him unmercifully. In December, 1940, he helped found *Christianity and*

Reinhold Niebuhr, "To Prevent The Triumph of An Intolerable Tyranny," *The Christian Century* LVII (December 18, 1940): 1578–80. Third in a series, "If America Enters the War." Copyright © 1940, Christian Century Foundation. Reprinted by permission of Christian Century Foundation.

Crisis, a magazine directed to the Protestant ministry, many of whose leaders were pacifists.

Niebuhr's article in the interdenominational *Christian Century*, printed below, reflects the sense of tragic realism, the universalism, and the moral passion that he unflinchingly applied to the world about.

The editor of *The Christian Century* has invited representatives of various shades of opinion to state what their attitude and conviction would be in the event of the involvement of this nation in the world war. The invitation of the editor begins with the following statement: "The cumulative steps taken by our government during the past year, culminating in the adoption of conscription, have brought the nation to a point where America's participation as a belligerent in the war is an imminent possibility."

It is indicative of the deep chasm which separates some of us in the Christian church today, that I cannot even accept this statement as presenting a true picture of the situation in which we stand. It implies that we have been brought to the edge of war primarily by contrivance of the administration. I should have thought that when a storm is raging in the seven seas of the earth, one could hardly hold any pilot responsible for not steering the ship of state in such a way as to avoid the storm. Living in an age of war and revolution, no possible statesmanship could have avoided at least the danger of involvement. But perhaps I am plunging into the argument too hurriedly by this introduction.

No Rush Toward War

I will therefore begin again with the simple statement, that if our nation should be involved in the world conflict I will have no hesitancy in supporting the war effort of the nation. I am assuming, in making such an unqualified statement, that the nation will not be drawn into the war if there is a decent and honorable way of remaining out of it. The suspicion in which the isolationists hold the international policy of the administration will of course prompt them to challenge this assumption. But I believe that contemporary history refutes the idea that nations are drawn into war too precipitately. It proves on the contrary that it is the general inclination, of democratic nations at least, to hesitate so long before taking this fateful plunge that the dictator nations gain a fateful advantage over them by having the opportunity of overwhelming them singly instead of being forced to meet their common resistance. More than a half-dozen nations of Europe mourn the loss of their liberties today, who might have preserved them if extreme caution had not enervated their resolution of self-defense.

I shall seek to justify my determination to support the nation in war by a political and a religious analysis of the moral problems involved, since every moral problem is political on the side of its application and religious on the side of the basic presuppositions from which the moral judgment flows.

On the political side I view the situation which confronts us as follows: Germany on the pretext of righting the wrongs of Versailles is engaged in a desperate effort to establish her mastery over the whole continent of Europe. She may succeed. Nothing but the resistance of Great Britain now stands in her way. One nation after the other has collapsed before the might of her arms or before a diplomacy which knows how to exploit all the weaknesses and internal divisions of her adversaries. These imperial ambitions of Germany are in quality and extent perilous to all the nations outside Europe.

Peril to All Civilized Values

In quality they represent a peril to every established value of a civilization which all Western nations share and of which we are all the custodians. In extent the German ambitions must immediately reach beyond Europe, because Europe is not economically self-sufficient and a German-dominated slave economy would immediately stand in fateful competition with us and would use all means, fair and foul, to make us the subservient accomplices of its economic and political penetration. It is not necessary to fear an immediate invasion of our shores to regard the imperial expansion of Germany with apprehension. I have never shared the naive belief that all war could be avoided if only you could persuade nations not to cross each other's borders. I am perfectly certain that if an enemy of mine did not invade the sanctity of my home but posted sentries at my gate and pointed a gun into my windows and, by virtue of such threats, presumed to dictate my comings and goings or even dared to levy tribute on my trade, he would be no less an enemy of my liberties than if he invaded my home.

Far from believing that we can permit anything to happen in Europe while we enjoy peace and democracy upon an island of security in a tyrannically organized world, I am convinced that if Britain should fall and Germany should be triumphant we could do nothing but spend all our energies in the next decades in arming against all possible perils and attacks and in contriving to outwit a resourceful and ingenious foe. This is what we would do at best. There is a worse alternative. We might accept the advice of Colonel Lindbergh and other appeasers of his type and become the accomplices of such a victor. I fear there are many of us for whom nothing succeeds like success and who would be easily persuaded that after all nothing must interfere with the ultimate sanctity of ⌐ commercial society: trade.

Signs of Moral Confusion

On the point of the quality rather than extent of the German ambitions I must confess that I have found nothing so difficult to understand as the constant appeals of *The Christian Century* to the President to be more perfectly neutral in this conflict so as not to involve America in it by favoring one side. I regard such advice as the typical fruit of the moral confusion which issues from moral perfectionism, whenever moral perfectionism seeks to construct political systems.

A Fury Fed by Paganism

We have allowed ourselves to forget as much as possible that this resurgent Germany not only shares imperial ambitions with all strong nations, but that its fury is fed by a pagan religion of tribal self-glorification; that it intends to root out the Christian religion; that it defies all the universal standards of justice which ages of a Christian and humanistic culture have woven into the fabric of our civilization; that it threatens the Jewish race with annihilation and visits a maniacal fury upon these unhappy people which goes far beyond the ordinary race prejudice which is the common sin of all nations and races; that it explicitly declares its intention of subjecting the other races of Europe into slavery to the "master" race; that it intends to keep them in subjection by establishing a monopoly of military violence and of technical skill so that they will be subordinate in peace and in war; that it is already engaged in Poland and Czechoslovakia in destroying the very fabric of national existence by wholesale expulsion of nationals from their homeland and the forced colonization of Germans in their place; that, in short, it is engaged in the terrible effort to establish an empire upon the very negation of justice rather than upon that minimal justice which even ancient empires achieved.

If anyone believes that the peace of such a tyranny is morally more tolerable than war I can only admire and pity the resolute dogmatism which makes such convictions possible.

Since some of us who express convictions of the kind I have outlined have been accused of being swayed in our opinions by ties of family and friendship which bind us to Great Britain, I would like to add the personal word that I am an American of pure German stock, that I gained most of these convictions in many visits to Hitler's Germany, that I share them with pure Germans such as Thomas Mann and many others, and that far from being swayed by any ties with Britain, I thought Britain was much too slow in understanding or challenging the peril which nazi imperialism presented to both our common civilization and the vital interests of Britain, just as I believe that we have been too tardy in understanding this peril.

Challenge to Conscience

It will appear from the above analysis that my primary difficulty in recent months has been, not the fear of becoming involved in war but an uneasy conscience about living in security while other men are dying for principles in which I very much believe. The question whether or not we should declare war is therefore not primarily one of morals but of strategy in the sense that I believe we ought to do whatever has to be done to prevent the triumph of this intolerable tyranny.

This assertion brings us immediately to the deeper issues involved in the religious presuppositions of our moral judgments. As I understand those who regard such a position as I have stated with abhorrence to believe, to quote a recent letter in *The Christian Century*, that we are "crucifying the Lord afresh," they hold that the avoidance of conflict is in some sense the realization of the Christian law of love. They judge men's virtue by the degree of their non-involvement in conflict. Thus *The Christian Century*, in the months just preceding the invasion of the Low Countries, spoke of the little neutral nations as the "custodians" of European civilization. The nations at conflict had forfeited civilization since, in the view of *The Christian Century*, it is not possible to preserve civilization in conflict because war is the negation of civilization. I find it a little amusing to prefer Latvia to Great Britain as to the quality of its civilization because the one was at war and the other one was not, more particularly so since Latvia, and many similar small neutral nations, rather suddenly lost both their virtue and their lives by being gobbled up.

Perfectionism and Historical Reality

The fact is that this whole pitiless perfectionism, which has informed a large part of liberal Protestantism in America, is wrong not only about this war and the contemporary international situation. It is wrong about the whole nature of historical reality. It worries about some of us "crucifying the Lord afresh" by being involved in war and does not recognize that the selfishness of the best of us is constantly involved in the sin of crucifying the Lord afresh. It thinks there is some simple method of extricating ourselves from conflict, when as a matter of fact all justice which the world has ever known has been established through tension between various vitalities, forces and interests in society. All such tension is covert conflict and all covert conflict may on occasion, and must on occasion, become overt. . . .

No matter how they twist and turn, the protagonists of a political, rather than a religious, pacifism end with the acceptance and justification of, and connivance with, tyranny. They proclaim that slavery is better than war. I beg leave to doubt it and to challenge the whole system of sentimentalized Christianity which prompts good men to arrive at this perverse conclusion. This system must be challenged not only in this tragic hour of the world's history, lest we deliver the last ramparts of civilization into the hands of the new barbarians. It must be challenged in peace and in war because its analysis of human nature and human history is fundamentally false.

27. FRANKLIN D. ROOSEVELT

Remember the Nazi technique

By contrast with World War I, World War II was remarkably free of wholesale anti-immigrant sentiment directed against those of European origin. As Franklin Roosevelt's statement makes clear, the totalitarian racist menace discouraged group prejudice on the American scene.

I am deeply concerned over the increasing number of reports of employers discharging workers who happen to be aliens or even foreign-born citizens. This is a very serious matter. It is one thing to safeguard American industry, and particularly defense industry, against sabotage; but it is very much another to throw out of work honest and loyal people who, except for the accident of birth, are sincerely patriotic.

Such a policy is as stupid as it is unjust, and on both counts it plays into the hands of the enemies of American democracy. By discharging loyal, efficient workers simply because they were born

Roosevelt, Statement, January 2, 1942, from *The Public Papers and Addresses of Franklin Delano Roosevelt*, ed. Samuel I. Rosenman (New York: Random House, 1950), vol. 11, pp. 5–6. Copyright © 1950 by Random House, Inc. Reprinted by permission of Random House, Inc.

abroad or because they have "foreign-sounding" names or by refusing to employ such men and women, employers are engendering the very distrust and disunity on which our enemies are counting to defeat us.

Remember the Nazi technique: "Pit race against race, religion against religion, prejudice against prejudice. Divide and conquer!"

We must not let that happen here. We must not forget what we are defending: liberty, decency, justice. We cannot afford the economic waste of services of all loyal and patriotic citizens and non-citizens in defending our land and our liberties.

I urge all private employers to adopt a sane policy regarding aliens and foreign-born citizens, and to remember that the sons of the "foreigners" they discharged may be among those who fought and are fighting so valiantly at Pearl Harbor or in the Philippines.

There is no law providing against employment of aliens except in special defense work of a secret nature, and even in such work the employer may hire an alien with the permission of the Army or Navy, depending on the contract.

28. LEARNED HAND

Liberty lies in the hearts of men and women

On May 21, 1944, a vast "I Am an American Day" ceremony was held in New York's Central Park, marking the induction of a large number of aliens to American citizenship. At a critical time during World War II, Judge Learned Hand's brief tribute to a nation of immigrants and the descendants of immigrants made the libertarian tradition even more poignant. Widely distributed, this statement came to be regarded as the most succinct expression of its theme.

Learned Hand, from *The Spirit of Liberty, Papers and Addresses of Learned Hand*, ed. Irving Dilliard (New York: Alfred A. Knopf, 1952), pp. 189–91. Reprinted by permission of Alfred A. Knopf, Inc.

We have gathered here to affirm a faith, a faith in a common purpose, a common conviction, a common devotion. Some of us have chosen America as the land of our adoption; the rest have come from those who did the same. For this reason we have some right to consider ourselves a picked group, a group of those who had the courage to break from the past and brave the dangers and the loneliness of a strange land. What was the object that nerved us, or those who went before us, to this choice? We sought liberty; freedom from oppression, freedom from want, freedom to be ourselves. This we then sought; this we now believe that we are by way of winning. What do we mean when we say that first of all we seek liberty? I often wonder whether we do not rest our hopes too much upon constitutions, upon laws and upon courts. These are false hopes; believe me, these are false hopes. Liberty lies in the hearts of men and women; when it dies there, no constitution, no law, no court can save it; no constitution, no law, no court can even do much to help it. While it lies there it needs no constitution, no law, no court to save it. And what is this liberty which must lie in the hearts of men and women? It is not the ruthless, the unbridled will; it is not freedom to do as one likes. That is the denial of liberty, and leads straight to its overthrow. A society in which men recognize no check upon their freedom soon becomes a society where freedom is the possession of only a savage few; as we have learned to our sorrow.

What then is the spirit of liberty? I cannot define it; I can only tell you my own faith. The spirit of liberty is the spirit which is not too sure that it is right; the spirit of liberty is the spirit which seeks to understand the minds of other men and women; the spirit of liberty is the spirit which weighs their interests alongside its own without bias; the spirit of liberty remembers that not even a sparrow falls to earth unheeded; the spirit of liberty is the spirit of Him who, near two thousand years ago, taught mankind that lesson it has never learned, but has never quite forgotten;° that

---

° This clause was taken in substance from the following clause in H. G. Wells's *The Outline of History* (volume II, page 632, George Newnes, Ltd., London): ". . . whose pitiless and difficult doctrine of self-abandonment and self-forgetfulness we can neither disregard nor yet bring ourselves to obey." [L. H.]

there may be a kingdom where the least shall be heard and considered side by side with the greatest. And now in that spirit, that spirit of an America which has never been, and which may never be; nay, which never will be except as the conscience and courage of Americans create it; yet in the spirit of that America which lies hidden in some form in the aspirations of us all; in the spirit of that America for which our young men are at this moment fighting and dying; in that spirit of liberty and of America I ask you to rise and with me pledge our faith in the glorious destiny of our beloved country.

29. JAPANESE-AMERICANS

We should not be treated differently than Italians, Germans, Finns, Yugoslavs

If the attack on Pearl Harbor stunned most Americans, it virtually paralyzed Americans of Japanese origin. The dreaded war between Japan and the United States was now a reality. Unlike German and Italian aliens, who as Europeans were to be judged as individuals, persons of Asian origin—even when they were native-born Americans—were regarded collectively as guilty. Within two months, the American government decided to evacuate all persons of Japanese ancestry from the West Coast on the grounds of military necessity. By November 1942, 113,000 West Coast Japanese-Americans were confined behind barbed wire in ten War Relocation Authority camps in the states of California, Arizona, Idaho, Utah, Wyoming, Colorado, and Arkansas. These barren, remote sites were to be their homes until 1945. Then, despite persistent anti-Japanese sentiment in California, a majority of the Japanese-Americans returned to their despoiled homes, businesses, and lands. Others preferred not to return and settled elsewhere. A few thousand chose to depart for Japan. One of the sorriest episodes in American history had come to an end.

U. S. Congress, House, Select Committee Investigating National Defense Migration, *San Francisco Hearings Pursuant to H. Res. 113, Part 29: Problems of Evacuation of Enemy Aliens and Others from Prohibited Military Zones*, 77th Cong., 2nd sess., February 21 and 23, 1942, pp. 11217–28 passim.

Beginning in late February 1942, a Congressional committee, headed by Representative John H. Tolan of California, originally created to investigate "National Defense Migration," conducted a series of hearings on the West Coast in which Japanese-Americans especially were questioned. The simple testimony revealed the hopeless dilemma that Japanese-Americans confronted when forced to demonstrate their loyalty in the face of charges of racial conspiracy.

THE CHAIRMAN. Where were you born?

MR. OGAWA. In Hawaii, on the island of Maui. . . .

THE CHAIRMAN. How long have you resided in the United States?

MR. OGAWA. Ever since 1915, during the first San Francisco Fair. . . .

THE CHAIRMAN. . . . You are not in business now; are you?

MR. OGAWA. No, sir.

THE CHAIRMAN. What caused you to go out of business?

MR. OGAWA. I think it is due to—I don't know exactly—but I think it is due mostly to depression.

THE CHAIRMAN. What?

MR. OGAWA. Depression. I think so, but not exactly discrimination, but business fell off.

THE CHAIRMAN. You have been 12 years in business. It took quite a while for depression to catch up with you, didn't it?

MR. OGAWA. Yes, sir; it finally caught up with me.

THE CHAIRMAN. That partner didn't help you out any, did he, the partner that you had in business?

MR. OGAWA. Not very much.

THE CHAIRMAN. Except to help you out of business, is that the idea?

MR. OGAWA. Yes; that is right, sir.

THE CHAIRMAN. Was he a Japanese?

MR. OGAWA. Yes, sir.

THE CHAIRMAN. How long were you in partnership with him?

MR. OGAWA. Ever since we started in together.

THE CHAIRMAN. Don't you think that that was the real depression that caused your loss of business, this partnership as much as anything?

MR. OGAWA. Probably so; yes.

THE CHAIRMAN. He sort of held out on you, didn't he?

MR. OGAWA. Well, I don't like to say.

THE CHAIRMAN. Did you ever serve in the armed forces of the United States?

MR. OGAWA. I am glad to say I did, sir.

THE CHAIRMAN. For how long?

MR. OGAWA. From October 1917 until discharged in April 1919.

THE CHAIRMAN. Did you go to Europe?

MR. OGAWA. Yes, sir. I served with Company G, Three hundred and Sixty-fourth Infantry, Ninety-first Division. . . .

THE CHAIRMAN. Were you wounded?

MR. OGAWA. I was wounded on the morning of October 2, 1918, at Meuse-Argonne offensive. . . .

THE CHAIRMAN. What are you doing now?

MR. OGAWA. I am working at the Moore Shipyard. . . .

THE CHAIRMAN. How much money are you making now? . . .

MR. OGAWA. It varies from $35 to $50.

THE CHAIRMAN. Where is your family?

MR. OGAWA. My wife and four children are back in Hawaii visiting. She was just about ready to return when war was declared.

THE CHAIRMAN. They went before the Pearl Harbor attack?

MR. OGAWA. Yes; she left here last July.

MR. SPARKMAN. Are you a citizen of the United States?

MR. OGAWA. I am glad to say that I am, sir.

MR. SPARKMAN. Do you anticipate that you are to be affected in any way by any of these orders, that is, do you live within a restricted area?

MR. OGAWA. My home is in a restricted zone.

MR. SPARKMAN. Not in a prohibited zone?

MR. OGAWA. Well, I am in the north of University Avenue and west of Grove Street [Berkeley].

MR. SPARKMAN. Are you going to be required to move out tomorrow, day after tomorrow?

Mr. Ogawa. I haven't heard anything like that yet.

Dr. Lamb. You are in the curfew zone, aren't you?

Mr. Ogawa. I don't know just how it is.

Mr. Sparkman. There is no order that applies to you as yet?

Mr. Ogawa. No.

Mr. Sparkman. You simply anticipate that there may be some order later?

Mr. Ogawa. If it comes through; yes.

Mr. Sparkman. Is there any likelihood of your losing your job?

Mr. Ogawa. The dark cloud seems to be hanging before me now and I may lose my job tomorrow, or at least in a very short time.

Mr. Sparkman. No one has actually told you so?

Mr. Ogawa. I was called into the office last Thursday afternoon and I was surprised to hear that my services were no longer needed at the Moore Shipyard. . . .

Mr. Arnold. We have two witnesses next, Mr. Kunitani and Mr. Iiyama, appearing in behalf of the Nisei Democratic Club of Oakland.

The committee will be glad to have you proceed in as brief a manner as you can. I have no questions. Just make your own statement. . . .

Mr. Iiyama. We were organized during the 1938 campaign, and the purpose of our organization was to bring about democratic education of Nisei Japanese and also action in the political field.

Our members are Young Democrats. We have approximately 50 members now.

Mr. Sparkman. Is your organization opposed to Republicans or any other political party?

Mr. Iiyama. We were affiliated with the Young Democrats, Inc., of California . . . until the Young Democrats split, and although we are not members of the organization now we are still Young Democrats.

The Chairman. You don't mean to tell the committee that Democrats ever split, do you?

MR. IIYAMA.   There was some difference, I believe. . . .

MR. KUNITANI.   . . . We come here as Americans, not by virtue of our birth in America, but by virtue of the social and cultural forces in America. We come here to be treated as Americans and we want to live as Americans in America.

As I say, we are Americans, not by the mere technicality of birth, but by all the other forces of sports, amusements, schools, churches, which are in our communities and which affect our lives directly.

Some of us are Yankee fans; some of us are Dodger fans; some like to sip beer; some like to go up to the Top of the Mark once in a while; we enjoy Jack Benny; we listen to Beethoven, and some of us even go through the Congressional Record. That is something.

The main idea that our group wanted to present here today was that we didn't want to be treated as a special group of enemy aliens and as descendants of enemy aliens. We want to be treated as Americans, or as other groups, such as Italians, Yugoslavs, or Finns.

It seems that among the reasons put forth by the committee, and the witnesses who testified this morning, and last Saturday, on why they thought that we should be treated as a special group were the following:

No. 1. Our physical characteristics.

No. 2. The question of dual citizenship.

No. 3. The vague question of Shintoism and national religion.

No. 4. The question of the language schools which many of us have attended.

Our group is in favor of evacuation if the military authorities of the United States deem it necessary. But if we do evacuate we think certain considerations should be taken into account:

No. 1. If we are evacuated we would like to have food, shelter, and clothing, whether it be in North Dakota, Arizona, or Florida.

No. 2. We think some plan should be instituted so that the evacuees can participate positively in the defense effort and that we can, by our efforts in some way help gain a quicker victory for the anti-Fascist forces.

No. 3. We want the evacuees who are in the various professions, such as doctors, opticians, lawyers, and so on, to continue to act in that capacity.

I would like to touch on the question of loyalty. There has been a hue and cry by a lot of the people in California that there has been no anti-Fascist action on the part of any Japanese group. I would like to refute that statement right here and now.

Our organization, since the Democratic campaign of 1938, has come out on numerous occasions against shipments of oil and scrap iron to the Fascist war lords of Japan, and we opposed aggression in Ethiopia. Our records are filled with communications to our Congressmen, even to our Representative, who happens to be Mr. Tolan, urging them to vote against such measures in Congress.

I want to touch upon the question of the language schools. I would like to point out to the members of the committee that our parents, most of them, have had very little education. You will find in any group, whether they be Jews, Yugoslavs, Finns, Danes, or Japanese, that the people who do migrate to other lands are usually those who have not had economic security in their native lands and, therefore, have come to new areas in order to gain a livelihood. Most of our parents fall into that category.

They set up these language schools for various reasons.

No. 1. They thought that since they enjoyed the fruits of American life that they should contribute something to America. They thought that the fine parts of Japanese culture could be integrated into American life and that the second generation of Japanese, if they were able to read and write, could thereby discover the better side of Japanese culture and they could give that as their contribution to America and, if they could do that, the parents would die happy.

No. 2. This so-called indoctrination on the part of our parents hasn't been only along Japanese lines, but it has also followed American lines. We had 500 students registered at the University of California last semester. That is the largest enrollment of any minority group in the State of California. The record will also show a large number of Japanese students attending universities and high schools.

There is another reason why a study of the Japanese language is encouraged and that is because a knowledge of the Japanese language is essential to the economic picture into which the Japanese man or woman has to fit. At least, in this generation most of our employers happen to be Japanese.

We were discriminated against in private industry and, therefore, the only other channel into which the Japanese people could gain an economic livelihood was in the Japanese group. It was essential for us to learn the Japanese language so that we could converse intelligently with our employers.

Another point that I want to bring out is that there aren't very many Japanese in the civil service of the Federal Government, or in the State and local governments. That those who are working for the Federal Government are in there because they are discriminated against in private industry. It is usually in the case of professional workers rather than, we will say, those who fall in the category of laborers.

Another point I want to bring out is that the time spent in language schools amounts to about an hour a day, maybe two or three times a week.

Most of the time of the Japanese student is spent in the public schools. He spends from 6 to 8 hours in public schools. After school he goes into the extra-curricular activity of the public schools. His Sundays and Saturdays are taken up by participation in athletic events, Boy Scout activities, and such.

The time element there is not present in which the young Japanese could be indoctrinated with Shintoism or anything else.

MR. ARNOLD.   What is taught in those language schools?

MR. KUNITANI.   I went to a Japanese language school for about 4 years. I did not like to go at all. I went home and told my mother I had attended school when, as a matter of fact on some occasions I had not. She said, "What did you do?"

I lied, and said, "I did this and I did that."

I memorized a couple of poems. I knew that Yokohama was so

many miles away from Tokyo. I learned something about geography. There was nothing indoctrinating me in the worship of my ancestors, or anything like that. I didn't go high enough to learn what they taught in the higher grades. I just went to the equivalent of about the third grade in the Japanese school. Even then I attended only haphazardly.

My case, I think, is typical of most of the Japanese who attend Japanese language schools. . . .

Now, I want to touch on the question of dual citizenship. I do not know very much about its history and background, but I can present my case in point.

I didn't even know that I was a citizen of Japan until I was about 17 years old, and a freshman in college. My father happened to tell me that I was a citizen of Japan. Therefore, I went through the legal channels and expatriated myself.

MR. ARNOLD. You expatriated yourself as a Japanese?

MR. KUNITANI. Yes.

MR. ARNOLD. You have renounced your Japanese citizenship?

MR. KUNITANI. Yes, sir.

MR. ARNOLD. How did you do it?

MR. KUNITANI. The only legal channel set up at that time was to renounce your citizenship through the medium of the Japanese consulate. They sent some papers to my father's prefecture and they crossed my name off the record, or something like that.

I have a record of all that at home, but it is all in Japanese and it would have to be translated.

Another thing I would like to point out to the members of the committee is the indivisibility of citizenship in the eyes of American law. If we are citizens here that is enough. I don't think all this cry about the question of dual citizenship is that important. I mean it doesn't play a major role in our lives.

Another thing in connection with dual citizenship that I would like to point out is that since the only other channel of expatriation has been closed to us by the closing of Japanese consulates, we favor the bill which was before Congress which provides that legal means be set up so that Japanese who have dual citizenship could expatriate themselves through American courts. Our organization is in favor of such a measure and we have written to our Congressman to support it.

Another thing I would like to point out, and it is probably a question you would ask me, is this: What about the recent raids by the F. B. I., when they found thousands of rounds of ammunition, sabers, binoculars, flashlights, and what not, in some of the homes, after the date set for turning in such contraband?

Our answer to that question is this: That our organization has instructed its members many times to tell their friends, and their parents, to surrender such things. I think most Japanese people have done this, and have carried out the regulation of the Department of Justice and the War Department in that connection. . . .

Another point I want to bring out is about Pearl Harbor. We hear lots about sabotage at Pearl Harbor.

Mr. Tolan pointed out frequently this morning, and this afternoon, that he heard of Army trucks put in the road. I don't know where Mr. Tolan got that information. I don't know whether that is true or not. I cannot say. I can only go on the Roberts report, which was the only official United States document put out, as to what happened at Pearl Harbor, and why things happened as they did. I think if you gentlemen look into the Roberts report again you will find that no mention was made of sabotage on the part of Japanese-Americans. They pointed out that 200 members operating out of the Japanese consulate were the most active participants in fifth column activities in Hawaii.

I mean to say the average Japanese in California isn't intelligent enough to go about and engage in fifth column activities. The odds are against him. He has an oriental face that can be easily detected.

I am not saying there wasn't any fifth column activity in Pearl Harbor on the part of Japanese, but I don't think there was wholesale fifth column activity on the part of the Japanese-Americans or the aliens in Pearl Harbor.

THE CHAIRMAN. You don't want to leave the impression that Japanese are not smart, do you?

MR. KUNITANI.   No, not that. I think some of them are alert and intelligent.

THE CHAIRMAN.   Did you read the report of Secretary Knox about sabotage in Pearl Harbor?

MR. KUNITANI.   As I said before, the only report that I could believe, as a citizen, is the official report of the Government, and that was the Roberts report.

I think President Roosevelt said in his press conference the other day, when asked by Pearson, and some of the other reporters, if it were not true that even the Spaniards and Arabs knew about what happened at Pearl Harbor, his answer was, "Complete rot," and he spelled out r-o-t. That is the report I got. As far as our organization is concerned, it is standing by the only official report put out by the United States Government, which is the Roberts committee report. . . .

Our organization has a definite plan as to what should be done about such cases if evacuation is to be instituted here in California.

No. 1. Our prime purpose is that we should not be treated any differently than Italians, Germans, Finns, or Yugoslavs. We want to be treated equally.

No. 2. We think that the Federal authorities should handle such cases. We don't believe that local authorities have the time, or the money, to set up agencies to take care of such cases.

We believe that the Federal Security Administration, under the able direction of Paul G. McNutt, should take the matter into its hands. I don't think the Army and Navy should do it. They have a big fight on their hands outside. I think they would be willing to let civilian bureaus handle this job of hardship cases. We think that the United States Employment Service, or the State social security board, should take such cases and deal with them.

I do not think any individual in America has any idea as to the numerous problems which will arise when you transplant a whole economy from one area to another. There are so many variables involved that I do not think anybody could begin to comprehend them.

We have tried to point out what, in our opinion, should be done. . . .

MR. ARNOLD. I might ask Mrs. Kunitani the same question I asked an Italian lady this morning.

Is your husband a 100 percent loyal American?

MRS. KUNITANI. He is a Democrat and has been ever since I have known him. Does that make him a 100-percent American?

MR. KUNITANI. That puts me on the spot.

THE CHAIRMAN. Do you think that the Democrats alone can win the war in this country?

MRS. KUNITANI. Not necessarily.

MR. ARNOLD. As one Democrat to another, I want to commend you—

MRS. KUNITANI (interposing). I might tell you it was on the basis of his anti-Fascist activities that I met him and married him.

THE CHAIRMAN. Are you sorry?

MRS. KUNITANI. Not as yet.

MR. ARNOLD. Does that include anti-Japanese activity?

MRS. KUNITANI. Oh, yes. We don't discriminate among the Fascists.

MR. ARNOLD. Japan became a member of the Axis after Italy did.

MRS. KUNITANI. Yes. I want to bring out the fact that both the president of our organization and my husband have been to Japan and their reaction to what they saw there in the way of military activity did not affect them favorably. It had just the opposite effect. It was because of what they saw there that they have become especially ardent in championing the cause against the Axis Powers.

MR. ARNOLD. I think perhaps your statement has more effect in the record than what these two gentlemen have said.

MRS. KUNITANI. I think you are prejudiced.

THE CHAIRMAN. Well, a woman must always have the last word.

What do you think about this proposition: Do you think the United States today is more in danger of sabotage from Germans and Italians than it is from Japanese?

MRS. KUNITANI.   No; I wouldn't say that they are in greater danger. But I think there is just as much danger. Of course, here on the Pacific coast I think everyone has a tendency to be prejudiced more against the Japanese as a potential saboteur than against the others, because the danger seems more imminent.

As my husband stated, we feel we would be perfectly willing to abide by the regulations set down by the Federal Government, provided they are set down with equality toward all of these descendants of Axis aliens.

Another thing we forgot to mention is the fact that in our own membership we have had people who actually reported fifth-column activity. I don't care to divulge the names in public, but if you care to have them—

THE CHAIRMAN.   Reports against Japanese fifth columnists?

MRS. KUNITANI.   Yes.

THE CHAIRMAN.   Then there are some fifth-column Japanese?

MRS. KUNITANI.   Yes—if not actual fifth-column activity, there are people who have definite pro-Japanese sympathies.

MR. KUNITANI.   I think that the Army and Navy Intelligence, and the F. B. I. have known that for a long time. I wouldn't say at the present time there aren't foreign agents here. I think there are lots of them here, as well as native agents—I mean people who are Americans and who would like to see our country defeated. This question of fascism is not delegated to one country or to one race. It is universal, a universal pattern. . . .

PART SEVEN

The Self-Determination of Nations

30. Louis D. Brandeis

Your loyalty to America should lead you to support the Zionist cause

The outbreak of World War I heightened the interest of America's immigrants—particularly those linked to Europe's minority nationalities —in the fate of their kinsmen. Indeed, their concern for their homelands legitimized their position in the United States. Like other immigrants, American Jews were concerned for the minority rights of their co-religionists in Eastern Europe, but they were equally determined that a Jewish homeland be established in Palestine, so that Jews would be like other nations and that the Zionist aspiration would be honored as well. The hapless position of the Jews of Eastern Europe massed in the war zone intensified the Zionist impulse to redeem the ancient homeland.

No one was more sensitive to the demands of the times than was the newly chosen leader of America's Zionists. For Louis D. Brandeis (1856–1941), known as the "People's Attorney," Zionism came to represent in Jewish life what Progressivism did in general American life. His appointment to the Supreme Court in 1916 by President Wilson, the first Jew to be elevated to the nation's highest tribunal, confirmed his position as a major figure in American political life. His unimpeachable American credentials, great prestige, and organizational and intellectual gifts assured Zionists and all minority leaders that their cause was both just and patriotic.

Brandeis's address of 1915 became the classic American statement identifying Zionism with Americanism and was widely distributed in pamphlet form. In 1917, shortly after the United States declared war, Arthur Balfour came to Washington to coordinate the war effort. There, the British Foreign Minister discussed the future of Palestine with the Supreme Court Justice. On November 2, 1917, the Balfour Declaration was issued, with American approval, favoring "the establishment in Palestine of a national home for the Jewish people."

Louis D. Brandeis, "Zionism and Patriotism" (New York: Federation of American Zionists, 1915), pp. 1–4, 7. Reprinted by permission of Brandeis's daughters.

During most of my life my contact with Jews and Judaism was slight, and I gave little thought to their problems save by asking myself from time to time whether we were showing by our lives due appreciation of the opportunities which this hospitable country affords. My approach to Zionism was through Americanism. Practical experience and observation convinced me that to be good Americans, we must be better Jews, and to be better Jews we must be Zionists.

Lest there be misunderstanding, let me state at the outset what Zionism is and what it is not.

It is not a movement to remove all the Jews of the world compulsorily to Palestine. In the first place there are 14,000,000 Jews, and Palestine would not accommodate more than one-fifth of that number. In the second place, it is not a movement to compel anyone to go to Palestine. It is essentially a movement to give to the Jew more, not less freedom,—it aims to enable the Jews to exercise the same right now exercised by practically every other people in the world: to live at their option either in the land of their fathers or in some other country; a right which members of small nations as well as of large,—which Irish, Greek, Bulgarian, Servian, or Belgian, may now exercise as fully as Germans or English.

Furthermore, Zionism is not a movement to wrest from the Ottoman the sovereignty of Palestine. Palestine merely seeks to establish in Palestine, as part of the Turkish Empire, for such Jews as choose to go and remain there, and for their descendants, a legally secured home, where they may live together and lead a Jewish life; where they may expect ultimately to constitute a majority of the population, and may look forward to what we should call home rule.

Since the destruction of the Temple, nearly two thousand years ago, the longing for Palestine has been ever present with the Jew. It was the hope of a return to the land of his fathers that buoyed up the Jew amidst persecution, and for the realization of which the devout ever prayed. Until a generation ago this was a hope merely—a wish piously prayed for but not worked for. The Zionist movement is idealistic, but essentially practical. It seeks to realize that hope, to make the dream of a Jewish life in a Jewish land come true as other great dreams of the world have been realized—by men working with devotion, intelligence, and self-sacrifice. It was thus the dream of Italian independence and unity, after centuries of vain hope, came true through the efforts of Mazzini, Garibaldi and Cavour; that the dream of home rule in Ireland has just been realized; that the dream of Greek, of Bulgarian and of Servian independence became facts.

The rebirth of the Jewish nation is no longer a mere dream. It is in process of accomplishment in a most practical way; and the story is a most wonderful one. A generation ago a few Jewish emigrants from Russia and from Roumania, instead of proceeding Westward to this hospitable country where they might easily have secured material prosperity, turned Eastward for the purpose of settling in the land of their fathers. They came from countries where the Jews were persecuted and subjected to the gravest injustice; but the desire to avoid persecution and injustice was not the main cause of their settling in Palestine. Some of them were devoutly orthodox; but religious devotion was not the main cause of their settling in Palestine. They went to Palestine because they were convinced that the undying longing of Jews for Palestine was a fact of deepest significance; that it was a manifestation in the struggle for existence by an ancient people which had established its right to live—a people whose three thousand years of civilization had produced a faith, culture, and individuality which enable them to contribute largely in the future, as they had in the past, to the advance of civilization; and that it was not a right view, that it was not a right merely, but a duty of the Jewish nation to survive and develop.

These new Pilgrim Fathers sought, therefore, to restore in the land of their fathers the Jewish national life. They believed that there only could Jewish life be protected from the forces of disintegration; that there alone could the Jewish spirit reach its full and natural development; and that by securing for those Jews who wish to settle in Palestine the opportunity to do so, not only those Jews, but all other Jews would be benefited and that the long perplexing Jewish problem would at last, find solution.

To the worldly wise these efforts at colonization appeared very foolish. Nature and man presented obstacles in Palestine which appeared to them insuperable; the colonists were in fact ill-equipped for their task, save in their spirit of devotion and self-sacrifice. The land, harassed by centuries of misrule, was treeless and apparently sterile; and it was infested with malaria. The Government offered them no security, either as to life or property. The colonists themselves were not only unfamiliar with the character of the country, but were ignorant of the farmer's life which they proposed to lead; for the Jews of Russia and Roumania had been generally denied the opportunity of owning or working land. Furthermore, these colonists were not inured to the physical hardships to which the life of a pioneer is necessarily subjected. To these hardships and to malaria the men succumbed. Those who survived were long confronted with failure. But at last success came. Within a generation these Jewish Pilgrim Fathers, and those who followed them, had succeeded in establishing these two fundamental propositions:

First—That Palestine is fit for the modern Jew.

Second—That the modern Jew is fit for Palestine.

This land, then treeless and supposed to be sterile and hopelessly arid, has been shown to have been treeless and sterile only because of man's misrule. It has been shown to be capable of becoming again a land "flowing with milk and honey." Oranges and grapes, olives and almonds, wheat and other cereals are now growing there in profusion. Those who undertake to describe Palestine are apt to speak of it as a miniature California, in its climate, its topography and its agricultural possibilities. Others have compared it with Sicily—long the granary of Rome.

Much patience and perseverance and faith have been required to develop these possibilities in Palestine; and very much remains to be done to make the life of the Jewish settler what it should be. But the commercial test has been made. The progress is obvious to every traveller; and it may already be measured in statistics. In a single generation the export of oranges increased from 60,000 boxes to 1,500,000 and in recent years the groves have been so largely extended that exports to twice this amount are expected within a few years when these trees shall begin to bear fruit. The grape, the almond and the olive culture have prospered likewise, and there are important exports of wheat and other cereals.

This material development has been attended by a spiritual and social development no less extraordinary; a development in education, in health and in social order; and in the character and habits of the population. Perhaps the most extraordinary achievement of Jewish nationalism is the revival of the Hebrew Language, which has again become a language of the common intercourse of men. The Hebrew tongue, called a dead language for nearly two thousand years, has, in the Jewish colonies and in Jerusalem, become again the living mother-tongue. The effect of this common language in unifying the Jews is, of course, great; for the Jews of Palestine came literally from all the lands of the earth, each speaking, except for the use of Yiddish, the language of the country from which he came, and remaining, in the main, almost a stranger to the others.

But the effect of the renaissance of the Hebrew tongue is far greater than that of unifying the Jews. It is a potent factor in reviving the essentially Jewish spirit. It was a bold dream to plan the foundation of a new Jewish nation in Palestine by giving a common language to the natives of so many lands, particularly so when it is remembered that the language, long called dead, had not only to be introduced, but to be adapted to modern use. Yet this has actually been accomplished, in a single generation; and the man who took the first practical step, Eliezer Ben Jehuda—is still in Jerusalem, engaged in furthering the work.

Ben Jehuda's story will have a place in history. In 1880, living comfortably in Paris, he wrote an article for a Jerusalem paper, demanding that Hebrew become the language of intercourse in the Talmud Torahs and Yeshibahs of Palestine. The editor of the paper in which that article was published spoke of the proposition as "a pious wish;" but Ben Jehuda was not content that it should remain a wish. He proposed that the wish become a fact, so he went to Palestine himself. He conducted [sic] that if Hebrew was to become a spoken language, the way to begin with Hebrew, as with charity, was at home. He said he would marry no woman who did not speak Hebrew fluently. Fortunately, he found one who could; and Hebrew became the language of his own household. Then he declared that he would deal only with those who could speak Hebrew. He was naturally regarded as half-crazy. But soon others followed his example!

And before a generation had passed, Hebrew became the language of kindergartens, of primary schools and of higher institutions of learning. Daily papers and magazines are now published, public lectures are delivered and plays performed in Hebrew. Many were the parents who learned Hebrew from their children! and there are instances also of non-Jews learning Hebrew in order to avail themselves of the advantages offered by the Hebrew educational and cultural institutions.

It was no ordinary sense of piety that made Ben Jehuda seek to introduce the Hebrew language. He recognized what the leaders of other peoples, seeking re-birth and independence, have recognized: that it is through the national language expressing the people's soul that the national spirit is aroused and the national power restored. In spite of the prevalence of the English tongue in Ireland, the revival of Gaelic was one of the most important factors in the movement which has just resulted in securing for the Irish their long-coveted home rule. The revival of Flemish was a potent factor in the re-birth of the Belgian people, who have now given such good account of themselves. And so it was with the revival of Greek, of Bulgarian and of Servian.

The intensity of conviction and the devotion which the revival of Hebrew has developed was shown in the struggle for its maintenance last year (1914) in the Palestinian schools. Believing that an effort was being made to supersede it in some of the schools, practically every teacher—two hundred in all—struck, giving up their only means of livelihood rather than submit to the impairment of the position of the Hebrew language. Pupils followed teachers, and parents aided by others in the community willingly faced, despite their poverty, the burden of establishing new national schools, so that their new-old national language might predominate. This is stuff out of which nations can be built! . . .

There is one other consideration to which the Jews of America should give thought. Though the result of this war should be as we hope, the removal or lessening of the disabilities under which the Jews labour in Eastern Europe, nevertheless, when peace comes, emigration from the war-stricken countries will certainly proceed in large volume, because of the misery incident to the war's devastation. More than one-half of the Jews of the whole world live in that territory near the western frontier of Russia, which has become one of the two vast battlefields of the nations. Is it desirable that America should be practically the only country to which the Jews of Eastern Europe may emigrate? Is it not desirable that Palestine should give a special welcome to the Jews, as the Zionists propose?

I am impelled all the more to ask for your support, both moral and financial, because at this critical juncture we should all stand together, so that when the occasion arises, we may be of lasting service to our people. Now is not the time to foreshadow the policy which we should engage upon. But when the nations approach peace, the Jews of America, if united, may be factors in obtaining for the Jews of the other parts of the world something more real than promises of amelioration; something more lasting than philanthropy. And this greater undertaking depends upon the readiness with which you rally in every possible form to the cause.

Your loyalty to America, your loyalty to Judaism, should lead you to support the Zionist cause.

31. THOMAS G. MASARYK

Our American colonies contributed to our conquest of freedom

From Thomas Garrigue Masaryk, *The Making of a State: Memories and Observations 1914–1918*, an English version, arranged and prepared with an introduction by Henry Wickham Steed (New York: Frederick A. Stokes, 1927), pp. 218–20, 224. Reprinted by permission of Violet S. Steed.

No new state so brilliantly exemplified the ideals of political and cultural justice as did the new Czechoslovakia. With its Czech, Slovak, Hungarian, German, and Ruthenian minorities, it came to represent the model political and ethnic democracy. The first president of the Czechoslovak republic, Thomas Garrigue Masaryk (1850–1937), came to be regarded as the foremost creative statesman of the new Europe. Born in Moravia of peasant stock, Masaryk attained fame as a philosopher and historian at the University of Prague. Throughout the Slavic world, this "lonely Slovak," who seemed a combination of Leo Tolstoy and Walt Whitman, inspired the younger generation.

A close student of American democracy, Masaryk visited the United States for the first time in 1878. After marrying an American, he returned there many times and in 1902 lectured at the University of Chicago. In 1907, upon his reelection to the Austrian Parliament, he became an outstanding figure in public life and revisited Chicago—next to Prague, the city with the greatest number of Czechs in the world. With the outbreak of World War I, Masaryk fled Austria to begin abroad the fight for national liberation. On May 5, 1918, at Chicago's Northwestern Station, one hundred thousand Czechs and Slovaks greeted Masaryk in an unprecedented welcome. Although the Czechs and Slovaks in the United States had organized to make their demands for national independence known to other Americans, not until the coming of Masaryk did the full significance of their self-determination become apparent.

In *The Making of a State*, Masaryk left a detailed record of the great international effort that was required to achieve his goal. These excerpts focus on his American visit, his role as president of the Mid-European Democratic Union, and his American strategy for recasting the map of Central and Eastern Europe so as to liberate its peoples.

. . . We left Vancouver on April 30 [1914], traveling through Western Canada to Chicago and breaking the journey at St. Paul so that I might see my fellow-countrymen, many of whom I had met there before. Chicago was reached on May 5. Here a new phase of activity began—and on a big scale from the start.

After the American fashion, our people in Chicago had arranged a spectacular reception for me. Next to Prague, Chicago was the largest Czech city in the world and it was also the center of our financial organization. It was the home of Mr. Štěpina whom I had begun to bombard with appeals for money as soon as I got to Venice at the end of 1914; of Dr. Fisher, the head of the Czech Alliance; and of Vojta Beneš (a brother of Dr. Beneš) who had gone the round of our colonies in America to collect the funds for our liberation. Our people had managed to win the goodwill of practically the whole of Chicago, the Americans as well as the Slavs. From the railway station to the hotel there was a huge procession; the city was beflagged with Czech and Slav colors; and during the procession English and Czech speeches were made in the streets. The reception was splendid and served as an example for other cities with Czech and Slovak colonies. It was followed by a number of meetings, great and small, Czech and Czecho-American. Towards the end of May, I had to return to Chicago in order to hold meetings of our various organizations. Then I spoke at the University, in the Press Club and elsewhere. At Chicago University I had already lectured in 1902, when I had made many friends among the Czechs and Americans; and Mr. Judson, now President of the University, had helped me very liberally.

Receptions and meetings like those at Chicago took place later on in New York, Boston, Baltimore, Cleveland, Pittsburgh and Washington. Everywhere things were so organized as to arouse American interest. Our national costumes, colors and emblems and the artistic arrangement of the processions were pleasing and drew the attention of the masses to our movement for independence. Before the war I used to denounce "flag-wagging"; but, in America, I realized that in so doing I had overshot the mark. Professor as I then was, I had failed to see that a well-organized procession may be worth quite as much as an ostensibly world-shaking political article or a speech in Parliament. During the Chicago procession I well remember thinking of the well-known British preacher, Spurgeon, who said he would be willing to stand on his head if, by so doing, he could call attention to a good cause—this in a church, then why not in the street?

At first there had been personal and political dissensions in our American colonies as elsewhere. America was then neutral; and German, Austrian and Magyar influences were strong. Some of

our people distrusted the revolutionary character of our movement and among them were quite a number of pro-Austrians. But
our movement made headway, the leadership of the National
Council was recognized, the pro-Austrians no longer carried
weight, and though the Dürich affair caused some excitement no
political damage was done. Naturally our colonies were greatly
and, in many cases, decisively influenced by the American
declaration of war on Germany on April 6, 1917. Then doubts
disappeared and unanimity prevailed, as the collections for our
funds testified.

Two consequences deserve special mention. The first was that
our Catholics went hand in hand with our "Freethinkers" and
Socialists—so strong was the unifying force of the movement for
liberation, as those will appreciate who know what the relations
between the Catholics and the non-Catholics had been before. . . .

The other weighty consequence lay in the negotiations at
Pittsburgh between Czechs and Slovaks. There, on June 30, 1918,
I signed the Convention (the "Czechoslovak Convention"—not
Treaty) between the Slovaks and the Czechs of America. It was
concluded in order to appease a small Slovak faction which was
dreaming of God knows what sort of independence for Slovakia,
since the ideas of some Russian Slavophils, and of Štúr[1] and
Hurban-Vajanský,[2] had taken root even among the American
Slovaks. . . . From the beginning of the war they [Czech and
Slovak colonies in America] engaged in political propaganda and,
through their organizations, exercised considerable influence upon
the American public—an influence the more important because
America remained neutral for two and a half years. In 1916 our
"National Alliance" in America issued a manifesto explanatory of
our struggle for freedom. In May 1917 it and the "Slovak League"
presented to President Wilson, through the intermediary of

1. Ludevit Štúr (1815–1856), a Slovak Protestant leader and writer who organized the Slovak Protestants as a party in 1844, and helped to establish Slovak as
a literary language.

2. Svetozar Hurban-Vajanský (1847–1916), a Russophil Slovak poet and writer
who had been influenced by the works of Štúr.

Colonel House, a memorandum setting forth our political aspirations; and in February 1918 a further memorandum put the Foreign Relations Committee of the Senate on its guard against Austrian promises of autonomy. On May 25, 1917, Mr. Kenyon, the Senator of Iowa, whose goodwill our people had won, moved a resolution demanding the liberation of the Czechs and Slovaks as a condition of peace; and a year later (May 31, 1918) Mr. King, Senator for Utah, put forward the same demand. In this way and by organizing numerous public lectures and meetings, our American colonies contributed politically as well as financially to our conquest of freedom—politically, perhaps, even more than financially. After I reached Washington our "National Alliance" induced Congress, on June 29, so to amend the Immigration Law that, like the American volunteers who had joined the Allied armies, our Legionaries should be allowed to return unhindered to the United States.

32. EAMON DE VALERA

Ireland's title to self-determination on the basis of American principles

More than that of any other people, the Irish commitment to self-determination and independence had been associated with the American spirit of '76. Both Ireland and the Thirteen Colonies had been dependencies of the British Empire at the time of the American Revolution, and Ireland never forgot the American example. Although Woodrow Wilson recognized that Ireland represented "the outstanding case of the small nationality," he found it impossible to deal with the Irish question in the terms that had been broadcast for Europe's other nationalities.

Eamon De Valera (1882–1975), was President of Sinn Fein, 1917–1921; President of the Irish Republic, 1919–1922; founder and President

From Eamon De Valera, *Ireland's Request to the Government of the United States of America For Recognition as a Sovereign Independent State* (Washington: Irish Diplomatic Mission, 1920), pp. 3–6, 10, 20–21.

of Fianna Fail, 1926–1959; and first prime minister of the Irish Free State
when it adopted the name of Eire in 1938, and subsequently its president.
More than any other person, he has been identified with the Irish cause.
Born in New York City, he was the son of an Irish mother and a Spanish
father, who died when he was not yet three years old. Young Edward,
whose name was changed to its Gaelic equivalent, Eamon, was sent to
live with his grandmother in Limerick, Ireland. While at the National
University of Ireland, where he became a brilliant mathematician, he
learned Gaelic, became a nationalist and revolutionary, and in 1916
became a leader of the Easter Rebellion. Of the leaders of the rebellion,
De Valera was one of the few to elude execution. After a sensational
escape from prison, he made a whirlwind tour of the United States in
1919 and 1920 in an effort to gain recognition for the Irish Republic,
which culminated in a formal request calling for American recognition.

To His Excellency, The President of the United States

MR. PRESIDENT:

I have the honor on behalf of the people and Government of
Ireland to request from the United States Government the
recognition of the Republic of Ireland. In support of that request,
I beg to submit the following facts and considerations.

When the people of a nation have proved beyond question their
desire for an independent government of their own by the
civilized as well as decisive test of the ballot; when they have,
with scrupulous regard to propriety in method taken all the
measures necessary to establish such a government; and when,
having established it, they have, through voluntary acceptance of
that government's decrees and obedience to them, succeeded in
making it the *de facto* ruling authority of their country, functioning in every department of civil administration—no State which
denies them recognition can maintain at the same time that it
upholds the principle of "government by the consent of the
governed." Particularly is this true at this moment of history when
the greatest war of all time has just been fought to establish as
moral and political principles of universal application the rights
of nations great and small, to life, liberty, and the pursuit of
happiness, and,

the privilege of men everywhere to choose their way of life and obedience.

The people of Ireland are a people and the government of the Republic of Ireland is a government exactly such as described. Hence, as it is not to be believed that the United States would abandon the principle of "government by the consent of the governed," which has always been a fundamental guiding principle of its national policy, reiterated with special emphasis during the war by you, Sir, as the necessary basis of any peace which the United States would feel itself justified in guaranteeing, the people of Ireland and their government are confident that their claim to recognition will not be refused or ignored by the Government of the United States.

Summarized, the fundamental facts on which Ireland's claim is based are:

1. That the people of Ireland constitute a distinct and separate nation, ethnically, historically, and tested by every standard of political science; entitled therefore, to self-determination;

2. That Ireland never voluntarily accepted British domination and that that domination has been consistently challenged through the centuries;

3. That the people of Ireland in a general and regular parliamentary election, in effect a national plebiscite, held under British supervision (thus eliminating completely any question of illegitimate influences in favor of the Republic) declared unmistakably by an overwhelming majority, their desire to be an Independent Republic—which is, therefore, and ought to be accepted by other nations as Ireland's definite choice by self-determination;

4. That the people's representatives elected for the purpose and summoned to meet in a National Congress (Dail Eireann) duly met in public session in the nation's capital at Dublin, formally proclaimed Ireland's independence as a Republic, and notified its establishment as a Republic to all the nations of the world;

5. That the National Congress thus assembled elected and set up a government, which government is, on democratic principles,

the *de jure*, and has ever since been functioning in fact as the obeyed, *de facto* government of Ireland, entitled, therefore, to international recognition as the rightful and actual government of Ireland;

6. That the rival (British) authority in Ireland is an alien usurping authority, commanding neither the respect nor the obedience of the people of Ireland, unable even to maintain discipline among its own forces—ignored and "non-existent" save within the immediate shadow of the fortresses of the Army of Occupation, without a title, therefore, either in morality or in fact to recognition as the government of Ireland, unless, as President Cleveland expressed it, "the will of the military officer in temporary command of a particular district can be dignified as a species of government."

7. That the standards heretofore announced in principle and approved in practice by the United States, entitle Ireland to recognition from the United States.

In the face of indisputable facts such as these the right of self-determination would be but a "mere phrase" indeed were the Republican Government of Ireland now to be denied recognition.

Ireland a Nation

The people of Ireland undoubtedly constitute a nation—one of the oldest and most clearly defined in Europe. Their nation is not a nation merely—in the sense of modern political science it was a sovereign independent state for over a thousand years knowing no external master but moulding its own institutions to its own life in accordance with its own will.

The original Norman came as an invader and an aggressor, and down through the long seven centuries and one-half during which his successors have sought to secure their domination in Ireland the Irish have consistently challenged their authority and have resisted it with a courage and a perseverance for which there is no parallel in history. Neither Czecho-Slovakia nor Jugo-Slavia, nor Finland nor Armenia nor Poland itself, nor any of the other newly established states of Europe, whose independence is now rightly recognized, even approach the perfection of nationhood manifested by Ireland nor can their claim compare with Ireland's on other grounds. These nations, for instance, had no elected or organized government of their own to point to as Ireland has, ready to discharge the duties of a responsible government, not only, but actually discharging the most essential of them.

Ireland's Title to Self-Determination on the Basis of American Principles

The entry of the United States into the late war raised that struggle once for all from the slough of contending imperialisms to the level of a crusade for "the inviolable rights of peoples and mankind."

Long before the United States had declared war, you, Sir, had well expressed it, May 27, 1916, as the "passionate conviction of America" that

> . . . the principle of public right must henceforth take precedence over the individual interests of particular nations.
>
> . . . every people has a right to choose the sovereignty under which they shall live.
>
> . . . the world has a right to be free from every disturbance of its peace that has its origin in aggression and disregard of the rights of peoples and nations,

and as the war approached, you confirmed these views in a famous address to the Senate:

> . . . No peace can last or ought to last which does not recognize and accept the principle that governments derive all their just powers from the consent of the governed . . .

taking it for granted that statesmen everywhere were agreed that

> . . . henceforth inviolable security of life, of worship, of industrial and social development should be guaranteed to all peoples who have lived hitherto under the power of governments devoted to a faith and purpose hostile to their own,

and proposing that

> . . . no nation should seek to extend its polity over any other nation or people but that every people should be left free to determine its own polity, its own way of development unhindered, unthreatened, unafraid, the little along with the great and powerful,

concluding

> These are American principles, American policies. We could stand for no others. . . . They are the principles of mankind and must prevail.

These principles were the fundamental ones in the program with which you, Sir, went before the Nation. They are embodied as a plank in the platform of the Democratic Party, adopted in St. Louis in 1916, and were emphatically endorsed by the American people at the elections.

> We believe that every people has the right to choose the sovereignty under which it shall live; that the small states of the world have a right to enjoy from other nations the same respect for their sovereignty and for their territorial integrity that great and powerful nations expect and insist upon; and that the world has a right to be free from every disturbance of its peace that has its origin in aggression or disregard of the rights of peoples and nations. At the earliest practical opportunity our country should strive earnestly . . . that all men shall enjoy equality of right and freedom . . . in the lands wherein they dwell.

The responsible spokesman of the American people had in these words made clear to the masses everywhere that their thought was also his thought, and they knew that America's President, proclaiming such principles and with the will to realize them, backed by America's might, could achieve the common ideal, could, in the conditions prevailing, really reform the world and reconstruct it on a basis of justice, bringing to war-weary and harassed humanity the secure and lasting peace for which it yearned. . . .

England's Pleas

Britain claims national self-determination was not intended to apply to nations like Ireland, because Ireland had been for a long time in the British political system—but Czecho-Slovakia had long been in the political system of Austria, and Poland in the political systems of Germany, Austria, and Russia. Self-determination was obviously not meant for the free nations who already had it, but principally for such nations as Ireland "held in forced bondage by powerful imperial neighbors." England's hold on Ireland in the past has been maintained by force alone, and by force is maintained whatever hold she has on Ireland today—by machine guns, aeroplanes, tanks, bayonets—not by the consent of the people.

England claims that the establishment of Ireland as an independent nation would be an act of "secession." Secession presupposes a previous voluntarily contracted union—there has been no such contract between Ireland and England. As shown in (Appendix) the methods by which the so-called "United Kingdom" was created, and the Act of "Union" passed were, as Gladstone puts it, "so foul and vile" that it has "no moral title to existence whatever." That union was simply, to use Lloyd George's own term, "the union of the grappling hook" or as Lord Byron puts it, the "union of the shark with its prey." The separation of Poland or Finland from its conquerors is not considered an act of secession.

Another form of the above pretence is that the Irish question is a domestic question for Britain—one for her alone to settle. The struggle of the American Colonies to obtain their freedom from England in 1776 was similarly claimed to be a "domestic question." But even before the Continental Congress sent Franklin, Adams, Dean, Lee and Dana to visit the courts of Europe to seek recognition, the American Revolution had ceased to be a "domestic question." Every foreign tyrant that has ever sought to be allowed to do as he wills with a subject people has claimed that the determination of his relations with them was purely a domestic question for himself. If the argument that Britain seeks to have applied to Ireland were accepted in the case of other countries, then Greece and other nations of the Near East would still be struggling with the Sultan, and the countries of Latin America still be subject to Spain. That Ireland is not in any real sense a domestic question for England has already been recognized by the people of America, by the Legislatures of many of its States, and by the House of Representatives and the Senate. . . .

To repudiate the evidence of the ballot, the most civilized method of declaring the national will, and to demand that, as a condition of recognition, the bullet be more effectively used, is to introduce into international relations an inhuman principle of immorality. Ireland's claim today, measured by all the moral and legal standards the United States has established since its infancy and measured by the moral principles upon which the greatest war in history was fought, is as strong as any additional bloodshed can make it. Further bloodshed would not more decisively prove the national will of the people of Ireland, but a refusal of recognition now would invite it.

Nor in requesting executive recognition at this time, do we ask you, Mr. President, to move far in advance of your people. Both branches of Congress have made manifest their will by recognizing that the case of Ireland was a proper one to be heard at the Peace Conference, and by expressing their sympathy with the Irish people's effort to establish a government of their own choice. We now ask you, in your capacity as spokesman and chief executive of the American people, to take executive notice of this action of Congress "as the Council associated with (you) in the final determination of (America's) international obligations." Ireland's right to independence has been already admitted, by implication, in the decision to exempt her nationals in the United States from the application of the British-American military service convention of March, 1918. Ireland merely asks that the implied recognition be now made explicit.

I have the honor, Mr. President, to avail myself of this opportunity to express the assurances of my profound consideration and esteem.

October 27, 1920.

> *Eamon De Valera*
> *President of the Republic of Ireland*

33. MARCUS GARVEY

Restore Africa to her scattered and abused children

The call to national self-determination that inspired Europe's minority peoples and their American immigrant cousins in the early twentieth century had a counterpart among people of African origin in the United States. When Marcus Garvey (1887–1940) arrived in New York from the West Indies in 1916, determined to establish a New York chapter of the Universal Negro Improvement Association, he could have chosen no more propitious time to gain an audience and a following. Rootless Negro migrants from the Southern states and the West Indies were waiting to respond to Garvey's vision of Negro "nationhood," of a noble black past, and a promising black future in an independent African republic.

A blueprint of black Zion offered a dream to those who were oppressed and starved for a sense of place and dignity in a time of mounting anti-Negro prejudice, violence, unemployment, and urban chaos. Indeed, it generated the first and greatest Negro mass movement in American history. If Garvey did not gain the millions of adherents that his admirers claimed, he did attract them by the hundreds of thousands. If the association's table of organization, titles, parades, uniforms, and general fanfare lent little more than festive pride to gray daily lives, the bracing rhetoric of the fierce black nationalist was overpowering in its effects.

Unfortunately, Garvey's business acumen failed to match his formidable forensic gifts and soon brought disaster to both leader and movement. But his influence endured. Garvey himself was never to set foot on the African continent, but Kwame Nkrumah and other leaders of the new African nations, as well as a new generation of black Americans, came to recognize him as the father of black nationalism and race pride, even though stirrings of black nationalism go back to the early days of the American republic. Garvey's keen sense of history was no better demonstrated than in his speech at Madison Square Garden in 1924, "In Honor of the Return to America of the Delegation Sent to Europe and Africa by the Universal Negro Improvement Association to Negotiate for the Repatriation of Negroes to a Homeland of Their Own in Africa."

Marcus Garvey, *Speech Before Negro Citizens of New York*, at Madison Square Garden, Sunday, March 16, 1924, at 4 o'clock, pp. 2–11. Reprinted by permission of Mrs. A. Jacques Garvey.

FELLOW CITIZENS:

The coming together, all over this country, of fully six million people of Negro blood, to work for the creation of a nation of their own in their motherland, Africa, is no joke.

There is now a world revival of thought and action which is causing peoples everywhere to bestir themselves towards their own security, through which we hear the cry of Ireland for the Irish, Palestine for the Jew, Egypt for the Egyptian, Asia for the Asiatic, and thus we Negroes raise the cry of Africa for the Africans, those at home and those abroad.

Some people are not disposed to give us credit for having feelings, passions, ambitions and desires like other races; they are satisfied to relegate us to the back-heap of human aspirations; but this is a mistake. The Almighty Creator made us men, not unlike others, but in His own image; hence, as a race, we feel that we, too, are entitled to the rights that are common to humanity.

The cry and desire for liberty is justifiable, and is made holy everywhere. It is sacred and holy to the Anglo-Saxon, Teuton and Latin; to the Anglo-American it precedes that of all religions, and now come the Irish, the Jew, the Egyptian, the Hindoo, and, last but not least, the Negro, clamoring for their share as well as their right to be free.

All men should be free—free to work out their own salvation. Free to create their own destinies. Free to nationally build by themselves for the up-bringing and rearing of a culture and civilization of their own. Jewish culture is different from Irish culture. Anglo-Saxon culture is unlike Teutonic culture. Asiatic culture differs greatly from European culture; and, in the same way, the world should be liberal enough to allow the Negro latitude to develop a culture of his own. Why should the Negro be lost among the other races and nations of the world and to himself? Did nature not make of him a son of the soil? Did the Creator not fashion him out of the dust of the earth?—out of that rich soil to which he bears such a wonderful resemblance?—a resemblance that changes not, even though the ages have flown? No, the Ethiopian cannot change his skin; and so we appeal to the conscience of the white world to yield us a place of national freedom among the creatures of present-day temporal materialism.

We Negroes are not asking the white man to turn Europe and America over to us. We are not asking the Asiatic to turn Asia over for the accommodation of the blacks. But we are asking a just and righteous world to restore Africa to her scattered and abused children.

We believe in justice and human love. If our rights are to be respected, then, we, too, must respect the rights of all mankind; hence, we are ever ready and willing to yield to the white man the things that are his, and we feel that he, too, when his conscience is touched, will yield to us the things that are ours.

We should like to see a peaceful, prosperous and progressive white race in America and Europe; a peaceful, prosperous and progressive yellow race in Asia, and, in like manner, we want, and we demand, a peaceful, prosperous and progressive black race in Africa. Is that asking too much? Surely not. Humanity, without any immediate human hope of racial oneness, has drifted apart, and is now divided into separate and distinct groups, each with its own ideals and aspirations. Thus, we cannot expect any one race to hold a monopoly of creation and be able to keep the rest satisfied.

From our distinct racial group idealism we feel that no black man is good enough to govern the white man, and no white man good enough to rule the black man; and so of all races and peoples. No one feels that the other, alien in race, is good enough to govern or rule to the exclusion of native racial rights. We may as well, therefore, face the question of superior and inferior races. In twentieth century civilization there are no inferior and superior races. There are backward peoples, but that does not make them inferior. As far as humanity goes, all men are equal, and especially where peoples are intelligent enough to know what they want. At this time all peoples know what they want—it is liberty. When a people have sense enough to know that they ought to be free, then they naturally become the equal of all in the higher calling of man to know and direct himself. It is true that economically and scientifically certain races are more progressive than others; but that does not imply superiority.

For the Anglo-Saxon to say that he is superior because he introduced gunpowder to destroy life, or the Teuton because he compounded liquid gas to outdo in the art of killing, and that the Negro is inferior because he is backward in that direction is to leave one's self open to the retort of "Thou shalt not kill" as being the divine law that sets the moral standard of the real man. There is no superiority in the one race economically monopolizing and holding all that would tend to the sustenance of life, and thus cause unhappiness and distress to others; for our highest purpose should be to love and care for each other and share with each other the things that our Heavenly Father has placed at our common disposal; and even in this the African is unsurpassed, in that he feeds his brother and shares with him the product of the land. The idea of race superiority is questionable; nevertheless, we must admit that, from the white man's standard, he is far superior to the rest of us, but that kind of superiority is too inhuman and dangerous to be permanently helpful. Such a superiority was shared and indulged in by other races before, and even by our own, when we boasted of a wonderful civilization on the banks of the Nile, when others were still groping in darkness; but because of our unrighteousness it failed, as all such will. Civilization can only last when we have reached the point where we will be our brother's keeper. That is to say, when we feel it righteous to live and let live.

Let no black man feel that he has the exclusive right to the world and other men none, and let no white man feel that way, either. The world is the property of all mankind, and each and every group is entitled to a portion. The black man now wants his, and in terms uncompromising he is asking for it.

The Universal Negro Improvement Association represents the hopes and aspirations of the awakened Negro. Our desire is for a place in the world; not to disturb the tranquillity of other men, but to lay down our burden and rest our weary backs and feet by the banks of the Niger, and sing our songs and chant our hymns to the God of Ethiopia. Yes, we want rest from the toil of the centuries, rest of political freedom, rest of economic and industrial liberty, rest to be socially free and unmolested, rest from lynching and burning, rest from discrimination of all kinds.

Out of slavery we have come with our tears and sorrows, and we now lay them at the feet of American white civilization. We cry to the considerate white people for help, because in their midst we can scarce help ourselves. We are strangers in a strange land. We cannot sing, we cannot play on our harps, for our hearts are sad. We are sad because of the tears of our mothers and the cry of our fathers. Have you not heard the plaintive wail? It is your father and my father burning at stake; but, thank God, there is a larger humanity growing among the good and considerate white people of this country, and they are going to help. They will help us to find and know ourselves. They will help us to recover our souls.

As children of captivity we look forward to a new day and a new, yet ever old, land of our fathers, the land of refuge, the land of the Prophets, the land of the Saints, and the land of God's crowning glory. We shall gather together our children, our treasures and our loved ones, and, as the children of Israel, by the command of God, face the promised land, so in time we shall also stretch forth our hands and bless our country.

Good and dear America that has succored us for three hundred years knows our story. We have watered her vegetation with our tears for two hundred and fifty years. We have built her cities and laid the foundation of her imperialism with the mortar of our blood and bones for three centuries, and now we cry to her for help. Help us, America, as we helped you. We helped you in the Revolutionary War. We helped you in the Civil War, and, although Lincoln helped us, the price is not half paid. We helped you in the Spanish-American War. We died nobly and courageously in Mexico, and did not we leave behind us on the stained battlefields of France and Flanders our rich blood to mark the poppies' bloom, and to bring back to you the glory of the flag that never touched the dust? We have no regrets in service to America for three hundred years, but we pray that America will help us for another fifty, until we have solved the troublesome problem that now confronts us. We know and realize that two ambitious and competitive races cannot live permanently side by side, without friction and trouble, and it is for that that the white race wants a white America and the black race wants and demands a black Africa.

Let white America help us for fifty years honestly as we have helped her for three hundred years, and before the expiration of many decades there shall be no more race problem. Help us to gradually go home, America. Help us as you have helped the Jews. Help us as you have helped the Irish. Help us as you have helped the Poles, Russians, Germans and Armenians.

The Universal Negro Improvement Association proposes a friendly co-operation with all honest movements seeking intelligently to solve the race problem. We are not seeking social equality; we do not seek intermarriage, nor do we hanker after the impossible. We want the right to have a country of our own, and there foster and re-establish a culture and civilization exclusively ours. Don't say it can't be done. The Pilgrims and colonists did it for America, and the new Negro, with sympathetic help, can do it for Africa.

The thoughtful and industrious of our race want to go back to Africa, because we realize it will be our only hope of permanent existence. We cannot all go in a day or year, ten or twenty. It will take time under the rule of modern economics to entirely or largely depopulate a country of a people who have been its residents for centuries, but we feel that, with proper help for fifty years, the problem can be solved. We do not want all the Negroes in Africa. Some are no good here, and naturally will be no good there. The no-good Negro will naturally die in fifty years. The Negro who is wrangling about and fighting for social equality will naturally pass away in fifty years, and yield his place to the progressive Negro who wants a society and country of his own.

Negroes are divided into two groups, the industrious and adventurous, and the lazy and dependent. The industrious and adventurous believe that whatsoever others have done it can do. The Universal Negro Improvement Association belongs to this group, and so you find us working, six million strong, to the goal of an independent nationality. Who will not help? Only the mean and despicable "who never to himself hath said, this is my own, my native land." Africa is the legitimate, moral and righteous home of all Negroes, and now, that the time is coming for all to assemble under their own vine and fig tree, we feel it our duty to arouse every Negro to a consciousness of himself.

White and black will learn to respect each other when they cease to be active competitors in the same countries for the same things in politics and society. Let them have countries of their own, wherein to aspire and climb without rancor. The races can be friendly and helpful to each other, but the laws of nature separate us to the extreme of each and every one developing by itself.

We want an atmosphere all our own. We would like to govern and rule ourselves and not be encumbered and restrained. We feel now just as the white race would feel if they were governed and ruled by the Chinese. If we live in our own districts, let us rule and govern those districts. If we have a majority in our communities, let us run those communities. We form a majority in Africa and we should naturally govern ourselves there. No man can govern another's house as well as himself. Let us have fair play. Let us have justice. This is the appeal we make to white America.

PART EIGHT

World Revolution

34. THE PROTOCOLS OF THE WISE MEN OF ZION

The great conspiracy of destruction threatening the peace of the world

After World War I, the Russian Revolution continued to stir New York's Lower East Side, hub of the great Russian immigration. The mounting hostility to everything that suggested cultural complexity, international unrest, or even moderate dissent inevitably turned America's Jews into an easy target of nativist agitation. The ancient bogie of the International Jew acquired an unusual potency. In this atmosphere, the prime anti-Semitic document of the early twentieth century gained wide currency in the United States, especially after a national folk hero, Henry Ford, contributed to its credibility and dissemination.

The Protocols of the Elders of Zion that gave popular form to the myth of a world Jewish conspiracy originated from remote superstitions that compounded demonology, sorcery, and ritual murder. Originally concocted around 1895 by the Tsarist secret police, the fabricated document did not gain much notice, even inside Russia, until the Bolshevik Revolution when the Protocols were distributed among the "white" armies to persuade the troops that they were engaged not in a civil war but in a holy struggle to liberate their country from the underground Jewish conspiracy, its quest for world dominion, and its scheme to promote financial monopoly, chaos, war, and revolution. Apocalyptic, labored, and diffuse, the twenty-four "Protocols" with prologue and epilogue ground out the plot, the incantations, and the sinister methods by which Jewish world control was to be achieved, Christianity subdued, and the future world state established.

In 1920 the Protocols were imported into the United States by Tsarist

From *Praemonitus Praemunitus, The Protocols of the Wise Men of Zion, Translated from the Russian to the English Language for the information of all True Americans to confound enemies of democracy and the Republic also to demonstrate the possible fulfillment of Biblical prophecy as to world domination by the Chosen People* (New York, Beckwith Company, 1920), pp. iii–iv, 9–17.

sympathizers and published in a full American edition. In May of that year they also began to appear in installments in Henry Ford's *Dearborn Independent* and were subsequently reprinted as *The International Jew,* gaining wide circulation. After seven years of silence, the credulous billionaire at last recanted publicly and apologized to the nation's Jews. But by then the Protocols had acquired a life of their own, the ready staple of peddlers of fear and suspicion, promoting the hallucination of a world Jewish conspiracy to foment world revolution. In the Hitlerian era, the reluctance of people to come to the aid of Jews in Europe was fed by the delusion that even if there were no Elders of Zion, Jews were uncanny, even in the pursuit of liberty and of their very lives.

Reprinted below are the Prologue and Chapter I, which document the perverse turn of mind that would revel in such obscene fantasy.

Prologue

The Protocols of the Wise Men of Zion are presented herewith to the American public with the hope that they may throw some light upon the great conspiracy of destruction which at present is threatening the peace of the world and Christian civilization.

The origin of this document is lost in obscurity. Whether it is the work of a group of men sitting in session as it purports to be, or of one man of literary genius and masterly intellect, or is a collection of rules and precepts which have come down through the centuries, we do not know. One thing, however, is obvious, no such brilliant piece of psychology, however perverted, could have been written with the purpose of throwing discredit upon a race. The diabolic cleverness of the whole plan must have been the work of a man or men inspired by religious enthusiasm and guided by years of study and precept. Internal evidence would lead us to suppose that it was written about 1893. It is known to have been in existence before 1905 and was in the British Museum in 1906.

If there were no evidence in the world to-day which would point toward the fulfillment of this plan, the document would be interesting only as a psychological study of religious and race fanaticism. It would have no practical bearing. But the most startling thing about these Protocols is the way in which they describe the plan of campaign which has been followed to a large extent by the Bolsheviki of Russia and by those who are directly or indirectly playing the game of a world revolution.

The plan to break down modern government by teaching the masses a distrust of their own leaders, and in the consequent confusion to seize the power and establish a dictatorship of a small minority, is here laid down in great detail, and many of the inexplicable happenings of modern political life are described and given their place in the general scheme.

It seems incredible that the radical revolutionary movement, based upon false economic premises and upon a complete distortion of human nature, should be carried on entirely by a group who have been converted spontaneously to communist ideas. Is it not possible that behind this well-organized and well-financed world movement, there lies another motive which is not apparent upon the surface? Is it not possible that this document explains the inner nature of that motive and the racial and religious fervor which gives it its rapid growth and its terrific power?

No one wishes to fan the flames of racial prejudice unnecessarily, but if history has taught the world any lesson, it is that no race has a right to dominate by force or cunning. Many great nations have tried to conquer the world. It is not beyond the limits of possibility that another such attempt is now in progress. If so the world has a right to know who is making this attempt and what are the ambitions behind the mystery.

If the publication of this document brings into the light of day any of the hidden plans beneath the world confusion or opens for discussion any dark chapter of the human lust for power, it will have justified itself.

The background of the book and the history of the manuscript are described in the epilogue. Our only reason for presenting it to the public is a desire that all may view from every possible angle the motives of those who do not believe either in a republican government or the moral principles accepted by civilized countries throughout the world.

THE BASIC DOCTRINE—"RIGHT LIES IN MIGHT"

Formulation of the system = Mankind essentially selfish and yields only to force = Political freedom is non-existent and such an idea can be used only for political ends = A new authority supercedes a government weakened by liberal ideals = The power of gold has replaced faith = Masses are not guided by academic argument but by passions and sentiment = Politics and morals have nothing in common = Right lies in might = Do evil that good may come = Necessity overrules the moral = The masses are blind and led by upstarts who have no political sensibilities = Power and hypocrisy, violence and cunning, bribery and treason, all help to reach the goal and are therefore duties = Terrorism leads to blind submission = Prosperity and Gentile government = The abolition of privileges which were the last bulwark of the people = Greed and material desires stifle initiative = Any government may be changed like a pair of worn-out gloves.

Protocol I

Disregarding mere words and phrases, we will analyze the significance of every thought, and interpret events in the light of comparisons and deductions. I will formulate our system, both from our standpoint and from that of the Gentiles.

It should be noted that people with evil instincts are more numerous than those with good ones; therefore, the best results in governing them are attained by intimidation and violence, and not by academic argument. Every man aims for power; everyone desires to be a dictator, if possible; moreover, few would not sacrifice the good of others for the attainment of their own ends.

What has controlled the wild animal called man? What has ruled him until the present time?

At the beginning of social organization, men submitted to brute force; later, they obeyed the law, which is the same force, only in a masked form. Consequently, I draw the conclusion from this, that, according to the laws of nature, right lies in might.

Political freedom is an idea, not a fact. It is necessary to know how to apply this idea when there is need of a clever bait to gain the support of the people for one's party, if such a party has undertaken to defeat another already in power. This task is made easier if the opponent has himself been infected by principles of freedom or so-called liberalism, and for the sake of the idea will yield some of his own power. It is in this that the triumph of our theory appears: the weakened reins of government are immediately grasped by a new hand in compliance with the laws of existence, for the blind force of the people cannot exist without leadership even for a day. The new authority simply steps into the position of the old, already weakened by liberalism.

In our times, the power of gold has become the substitute for the rulership of liberalism. Faith ruled at one time. Liberty, however, is unattainable, because no one knows how to use it within bounds. It is sufficient to give the people self-government for a time for that government to become dissolute. Then come dissensions and strife steps in, followed by class struggles. Governments are thus destroyed and their significance turned to ashes.

Whether the government exhausts itself, or whether internal strife places it in the hands of external enemies, in either case it may be considered as irretrievably lost; it is in our power. The despotism of capital, which is entirely in our hands, stretches forth a straw that the governments must grasp, or plunge into the abyss.

I would ask the following question of him who, from a liberal heart, regards such arguments as unprincipled: if every government has two enemies and it is permissible to use all methods of warfare against the external enemy, and it is not considered unprincipled to do so,—as for example to keep the enemy in ignorance of plans of attack and defense, in the use of night attack or attack by unequal forces,—why should similar methods towards a worse foe, one who transgresses against social order and prosperity, be called unallowable or immoral?

Can a sound and logical mind hope to govern successfully the masses by arguments and reasoning, when there is the possibility of counter-arguments, perhaps even stupid, but which nevertheless might present themselves as more agreeable to their superficial minds? People in masses and people of the masses are guided by exceptionally shallow passions, beliefs, customs, traditions and sentimental theories and are inclined towards party divisions, a fact which prevents any form of agreement, even when this is founded on a thoroughly logical basis. Every decision of the mob depends upon an accidental or prearranged majority, which, owing to its ignorance of the mysteries of political secrets, gives expression to absurd decisions that introduce anarchy into the government.

Politics have nothing in common with morals. The ruler guided by morality is not a politician, and consequently he is not seated firmly on the throne. He who desires to rule must do so by cunning and hypocrisy. The great qualities of the people— honesty and frankness—are essentially vices in politics, because they dethrone more surely and more certainly than does the strongest enemy. These qualities are attributes of Gentile rule; we certainly must not be guided by them.

Our right lies in force. The word "right" expresses an abstract idea. It has no proof. The word means nothing more than: "Give me what I want, that I may have the evidence of my superior strength over you."

Where does right begin? Where does it end?

In a government with poorly organized authority, in which the laws and the ruler are powerless amid the flood of rights ever multiplying out of liberalism, I find that there exists a new right: the right of the stronger to attack and destroy all existing regulations and statutes, to take the law into his own hands, to change all institutions and become the ruler of those who give that right by yielding it voluntarily through their liberalism.

With the present instability of all authority, our power will be more unassailable than any other, because it will be invisible until it has gained such strength that no cunning can undermine it.

Out of the temporary evil to which we are now forced to resort will emerge the good of a permanent government, which will restore the orderly functioning of the mechanism of people's existence, now shaken by liberalism. The result will justify the means. In laying our plans, we must turn our attention not so much to the good and the moral as to the necessary and the useful. Before us lies a project embodying a strategical line of action, from which we must not diverge if we are to avoid the risk of a collapse of the work of many centuries.

In working out an expedient plan of action, it is necessary to take into consideration the meanness, the vacillation, the changeability of the crowd; its inability to appreciate and respect the conditions of individual life and well-being. It is necessary to realize that the force of the masses is blind, unreasoning, and unintelligent, prone to listen now to the right and now to the left. The blind cannot guide the blind, without leading them to the precipice; consequently, units from the crowd, upstarts from among the people, even if extremely gifted with cleverness, but without political understanding, cannot come forth as leaders of the masses without ruining the entire nation.

Only the person educated from childhood for rulership can understand the words which are spelled with the letters of politics.

The masses left to themselves, that is, to the direction of upstarts from among them, wreck themselves by party divisions created by the struggle for authority and honors, and the disorders arising therefrom. Is it possible for the masses of the people quietly and without rivalry to judge impartially and manage properly the affairs of a nation in such a manner that they will not become tangled with personal interests? Can they protect themselves from external enemies? It is unthinkable, since a plan split up into as many parts as there are heads in the crowd loses its unity and consequently becomes incomprehensible and impracticable.

Only the plans of an autocrat can be laid out on a broad scale, clearly and in order, distributing everything properly in the mechanism of the government machinery. From this the conclusion is inevitable that the best government is one that is concentrated in the hands of one responsible person. Civilization cannot exist without absolute despotism, exercised not by the masses but by their leader, no matter who he may be. The barbarous crowd shows its barbarism on every occasion. When the mob grasps liberty in its hands, it soon changes it into anarchy, which is in itself the highest degree of barbarism.

Look at these beasts, steeped in alcohol, stupefied by wine, the unlimited use of which is granted together with liberty. Surely we cannot allow our own people to come to this. The people of the Gentiles are stupefied by spirituous liquors; their young people are insensible to aught else than classicism and early vice, which has been encouraged in them by our agents—tutors, footmen, and governesses in the houses of the rich, by clerks and others, and by our women in places of dissipation frequented by Gentiles. Among the latter, I classify so-called society women, voluntary followers of vice and luxury.

Our password is force and hypocrisy, for only force can conquer in the realm of politics, especially if it is concealed in the talents essential to statesmen. Violence must be the principle, hypocrisy and cunning the rule of governments which do not wish to lose their power. This evil is the sole means of reaching the goal of good. For this reason, we must not hesitate at bribery, deceit and treachery, when these can help us to achieve our end. In the field of politics, it is necessary to take the property of others without hesitation, if by that means we secure submission and authority.

Our government, following a line of peaceful conquest, has a right to substitute for the horrors of war less apparent and more effective executions of people, by which terrorism can be supported, thus bringing about blind submission. Just but merciless severity is the greatest factor in the strength of government. We must follow a program of violence and hypocrisy, not only for the sake of gain, but also as a duty and for the sake of victory. The doctrine of self-interest is as potent as are the methods employed by it. Consequently, we shall triumph, not so much by the methods employed, as by the doctrine of severity, and shall subjugate all the governments to our super-government. It is sufficient for all to know that we are inexorable, and disobedience will cease.

Already in ancient times, we were the first to shout the words, "Liberty, Equality, Fraternity", among the people. These words have been repeated many times since by unconscious poll-parrots, flocking from all sides to this bait, with which they have ruined the prosperity of the world and true personal freedom, before so well protected from the pressure of the mob. The presumably clever and intelligent Gentiles did not understand the symbolism of the uttered words; did not observe their contradiction in meaning and their interrelation; did not notice that in nature there is no equality; that there can be no liberty, since nature herself has established the inequality of brains, character and ability and has established subjection to her laws. They did not reason that the power of the crowd is blind, that the upstarts selected from it for government are just as blind in politics as is the crowd itself, whereas the initiate even though a fool, can rule, while the uninitiate, though a genius, will understand nothing in politics. All this has been overlooked by the Gentiles.

Meanwhile, dynastic government has rested on this, the father passing on the knowledge of the course of political affairs to his son, so that nobody except the members of the dynasty understands, or could disclose such secrets to the people whom they ruled. As time went on, the significance of the dynastic transmission of the true situation of political affairs was lost, thus aiding the success of our undertaking.

From all ends of the world, the words, "Liberty, Equality, Fraternity", brought whole legions into our ranks, through our blind agents carrying our flag with delight. Meanwhile, these words were canker-worms at work, undermining the prosperity of the Gentiles, everywhere destroying peace, quiet, and solidarity, wrecking all the foundations of their governments. You will see finally that it assisted our triumph, for it gave us incidentally the opportunity to grasp the trump card, the abolition of privileges, in other words the very basis of the Gentile aristocracy, the only protection which peoples and nations had against us.

On the ruins of the natural and hereditary aristocracy of the Gentiles we have set up the aristocracy of our educated class and over all the aristocracy of money. We have established the position of this new aristocracy on the basis of riches, which we control and on the science guided by our wise men.

Our triumph has also been made easier because, in our relations with the people necessary to us, we have always played upon the most sensitive strings of the human mind—on calculation, greed and the insatiable material desires of men. Each of these human weaknesses, taken separately, is capable of paralysing initiative and of placing the will of the people at the disposal of the purchaser of their activities.

The abstract conception of liberty made it possible for us to convince the crowd that government is only the management for the owner of the country, the people, and that the steward can be changed like a pair of worn-out gloves. The possibility of changing the representatives of the people has placed them at our disposal and, as it were, has placed them in our power as creatures of our purposes.

35. Nicola Sacco and Bartolomeo Vanzetti

Speeches to the court

In 1921, in the wake of the Red Scare, two Italian anarchists and draft-evaders were convicted of murdering a paymaster and guard in South Braintree, Massachusetts, the previous year. The court appeared to be more persuaded by Sacco and Vanzetti's radical beliefs and Italian origins than by the evidence. Judge Webster Thayer, after privately referring to the defendants as "those anarchist bastards," sentenced them to death.

The Sacco-Vanzetti case proved to be the Haymarket Affair of the 1920s. In the subsequent six years of appeal and reappeal, Sacco and Vanzetti gained international sympathy and attention. Although the evidence was clearly prejudiced and inadequate, efforts to prevent their execution proved futile.

On August 22, 1927, just after midnight, Nicola Sacco and Bartolomeo Vanzetti went to their deaths.

Before their electrocution, the defendants availed themselves of the opportunity to address the court. The almost inarticulate Sacco spoke briefly. The more eloquent Vanzetti spoke at length.

Clerk Worthington: *Nicola Sacco,* have you anything to say why sentence of death should not be passed upon you?

From *Letters of Sacco and Vanzetti,* ed. Marion Denman Frankfurter and Gardner Jackson, pp. 361–65, 369–71, 376–77. Copyright © 1928, renewed 1956 by The Viking Press, Inc. Reprinted by permission of The Viking Press, Inc.

Nicola Sacco: Yes, sir. I am no orator. It is not very familiar with me the English language, and as I know, as my friend has told me, my comrade Vanzetti will speak more long, so I thought to give him the chance.

I never knew, never heard, even read in history anything so cruel as this Court. After seven years prosecuting they still consider us guilty. And these gentle people here are arrayed with us in this court today.

I know the sentence will be between two classes, the oppressed class and the rich class, and there will be always collision between one and the other. We fraternize the people with the books, with the literature. You persecute the people, tyrannize them and kill them. We try the education of people always. You try to put a path between us and some other nationality that hates each other. That is why I am here today on this bench, for having been of the oppressed class. Well, you are the oppressor.

You know it, Judge Thayer—you know all my life, you know why I have been here, and after seven years that you have been persecuting me and my poor wife, and you still today sentence us to death. I would like to tell all my life, but what is the use? You know all about what I say before, that is, my comrade, will be talking, because he is more familiar with the language, and I will give him a chance. My comrade, the kind man to all the children, you sentenced him two times, in the Bridgewater case and the Dedham case, connected with me, and you know he is innocent.

You forget all this population that has been with us for seven years, to sympathize and give us all their energy and all their kindness. You do not care for them. Among that peoples and the comrades and the working class there is a big legion of intellectual people which have been with us for seven years, to not commit the iniquitous sentence, but still the Court goes ahead. And I want to thank you all, you peoples, my comrades who have been with me for seven years, with the Sacco-Vanzetti case, and I will give my friend a chance.

I forget one thing which my comrade remember me. As I said before, Judge Thayer know all my life, and he know that I am never guilty, never—not yesterday, nor today, nor forever.

CLERK WORTHINGTON: *Bartolomeo Vanzetti*, have you anything to say why sentence of death should not be passed upon you?

BARTOLOMEO VANZETTI: Yes. What I say is that I am innocent, not only of the Braintree crime, but also of the Bridgewater crime. That I am not only innocent of these two crimes, but in all my life I have never stolen and I have never killed and I have never spilled blood. That is what I want to say. And it is not all. Not only am I innocent of these two crimes, not only in all my life I have never stolen, never killed, never spilled blood, but I have struggled all my life, since I began to reason, to eliminate crime from the earth.

Everybody that knows these two arms knows very well that I did not need to go into the streets and kill a man or try to take money. I can live by my two hands and live well. But besides that, I can live even without work with my hands for other people. I have had plenty of chance to live independently and to live what the world conceives to be a higher life than to gain our bread with the sweat of our brow.

My father in Italy is in a good condition. I could have come back in Italy and he would have welcomed me every time with open arms. Even if I come back there with not a cent in my pocket, my father could have give me a position, not to work but to make business, or to oversee upon the land that he owns. He has wrote me many letters in that sense, and as another well-to-do relative has wrote me letters in that sense that I can produce.

Well, it may be said to be a boast. My father and my aunt can boast themselves and say things that people may not be compelled to believe. People may say they may be poor when I say that they are in good condition to give me a position any time that I want to settle down and form a family and start a settled life. Well, but there are people maybe in this same court that could testify to what I have said and that what my father and my aunt have said to me is not a lie, that really they have the means to give me a position any time that I want.

Well, I want to reach a little point farther, and it is this, that not only have I not been trying to steal in Bridgewater, not only have I not been in Braintree to steal and kill and have never stolen or killed or spilt blood in all my life, not only have I struggled hard against crimes, but I have refused myself of what are considered the commodity and glories of life, the prides of a life of a good position, because in my consideration it is not right to exploit man. I have refused to go in business because I understand that business is a speculation on profit upon certain people that must depend upon the business man, and I do not consider that that is right and therefore I refuse to do that.

Now, I should say that I am not only innocent of all these things, not only have I never committed a real crime in my life—though some sins but not crimes—not only have I struggled all my life to eliminate crimes, the crimes that the official law and the moral law condemns, but also the crime that the moral law and the official law sanction and sanctify,—the exploitation and the oppression of the man by the man, and if there is a reason why I am here as a guilty man, if there is a reason why you in a few minutes can doom me, it is this reason and none else.

There is the best man I ever cast my eyes upon since I lived, a man that will last and will grow always more near to and more dear to the heart of the people, so long as admiration for goodness, for virtues, and for sacrifice will last. I mean Eugene Victor Debs.

He has said that not even a dog that kills chickens would have found an American jury disposed to convict it with the proof that the Commonwealth has produced against us. That man was not with me in Plymouth or with Sacco where he was on the day of the crime. You can say that it is arbitrary, what we are saying from him, that he is good and he applied to the other his goodness, that he is incapable of crime, and he believed that everybody is incapable of crime.

Well, it may be like that but it is not, it could be like that but it is not, and that man had a real experience of court, of prison and of jury. Just because he wanted the world a little better he was persecuted and slandered from his boyhood youthness to his old age, and indeed he was murdered by the prison.

He knew, and not only he knew, but every man of understanding in the world, not only in this country but also in other countries, men to whom we have provided a certain amount of the records of the case at times, they all know and still stick with us, the flower of mankind of Europe, the better writers, the greatest thinkers of Europe, have pleaded in our favor. The scientists, the greatest scientists, the greatest statesmen of Europe, have pleaded in our favor. . . .

We were tried during a time whose character has now passed into history. I mean by that, a time when there was a hysteria of resentment and hate against the people of our principles, against the foreigner, against slackers, and it seems to me—rather, I am positive of it, that both you and Mr. Katzmann have done all what it were in your power in order to work out, in order to agitate still more the passion of the juror, the prejudice of the juror, against us.

I remember that Mr. Katzmann has introduced a witness against us, a certain Ricci. Well, I have heard that witness. It seems that he has nothing to say. It seemed that it was a foolishness to produce a witness that has nothing to say. And it seemed as if he were called by the Commonwealth to tell to the jury that he was the foreman of those laborers who were near the scene of the crime and who claimed, and who testified in our behalf, that we were not the men, and that this man, the witness Ricci, was their foreman, and he has tried to keep the men on the job instead of going to see what was happening so as to give the impression that it was not true that the men went towards the street to see what happened. But that was not very important. The real importance is what that man said and that was not true, that a certain witness who was the water boy of the gang of the laborers testified that he took a pail and went to a certain spring, a water spring, to take water for the gang—Ricci testified it was not true that that man went to that spring, and therefore it was not true that he saw the bandit, and therefore it was not true that he can tell that neither I nor Sacco were the men. But Ricci was introduced to show that it was not true that that man went to that spring, because he knew that the Germans had poisoned the water in that spring. That is what he, Ricci, said on that stand over there. Now, in the world chronicle of the time there is not a single happening of that nature. Nobody in America—we have read plenty things bad that the Germans have done in Europe during the war, but nobody can prove and nobody will say that the Germans are bad enough to poison the spring water in this country during the war.

Now, this, it seems, has nothing to do with us directly. It seems to be a thing said by incident on the stand between the other things; why, whereas, that is the essence here. Because the jury were hating us because we were against the war, and the jury don't know that it makes any difference between a man that is against the war because he believes that the war is unjust, because he hate no country, because he is a cosmopolitan, and a man that is against the war because he is in favor of the other country that fights against the country in which he is, and therefore a spy, an enemy, and he commits any crime in the country in which he is in behalf of the other country in order to serve the other country. We are not men of that kind. Nobody can say that we are German spies or spies of any kind. Katzmann knows very well that. Katzmann knows that we were against the war because we did not believe in the purpose for which they say that the war was fought. We believed that the war is wrong, and we believe this more now after ten years that we studied and observed and understood it day by day,—the consequences and the result of the after war. We believe more now than ever that the war was wrong, and we are against war more now than ever, and I am glad to be on the doomed scaffold if I can say to mankind, "Look out; you are in a catacomb of the flower of mankind. For what? All that they say to you, all that they have promised to you—it was a lie, it was an illusion, it was a cheat, it was a fraud, it was a crime. They promised you liberty. Where is liberty? They promised you prosperity. Where is prosperity? They have promised you elevation. Where is the elevation?" . . .

What I want to say is this: Everybody ought to understand that the first beginning of our defense has been terrible. My first lawyer did not try to defend us. He has made no attempt to collect witnesses and evidence in our favor. The record in the Plymouth court is a pity. I am told that they are part or almost one-half lost. So that later on the defense have had a tremendous work to do in order to collect some evidence, to collect some testimony to offset and to learn what the testimony of the State had been. And in this consideration it must be said that even if the defense take double time of the State about delays, double time than they (the State) delayed the case, it would have been reasonable just the same, whereas it took less than the State.

Well, I have already say that I not only am not guilty of these two crimes, but I never committed a crime in my life,—I have never stolen and I have never killed and I have never spilt blood, and I have fought against crime, and I have fought and I have sacrificed myself even to eliminate the crimes that the law and the church legitimate and sanctify.

This is what I say: I would not wish to a dog or to a snake, to the most low and misfortunate creature of the earth—I would not wish to any of them what I have had to suffer for things that I am not guilty of. I am suffering because I am a radical and indeed I am a radical; I have suffered because I was an Italian, and indeed I am an Italian; I have suffered more for my family and for my beloved than for myself; but I am so convinced to be right that you can only kill me once but if you could execute me two times, and if I could be reborn two other times, I would live again to do what I have done already.

I have finished. Thank you.

PART NINE

Restriction and Race

36. John R. Commons

Race and democracy

The mounting pressure for immigration restriction found an avid advocate in John R. Commons (1862–1945), Progressive, reformer, and labor historian. Of New England stock on his mother's side, and Carolinian on his father's, this Oberlin graduate and Johns Hopkins Ph.D. mixed social reform with the study of labor economics and immigration. For nearly two generations Commons was an arch-exponent of Anglo-Saxon superiority, an ever-reliable advisor to the Immigration Restriction League, and a readily available expert at Congressional immigration hearings.

In the opening chapter of *Races and Immigrants in America*, Commons pursued the logic of the racist argument to its ultimate conclusion: The equalitarian assumptions of the Declaration of Independence were no longer—if they ever had been—tenable, for race and heredity continued to be the decisive factors in shaping social institutions. An immigration policy that continued to disregard such realities threatened to undermine the American republic, insisted Commons.

"All men are created equal." So wrote Thomas Jefferson, and so agreed with him the delegates from the American colonies. But we must not press them too closely nor insist on the literal interpretation of their words. They were not publishing a scientific treatise on human nature nor describing the physical, intellectual, and moral qualities of different races and different individuals, but they were bent upon a practical object in politics. They desired to sustain before the world the cause of independence by such appeals as they thought would have effect; and certainly the appeal to the sense of equal rights before God and

From John R. Commons, "Races and Democracy," *Chautauquan* 38 (September, 1903): 33–35.

the law is the most powerful that can be addressed to the masses of any people. This is the very essence of American democracy, that one man should have just as large opportunity as any other to make the most of himself, to come forward and achieve high standing in any calling to which he is inclined. To do this the bars of privilege have one by one been thrown down, the suffrage has been extended to every man, and public office has been opened to any one who can persuade his fellow-voters or their representatives to select him.

But there is another side to the successful operations of democracy. It is not enough that equal opportunity to participate in making and enforcing the laws should be vouchsafed to all—it is equally important that all should be capable of such participation. The individuals, or the classes, or the races, who through any mental or moral defect are unable to assert themselves beside other individuals, classes, or races, and to enforce their right to an equal voice in determining the laws and conditions which govern all, are just as much deprived of the privilege as though they were excluded by the constitution. In the case of individuals, when they sink below the level of joint participation, we recognize them as belonging to a defective or criminal or pauper class, and we provide for them, not on the basis of their rights, but on the basis of charity or punishment. Such classes are exceptions in point of numbers, and we do not feel that their non-participation is a flaw in the operations of democratic government. But when a social class or an entire race is unable to command that share in conducting government to which the laws entitle it, we recognize at once that democracy as a practical institution has in so far broken down, and that, under the forms of democracy, there has developed a class oligarchy or a race oligarchy.

Two things, therefore, are necessary for a democratic government such as that which the American people have set before themselves: equal opportunities before the law, and equal ability of classes and races to use those opportunities. If the first is lacking, we have legal oligarchy; if the second is lacking, we have actual oligarchy disguised as democracy.

Now it must be observed that, compared with the first two

centuries of our nation's history, the present generation is somewhat shifting its ground regarding democracy. While it can never rightly be charged that our fathers overlooked the inequalities of races and individuals, yet more than the present generation did they regard with hopefulness the educational value of democracy. "True enough," they said, "the black man is not equal to the white man, but once free him from his legal bonds, open up the schools, the professions, the businesses, and the offices to those of his number who are most aspiring, and you will find that, as a race, he will advance favorably in comparison with his white fellow-citizens."

It is now nearly forty years since these opportunities and educational advantages were given to the negro, not only on equal terms, but actually on terms of preference over the whites, and the fearful collapse of the experiment is recognized even by its partisans as something that was inevitable in the nature of the race at that stage of its development. We shall have reason in the following pages to enter more fully into this discussion, because the race question in America has found its most intense expression in the relations between the white and the negro races, and has there shown itself to be the most fundamental of all American social and political problems. For it was this race question that precipitated the Civil War, with the ominous problems that have followed upon that catastrophe; and it is this same race problem that now diverts attention from the treatment of those pressing economic problems of taxation, corporations, trusts, and labor organizations which themselves originated in the Civil War. The race problem in the South is only one extreme of the same problem in the great cities of the North, where popular government, as our forefathers conceived it, has been displaced by one-man power, and where a profound distrust of democracy is taking hold upon the educated and property-holding classes who fashion public opinion.

This changing attitude toward the educational value of self-government has induced a more serious study of the nature of democratic institutions and of the classes and races which are called upon to share in them. As a people whose earlier hopes have been shocked by the hard blows of experience, we are beginning to pause and take invoice of the heterogeneous stocks of humanity that we have admitted to the management of our great political enterprise. We are trying to look beneath the surface and to inquire whether there are not factors of heredity and race more fundamental than those of education and environment. We find that our democratic theories and forms of government were fashioned by but one of the many races and peoples which have come within their practical operation, and that that race, the so-called Anglo-Saxon, developed them out of its own insular experience unhampered by inroads of alien stock. When once thus established in England and further developed in America we find that other races and peoples, accustomed to despotism and even savagery, and wholly unused to self-government, have been thrust into the delicate fabric. Like a practical people as we pride ourselves, we have begun actually to despotize our institutions in order to control these dissident elements, though still optimistically holding that we retain the original democracy. The earlier problem was mainly a political one—how to unite into one self-governing nation a scattered population with the wide diversity of natural resources, climates, and interests that mark a country soon to stretch from ocean to ocean and from the arctics to the subtropics. The problem now is a social one,—how to unite into one people a congeries of races even more diverse than the resources and climates from which they draw their subsistence. That motto, *"E pluribus unum,"* which in the past has guided those who through constitutional debate and civil war worked out our form of government, must now again be the motto of those who would work out the more fundamental problem of divergent races. Here is something deeper than the form of government—it is the essence of government—for it is that union of the hearts and lives and abilities of the people which makes government what it really is.

The conditions necessary for democratic government are not merely the constitutions and laws which guarantee equality, liberty, and the pursuit of happiness, for these after all are but paper documents. They are not merely freedom from foreign power, for the Australian colonies enjoy the most democratic of all governments, largely because they are owned by another country which has protected them from foreign and civil wars. Neither are wealth and prosperity necessary for democracy, for these may tend to luxury, inequality, and envy. World power, however glorious and enticing, is not helpful to democracy, for it inclines to militarism and centralization, as did Rome in the hands of an emperor, or Venice in the hands of an oligarchy. The true foundations of democracy are in the character of the people themselves, that is, of the individuals who constitute the democracy. These are: first, intelligence—the power to weigh evidence and draw sound conclusions, based on adequate information; second, manliness, that which the Romans called virility, and which at bottom is dignified self-respect, self-control, and that self-assertion and jealousy of encroachment which marks those who, knowing their rights, dare maintain them; third, and equally important, the capacity for coöperation, that willingness and ability to organize, to trust their leaders, to work together for a common interest and toward a common destiny, a capacity which we variously designate as patriotism, public spirit, or self-government. These are the basic qualities which underlie democracy,— intelligence, manliness, coöperation. If they are lacking, democracy is futile. Here is the problem of races, the fundamental division of mankind. Race differences are established in the very blood and physical constitution. They are most difficult to eradicate, and they yield only to the slow processes of the centuries. Races may change their religions, their forms of government, their modes of industry, and their languages, but underneath all these changes they may continue the physical, mental, and moral capacities and incapacities which determine the real character of their religion, government, industry, and literature. Race and heredity furnish the raw material, education and environment furnish the tools, with which and by which social institutions are fashioned; and in a democracy race and heredity are the more decisive, because the very education and

environment which fashion the oncoming generations are themselves controlled through universal suffrage by the races whom it
is hoped to educate and elevate.

37. WOODROW WILSON

Not tests of quality
but of opportunity

The first device proposed for restricting immigration was the literacy test.
On four successive occasions, in 1896, 1913, 1915, and 1917, the Congress
passed literacy test bills. Presidents Cleveland, Taft, and Wilson vetoed
these bills in turn. But in 1917, after Wilson rejected the literacy test bill
for a second time, a more restrictionist-minded Congress than ever
overrode the veto.

Wilson's veto message of 1915 succinctly summarized the American
tradition of free immigration.

To the House of Representatives:

It is with unaffected regret that I find myself constrained by
clear conviction to return this bill (H. R. 6060, "An act to regulate
the immigration of aliens to and the residence of aliens in the
United States") without my signature. Not only do I feel it to be a
very serious matter to exercise the power of veto in any case,
because it involves opposing the single judgment of the President
to the judgment of a majority of both the Houses of the Congress,
a step which no man who realizes his own liability to error can
take without great hesitation, but also because this particular bill
is in so many important respects admirable, well conceived, and
desirable. Its enactment into law would undoubtedly enhance the
efficiency and improve the methods of handling the important
branch of the public service to which it relates. But candor and a

U. S., Congress, House, *Congressional Record,* 63rd Cong., 3rd sess., Jan. 28, 1915,
LII, pp. 2481–82.

sense of duty with regard to the responsibility so clearly imposed upon me by the Constitution in matters of legislation leave me no choice but to dissent.

In two particulars of vital consequence this bill embodies a radical departure from the traditional and long-established policy of this country, a policy in which our people have conceived the very character of their Government to be expressed, the very mission and spirit of the Nation in respect of its relations to the peoples of the world outside their borders. It seeks to all but close entirely the gates of asylum which have always been open to those who could find nowhere else the right and opportunity of constitutional agitation for what they conceived to be the natural and inalienable rights of men; and it excludes those to whom the opportunities of elementary education have been denied, without regard to their character, their purposes, or their natural capacity.

Restrictions like these, adopted earlier in our history as a Nation, would very materially have altered the course and cooled the humane ardors of our politics. The right of political asylum has brought to this country many a man of noble character and elevated purpose who was marked as an outlaw in his own less fortunate land, and who has yet become an ornament to our citizenship and to our public councils. The children and the compatriots of these illustrious Americans must stand amazed to see the representatives of their Nation now resolved, in the fullness of our national strength and at the maturity of our great institutions, to risk turning such men back from our shores without test of quality or purpose. It is difficult for me to believe that the full effect of this feature of the bill was realized when it was framed and adopted, and it is impossible for me to assent to it in the form in which it is here cast.

The literacy test and the tests and restrictions which accompany it constitute an even more radical change in the policy of the Nation. Hitherto we have generously kept our doors open to all who were not unfitted by reason of disease or incapacity for self-support or such personal records and antecedents as were likely to make them a menace to our peace and order or to the wholesome and essential relationships of life. In this bill it is proposed to turn away from tests of character and of quality and impose tests which exclude and restrict; for the new tests here embodied are not tests of quality or of character or of personal fitness, but tests of opportunity. Those who come seeking opportunity are not to be admitted unless they have already had one of the chief of the opportunities they seek, the opportunity of education. The object of such provisions is restriction, not selection.

If the people of this country have made up their minds to limit the number of immigrants by arbitrary tests and so reverse the policy of all the generations of Americans that have gone before them, it is their right to do so. I am their servant and have no license to stand in their way. But I do not believe that they have. I respectfully submit that no one can quote their mandate to that effect. Has any political party ever avowed a policy of restriction in this fundamental matter, gone to the country on it, and been commissioned to control its legislation? Does this bill rest upon the conscious and universal assent and desire of the American people? I doubt it. It is because I doubt it that I make bold to dissent from it. I am willing to abide by the verdict, but not until it has been rendered. Let the platforms of parties speak out upon this policy and the people pronounce their wish. The matter is too fundamental to be settled otherwise.

I have no pride of opinion in this question. I am not foolish enough to profess to know the wishes and ideals of America better than the body of her chosen representatives know them. I only want instruction direct from those whose fortunes, with ours and all men's, are involved.

The White House, January 28, 1915.

38. WILLIAM N. VAILE

We prefer to base quotas on established groups

The mounting sentiment for the restriction of immigration from Europe reached its peak between 1920 and 1924. The provisional Johnson law of 1921 was followed by the act of 1924 establishing an annual quota of 150,000 for the countries of Europe. The quotas for the individual countries were based on the number of foreign-born of each nationality living in the United States in 1890. This system was modified slightly in favor of a national origins quota system before the final immigration act was passed in 1929.

The vigorous debate of the immigration issue in Congress was vividly reflected in the statements of Colorado Congressman William N. Vaile (1876–1927), a dedicated proponent of drastic immigration controls on racial and nationalistic grounds. His comments and graphic representations vividly define the immigration controversy.

The present law, our first numerical limitation of immigration, which has been in effect for three years, admits from any country—with certain exceptions not involved in this inquiry— 3 per cent of the number of persons born in that country who were resident in the United States by the census of 1910. The total quota is 357,803.

The Johnson bill, now pending, proposes to admit from any country 2 per cent of the number of persons born in such country who were resident in the United States by the census of 1890, and, in addition, 100 from each country. The total proposed quota is 161,184.

Now, people who have come here from Italy, Rumania, Greece, Czechoslovakia, and other countries of southern and eastern Europe claim that this "discriminates" against their countrymen. Why? The answer is a complete refutation of their own argument. The "discrimination" lies in the fact that, as they themselves

From U. S. Congress, House, *Congressional Record*, 68th Cong., 1st sess., April 1–14, 1924, 65, pt. 6, pp. 5643–45.

admit, the bulk of their immigration came after 1890, whereas the great bulk of immigration from northern and western Europe came before that year.

We would not want any immigrants at all unless we could hope that they would become assimilated to our language, customs, and institutions, unless they could blend thoroughly into our body politic. This would be admitted, I suppose, by the most radical opponent of immigration restriction. In fact, it is one of the stock arguments of these gentlemen that, although the immigrant himself may be assimilated slowly, his children, born here, become Americans in thought, action, speech, and character. That statement, often splendidly true, must nevertheless be accepted with many qualifications; but at least it is clear enough that the second generation will be assimilated quicker than the first—whatever may be the effect in many cases of such assimilation upon the United States. It would seem still clearer that the third and subsequent generations will be still more American than their predecessors.

It is also one of the stock arguments of the antirestrictionists that the immigrant has taken an important part in the building up of the country. Surely his children and grandchildren, both in numbers and in the quality of their work, have taken a still more important part.

Now, it seems rather illogical for gentlemen who vaunt the assimilability and the work of alien groups in our population to claim that those who have been for the shortest time in the process of assimilation and in the work of the Republic should have greater or even equal consideration because of this very newness. It would seem if those who came to the work at the eleventh hour are to have a penny, then at least those who have "borne the heat and burden of the day" should not be put off with a farthing.

It is a fact, not merely an argument, that this country was created, kept united, and developed—at least for more than a century of existence—almost entirely by people who came here from the countries of northern and western Europe. That people from southern and eastern Europe did not begin to come in large numbers until after 1890 certainly proves that those who came before them had built up a country desirable enough to attract these late comers.

Shall the countries which furnished those earlier arrivals be discriminated against for the very reason, forsooth, that they are represented here by from 2 to 10 generations of American citizens, whereas the others are largely represented by people who have not been here long enough to become citizens at all?

If there is a charge of "discrimination," the charge necessarily involves the idea that the proposed quota varies from some standard which is supposed to be not "discriminatory." What is that standard? From the arguments of those opposed to the bill it would appear that the census of 1910 is now regarded as not "discriminatory," or at least as less "discriminatory" than the census of 1890. It will be remembered that the census of 1910 was adopted as a base for emergency legislation, legislation not expected to be permanent, legislation not claimed to be exact, but intended to answer the purpose of an urgently needed restriction of the total volume of immigration. It has answered that purpose fairly well, but with some unnecessary hardships obviated by the present bill. The number admitted under it, however, has been far too great, and it is now proposed to cut the quota more than one-half.

But it is not the cut in the total which is so bitterly complained of. It is the change in the proportions, and it is interesting to note that those who violently opposed the passage of the 3 per cent law now with equal violence demand the retention of its proportions in the present legislation. But at least we can say that it has not been in operation long enough to have become an established and inviolable principle of distribution if some more equitable basis could be devised.

It is submitted that the Immigration Committee might fairly have determined to disregard the claims of very recently arrived immigrants that they should be figured at all as a basis for the admission of others. Congress might reasonably say, "Your value to the United States may be proved. We hope it will be. But it has not yet been fully proved, and we prefer to base our quotas on groups whose value has been established through several generations. We will therefore endeavor to distribute immigration in proportion to the elements of our population as they existed a generation ago."

But the committee did nothing of the sort, and the use of the 1890 census proposes nothing of the sort. Whatever our inducement to question it, we did accept the new immigration at its full face value, and we said, "We will distribute immigration in proportion to the elements of our population as they exist to-day. We will give you full credit for your recent additions to our population on exactly the same basis as we credit the contributions which started nearly a century and a half ago."

It is submitted that this is the very height of liberality to those who with ungrateful clamor are now complaining that they are being discriminated against. . . .

. . . The countries of northern and western Europe have contributed 85.02 per cent of our present white population (1920), and that under the present law they are entitled to only 56.33 per cent of our quota immigration, but that under the pending bill they will be entitled to 84.11 per cent of our annual quota immigration. In other words, for the last three years those countries have been having about two-thirds of their share of the immigration, while under the proposed quota they get within less than 1 per cent of their exact share.

On the other hand, the countries of southern and eastern Europe have furnished 14.62 per cent of our present—1920— white population, but under the present quota law those countries as a group are getting 44.64 per cent of our immigration. Under the proposed bill they will receive 1.88 per cent, which is about a quarter of 1 per cent more than their "share." . . .

In the grouping of countries the following are treated as southern and eastern countries, namely: Albania, Armenia, Austria, Bulgaria, Czechoslovakia, the Free City of Danzig, Greece, Hungary, Italy, Latvia, Lithuania, Poland, Portugal, Rumania, Russia, Spain, Yugoslavia, and "Other Europe."

The following are treated as northern and western countries, namely: Belgium, Denmark, Finland, France, Germany, Great

Britain and Ireland, Iceland, Luxemburg, Netherlands, Norway, Sweden, and Switzerland. . . .

It will be apparent on very brief consideration that no census base would work out complete proportional equality between all countries individually. Thus, taking the examples given in the chart, it will be noted that under the 1890 census base Great Britain and Ireland, which have furnished 60.74 per cent of our present (1920) white population, have been allowed to furnish, under the present law, 21.61 per cent of our immigration for the last three years. Under the pending bill the British Isles would be entitled to furnish 38.87 per cent of our new immigration. This is nearly twice what the British Isles can get under our present law, but it is still less than two-thirds of their "share" on the basis of their total contribution to our population.

Italy, which is one of the loudest complainers, is cut a little, because the great bulk of her immigration came very late, not only after 1890 but considerably after that date. She has furnished 3.92 per cent of our present white population. She will only be entitled to send 2.92 per cent of our future immigration. But for the last three years she has been sending 11.75 per cent of our total quota immigration, or nearly three times her "share" on the basis of her contribution to the population of the United States.

Poland, in whose behalf the welkin rings with cries of "unjust discrimination," has been receiving nearly three times her "share." She will be reduced to only a little less than twice her "share." This is doing pretty well for a country whose recently arrived population in one American city alone—Buffalo—out-numbers the native stock by 20,000 people.

PART TEN

A New American Culture

39. H. H. BOYESEN

How flavorless his soul appears to itself

Hjalmar Hjorth Boyesen (1848–1895), a graduate of the University of Christiania, migrated to the United States from Norway at the age of twenty, determined to succeed as an American man of letters. By all outward appearances, he did. Within a few years after his arrival, he had written the first novel by a Norwegian in America, was appointed to a professorship at Cornell University, and married an American. Subsequently a professor at Columbia University, he was the author of twenty-four books and hundreds of articles. A friend of Howells and Cleveland, Bjørnson and Turgenev, Boyesen wrote exclusively in English, insisted that he never spoke a word of Norwegian except when absolutely necessary, and urged fellow immigrants to follow his example.

But in the closing years of his life, Boyesen discarded the Viking literary posture and the false garb of romantic individualism that were strategic to his successful career. In a series of realistic novels, of which *The Mammon of Unrighteousness* was the most notable, he confessed his sense of failure and betrayal.

In the article below, Boyesen writes of the intractable problems of culture and personality that mocked the simplistic rules of individual success that he had prescribed for his countrymen.

Some years ago, a Norwegian who had spent twenty years in the United States and amassed a moderate fortune, came to me and announced that he was going back to Norway.

"For a visit?" I remarked interrogatively.

"No," he replied, with a jubilant force of conviction, "I am going for good. I shall never see this continent again."

Hjalmar Hjorth Boyesen, "The Emigrant's Unhappy Predicament," *Chautauquan* XV (August, 1892): pp. 607–10.

"Allow me to put a little interrogation mark after that," I observed smiling.

"You may put as many as you like," he ejaculated brusquely; "but that is as sure as the gospel, that I shall never put my foot on these blasted shores again."

I continued however in my skeptical mood, and tried to extort from him a promise not to invest any part of his fortune in Norway, until one year from the date of his arrival. But he was not to be prevailed upon. He had visions of a great estate, where, surrounded by docile and respectful tenants, he sat as lord of the manor and from the altitude of his wealth and foreign experience, received the homage of the simple folk who were to be his neighbors. It was of no use that I explained to him the changed conditions in Norway, and how woefully he would be disappointed if he expected the populace to stand at the roadside with bared heads, as they did in days of old, when the judge or the parson rode by. His heart was set upon his fanciful enterprise; and happy as a king he bounded down my front steps and swung his hat for a parting greeting.

In a year he returned and once more honored me with a call. A sadder man I have rarely seen, nor one more cruelly disillusioned.

"I really came to thank you," he said, after some introductory interjections and abjurgations, "for making me promise to wait a year before buying property."

"But you did not promise."

"Didn't I? Well, my impression was that I had. And I am glad if my memory played a trick on me. It was that which saved me."

It is not necessary to explain the man's predicament in all its details; for it was a long story, and by no means an unusual one. But one thing he said struck me very forcibly.

"The beastliness of the whole thing is that there is no remedy for it. No immigrant who has spent five or ten years in the United States will ever find himself contented in Europe, and he is not likely to be happy, in any real sense, in the United States either. He has just enough of each continent in him, to be uncomfortable in the other; and therefore I think that to emigrate from one's native land, unless it be to escape jail, is under all circumstances a mistake."

Though I am not in agreement with this gentleman's sentiments on all points, I am inclined (after a somewhat extended experience of both continents) to subscribe to the final conclusion. Whenever a countryman writes to me for advice (and I regret to say that a great many do) I invariably advise him to stay at home. A primitive existence close to the soil—with few wants and few aspirations—offers, I believe, better chances of contentment than a super-refined and highly organized one with many and complex wants and high aspirations.

I have expressed this in speech and writing to my friend Ole, a hundred times; but Ole, though he professes a high respect for my opinion, usually declines to act upon my advice. One fine morning in May or June I find him seated on my doorstep or groping his bewildered way through the labyrinthine corridors of Columbia College, intent upon finding my study, and, perhaps, desirous of borrowing enough money to take him to Chicago or Minneapolis or Fargo, as the case may be. I repeat my warning and preach him a little sermon on the folly of his course. He looks incredulously at me, and remarks, perhaps, that I seem to be pretty prosperous myself, and can surely have no ground of complaint against a country which has treated me so well. And after having talked for fifteen or twenty minutes, I begin to see the hopelessness of explaining the situation to Ole. I am dealing with altogether too subtle and impalpable values to impress his primitive mind; he merely stares at me with a sly intelligence; and I perceive that he is mentally imputing to me motives of which I should be ashamed. In my despair I therefore turn to my American reader (who has been the recipient of so many confidences) with a delightful certainty of being completely and sympathetically understood, and address to him my plea for primitive existence.

How much simpler and more unperplexed, how much more richly colored, for weal or for woe, is the life of the Norwegian peasant than that of the American farmer! The mountain above Ole's head, in which as a boy he saw grinning trolls' faces, which sheltered a host of delightful, mysterious, legendary creatures, may send freshets down upon him and damage his pastures; it may fling its huge shadow over his fields and compel him to cut his rye green in September; it may even darken his vision of life and set unsurpassable boundaries to his spirit, but the fact that it has thus chilled and bounded his race for a thousand years has made it his doom, his destiny—a part of himself—and if he migrates, it is a fatally detached and incomplete self he transfers to the western prairies. All the finest tendrils of the torn roots of his being remain in the old soil; and though he may thrive, in a crude fashion, after the transplantation, he loses in an indefinable way his distinctness of physiognomy; his individuality pales and flattens out, and he becomes frequently incredibly vulgarized.

A transplanted Norwegian farmer expressed, some years ago, a vague sentiment of this uncomprehended loss, to a newly arrived kinsman; and my informant, who sat behind them in a railway car, related to me the following conversation which he could not help overhearing. The elder settler who was named Lars was endeavoring to tone down the younger's somewhat high-pitched expectations. But in the face of the elder's rank prosperity, his kinsman refused to be discouraged.

"You are indeed a good deal bigger man to-day than you were when I last saw you," he remarked with youthful exuberance.

"Oh, yes," Lars replied sadly, "you may well say so."

"They say you are awfully rich now. You must have made a big pile of money."

"Oh, well, I've got all I need and perhaps some to spare."

"You must be glad of the day when you landed in this country?"

"Glad? no, I can't say I am glad of it."

"You are not glad of it—rich as you are and respected?"

"No; really glad—light of heart, and happy I have not been for a single day since I left home."

The younger sat and stared in dumb amazement.

"I'll tell you one thing," Lars resumed after a long meditative pause, "I don't think people in this country leave themselves any time to be happy. And as for me, I can only think of one thing that would make me right glad. On the day when I shall sit again on the Nordby mountain and look out over the valley, then, my boy, then I shall be glad."

But the saddest part of all is that he would not be glad. That final pathetic certainty is a hallucination. The mountain, on his return, would acknowledge him no more. It would be dumb and featureless. Its rills would sing no tunes to him, gay or mournful; and all its legendary inhabitants would retire into their shells with a surly uncommunicativeness and "refuse to play." He will be made to feel that he is an alien, a traitor who has forfeited his birthright.

The beggar at the roadside who sits trolling a ballad is richer than he; because he is still heir, by indefeasible right of entail, to the long past of the race; and the countless singing, fabling, and toiling generations lost in the deep and dusky centuries are living and singing and fabling in him. Tippling, shiftless cumberer of the ground though he be, he is a king on his own soil. He is invested with the race dignity as with a mantle. The race pride sits upon his tousled locks like a crown. And the returned emigrant stops and gazes enviously at him, and begins dimly to apprehend what he never before apprehended—the meaning, the magnitude, the irremediableness of his loss. It dawns upon him that in abandoning his country he abandoned more than he knew; nay, that nothing that he has gained or can gain is so precious as that impalpable something which evaporated out of his life during the ten or twenty years of his transatlantic sojourn.

How bare, how meager, how flavorless his soul appears to itself as he contemplates it in the mirror of reflection. Those thousand generations of the dead in whose shadow he once lived and in whose well-worn footprints he unconsciously walked—how could he have suspected in the heyday of his youth, that they were of any value to his own strong and self-reliant self? How willingly would he have sold them (if a buyer had presented himself) for a farthing and felt himself none the poorer. It was in the same light-hearted mood that Peter Schlemihl sold his shadow—an equally unsubstantial possession—and never knew a moment's peace or happiness afterwards. The consciousness of the absent shadow afflicted him with a vague oppression. The feeling that he differed in this one respect from his fellow-men made him shy and suspicious; and prevented him from asserting his full vigor in anything.

It is exactly this chilling sense of difference between him and the natives which dooms the immigrant to failure or to a success below the utmost reach of his powers. It constitutes a discount, and a heavy one, which is charged by the land of his adoption on his life's capital. Of that margin of superiority which determines survival and dominance, he is obliged to sacrifice much, if not all, in the mere effort at adaptation to new conditions.

He is more or less at a disadvantage and is apt to have a tormenting sense of misrepresenting himself, of having fallen short of high achievement, even when he is most vociferously applauded. If he be a poet he can but murmur in broken syllables (like a musician playing upon an untuned instrument) the song that in his native tongue would have burst clear and melodious from his breast. If he be a novelist (even though he be imbued with a deep love for the country of his adoption) he is constantly reminded by his critics that his point of view is that of an alien, and if he ventures upon a criticism of social or political conditions, it is promptly resented. He is told that, if this republic is not good enough for him, he ought to have stayed at home. Nobody asked him to come. If he be a merchant the process of adaptation, of commercial acclimatization, is so exhausting, so wasteful of vitality, that success is likely to be bought, if at all, by an expenditure of talent and energy, much in excess of what would be required of a native.

I am speaking now of eminent achievement, not of the mere making of a paltry living. If it be nevertheless a fact that so many immigrants accumulate great fortunes in commercial enterprises, it is because most of them possess a compensating advantage over the majority of native Americans in being inured to frugal habits, and demanding little of life, until their means justify them in demanding much.

If finally the immigrant be what most immigrants are, viz.: a farmer, he will indeed, in nine cases out of ten, improve his lot externally, and fill his belly with good things which at home he would have hankered for in vain. But if the Norwegian farmers with whom I have come in contact are in any sense typical, they buy their independence at a high price. Apart from the dangers which I have already pointed out, incident upon transplantation, it would seem that their minds, in emerging from the legendary dusk into the glaring American daylight, become, as it were, bleached and fade into a dire uniformity. They become like the prairie—blank, level, tedious, basking in a dreary, featureless prosperity. Though wealth, such as they now possess, would have been beyond their most daring aspiration at home, it rarely brings contentment. I should not venture to assert that they are conscious of their detachment from their own historic past, and feel it as a deprivation; but though they would be unable to formulate such a want, the more concrete ills from which they suffer and which they are amply able to formulate, are nevertheless fundamentally the results of the fortuity and isolation to which every uprooted and transplanted life must be subject. Every sapling, every flower, droops for a while in a new soil. It wilts, and seems on the point of dying. It takes long before it puts forth new roots and leaves and can draw its nourishment freely from the richer environment. It may, if the conditions be favorable, in the course of time, develop a vigor and lustihood which it never could have drawn from the old soil. But (like the finer qualities of European grapes which have become acclimated) it will lose its subtlest bloom and fragrance. It will become a coarser, cruder, more flavorless product.

Human transplantation is apt to involve a similar loss. A man really belongs only to the country of his birth. There are the spiritual soil and the climate most completely adapted to his needs. There alone, if anywhere, can he reach a full and perfect florescence. What he would attain elsewhere (though it need not be mean) will always be much below the climax of his powers. Therefore, if he be wise, let him, like Ulysses of old, close his ears to those alluring siren voices in the western wind that would entice him across the seas. America is a great and glorious land—to those who are born here. But the immigrant, through no fault of his own, was not born here; and can never fully reconquer here the birthright he forfeited at home.

40. CARL SCHURZ

Their sacred obligation to preserve the mothertongue

Most immigrants abandoned their mother tongue reluctantly, while many were committed to its perpetuation. German, especially, like French, occupied an enviable position, for it was not only a folk vernacular but a language of high culture, a vehicle for transmitting the knowledge of an advanced civilization. During the era of the great migration, it stood second only to English among the languages of the American nation. Spokesmen for German-America, such as Carl Schurz, were committed to encouraging bilingualism indefinitely. But World War I brought a tragic end to German-America and to the German tongue that went with it.

On January 9, 1897, Schurz paid tribute to his beloved mother tongue in an address before the Deutscher Liederkranz of New York City on that choral society's fiftieth anniversary. Delivered, of course, in German, it was later translated for publication by his daughter.

MY FRIENDS:—The toast to the German mothertongue ought to be responded to in music. This the Liederkranz has done so often and with so much feeling—and again only the other day—that it might be better were the chorus now to stand in my place, for to-day we celebrate more especially the German mothertongue as it speaks to us in song. There may indeed be other languages which on account of the resonance of their vowels and the softness of their consonants are better adapted to singing, but in no other language do people sing as much as in German and no

From *Speeches, Correspondence and Political Papers of Carl Schurz,* ed. Frederic Bancroft (New York: G. P. Putnam, 1913), vol. 5, pp. 334–38. Reprinted by permission of G. P. Putnam, original American publisher.

other nation has given us so great a treasure of melodies that people sing, songs of such deep feeling and of such virile force. Together with the mothertongue, the German *Lied* sprang from the German heart and it has made its way around the world. Whatever may resist German intellect and German enterprise— nothing can withstand German song.

We must be forgiven if, when speaking of our German mothertongue, we become a little sentimental, for that is not a sign of weakness. You may remember Heine's lines about the "sentimental oaks." The German mothertongue is a treasure for every thoughtful person who possesses it, the value of which is to him much more than a mere matter of sentiment. We Germans like to hear honesty spoken of as one of the prominent traits of the German national character; and I, for my part, am particularly pleased when the better elements of the American people rely upon the support of German-Americans when questions about honest government and honest money arise. Pardon me for referring to such questions here; I do so only because honesty is also one of the principal characteristics of the German mother-tongue.

Other languages, particularly the Romance, are distinguished for the refined and graceful elegance of their melodious diction. In these languages it is easy to say things that sound very pretty and that mean very little. In German that is more difficult. I would not imply that I consider it admirable, where a sign announces "German spoken here," for one to be as rude as one pleases—I mean rather that an insincere or stupid thought expressed in German really sounds so. And if you say anything clever or graceful in German, you cannot make it sound any more clever than it really is. In other words, the German mothertongue is not the language of vain display. Moreover, like a great organ it commands the whole range of musical expression, of force, of grandeur, of lofty enthusiasm, of passion, of delicate feeling. What is there in any other language that can excel the vigor of the German Bible, the powerful, sonorous sublimity of Schiller's dramas, the captivating word-music of Heine's lyrics?

It would be superfluous here to speak of the literature which has grown up in the German language and includes every field of intellectual activity, for its imposing scope has been recognized by the whole civilized world. But it is not only *German* literature which the mothertongue has to give us.

There is no language in the world which offers so many difficulties to the translator as the German, and none in which all the idioms and poetic meters of other languages can be so exactly rendered and which has so rich and complete a collection of translations. Homer, Dante, Hafiz, Shakespeare, Aristotle, Bacon, Thucydides, Tacitus, Macaulay, Victor Hugo, Walter Scott, Tolstoy—the poetry, philosophy, science, history, fiction of all times and of all nations have naturally found a home in the German language, through the translations which are worthy of the originals by their fidelity, their strength and beauty. Indeed, the German language opens up to us more than any other the wealth of the literature of the whole world.

We possess, in truth, a treasure which we cannot prize highly enough, especially we who have made a new home in a new world speaking another language. It is sometimes expected of our compatriots in America that they shall not only learn English, but that they shall entirely cast aside the old mothertongue. That is very unwise advice. Nobody will dispute that the German-American must learn English. He owes it to his new country and he owes it to himself. But it is more than folly to say that he ought, therefore, to give up the German language. As American citizens we must become Americanized; that is absolutely necessary. I have always been in favor of a sensible Americanization, but this need not mean a complete abandonment of all that is German. It means that we should adopt the best traits of American character and join them to the best traits of German character. By so doing we shall make the most valuable contribution to the American nation, to American civilization. As Americans we ought to acquire the language of the country, but we must not lose our German mothertongue.

The idea that the preservation of the German language together with the English may hinder the development of our American patriotism is as silly as it would be to say that it makes us less patriotic to be able to sing *Hail, Columbia* in two languages. There are thousands of Americans who study German without becoming less patriotic; it only makes them more cultured and more accomplished. They learn German with laborious effort, for German is very difficult. We German-Americans have brought this treasure over the ocean with us. We need not study German—we need only not to forget it. Our children will have without trouble what others can acquire only with great difficulty, if we are but sensible and conscientious enough to cultivate and to foster it in our families. That may not suffice to give our children as thorough a knowledge of the language as is desirable, but it will immensely facilitate the acquisition of what is lacking.

I am not preaching as one of whom it might be said: "Follow his words but not his deeds." I flatter myself that I am as dutiful an American as any one, and I have tried to learn English and so have my children. But in my family circle only German is spoken, much German is read and our family correspondence is carried on only in German. I may therefore be permitted to express myself strongly on this point. And so I say to you when I see how German-American parents neglect to secure for their children the possession of the mothertongue, often from mere indolence, how they wantonly cast aside the precious gift—then my German heart and my American common-sense rise up in indignant protest. Parents who neglect to give their children an opportunity to learn the German language without effort are sinning against their sacred obligation to preserve the mothertongue. All the more do I honor a German-American society in which the German language is valued and cherished as it is here; it is doing an incalculable service to our contemporaries as well as to coming generations.

May the Liederkranz, in the unnumbered years that we all hope are still in store for it, remain as faithful to this noble duty as it has been in the half-century just elapsed—for the mothertongue is the bond which holds and binds its members together. The German mothertongue, the dear, strong, noble, tender, sacred mother-tongue—may it live everlastingly here and all the world over!

41. SAMSON RAPHAELSON

A song number with a kick in it

In the 1920s New York's Lower East Side was melting into the Great
White Way, where a new American culture was being hammered out,
linking new Americans to old, in ways that were novel to both. In 1922,
the same year that saw Anne Nichols' *Abie's Irish Rose* begin its
record-smashing performance on Broadway, Samson Raphaelson's story
"The Day of Atonement," appeared in *Everybody's Magazine.* Slated for
melodrama on the boards as *The Jazz Singer,* it struck an unusually
responsive chord that mirrored, however mawkishly and naively, the
deep-seated yearning of the children of immigrants to blend the new with
the old.

"The Day of Atonement" is the story of Jack Robin, born Jakie
Rabinowitz, son of Cantor Yosele Rabinowitz of the Hester Street
Synagogue, who was on the verge of becoming America's greatest
ragtime singer. The marriage of Jew to Gentile and of poverty to wealth,
and the translation of traditional cantorial modes into a popular new
American idiom are key themes in this melting pot romance.

"What Jack Robin needs," said David Lee, who owns some of the
whitest of Broadway's white lights, "is a wife."

"What our Jakie needs," said Jack Robin's father, old Cantor
Rabinowitz, of the Hester Street Synagogue, "is a God."

"What I need," said Jack Robin, "is a song-number with a kick
in it. The junk that Tin Pan Alley is peddling these days is
rusty—that's all—*rusty.*"

And the sum and substance of it was a sober-faced Jack,
engaged fitfully in experiments with pleasure, a worried but
watchful David Lee, and a tragically lonely household on Hester
Street, where dwelt the aged cantor and his wife.

For Jack was no ordinary singer of ragtime. Those dark eyes of
his might have been the ecstatic eyes of a poet in the days when
the Chosen People lived sedately in the land of Canaan. They
might have been prophetic eyes, stern and stirring, in the years of

From Samson Raphaelson, "The Day of Atonement," *Everybody's Magazine* XLV
(January, 1922): pp. 44–55. Reprinted by permission of the author.

Zedekiah, son of Josiah, King of Judah, when Jerusalem "knew not its God." They might have been deep wells of lamentation even one generation ago had his lyric voice been born to cry the sorrows of Israel in a Russian synagogue.

But he lived in New York, and his slender, well-set-up figure was draped in perfectly fitting suits of Anglo-Saxon severity, and his dark hair was crisply trimmed and parted after the fashion of young America, and the black eyes in his thin, handsome face were restless, cynical and without joy.

That bewilderment, brooding and fitful, which was now so palpable, had vaguely begun to propel Jack in the days when, as Jakie Rabinowitz, he had drifted with a gang of Hester Street hoodlums. He was twelve then, rather tall and sturdy for his age, and for an exciting few weeks he enjoyed the thrills of looting fruit-stands, of stealing milk-bottles and of openly shooting craps. But the bliss of these few weeks came to a hysterical termination when he violated the code of the gang, and it was not until ten years later, when he knew Amy Prentiss, that he felt such happiness again.

The gang's code regarded certain acts of loyalty as religion; and certain epithets could be avenged only in blood—the blood of a bleeding nose or a lacerated lip. Foremost among the firebrand epithets was the term "sheeny." If some one called you a sheeny, only one thing could properly ensue—violent fistic battle. But Jakie, traversing Cherry Street, the Irish domain, received the stigma with indifference.

He and nine-year-old Hymie Cohen were on their way home from an East River salt-water swimming-shack, where for a dime they had received the use of faded trunks and the privileges of a moldy wooden tank. A barefoot young "mick," slighter than Jakie but of truculent demeanor, had united ten fingers with his nose in a trestle of vilification and cried: "Yah! Lookit the sheeny! Go back where yah came from, yah sheeny!"

Jakie shrugged his shoulders and passed on. Neither righteous indignation nor the tremors of fear had risen within him.

Little Hymie told his brother Joe of the humiliating incident, and that night Joe asked Jakie about it.

"Yah didn't fight, did yah?" he demanded. "Yah didn't do nothin'?"

"Why should I fight? I wasn't mad."

Joe stepped close to Jakie.

"You're yeller! Yah got a yeller streak a mile wide right t'rough to your liver! Yah can't hang around wit' de gang no more. Go 'way before I paste yah one on the jaw!"

This was disturbing. Jakie was not minded to obedient alacrity. He responded with a show of spirit,

"I'll go when I feel like it!"

Joe's response was a contemptuous slap over the eyes—a slap which stung and infuriated. Sobbing and seeing red, he fell upon Joe and blindly pommeled away with his fists.

After it was over and Jakie lay on the curb with a "shiner," a bleeding nose, and a perforated dental display, sobbing breathlessly and cursing in richly filthy East Side *argot*, Joe came up to him.

"I take it back, Jakie," he said, proffering his hand. "Y'ain't yeller. I——"

"Go to hell," Jakie panted, "you dirty sheeny!"

Jakie went directly home that night and endured stoically his father's scolding and his mother's running fire of questions. Dwelling in a passion of hatred for the complete order of things, his parents exasperated him into a seething calm beyond the point of articulate resentment. The next day he played truant from Hebrew school.

The *Melammed*, who was receiving a dollar a month extra for teaching the cantor's son, anxious to prepare him magnificently for the *Bar Mitzvah* recitative and speech in the synagogue, went out in search of the boy. He found Jakie playing basket-ball in the Hester Street playgrounds, dragged him back to the small, ill-smelling, gas-lit room where a few of the older boys still were singsonging the cadenced subtleties of *"Baba Kama,"* and flogged him until his body was purple.

Jakie came home that night somewhat terrified by the decision he had made, yet completely set in his determination. He was acute enough to speak to his mother first.

"Mamma, that *Rebi*—he ain't no good. He's so *dirty,* and he's always hollering, and, anyways, none of us kids ever learns anything. And he nearly killed me to-day, mamma, with a big strap— Look how sore my back is—and I never did nothing at all!"

"I'll tell papa," said his mother, busily applying goose-grease to his tortured back, "and he'll speak to the *Rebi* he shouldn't hit you no more."

"I don't wanna go to *Chaidar*," Jakie announced, with low-voiced intensity.

"Jakie! Your papa shouldn't hear you speak like this! How could you ever be a *Chazon*—a cantor in a big fancy synagogue—if you don't know good your Hebrew? I'll speak to papa he should find you a new *Chaidar* and a new *Rebi*."

"I don't want no new *Chaidar,* and I don't want to be a *Chazon* when I grow up!"

"Jakie! Eat your supper and don't speak it another word like this! Lucky your papa he's ain't home, or he would kill you."

The boy did not move toward the table. He raised a blazing face to his mother.

"If papa kills me," he said, "then I'll run away from home."

The old cantor did whip Jakie. It had long been a matter of profound distress to the cantor that a youth with so nimble a mind should be so diffident in the presence of the great culture of the noblest of all peoples. For ten generations, in Russia and now in America, the name "Rabinowitz" had stood for devout, impassioned *Chazonoth,* and Jakie's father was animated by the one desire that his son should become even a greater cantor than himself.

"I can see it comes a day when the Children of Israel will need it more *Chazonim*," the old father had said once to his young son. "It's too good here in America—too much money—too much telephones and trains and ragtime. A little bit more God ain't a bad thing, Jakie. Music is God's voice, and you make it your papa and mamma happy, Jakie, if you grow up to be a great *Chazon* like your grandfather in Vilna *olav-hasholom*."

"Aw, gee," Jakie had responded; "I wish the *Rebi* would comb his whiskers onct in a while!"

Fervently considering his God, the cantor had beaten Jakie soberly, and the boy had been inclined after that to listen in silence, if with resentment, to his pleas and homilies. That beating a year ago was the first Jakie had suffered from his father. The present belaboring was the second and last. That night, while his parents slept, Jakie, true to his word, did run away from home.

. A policeman found him, two days later, white with hunger and dragging his feet with weariness. His parents, who had become panic-stricken, overfed him and put him tenderly to bed. In the next few days they argued and pleaded with him, and, before they admitted defeat, wept before him.

"I'll sing in the choir every Sabbath," he said then. "But, honest, pa, *honest*, I'd quicker die than go every day to a *Chaidar*."

His father had to find comfort during the several years that followed in hearing the liquid golden tones of Jakie's alto voice in the choir only on Sabbath and on holy days.

"Maybe," he said to his wife, "maybe when he gets older, he'll see how beautiful is *Yiddishkeit*. Maybe he would stop hanging around music-places and singing these ragtime songs what all the bums they sing."

"I'm afraid, Yosele; I'm afraid," she sighed. "When he grows older, a job he'll get it—in a tailor shop, maybe—and right away with a girl he'll be running around."

"Better he should never marry," the cantor cried, "than with one of these peek-a-boo-waist girls with paint on the faces! Oy, Rivka mine, why ain't it here in America good healthy girls like you was?"

But girls were not in Jakie's mind. The few who moved through his life had laughed too much and listened too little. They were shrill creatures, made for anything but love. They were haughty when they should have been humbly eager, and they greedily mimicked things they should austerely have left alone.

He might have sunk to a Russian kind of morbidness if he had not been caught up in the stream of highly seasoned folk-song which poured constantly from Tin Pan Alley.

By the time he was eighteen he moved in an unreal, syncopated world of his own. If he had a sentimental grief, what better relief than sitting in the dark of his bedroom in the tiny Hester Street flat and howling dolefully the strains of "Down by the Old Mill Stream"? If the joys of being alive smote him, what could more sweetly ease the ache of happiness than the plaintive blare of "Alexander's Ragtime Band"?

So he haunted the motion-picture shows.

Then one night he got a job singing popular songs in the Great Alcazar Palace on Grand Street—one of the new movie-houses with rococo modeling in front, a house penetrating into the bowels of the building to a greater depth than its rickety, makeshift predecessors. And later that night his father told him never to show his face in the Hester Street home again.

"Better I shouldn't have it no son at all. Your loafer's talk stabs me in my heart. I couldn't bear to see your face no more—bum! In a synagogue you don't even put your head. For ten generations was every Rabinowitz a God-fearing *Chazon*, and you—my only son—street-songs you are singing! Go! Be a ragtime singer with the bums!"

How could the old cantor, or, for that matter, Jakie himself, understand that instead of being sinful and self-indulgent, loose and lazy, this grave-eyed boy with the ways of the street was sincerely carrying on the tradition of plaintive, religious melody of his forefathers—carrying on that tragic tradition disguised ironically with the gay trappings of Broadway and the rich vulgarity of the East Side? Instinctively the East Side responded to it, for people came hours early to the Great Alcazar Palace and stood in line twenty deep to hear Jakie, now Jack Robin, sing "Lovey Joe" or "When Dat Midnight Choo-Choo Leaves for Alabam'."

"Chee, but that baby can rag!" they said, as they swayed, hypnotized, to the caressing quavers of his voice. They knew only that he caught at their heart-strings. They failed to perceive that Jakie was simply translating the age-old music of the cantors— that vast loneliness of a race wandering "between two worlds, one dead, the other powerless to be born"—into primitive and passionate Americanese.

One year Jakie spent thus, and then David Lee, on a periodical scouting expedition, drifted into the Great Alcazar Palace. A short, fat man with cold blue eyes in a round pink face, Lee slipped unnoticed into the dark of the last row. He heard Jack Robin render "Underneath the Sugar Moon" with swifter, more potent tunefulness than a certain black-face comedian whom he was paying a thousand a week for singing the same song on Broadway. As a result, Jack Robin found himself booked on the great Keats vaudeville circuit.

"It's up to you," David Lee told him. "If you can put it over in vaudeville for a year or two, I'll place you on Broadway in electric lights."

With money and comfort and prestige tossed into his lap, a certain change came slowly over Jack. The clouds, lifting away, did not reveal sunshine, but a gray void. The clouds had been grim, inexplicable, tormenting—but they had inspired. The present void was reflected by emptiness in Jack. He was singing badly when he encountered Amy Prentiss, who was billed by the Keats people as "The World-Famous Dancer of Joyous Dances."

It was in San Francisco. Her act preceded his, and he stood in the wings, waiting his turn. Slender, dark-haired, blue-eyed, she had none of the Oriental instinct for undulation which Jack had understood so easily and to which he was so casually indifferent. Her open, frankly gay movements, her girlishly graceful fluttering pricked him to a breathless interest. She was bafflingly foreign to him—everything about her. Elusive, infinitely desirable to his naturally complex nature because of her simplicity, *she* was seeing the sunshine which for him did not exist. As he stood there watching, Henrietta Mooney, of the Mooney Ballet, joined him.

Henrietta's name off-stage was Sadie Rudnick. Jack had seen her performance several times in the past few years, and, while it was skilful and had its charm, its qualities were no mystery to him. Nor was Henrietta herself a mystery, for with one glance Jack knew her as baldly as he would a sister. "A clever Grand Street kid—in her second youth."

Henrietta listened in the wings at this Monday matinée while Jack went through his performance. She was there when he came off, and came directly up to him, saying without preliminaries,

"Kiddo, I heard you last September in Chicago, and you're losing the wallop."

Jack smiled without replying.

"What's wrong?" the girl persisted. "Booze?"

Jack shook his head amiably.

"Is it a skirt?"

"No; and it isn't an off day, either," he said wearily. "Guess I'm just getting tired of the game."

"Bunk!" was her scornful response. "You were born to the profession."

With the easy fellowship of the stage, they became chummy during the week. They would stand idly in the wings during the greater part of the performances, exchanging comments and gossip. Jack liked Henrietta's sturdy honesty, her slangy sophistication. Saturday evening, as he was hungrily following the fairylike movements of Amy Prentiss, Henrietta said,

"That girl's got your goat!"

"Do you think so?"

"Say—do I *think* so? I *know* it!"

"I wonder why," he mused audibly.

Henrietta looked him squarely in the eyes.

"You wonder why? She's a *Shiksa;* that's why! I've seen Jewish boys fall that way before. It ain't new to me." There was bitterness in her voice.

"But why?" Jack repeated, more to himself than to her. "Why?"

"You come from the Ghetto, and she studied fancy dancing in a private school. You're the son of a poor old *Chazon,* and she's the daughter of a Boston lawyer. You're— Aw, you make me sick!"

Abruptly Henrietta left him, and during the one remaining day of their stay in San Francisco she avoided him. But her words stayed with him; they pried brutally into his apathy; they jeered him from afar; they came terribly close and stung him. The thought of approaching this lovely dancer with the quiet eyes and the gentle mouth frightened him a little; but his fear angered him. As she came out into the wings Saturday night, she found him in her path.

"Say—" he began. She stopped, smiling uncertainly. Jack, to her, was a pleasingly debonair figure with a handsome face, glowing eyes. His manner she hadn't the time or the gift to analyze.

"I have to hand it to you," he went on, self-consciously, flushing to the roots of his hair. "You—you dance with more real class—I mean to say—you're darn good—" He paused, floundering.

It is a curious fact that often the only signs of yearning, of sincere and painful humbleness, of profound anxiety to express fine things consist of awkwardness—of a stilted nonchalance. His confusion served simply to embarrass her. She strove, not in vain, for poise to cover her embarrassment. Her only recourse was to smile vaguely and say, "Glad you liked—uh—" And then, fearing that he might gurgle more badly still, she passed on.

Jack hated her for having made it so hard for him.

"I know she don't care a damn about me," he told himself savagely. "But she didn't have to make a fool of me. She could have said a few civil words, even if I don't mean anything in her life."

In San Diego, in Dallas, in San Antonio, in New Orleans and in the other cities he made on the long swing back to New York, his eyes seemed to seek morbidly for further evidences of the simple, unruffled Anglo-Saxon quality of temperament. He found plenty of them, and, as the weeks passed, they served to beat him down into a soothing numbness, which was bad for the audiences, who sat stonily through his performances. Henrietta's words would constantly drum into his ears: "You come from the Ghetto, and she's the daughter of a Boston lawyer."

It was slowly, because he was fundamentally temperate, that he learned to seek self-respect in barrooms. No one else would have called it that. It had too little of the nature of peace. It brought back the invigorating uncertainty, the inspiring restlessness of his adolescent days. It eliminated, for the moment, this new numbness which had come upon him, this queer sensation of being softly strangled. And, since it substituted his old *Weltschmerz* for the feeling of being slowly buried into a grave of inarticulateness by the Amy Prentisses of the world, his ragtime singing got back some of its old lilting plaintiveness.

Jack saw his parents occasionally. His mother's furtive pride in the adulation which younger Hester Street gave to her son had even begun to reflect itself in a way in the old cantor.

"Every actor he's ain't a loafer, Yosele," she would say. "Look—is Jacob Adler a loafer? A finer man you couldn't find it if you should search a whole lifetime."

"But he's a *Yiddisher* actor, *Leben*. He feels the *Yiddishe* heart. And our Jakie sings ragtime—like a *Shagetz!*"

"I know—I know," she soothed him. "But he's an American boy. And he's a good boy. He's sending you and me presents only last month from New Haven. He lives a clean life, Yosele. Maybe soon he makes enough money and he goes into business and gets married and comes regular every Sabbath and holy day to the synagogue."

When he visited them in the summer, Jack's dumb unhappiness became apparent to them. They took it for a good sign—for indication of a new, more mature thoughtfulness. His booking for the year ended, he took a month's vacation and spent two weeks of it in New York. For two consecutive Sabbath days he attended the synagogue, and the old cantor, singing from the pulpit, exulted in the conviction that his son was returning to his God.

Indeed, Jack himself found a certain solace in it. As he sat on the old familiar wooden bench, clothed in the silk *Talis*—the prayer-shawl which his father had so solemnly presented to him on the occasion of his *Bar Mitzvah*—with good old Yudelson, the cobbler, on one side of him, and stout, hearty, red-bearded Lapinsky, the butcher, on the other, he felt a singular warmth and sweetness. And the voice of his father, still clear and lyric, rising in the intricacies of the familiar old lamenting prayers—prayers which he remembered perfectly, which he would never forget— the dissonant rumble of response from the congregation, the restive shufflings of youngsters—all these were to him blessedly familiar and blissful.

In the murmurous peacefulness of those two weeks his father talked to him constantly of the austere beauties of the ancient ways of his people, and it began to appear to Jack that there was indeed something to be said for them. He could not and did not dismiss his father's world as he used to—with a sneer and the words: "Dead! I tell you that stuff's behind the times." For he began to feel that if it was a dead or a dying world, still it possessed some reality, an orderly nobility; while the world he was alive to was chaotic, crassly unreal.

During the two weeks which followed in Atlantic City he thought a good deal on this, but the nearness of violins and cocktails, the flash of women and the glamour of moonlight on the sea made it easy for him to decide arbitrarily that it was rather an abstract problem.

In Buffalo, where he opened with his act, he began committing the unforgivable sin in the theatrical world—he began missing performances. He had lost all vital interest in his work.

By the time he was playing in Chicago, reports of his derelictions had reached David Lee, who, after long pondering, wrote a severe note.

"What Jack Robin needs," Lee said to Harry Anthony, his partner, "is a wife." In his note he said:

> If I can't depend on a performer being steadily on the job, no matter if he has the genius of Booth and the popularity of George Cohan, I will not have him in my employ. I don't know what's ailing you, but whatever it is, you must steady down. There isn't a producer or booking-office in New York that will gamble on you if you're not completely dependable, and we're no exception.

Jack smiled crookedly when he read this. It came at a most unfortunate time, for, having arrived in Chicago that morning, Jack had discovered that the sixth number on the bill with him at the Majestic was "The World-Famous Dancer of Joyous Dances."

And this discovery was sending him sauntering, blithely bitter, to Righeimer's bar.

It was two in the afternoon. His act went on at three. The act of the girl whose unseen nearness possessed the power to slash him into bewilderment would begin at four. If he left the theatre promptly after his act, most likely he could avoid seeing her. And, with a comforting cargo of Righeimer's product on board, he felt he would be able to give an account of himself on the stage.

To make doubly sure that the sense of Amy's nearness would not cause his heart to sink before the footlights, he took three or four extra drinks. They more than achieved their purpose. The world became an insignificant turmoil underneath his feet, and he strolled, his smile growing steadily more crooked, down Clark Street toward Madison, where at the Morrison bar they could mix the finest Tom Collins in the world. The words of David Lee's letter came into his mind. " 'Completely dependable—that's me! I'll drink all the Tom Collinses Jerry can mix—to the great god Dependability."

He halted in the crush of traffic on the corner, and, not two feet away from him, jammed by a fat woman on one side and grabbed at on the other by two sticky children, he saw Amy Prentiss. As his eyes glimpsed her proud little head, brown-toqued, quaintly half veiled, his lips compressed into a' straight line and he turned sharply away. But the crowd began to move; Amy had seen him, and she was already edging her way toward him. Her face smiled a friendly greeting, and involuntarily Jack looked behind him to see if it were not some one else she was addressing.

"Why, Mr. Robin!" she was saying. "I was just going to the house early to see your turn."

Jack was dumb. They crossed Madison Street together in the surge of the released crowd.

"How did you happen to recognize me?" he blurted.

"You recognized *me*, didn't you?"

"Oh, I recognized you, all right." Jack paused. He longed for an hour in solitude, so that he could think. "This gets me," he confessed. "Your knowing me so quickly, and your actually going early to see my act."

"You're funny. Hasn't anybody let you in on the secret that you're one of the few real rag-singers in America? As for remembering you, how could I ever forget your genuine little compliment on my act out on the Coast?"

They had turned the corner at Monroe Street and were at the entrance to the Majestic. Jack looked hurriedly at his watch.

"Listen," he said; "I have to speed like the deuce to make it. I want to see you—talk to you some more. Meet me after your turn."

His mind raced in zigzags as he hastened to his dressing-room. He searched his memory for the exact wording of Amy's remark that Saturday in San Francisco, for her expression. He tried to see and hear again the outward things and to give a new, inner meaning to them. But all he could recall was the bitterness in him, the significant and fateful words of Henrietta, and Amy's vagueness, which turned the knife in his wounded vanity. And now she had voluntarily talked to him; she was deliberately coming to see him perform; she had been pleasant, approachable, inviting. His mind could find no place for such a manifestation from this girl.

His performance that matinée was discouragingly poor. Amy made no comment on it when they met.

"Let's have dinner somewhere," Jack suggested. "That is"—a flicker of his old wretchedness returning—"that is, if you haven't made any other arrangements, and—and if——"

"I should be glad to."

They dined at the Café Lafayette, which has a sedate lower floor and an upper floor with an orchestra for dancing. It had been in Jack's mind to avoid the beat of syncopated music, but by the time they reached the restaurant, the sweet poise of the girl had filled him with unreasoning dismay at himself. The old familiar bewildered sinking of the heart followed. And so he led her up-stairs. A violin was weaving a slim pattern of simple melody, which was being tortured into savage bedlam by the bullet-like spitting of the drum and by the saxophone's gusts of passionate whining.

He felt instinctively that liquor was not on the cards. But he was tense, strung up, dreadfully nervous.

"Let's dance," he said.

The music was sending forth a one-step, and Jack gave himself to it hungrily. He seemed, somehow, to make of the simple steps a wild, heart-breaking aria, a mad pounding on the doors of heaven.

Back at the table they sat a while in silence. Amy studied his face. She said,

"You dance differently from any one I know."

Jack flushed.

"I don't suppose I dance very well. I—I wish I could dance standing straight and moving sort of—well, evenly and correctly, if you know what I mean. Like that fellow, for instance." He indicated a tall, stolid-looking youth who was soberly and skilfully maneuvering a sleek young creature about the polished floor.

"That's funny," Amy remarked. "I'm crazy about the way you dance. I never quite liked any one's dancing so well. You danced to-night the way you used to sing—the way you sang when I first heard you in New York."

"You *like* my dancing?" Jack leaned to her, unbelieving. His voice came huskily. "*You* don't dance that way—even on the stage. You dance more like that fellow. I don't mean stiff as him—not that. But you're his kind, if you know what I mean. I'm—I'm crazy about that quality in you. I'd give anything if I could have it—that careless, happy— Guess I'm talking like a fool," he ended lamely.

But Amy, her eyes aglow, was leaning to him.

"You're the *funniest* person! I've been crazy about the very thing in you that you're deprecating. I wish I had it. I'd give *anything* to have it. It—it hurt me a lot to find your performance to-day lacking in it."

They dined and danced together every day that week. There was no making of appointments after that evening; tacitly they met after Amy's turn and went out together. Jack went about in an unreal world. He tried to think, but his mind persisted in substituting the turn of Amy's wrist, the curve of her cheek, the gay animation of her eyes, the little liquid turns in her voice.

Each day he grew more afraid of her while she was with him and more desolate while she was not. His only interludes were when they danced. The blare of the orchestra had somehow for him become Music—a glorious substitute for tears, a gleaming speedway for a breathless race hand in hand with grief. Sunday evening—the last of the week they would have together—he found himself holding Amy crushingly close, and he relaxed sharply, dancing badly after that.

Back at the table, sitting side by side on an upholstered bench against the wall, Amy chattered happily until she became aware that Jack was not listening. His food untouched, he was staring with undisguised misery before him. Amy placed her hand lightly over his on the seat.

"What is it?" she asked.

He withdrew his hand, afraid. For a moment he was silent, and Amy repeated her question.

"I—I suppose you think I'm out of my head, but—I—I'm crazy about you."

"I'm crazy about you, too," said Amy promptly.

Jack looked at her then, a puzzled, imploring look.

"You don't know what I mean."

"What do you mean?"—with a flicker of a smile.

He breathed deeply.

"I mean that I love you—that I want to marry you."

"That," said Amy, "is what I thought you meant."

Late that night, in his room at the hotel Jack scribbled a note to David Lee and one to his mother. To Lee he wrote:

> You needn't worry any longer about my dependability. I'm engaged to be married. . . . She's the kind of a girl who could no more understand my not being on the job than she could understand quitting of any kind. I'm going to work my head off. If it's in me at all, I'll be on Broadway in a year.

To his mother he wrote briefly that he was to be married, mentioning the girl's name, Amy Prentiss.

His letters brought two prompt results. David Lee offered him a part in the coming "Frivolities" and instructed him to leave for New York at once for rehearsals. And old Cantor Rabinowitz, not so strong as he used to be, had a nervous collapse.

"A *Shiksa!*" he repeated over and over as he lay in his bed. "A *Shiksa!* Our Jakie should marry a *Shiksa!* God in heaven, why do you let me live to suffer like this?"

His white-haired wife, broken-hearted, tried to console him.

"What could you tell it from a name, Yosele? A name, it ain't. nothing. Look—our Jakie he goes by the name Jack Robin. Amy Prentiss—it could be she's a *Yiddishe* girl. Look—Jenny Levy from Ludlow Street is her name on the stage Genevieve Leeds. Wait we should hear from Jakie some more."

"It's a *Shiksa,*" her husband insisted. "If it was a *Yiddishe* girl, he would have written it in the letter. I feel it—I know it—it's a *Shiksa. Gott im Himmel,* help me to live out my last years!"

The next Tuesday evening Jack came unexpectedly. As he stepped into the spotless little flat, his father, who was sitting before the kitchen table in his shirt-sleeves, a skull-cap on his white head, reading loudly to himself from the *Mishna,* looked up mildly over his glasses and spoke the question he must have rehearsed scores of times to himself.

"To a *Shiksa* you're engaged, ain't it?"

Jack hesitated. The calmness of his father he sensed at once as being anything but indifference. He suddenly was swept with shame for not having thought more about what his engagement would mean to them.

The old man had turned back to the *Mishna.* Apparently, Jack's hesitation had replied adequately. And now his mother came into the kitchen from the narrow, dark corridor of the tenement. Jack kissed her wrinkled cheek. It was the first time in years that he had kissed her, and it thrilled the old woman. But in a moment she had observed the portentous absorption of her husband in his book of the Talmud.

"Yosele, don't you see our Jakie is here?"

The cantor continued with the low-murmured singsong as if he had not heard her. She turned to Jack, who gave her a queer smile and an almost imperceptible shrug of the shoulders.

"Then it's a *Shiksa?*" she whispered. Briskly she moved to the kitchen stove. "You'll stay for supper, Jakie?" she asked over her shoulder. "Sit down. I'll have it quick ready. The soup is already on the stove—*Borsht,* red-beets soup, Jakie—and to-night we got it cucumbers in sour cream, and cheese *Blintzes,* too."

The old cantor joined them at the table, but beyond the various ritual prayers he and Jack mumbled together, he did not utter a word. The old woman, pathetically striving to eke out some harmony from the situation, made not the slightest attempt to get Jack to talk of his *fiancée*.

"You are coming to the synagogue next Sabbath?"

"I'm sorry, ma. I'm going to be terribly busy. You see, this is my one big chance. Lee has been fine, and it's up to me to repay him. He's one of these men who doesn't do things half-way. Either he backs you to the limit or he drops you. He's watching me closely, and I have to prove I can be relied upon. He's not giving me a star part, but I'm a principal, and if I make a hit, I'll rise fast with David Lee. This is the first time, ma, that my future has meant anything to me, and I'm going to give all I have to rehearsals."

When the meal was cleared off the table, the old cantor moved with his tome to the smaller kitchen table, where he went on with his low-toned recitative of the Talmud. Jack and his mother sat in silence at the larger table. Then Jack placed his hand tenderly over hers.

"Ma, it's a funny thing, but I'm just beginning to appreciate what you and pa mean to me. I never realized it until suddenly last week. I——"

"Do you hear what our Jakie is saying, Yosele? He's saying that now he's grown up and he knows how good it is a papa and a mamma. He's saying——"

It was as if the old man had not heard.

They talked on softly, rapidly at first, exchanging ideas and comments, and then peaceful silences crept between them. After a rather long pause in the talk, his mother said, with a casual air:

"You know, Jakie, I was just thinking the other day—I was thinking that if a *Yiddishe* girl marries a *Goyisher* boy, then it's bad, because you know how it is in a house—everything is like the father wants. But if a *Yiddisher* boy marries a *Goyishe* girl, then it ain't so terrible. She could be learned to buy *Kosher* meat and to have two kinds of dishes, for *Fleischige* and for *Milchige*—and the children could be brought up like *Yiddishe* children; they could be sent to a *Chaidar*—I was just thinking like this only yesterday, Jakie. Ain't it funny I should think of it?"

Jack's hand tightened over hers.

"You're sweet, ma," he said slowly. "I'm afraid it can't be. I was brought up that way, ma, and I've been unhappy all my life. And Amy was brought up the other way, and she's been happy from the day she was a baby. I'll want my children to be happy like Amy is."

The sharp sound of a book snapping shut twisted their attention to the cantor. He had risen, and, eyes blazing, was pointing a shaking finger at Jack.

"Go out!" he cried. "Go out from my house—bum! Go!" A fit of coughing seized him, and he sank to his chair. They hastened to his side. The old man was unable to speak, but his eyes glared so that Jack stepped back. His mother turned, tragic-eyed, to him and said,

"Maybe you better go, Jakie."

There are few tasks more absorbing and exacting than that of rehearsing for the "Frivolities," and the days which followed for Jack were so full that he found time only to telephone his mother. As there was no connection directly to the flat on Hester Street, Jack had to call the drug store on the corner. He succeeded in getting her but twice in the five times he called. His father was well, she told him cheerfully, but naturally getting old and feeble. She doubted whether he would be able to continue as cantor for very many more years, but thanked God that he would be able to lead in the services for the coming holy day, Yom Kippur—the Day of Atonement. "Maybe you will come to the synagogue then, and fast the whole day?" she asked wistfully.

"Ma, I don't see how I can possibly come. It's the fifteenth, and our show opens on Broadway the same evening. I—I'd give anything, ma, to be able to come. I'd do it for my own sake as well as for papa's and yours. It's beginning to mean something to me—Yom Kippur. You see how it is, don't you, ma?"

"Yes," his mother sighed; "I see."

The second time, she brought up the subject again.

"Your papa he's ain't feeling so good, Jakie. Maybe this will be his last Yom Kippur. He talks about you. He is all the time talking about you. He says God has punished him enough for his sins that he should be the last Rabinowitz in ten generations to sing *Chazonoth* in a *Shool*. He don't *say* you should come on Yom Kippur—he didn't talk about that. But I think in his heart he means it, Jakie."

"I'll tell you what I'll do, ma," he replied, after some thought. "We open Monday night, and there probably will be a lot of changes made in the special rehearsal on Tuesday. But I'll try to dodge that Tuesday rehearsal and come to the synagogue for the morning and most of the afternoon."

"You're a good boy, Jakie."

Amy, who had swung West on the vaudeville circuit, was in Denver at this time. Jack wrote her every day—love-letters, almost childish in their outpouring of longing, full of high resolve, glowing with the miracle of the new insight he felt he was getting into life.

> I realize that with me it isn't a question of ability, but of character. I've seen enough of this show to believe that I can put my songs over so big that Lee will have to star me. But I must be unswervingly steady. I have to be as good at the end of the season as on the opening night. I have to be on hand all of the time. My health must be guarded as well as my impulses. I don't even want to miss a performance with illness as an excuse. I can see that some of them are a bit leery of me—they're not dead-sure they can depend on me. Lee is the only one who's different. He's like a rock. I'd rather break a leg than fail him. But your wonderful confidence and my own resolution make me smile at them. I know I'll come through.

Swiftly the last month of rehearsal went by, and then the great day came. At two Monday afternoon, David Lee, who had attended the dress-rehearsal, called a halt.

"That's all," he said. "Take it easy until to-night. Robin, I want to see you."

He took Jack aside in a corner of the shadowy theatre.

"You're a winner if you can come through. Not exactly a world-beater—Frank Binney and Hal Bolton and Eddie Loren and Helen Kennedy still have something you haven't got. I don't know what it is, but you have the *capacity* to get it. I've seen it show suddenly in talented performers, sometimes overnight. But you'll make the electric lights, and I'm behind you. Now beat it, and be sure to take it easy."

At three in the afternoon, Jack, in his suite at the family hotel on Seventy-ninth Street, was busily writing a letter to Amy, who was in Salt Lake City. He had taken a hot bath, intending to sleep off some of his nervousness after this note to his sweetheart. He finished the letter and had just sunk beneath the covers of his bed when the telephone-bell rang. It was old Chiam Yudelson, friend and neighbor of his parents, to tell him that his father had just died.

When Jack's taxi-cab drew up before his home in Hester Street, a harassed policeman was swinging his club in the effort to disperse the crowd in front of the tenement where the beloved cantor lay dead. Jack elbowed his way through. He was recognized, and a pathway was instantly made for him.

In the tiny flat were his mother, the *Shamas* of the synagogue, old Chiam Yudelson and his wife, and Lawyer Feldman, the friend of all Hester Street. Greater perhaps than her grief at the loss of the man who had loved her and his God with equal fervor for sixty years was Mrs. Rabinowitz's panic at the thought that it was Yom Kippur eve and that the lyric voice of a Rabinowitz would not be raised in supplication to wipe out the sins of the Chosen People before their Creator. When Jack crowded his way through the friends and neighbors who packed the dark, narrow corridor, she was clinging to the hand of Lawyer Feldman.

"Look, Mr. Feldman," she was saying; "it's only two hours to Yom Kippur. It's got to be a good *Chazon* to sing. The last words my Yosele he said to me, he said, 'Rivka, get our Jakie.' So low he says it, Mr. Feldman, I couldn't hardly hear him. His face was white like a *Yahrzeit* candle, and he says to me: 'Rivka, God will forgive our Jakie if he will sing *"Kol Nidre"* for me to-night. Maybe my dying,' he says, 'will make a *Chazon* from our Jakie. Tell him, Rivka,' he says. Look, Mr. Feldman; Jakie is maybe coming here. Maybe you could talk to him. In his heart he's a good boy. Tell him—tell him—his father is dead—tell him—oh, Mr. Feldman, my heart is breaking in pieces—I—I can't talk no more——"

"Here's Jakie!" Chiam Yudelson broke in.

The next moment his mother was in his arms. Lawyer Feldman drew her gently away, and she turned into the other room—the bedroom where her dead husband lay. Silence followed. Nervously Jack went after her, fearing that silence.

It was an immaculately clean room—so clean that every rip in the wall-paper, every stain on the plastered ceiling stared at them, hollow-eyed, terrible in nakedness. The bed, a thing of iron tubing, whose green paint had long since scaled off, stood head against an ancient oak bookcase, crammed with old-fashioned mahogany-colored books of the Talmud, the *Chumesh*, the various prayer-books, and a mass of huge music portfolios filled with note-scribbled sheets. On the bed lay his father's body. It had been covered completely with a white sheet, but his mother, flung across it, had drawn the sheet off so that the waxlike face and one thin old shoulder were revealed. Jack looked long at his father's face. It was beautiful in death. Every line in it spoke of a brave, poetic fight, of deep, fierce religious faith. His mother's body shuddered, and Jack reached over to take her hand.

She rose from the bed then, and son and mother stood alone.

"I—I came as soon as I—heard," Jack said.

His mother's hand rested lightly against his coat.

"He—he died this morning. It was a quarter to twelve. Yesterday he got sick. He talked about you—all the time about you, Jakie. At a quarter to twelve he died—a quarter to twelve. He just closed his eyes—like a baby, Jakie—and he said—he said: 'Rivka,' he said, 'God will forgive our Jakie if he will sing *"Kol Nidre"* for me to-night. Maybe,' he said, 'maybe—maybe—' Oh, Jakie, I—Jakie, *mein Kind,* your father is dead—I can't stand it——"

She was again in his arms. Lawyer Feldman appeared in the doorway.

"Better take her out of that room," he suggested. "It isn't doing her any good. Has she spoken to you about——"

Jack nodded. He gently led his mother toward the kitchen. As they passed him, the lawyer asked in a low tone,

"Are you going to do it?"

Jack placed his mother in a chair, where she sat blankly, looking first at the friends gathered in the kitchen, then out of the window where the crowds were still pushing and surging noisily, and then, in a most pathetic and forlorn way, down at her hands folded so helplessly in her lap.

The *Shamas*, who was there, mainly for the purpose of finding out whether Jack would serve as cantor that evening and the next day or whether he would have to step into the breach himself, was becoming nervous and impatient. He approached Jack, who looked unseeingly at him.

It was four-thirty. If he appeared in the show that evening, singing ragtime songs while his father lay dead—while the Hester Street Synagogue went cantorless for the first Day of Atonement in forty years—while his mother struggled under an unbearable double grief——

He turned to the *Shamas*.

"My father's *Talis*, it is at the synagogue?"

"Yes; everything is in the *Shool*, Mr. Rabinowitz," the *Shamas* replied eagerly.

"The tunes—the *Genigen*—of the choir—are they the same my father used ten, fifteen years ago?"

"The same *Genigen*, exactly."

"All right. I'll be there at six o'clock."

As Jack took his mother in his arms to sit out the next hour with her and to comfort her, the tears for the first time since her husband died flowed from her eyes, and she said over and over to him:

"In your heart you're a good boy. I always told him that in your heart you're a good boy."

News travels like lightning in the East Side. "Jack Robin—the vaudeville headliner—is singing as cantor at the Hester Street Synagogue this Yom Kippur!" It might have been a newspaper scare headline, for by six-thirty that evening the slowly arriving members of the Hester Street Synagogue congregation had almost to fight their way through the mob that packed the street up to the corners of both Norfolk and Essex Streets. Wealthy East Siders, who had paid their ten and twelve dollars for pews in the much larger Beth Medresh Hagadol, neglected that comparatively splendid house of prayer to stand in the crammed lobby of the Hester Street Synagogue and listen to the golden notes of this young singer of ragtime as he rendered *"Kol Nidre"* with a high, broken sobbing which, they insisted critically, surpassed his father's in his best days.

Every twist and turn of his father's had been branded unforgettably in Jack's memory from childhood days, but he sang the grief-laden notes with a lyric passion that was distinctly his own. The low-hanging rafters of the old synagogue, the cheap, shiny chandeliers of painted gold, the faded velvet hangings on the holy vault where the parchments of the Old Testament stood, the gold-fringed, worn white-silk cloth that covered the stand in the pulpit where he prayed—these called to something surging and powerful in him, something which made his whole life since his boyhood seem blurred and unreal.

When, with the congregation standing and swaying in humility before their Creator, he uttered that refrain which asks forgiveness for every sin of mankind from evil thoughts to murder, rising from a low singsong into a quivering, majestic wail and then breaking into incoherent plaintiveness, the sobs choked his throat.

His mother sat in the small gallery at the back reserved for women, and he saw her when, after marching slowly forward with the choir, he had flung open the hangings before the holy vault and turned to face the congregation as he led in the appeal that the "prayers of this evening shall come before the Divine Presence in the morning and by nightfall bring redemption for all sins."

When he finished the high melodious strains of this triumphant yet humble and supplicating piece, there was a low murmur of approbation throughout the synagogue.

The rabbi, a rotund little man in the front pews, turned to his neighbor and remarked:

"Even Rosenblatt, when I heard him in Moscow, didn't give a *'Yaaleh'* like this. *Aza Singen nehmt by die Harz!*"

When the time came for *Kadish*, the prayer uttered only by those in mourning their dead, the whole congregation rose in silence in honor of the cantor who was dead and his son and wife. The other mourners subdued their customary loud recital, and the voices of Jack and his mother, the one flowing and resonant, the other high and broken with sobs, were heard clearly.

Crowds followed the couple as they slowly walked the half-block to the tenement-house that evening. As they paused on the stoop, Jack turned to the gathering people and in a low voice asked them to be good enough to leave his mother and himself alone with their grief. Instantly a cry was raised:

"Beat it!"

"Go home, bums, loafers! Ain't you got no respect for the *Chazon?*"

"G'wan! Can't you leave some peace be even on Yom Kippur—*Paskudniks!*"

The crowd dispersed.

Jack sat up until midnight that night with his mother, and then, completely weary, he fell asleep, to dream fitfully of Amy and of David Lee, of David Lee and of Amy, until morning.

David Lee slept fitfully also that night.

Jack's failure at the last moment to appear on the opening night had ruined three numbers and had made two others awkward, and Lee had a difficult job ahead of him in the next twenty-four hours. He wasted no time thinking about the delinquent. "*He's* going to do the worrying, not me," he said grimly to Harry Anthony. He stayed up until four in the morning, telephoning and telegraphing in the effort to get a substitute so much better than Jack that the reviews of Tuesday, probably derogatory, would be reversed on Wednesday morning.

His efforts did not meet with success, and he left word with his man to wake him early Tuesday. When his man called him, he asked for the morning papers.

He was about to turn to the theatrical page, when his eye was caught by a headline on the front sheet. Sitting on the edge of the bed, he read, and, as he read, a low whistle escaped him. He dropped the first paper and took another. He swore softly.

"That damn kid!" he murmured gleefully. "That damn kid! Stevens, tell Herman to have the car out in a half-hour."

He had to slip a crisp green bank-note into the hand of the policeman before room was made for him to stand in the crush in the narrow lobby of the Hester Street Synagogue. Jack Robin, swathed in the folds of a great black-striped linen *Talis*, an elaborate and stiff black-plush skull-cap on his head, his thin, handsome face deadly white, his dark eyes afire, was singing that splendid aria of his father's—"*Hamelech*," "The King"—and as the majesty of it rolled forth, broke, and narrowed into rivulets of humility, David Lee pinched himself to see if he were asleep.

Then, after a few moments of quick rattling recitative, Jack went on into a clear, low-toned series of sound which had the effect of musical talking, of superbly self-contained remonstrance. This speech gradually rose to a fluttering uncertainty, a bewildered pleading, and then the climax came—a flood of confession.

Excitedly Lee elbowed his way out of the crowd.

"Where's the nearest telephone?" he asked the policeman.

"Right on the corner—the drug store, sir."

In five minutes Harry Anthony was on the wire.

"Harry," said Lee, "do you want to hear the greatest ragtime singer in America in the making? A wonder, Harry, a wonder! Got Hal Bolton mopped off the boards. Come down right away. It's a dirty little hole down on the East Side called the Hester Street Synagogue. I'll meet you on the corner of Hester and Norfolk."

42. SAMSON RAPHAELSON

Jazz is prayer

Samson Raphaelson, ironically a former student of Stuart P. Sherman, arch-apostle of the American and the genteel at the University of Illinois, saw in the jazz delirium an awakening of all the inchoate yearnings of uprooted Americans. Raphaelson's *The Jazz Singer* had little to do with jazz. But when the author argued in the preface to the published play

Samson Raphaelson, *The Jazz Singer* (New York: Brentano's, 1925), pp. 9–10. Reprinted by permission of the author.

that jazz had become uniquely emblematic of the nation's new urban mass culture, he was persuasive.

In seeking a symbol of the vital chaos of America's soul, I find no more adequate one than jazz. Here you have the rhythm of frenzy staggering against a symphonic background—a background composed of lewdness, heart's delight, soul-racked madness, monumental boldness, exquisite humility, but principally prayer.

I hear jazz, and I am given a vision of cathedrals and temples collapsing and, silhouetted against the setting sun, a solitary figure, a lost soul, dancing grotesquely on the ruins. . . . Thus do I see the jazz singer.

Jazz is prayer. It is too passionate to be anything else. It is prayer distorted, sick, unconscious of its destination. The singer of jazz is what Matthew Arnold said of the Jew: "lost between two worlds, one dead, the other powerless to be born." In this my first play, I have tried to crystallize the ironic truth that one of the Americas of 1925—that one which packs to overflowing our cabarets, musical revues, and dance halls—is praying with a fervor as intense as that of the America which goes sedately to church and synagogue. The jazz American is different from the dancing dervish, from the Zulu medicine man, from the negro evangelist only in that he doesn't know he is praying. . . .

43. H. L. MENCKEN

Every fresh wave of immigrants has brought in new loan words

In 1910 Henry L. Mencken (1880–1956) casually began writing about the American form of the English language in the *Baltimore Evening Sun*. If

From H. L. Mencken, *The American Language*, ed. Raven L. McDavid, Jr., and David W. Maurer, fourth edition and two supplements, *Abridged*, with annotations not for the outbreak of World War I, Mencken recalled, his most lasting work would never have been done. But the exigencies of war and his pro-German views forced him to turn from pro-German editorials to extended philological comment. The result was *The American Language.* Published in 1919 in a limited edition, its great popularity quickly established it as the standard work. In subsequent decades, Mencken revised and recast his work three times. Although Craigie and Hurlbert's *A Dictionary of American English* and Mathews' *A Dictionary of Americanisms* have added much to our knowledge of the subject, *The American Language*, updated by Mencken's literary executors, continues to be current.

In the first edition of his book, Mencken emphasized the increasing divergence between American and English, predicting their increasing separation. By 1936, however, he concluded that American was so influencing English that they were growing together rather than apart and that future scholars might well study English as a dialect of American.

The following selection focuses on the naturalization of foreign words and phrases and their incorporation into the American language.

Of the 13,366,407 foreign-born whites in the country in 1930, 13,216,928 were ten years old or older, and of this number only 3,907,021 spoke English as their native language. Nevertheless, all save 869,865 of the remainder managed to convince the census enumerators that they had acquired a workable command of the language. The immigrants of the older immigrations had naturally made the most progress. The Scandinavians, about half of whom arrived before 1900, topped the list, with hardly more than 2% of them unable to speak English, and less than 1% of the males. Next came the Germans: 58.3% of them arrived before 1900, and all save 1.9% (1.8% of males) could speak English. The Poles, Russians, Italians, Greeks and Czechs, and the Baltic and Balkan peoples, most of whom came in between 1900 and 1914, fell much behind. Of the Poles, for example, 12.8% were still unable to speak English in 1930 (7.7% of males and 18.7% of females), and of Italians 15.7% (8.9% and 25.1%). Here something more than mere duration of residence in the country seems to have had some influence, for though 12.7% of the Germans came in after 1925, only 2.9% were without English in 1930. These late-coming Germans were, on the whole, much better educated than the Eastern and Southern Europeans who arrived at the same time, and large numbers of them had probably received some instruction in English at home. Moreover, they dispersed themselves throughout the country, and did not collect in ghettoes, like a majority of the Italians, Slavs and Jews. Of the 1,808,289 Italians here in 1930, more than 1,500,000 were crowded into relatively few cities, and of the 1,222,658 Jews who reported Yiddish as their native language, all save 19,000 were living in cities. [By and large, these latest immigrants have given far fewer words to the American vocabulary than their numbers might suggest, possibly because urban contacts between ethnic groups are less persistent than rural, possibly because these recent groups were largely peasants, with little literacy and less regard for their cultural traditions. At all events, in cities such as Cleveland and Chicago it is a rare second-generation American of Polish, Hungarian or Croatian stock who even pretends to know his parents' native language. In rural and small town settlements, of course, the foreign influence lasts longer.] How long may be observed in the so-called Pennsylvania-Dutch region of Pennsylvania, where a dialect of German is still a living speech after more than 250 years of settlement and the local dialect of English shows plain traces of it, both in vocabulary and in pronunciation. In the same way, the everyday speech of lower Louisiana is full of French terms not in use elsewhere, *e.g., brioche, lagniappe, jambalaya* and *bogue*. In Minnesota and adjacent states many Swedish and Dano-Norwegian terms are in common use. From Swedish come *lutfisk* (a fish delicacy), *lingnon* (a berry), *lefse* (a potato pancake) and *lag* (an association of Swedes from the same province); from Dano-Norwegian, *gubbefest* (a men's party) and *lefsi* (a pastry served with coffee). There is also a considerable borrowing of Scandinavian idioms, as in *to cook coffee (koka kaffe), forth and back (fram och tillbaka)* and *to hold with (håller med)* in place of *to agree with.*

In the same way Czech words have got into American, and Czech idioms have influenced usage in the regions in which Bohemian immigrants are numerous. One of the former, listed in Webster 1961, is *kolacky* or *kolach,* defined as "a bun made of rich sweet yeast-leavened dough filled with jam or fruit pulp." *Kolach* is the Czech *koláč,* with its accent lost in the melting pot. Other Czech loan words and phrases in local use are *rohlík* (a roll brushed with egg yolk, salted and sometimes sprinkled with caraway or poppy seeds), *povidla* (a prune marmalade), *buchta* (a coffeecake), *počkej* (wait, hold on), *sokol* (literally, a falcon, but used to designate an athletic association), and *to soč* (from the verb *sočiti,* meaning to scold or grumble). *Pantáta* (literally, Mr. Father, and signifying a father-in-law) was apparently once in use in New York to designate a corrupt police captain, but it has gone out. . . .

Since the Civil War the chief contribution of German has been the domestication of the suffix *-fest.* It came in with *sängerfest* and *turnfest* in the early 1850s, but the manufacture of American analogues did not begin until 1900 or thereabout. In 1916 Louise Pound rounded up twenty-three specimens from the current vocabulary: *Ananiasfest, batfest* (a baseball game), *blarneyfest, bloodfest* (war), *crabfest, eatfest, gabfest, gabblefest, gadfest, grubfest, jawfest, olymphest, singfest, slugfest* (a prize fight), *smilefest, smokefest, sobfest, songfest, spooffest, stuntfest, swatfest* (a baseball game marked by many hits), *talkfest* and *walkfest.* Many others appeared during the years following, *e.g., hoochfest, lovefest, bullfest, boozefest, bookfest* and *applefest,* and in 1918 Miss Pound herself added *chatfest, egofest, funfest* and *gossipfest.* Since then linguistic explorers have unearthed *beerfest, hymnfest, gagfest, hamfest, suitfest, bundesfest, blabfest, chawfest, chinfest, gasfest, hashfest, pipefest, joshfest, laughfest, nudefest, stripfest, pepfest, folkfest* and *henfest.* On April 9, 1927, the Pittsburgh *Courier* announced that the Northside Community Club of that city, a colored organization, was about to hold a *sangerfest* (no umlaut). The Spanish *fiesta* seems to have reinforced *fest* in the West, and *funfesta, jubilesta* and *hallowesta* have been reported. The DA [Dictionary of Americanisms] traces *sängerfest* to 1865, and *schützenfest* (an entertainment, usually a picnic, at which rifle-shooting competitions were held), to 1870. Webster 1961 lists both, along with *sängerbund*. There was a fashion about 1900 for words in *-bund*, and *moneybund* and *plunderbund* were in wide use. The pejorative significance of the suffix was accentuated when the FBI began running down *bundists, i.e.,* members of the German-American *Bund*, a Nazi-oriented organization. The latest word in *-bund* seems to be *smearbund*, signifying a band of defamers. Other German suffixes that have produced progeny in American are *-lust, -heimer* and *-burger*. The first was introduced by *wanderlust*, which was in wide use for some years, and produced the derivatives *wanderluster* (Eng. *rambler*), *wanderlust club* (Eng. *rambling club*), *wanderlusting* and *wanderlustful*. In 1933 the Hon. Louis Ludlow, a member of Congress from Indiana, launched *squanderlust* in a book, "America Go Bust," but it did not catch on. The suffix *-heimer* begat *wiseheimer* and various other terms. It was probably helped into American English by Yiddish influence. Along with it came *-sky* or *-ski*, as in *allrightsky, buttinski* and *damfoolski*, but of these only *buttinski* shows any sign of surviving. All the American words in *-burger* appear to be derived from *hamburger*. In its early days in the United States the chopped beef now known as a *hamburger* was called a *hamburg steak*, and was served like any other steak, not in the form of a sandwich. The DAE [Dictionary of American English] traces *hamburg steak* to 1884 and it is probably older. By 1889 it had become *hamburger steak*, and soon afterward it degenerated from the estate of a steak to that of a sandwich and became a simple *hamburger*. It began to produce numerous offspring. As Arnold Williams says, "*-burger* has come to mean almost any meat or meat-substitute ground or chopped and, fried or grilled, made into sandwiches." . . .

There are many German loan words in Yiddish, and one of them, *kibitzer*, has come into American by the Yiddish route. In German, *Kiebitz* signifies the peewit or lapwing, and has long been in figurative use to designate a looker-on at cards, and especially one who offers unsolicited advice. The word apparently acquired the agent suffix *-er* on coming into American. Another contribution is *schul* (the German word for school), used to designate a synagogue. . . .

[The most fruitful sources of Yiddish loans are the media of mass communication—journalism, radio and television. In addition to *schlemiehl, schmaltz* and *schnook,* commonly heard currently, there is the deprecatory rhyming slang with *schm-* substituted in the second element, as in *phonemeschmoneme,* often with an explanatory clause following, as in the joke, "*Oedipus-schmoedipus,* so long as he loves his mother." The final intensive *yet,* as in "Five programs a week, *yet,*" comes from a similar use of *noch.* Other partial or complete translations of Yiddish expressions, some familiar from at least the 1930s, are: "I should worry," "I should live so long," "If you'll excuse the expression," "Get lost," "He don't know from nothing," "I need it like a hole in the head" (or "a third leg," or something equally useless) and "Give a look."]

"We may take it as a fixed rule," said Engelbrecht Kaempfer in his "History of Japan," "that the settlement of foreigners in a country will bring a corresponding proportion of foreign words into the language; these will be naturalized by degrees, and become as familiar as the native words themselves." The truth of this is well demonstrated by the foregoing record. Every fresh wave of immigrants has brought in new loan words, and some of them have become so thoroughly imbedded in the language that they have lost their air of foreignness, and are used to make derivatives as freely as native words, *e.g., peonage* (from the Spanish *peón,* traced to 1849), *spaghetti joint* and *to stevedore* from the noun (Spanish *estivador,* a stower of cargo). Not infrequently naturalization brings in a change of meaning, as when the Spanish *silo,* signifying an underground chamber for the storage of grain, came to mean, in most states, an aboveground structure in which green crops are fermented, and *rodeo,* originally a cattle roundup, was transferred to an exhibition of cowboy tricks. *Alfalfa,* also from the Spanish, is not an Americanism, but only in the United States has it picked up such connotations as are to be seen in *Alfalfa Bill* and *Farmer Alfalfa*. As previously noted, American has probably made more loans from the Spanish than from any other language. They are, indeed, coming in all the time. *Marijuana* dates from 1894. The Spanish-American War added *trocha, ladrone, incommunicado* and *ley fuga*, some of which are already obsolete; and the popularity of Western movies and fiction has brought in a few more, *e.g., wrangler* (from *caballerango*, a horse groom), and greatly increased the use of others. *Chile con carne* did not enter into the general American dictary until after 1900. The suffix *-ista* came in during the troubles in Mexico, following the downfall of Porfirio Díaz in 1911. *Politico* appeared in the 1920s; *pachuco* in the 1940s; [and the recent influx of Puerto Ricans has spread *bodega* (a grocery-*cum*-liquor store) and given New York City (especially East Harlem—now often called *Spanish Harlem*) the nickname of *El Barrio* (the community). Spanish may share with Italian the credit for the current vogue of *marina,* as a de luxe designation for a yacht basin. The term has spread as far north as New Brunswick, and a new luxury river-front apartment development in downtown Chicago is called *Marina City*.]

There are other related loan words from immigrant languages, notably the Swedish *smörgåsbord,* which has been taken in since World War I, with the loss of its diacritical marks. From French there is a continual borrowing, *e.g., brassière* (commonly shortened to *bra*), which did not appear till *c.* 1910. The Italian *macaroni* had been in American use since 1802, and *spaghetti* since the 1880s, but *ravioli, pizza* and *espresso* are more recent. *Policy* (from Italian *polizza*), a type of poor man's gambling, is traced to 1830. It has largely been supplanted by *numbers. Policy ticket* is recorded in 1872, *policy dealer* in 1865, *policy backer* and *to play policy* in 1882 and *policy shop* in 1858.

The contributions of Chinese to the American vocabulary are few in number, and most of them are confined to the Pacific coast and its immediate hinterland. The DA traces *chow mein* to 1927 and *chop suey* to 1903, but they must be much older. *Chow mein* means, primarily, fried noodles, and is derived from the Chinese

words *ch'ao,* to fry, and *mien,* flour. *Chop suey* represents the
Cantonese cognate of the standard Chinese *tsa-sui,* meaning
miscellaneous pieces. *Joss* and its derivations got into English in
the Eighteenth Century, but they seem to have been taken into
American independently. The DAE traces *joss* in American use to
1873, and *joss house* and *joss stick* to 1871. *Tong* came in in the
early 1880s and was soon followed by *tong war. Highbinder,* as we
have seen, was first used in 1806 to designate a variety of Irish
gangster in New York; it was not applied to Chinese until the late
1870s. The Chinese loan *yuen,* a vegetable garden, is known only
on the West Coast. *Brainwash,* a loan translation, came in during
the Korean police action. The Chinese, it should not be forgotten,
also contributed one of the most pungent American proverbs: "No
tickee, no shirtee." . . .

44. RICHARD GAMBINO

The Italian-American, paralyzed by his pervasive identity crisis

New Americans with value systems out of phase with the American
pattern were particularly vulnerable to attack for transgressing traditional codes that old Americans often ignored with impunity. No
immigrant group proved more susceptible to censure on the grounds of
morality than did Italian newcomers. Beginning with the 1891 lynching
of eleven Italian immigrants accused of murdering the police chief of
New Orleans, Italians were stereotyped as peculiarly prone to crime.
Along with the Black Hand, Camora, Unione Siciliana, and the Mafia,
Italian ethnics became associated with violence and crime. The corporate, national, and international dimensions of the Cosa Nostra and the
Syndicate were so alarming in their implications that Americans were
readily persuaded that an international Mafia conspiracy—once confined

Richard Gambino, "Twenty Million Italian-Americans Can't Be Wrong," *The New
York Times Magazine,* April 30, 1972, p. 20ff. Reprinted by permission of the
author.

to bootlegging, gambling, prostitution, and loan-sharking—had infiltrated nearly every phase of American life. By implication and association, the indictment of the Mafia was an indictment of all Americans with Italian names or Italian ancestors.

In the following article, Richard Gambino, Assistant Professor of Educational Philosophy, Queens College, City University of New York, shifts the perspective from the Mafia stereotype to the larger context of Italian-American family culture illuminating the special dilemmas of invisible third generation Italian-Americans.

The persistent myth of a monolithic Italian-American subculture called the Mafia presents a set of dilemmas for Italian-Americans. To the average person in this country, the Sicilian-American norm is seen as identical with Mafia in a self-locking stereotype. Italian-Americans are offered a bigoted choice of two identities somewhat paralleling the two imposed on blacks. Blacks could be child-like, laughing, Uncle Tom figures, or sullen, incorrigible, violent, knife-wielding criminals. Similarly, the nativistic American mentality, born of ignorance and nurtured by malice, insists that Italian-Americans be either/or creatures. They must be either spaghetti-twirling, opera-bellowing buffoons in undershirts (as in the TV commercial with its famous line, "That'sa some spicy meatball"), or swarthy, sinister hoods in garish suits, shirts and ties. The incredible exploitation of "The Godfather" testifies to the power of the Mafia myth today.

To understand the special identity problems of Italian-Americans, we must begin with a very popular Sicilian proverb quoted by Leonard Covello in his pioneering work, "The Social Background of the Italo-American School Child": *"Che lascia la via vecchia per la nuova, so quel che perde e non sa quel che trova"*—"Whoever forsakes the old way for the new knows what he is losing, but not what he will find."

In Sicily, *la via vecchia* was family life. The Sicilian immigrants to America were mostly *contadini* (peasants) to whom there was one and only one social reality, the peculiar mores of family life. *La Famiglia* and the personality it nurtured was a very different thing from the American nuclear family with the personalities that are its typical products. The *famiglia* was composed of all of one's "blood" relatives, including those relatives Americans would consider very distant cousins, aunts and uncles, and extended clan with a genealogy traced through paternity. The only system to which the *contadino* paid attention was *l'ordine della famiglia*, the unwritten but all-demanding and complex series of rules governing one's relations within, and responsibilities to, his own family. All other social institutions were seen within a spectrum of attitudes ranging from indifferences to scorn and contempt.

One had absolute responsibilities to family superiors and absolute rights to be demanded from subordinates in the hierarchy. All ambiguous situations were arbitrated by the *capo di famiglia* (head of the family), a position held within each household by the father, until it was given to—or taken away by—one of the sons, and in the larger clan, by the male "elder." The *contadino* showed calculated respect to members of other families which were powerful, and haughtiness or indifference toward families less powerful than his own. He despised as a *scomunicato* (pariah) anyone in any family who broke the *ordine della famiglia* or otherwise violated the *onore* (honor, solidarity, tradition, "face") of the family.

Thus, Sicily survived a harsh history of invasion, conquest and colonization by a procession of tribes and nations. What enabled Sicilians to endure was a system of rules based solely on a phrase I heard uttered many times by my grandparents and their contemporaries in Brooklyn's "Little Italy": *sangu di me sangu*, Sicilian dialect for "blood of my blood." (As is typical of Sicilian women, my grandmother's favorite and most earnest term of endearment when addressing her children and grandchildren, and when speaking of them to others, was *sangu mio*—literally, "my blood.")

It was a norm simple and demanding, protective and isolating, humanistic and cynical. The unique family pattern of Sicily constituted the real sovereignty of that island, regardless of which government nominally ruled it.

As all of us are confronted with the conflicts of our loyalty to a sovereign state versus our cosmopolitan aspirations, so the Italian-

American has found himself in the dilemma of reconciling the psychological sovereignty of his people with the aspirations and demands of being American. Most Italian-Americans are derived from areas of Italy south of Rome, about 25 percent of them from Sicily. In his book, "The Italians," Luigi Barzini reminds us that "Goethe was right when he wrote: 'Without seeing Sicily one cannot get a clear idea of what Italy is.' Sicily is a schoolroom model of Italy for beginners, with every Italian quality and defect magnified. . . ."

This background illustrates the confused situation of Italian-Americans. It would not be an exaggeration to say that to Middle America the Chinese character is more scrutable than that of the Italian-American. Although the problems of Italian-Americans are less desperate than those of groups whose fate in this country has been determined by color, they are no less complicated. And they are rising to a critical point.

The solutions have been too long delayed, and we have thus lagged behind other large groups of European "ethnics," notably Jews and Irish-Americans, in social and economic terms. We live in a time of ethnic consciousness, when each group asserts its presence and insists on determining its character and destiny. It remains to be seen how the 20 million to 23 million Italian-Americans, many of them third- and fourth-generation citizens, will determine theirs—and how much upset it will bring.

To the immigrant generation of Italians, the task was clear: Hold to the psychological sovereignty of the old ways and thereby seal out the threats of the new "conqueror," the American society that surrounded them. This ingrained disposition was strongly reinforced by the hatred and insult with which the Italian immigrant was assaulted by American bigots who regarded him as racially inferior—a "dago," a "wop," a "guinea." Although one might assume that such indignity has altogether disappeared, we need only recall well-known tests used to identify these prejudices. In one study, American college students were shown photographs of members of the opposite sex with what purported to be the name of each person on the photograph. The students were asked to evaluate the attractiveness of the person in the photograph. Then, some time afterward, names were changed and the procedure repeated with the same students. The result was that those people who were regarded as "handsome" or "pretty" when they had names like "Smith" were found not attractive when their names were changed to Italian ones. (The same result was found using names commonly thought of as Jewish.)

As a blond, blue-eyed American who was never spotted as Italian, I was sometimes exposed to gibes and jokes such as the one I overheard at the University of Illinois in 1961. Question: "What sound does a pizza make when you throw it against the wall?" Answer: "Wop!" The joke was greeted with much laughter, not by red-necks, but by a roomful of graduate students, some of whom became belligerent rather than embarrassed when as a Sicilian-American I expressed irritation at the joke.

Discriminatory attitudes toward Italians are also indicated in the restrictionist immigration policies aimed at them. Not only did these continue until 1968, but they were made more stringent in recent times than in the period following the flood of immigrants before World War I. Whereas the Emergency Quota Law of 1921 imposed an annual limit of 42,000 Italian immigrants, the Immigration and Nationality Act of 1952 dropped the Italian quota to its lowest point in history, less than 6,000 per year. The law was passed by Congress over the veto of President Truman.

The Italian immigrants admitted in the earlier years responded to an alien, hostile society by clustering together in crowded Italian "ghettos," euphemistically called "Little Italies," and exhausted their energies in America's sweatshops. So desperate was the poverty of Southern Italy from which they had escaped (my father came to this country as a boy with rags wrapped around his feet because his family could not afford shoes) that their lives in the promised land was regarded as progress. Oppression and economic exploitation were woven into the fabric of life in Southern Italy. Most of Sicily's foreign governors had two things in common: The subjugation of Sicilians, and systematic exploitation of them and their land. The first was done by force, the second by perennial systems of absentee landlordships.

The complicated customs and institutions developed by the

Sicilians were marvelously effective in neutralizing the influence of the various alien masters. The people of the island survived and developed their own identity not so much by overtly opposing the oppressor, a suicidal approach given the small size, exposed location and limited resources of the island, but by *sealing out* the influence of the strangers.

The sealing medium was not military or even physical. It was at once an "antisocial" mentality and a supremely social psychology, for it forms the very stuff of Sicilian society. It constitutes the foundation and hidden steel beams of a society that historically has been denied the luxury of more accessible (and vulnerable) foundations or superstructure. This is the reason for the Sicilians' pride. A system of social attitudes, values and customs that is impenetrable to the *sfruttamento* (exploitation) of any *stranieri* (strangers), no matter how powerful their weapons or clever their devices. But like all defenses, their life-style has exacted costs from the people of Sicily—the vexing social and economic problems that Italians lump together as the *Problema del Mezzogiorno*, or *Questione Meridionale*, meaning "the Southern Problem."

This year, I saw evidence of the continuing conflict between Northern and Southern Italy. Three companions and I hired a car in Rome to drive south to the area of Naples. Our driver and guide was a native Roman in his thirties, a graduate of Boston University. His sophisticated and friendly manner changed as we drove south. He spoke rather rudely to everyone in the South, except policemen. At a restaurant in Naples, he found fault with everything and expressed it loudly to the staff and other patrons. Yet, in my observation, the restaurant was as good as any I had seen in Rome, Florence or Venice. Our guide explained to me that Southerners are uncultured, brutish creatures, even as they treated me in a warm, civilized way. He called them "not really Italian," a phrase that evoked an incident in my childhood.

I attended P. S. 142 in Brooklyn for eight years, a school about 90 percent Italian-American in my recollection. One day, when I was about nine years old, I was told by one of my teachers (a non-Italian, like almost all the staff), "You're not *real* Italians."

When I went home that day, I asked my immigrant grandfather what the teacher meant. He sat there, looked me level in the eye, shook his head slowly and said simply *"I Americani!"* (To Italian immigrants, all other people in this country were "Americans," whatever their ethnic background.) The prejudice of the Northerners, experienced by my grandfather in the old land, had been transplanted to his new home and visited upon his grandchild. For this reason, among others, the mores the immigrants brought with them from the old land gave them psychological stability, order and security, and were held to tenaciously. But in the United States, the price was isolation from the ways of the larger society.

The immigrants' children, the "second generation," faced a challenge more difficult to overcome. They could not maintain the same degree of isolation. Indeed, they had to cope with American institutions, first schools, then a variety of economic, military and cultural environments. In so doing, what was a successful social strategy for their parents became a crisis of conflict for them. Circumstances split their personalties into conflicting halves. Despite parental attempts to shelter them from American culture, they *attended* the schools, *learned* the language and confronted the culture.

It was a rending confrontation. The parents of the typical second-generation child ridiculed American institutions and sought to nurture in him *la via vecchia.* The father nurtured in his children (sons especially) a sense of mistrust and cynicism regarding the outside world. And the mother bound her children (not only daughters) to the home by making any aspirations to go beyond it seem somehow disloyal and shameful. Thus, outward mobility was impeded. Boys were pulled out of school and sent to work at the minimum legal age, or lower, and girls were virtually imprisoned in the house. Education, the means of social and economic mobility in the United States, was largely blocked to the second generation, because schools were regarded not only as alien but as immoral by the immigrant parents. When members of this generation did go to school the intrinsic differences between American and Southern-Italian ways were sharpened even further for them. The school, the employer and the media taught them, implicitly and often perhaps inadvertently, that Italian ways were inferior, while the immigrant community constantly sought to reinforce them.

Immigrants used "American" as a word of reproach to their children. For example, take another incident from my childhood: Every Wednesday afternoon, I left P. S. 142 early and went to the local parish church for religious instruction under New York State's Released Time Program. Once I asked one of my religious teachers, an Italian-born nun, a politely phrased but skeptical question about the existence of hell. She flew into a rage, slapped my face and called me a *piccolo americano*, a "little American." Thus, the process of acculturation for second-generation children was an agonizing affair in which they had not only to "adjust" to two worlds, but to compromise between their irreconcilable demands. This was achieved by a sane path of least resistance.

Most of the second generation accepted the old heritage of devotion to family, and sought minimal involvement with the institutions of America. This meant going to school but remaining alienated from it. One then left school at the minimum legal age and got a job that was "secure" but made no troubling demands on one's personality, or the family life in which it was imbedded. This explains why so many second- and even third-generation Italians fill civil service, blue-collar and low-echelon white-collar jobs—many of those in the last category being employed in more static, low-growth industries: for example, utilities like Con Edison, where my father worked for 40 years. So we see in New York City that the Fire Department, Police Department and Sanitation Department are filled with Italians. The top positions in these services and in their counterpart private corporations remain conspicuously and disproportionately free of Italian-Americans.

Another part of the second-generation compromise was the rejection of Italian ways which were not felt vital to the family code. They resisted learning the Italian culture and language well, and were ill-equipped to teach it to the third generation.

Small numbers of the second generation carried the dual rebellion to one extreme or the other. Some became highly

"Americanized," giving their time, energy and loyalty to schools and companies and becoming estranged from the clan. The price they paid for siding with American culture in the culture-family conflict was an amorphous but strong sense of guilt and a chronic identity crisis not quite compensated for by the places won in middle-class society. At the other extreme, some rejected American culture totally in favor of lifelong immersion in the old ways, which through time and circumstance virtually dissipated in their lifetimes, leaving underdeveloped and forlorn people.

The tortured compromise of the second-generation Italian-American thus left him permanently in lower middle-class America. He remains in the minds of Americans a stereotype born of their half-understanding of him and constantly reinforced by the media. Oliver Wendell Holmes said a page of history is worth a volume of logic. There are, with very few exceptions, no serious studies of the history of Italian-Americans. It is easy to see why this has left accounts of their past, their present and their future expressed almost exclusively in the dubious logic of stereotypes.

The second-generation Italian-American is seen as a "good employee," i.e., steady, reliable, but having little "initiative" or "dynamism." He is a good "family man," loyal to his wife and a loving father vaguely yearning for his children to do "better" in their lifetimes, but not equipped to guide or push them up the social ladder. He maintains his membership in the church, but participates in it little beyond ceremonial observances; while he often sends his children to parochial schools, this represents more his social parochialism than enthusiasm for the American Catholic Church, which has very few Italian-Americans at the top of the hierarchy and has never had an Italian-American cardinal. (Since the Irish immigrants who controlled the Church in its earlier years often discriminated against them, the Italian-Americans tended to view it as an alien "Irish institution.")

He is a loyal citizen of America, but conceives of his political role as protecting that portion of the status quo which he has so painfully carved out by his great compromise. Thus, his political expressions are reactive rather than active. He tends to feel threatened by social and political change, and he is labeled "conservative" or "reactionary" by the larger society. His political reactions are usually to *ad hoc* situations and individual candidates. A bloc of Italian-American voters has not been identified. And with few exceptions, Italian-Americans have not achieved visible positions of major political power. There was not an Italian-American in a Cabinet post until 1962 and none in the Senate until 1950. And even on state and local levels, this ethnic group remains under-represented, although it constitutes 11 or 12 per cent of the national population.

Clearly the most prominent—and pernicious—element in the Italian-American stereotype is that of the Mafia. The Italian immigrant carried with him a memory of the Mafia in Sicily as a kind of ultimate family. Formed in feudal times, the organization began with bands of men who were secretly organized on *ad hoc* bases to protect families (and their customs) from foreign oppression. The term Mafia is thought to be an acronym of the 13th-century Sicilian battle cry, *"Morte ai francesi gl'italiani anelano!"* ("Death to the French in Italy"), part of a violent rebellion against French oppression that began in Palermo on Easter Sunday, 1282, and spread to all of Sicily. Almost all of the French on the island were in fact killed. With characteristic sarcasm, "Sicilian Vespers."

The early Mafia bands defended the people by appropriating two old Sicilian institutions: (a) they adopted as their own code the traditional family code, and (b) they adopted the *vendetta,* i.e., revenge against the enemy by deadly violence, and terrorism. These *vendette* were not just political wars. They were struggles of honor, demanding total allegiance and sacrifice. By the late 19th century, the Mafia had become an institutional force in the life of Western Sicily. But by this time it had lost its role of defender of the Sicilian morality and people. The code of family honor had become hopelessly corrupt. With its members bribed by alien rulers and growing in greed, the Mafia became, over the years, a federation of gangs controlling Western Sicily largely for its own profit and power. To the Italian immigrant in America, the Mafia was both feared in its present form and respected in its archaic ideal as the supreme representative and protector of the family morality. *Rispetto* (respect in the sense of awe of this ideal) was expressed in colloquialisms he brought from Sicily. The immigrant used the word *Mafioso* as an adjective synonymous with "good" and "admirable." For example, he would speak of a *Mafioso* horse, meaning the animal was strong and spirited. Similarly, he would say of a fine specimen of a man, *"Che Mafioso!"*

Every group living in poverty in this country—or any country—has spawned crime. The poor Italian ghettos spawned criminals whose inherited Southern-Italian morality led them naturally to band together into groups that combined both elements of that morality and their own criminal bent. This amalgam is what the so-called Mafia was, and perhaps still is, in America. *The common characteristic of the at most 5,000 to 6,000 Italian-American gangsters claimed by governmental agencies, and the 23 million other Italian-Americans, is the family morality. The distinguishing characteristic that separates the relatively few gangsters from the millions of law-abiding Italian-Americans is that the gangsters have turned that morality to serve criminal ends.*

The responses to this by Italian-Americans of the second generation have fallen into several categories:

(1) Some have adopted as the lesser of two evils the "Uncle Giovanni" image. Interestingly, Sicilians have a contemptuous word for this kind of vulgar fool, *cafone.*

(2) Some have sought to get some public-relations mileage out of what has today become a kind of "Mafia chic" by half-jokingly adopting the Mafia myth. For example, I arrived at a plush restaurant at the Plaza Hotel recently and gave my name to the maitre d' in charge of reservations. He looked at me and said hello in Italian, and we exchanged a few words in the language. Then, searching for something else in our common background, he said, jokingly, referring to my name: "I expected somebody for 'The Godfather'."

At least the *Mafioso* is taken seriously as an individual of some importance, an improvement over being considered a buffoon, or being ignored. Moreover, the myth of an extrasocietal, almost omnipotent power has great appeal to people in a complex society who are exasperated by feelings of confusion, impotence and defeat.

(3) Some have patiently repeated, "We are not criminals. . . . The percentage of racketeers among us is small." In the scream of the public media-exploitation of Mafia chic, such voices are, year after year, all but lost. Through the power of the media, Mafia chic has even crossed the Atlantic to Italy itself. In bookstores in Italy, I saw copies of a translation of "The Godfather," called *"Il Padrino,"* a very popular book there. And even in Florence I was asked, as I have been for years in the United States, whether I am related to the reputed boss of the American Mafia, Carlo Gambino. (I am not.)

(4) Some recently have begun denying that the Mafia exists in this country at all. This hyperdefensive reaction is in reality an expression of rage, a reaction to years of abuse. The fact that some racketeers attempt to exploit the outrage for their own ends is beside the point. There is opportunism in every social expression.

Most recently, the media have gone beyond their role in transforming a difficult social problem of organized crime into a romantic myth of fantastic proportions. Just as many media people found that the creation and exploitation of the fantasy was lucrative, so many are discovering that ridiculing over-statements of denial of the fantasy is also lucrative. (At the height of the Italian Civil Rights League's campaign to deny that the Mafia exists, *New York Magazine* ran a parody of a fictional gangster named Salvatore Gambino who kept insisting there is no such thing as the Mafia.)

But the Mafia issue must be kept in perspective. The myth has become an example of an interesting expression I heard used in Italy, *americanata,* meaning something spectacular, wild, exaggerated. We are in danger of focusing only on this side show, which merely diverts attention from the larger issues. So far, none of the responses of Italian-Americans to the old Mafia myth and the new Mafia chic have been effective in improving either their image or their real, complex problems.

We come at last to the compound dilemma of the third- and fourth-generation Italian-Americans, who are now mostly young adults and children with parents who are well into their middle age or older. (The number of those in the third and fourth generations is estimated as at least 10 million, compared to more than 5 million in the second generation.) The difference between the problems of the second and those of the third generation is great—more a quantum jump than a continuity.

Perhaps a glimpse at my own life will serve as an illustration. I was raised simultaneously by my immigrant grandparents and by my parents who were second generation, notwithstanding my father's boyhood in Italy. So I am both second and third generation at one time. I learned Italian and English from birth, but have lost the ability to speak Italian fluently. In this, my third-generation character has won out, although I remain of two generations, and thus perhaps have an advantage of double perspective.

My grandfather had a little garden in the back yard of the building in which we all lived in Brooklyn. In two senses, it was a distinctly Sicilian garden. First, it was the symbolic fulfillment of every *contadino's* dream to own his own land. Second, what was grown in the garden was a far cry from the typical American garden. In our garden were plum tomatoes, squash, white grapes on an overhead vine, a prolific peach tree, and a fig tree! As a child, I helped my grandfather tend that fig tree. Because of the inhospitable climate of New York, every autumn the tree had to be carefully wrapped in hundreds of layers of newspaper. These in turn were covered with waterproof linoleum and tarpaulin. The tree was topped with an inverted, galvanized bucket for final protection. But the figs it produced were well worth the trouble. Picked and washed by my own hand, they were as delicious as anything I have eaten since. And perhaps the difference between second- and third-generation Italian-Americans is that members of the younger group have not tasted those figs. What they inherit from their Italian background has become so diluted as to be not only devalued but quite unintelligible to them. It has been abstracted, removing the possibility of their accepting it or rebelling against it in any satisfying way.

I was struck by this recently when one of my students came to my office to talk with me. Her problems are typical of those I have heard from Italian-Americans. Her father is a fireman and her mother a housewife. Both want her to "get an education" and "do better." Yet both constantly express fears that education will "harm her morals." She is told by her father to be proud of her Italian background, but her consciousness of being Italian is limited to the fact that her last name ends in a vowel. Although she loves her parents and believes they love her, she has no insight into their thoughts, feelings or values. She is confused by the conflicting signals given to her by them: "Get an education, but don't change"; "go out into the larger world but don't become part of it"; "grow, but remain within the image of the 'houseplant' Sicilian girl"; "go to church, although we are lacking in religious enthusiasm." In short, maintain that difficult balance of conflicts which is the second-generation's life-style.

Her dilemma becomes more widespread as unprecedented numbers of Italian-Americans enter colleges today. The 1970s are bound to see a sharp increase in the number of Italian-American college graduates. (In New York City only 5 per cent of native-born Italian-Americans graduated from college during the 1960s. One reason the figure is bound to jump during this decade is that large numbers of Italian-Americans, along with other lower middle-class whites, have taken advantage of the open-admissions policy of the City University of New York.) Moreover, my impression is that Italian-American college students are more inclined to move into areas of study other than the "utilitarian" ones preferred by their predecessors, which for boys were chiefly engineering, music for entertainment, and occasionally pharmacology or medicine, and for girls were teaching and nursing.

When the third-generation person leaves school and his parents' home, he finds himself in a peculiar situation. A member of one of the largest minority groups in the country, he feels isolated, with no affiliation with or affinity for other Italian-Americans. This young person often wants and needs to go beyond the minimum security his parents sought in the world; in a word, he is more ambitious. But he has not been given family or cultural guidance upon which this ambition can be defined and pursued. Ironically, this descendant of immigrants despised by the old WASP establishment embodies one of the latter's cherished myths. He sees himself as purely American, a blank slate upon which his individual experiences in American culture will inscribe what is to be his personality and his destiny.

But it is a myth that is untenable psychologically and sociologically. Although he usually is diligent and highly responsible, the other elements needed for a powerful personality are paralyzed by his pervasive identity crisis. His ability for sustained action with autonomy, initiative, self-confidence and assertiveness is undermined by his yearning for ego integrity. In addition, the third generation's view of itself as a group of atomistic individuals leaves them politically unorganized, isolated, diffident and thus powerless in a society of power blocs.

The dilemma of the young Italian-American is a lonely, quiet crisis, so it has escaped public attention. But it is a major ethnic group crisis. As it grows, it will be more readily recognized as such, and not merely as the personal problem of individuals. If this is to be realized sooner rather than later, then these young people must learn whence they came and why they are as they are. A "page of history" will expose the logic of their problems and thus make them potentially solvable. How they will solve them is unpredictable.

They may opt for one of the several models that have served other ethnic groups. For example, they may choose to cultivate their Italian culture, pursue personal career and fuse the two into an energetic and confident relationship—which has been characteristic of the Jewish-Americans. They may also turn toward the church, revive it and build upon its power base a political organization and morale, as Irish-Americans did. Or, they may feel it necessary to form strictly nationalistic power blocs, as some black-Americans are doing. On the other hand, they may forge their own models of individual and group identity out of an imaginative use of their unique inheritance.

. . . No group of young people surpasses Italian-American youth in its sense of the power of work, which, although derived from the old notion of labor for the family, is now, in the third generation, independent of it. It now remains for young Italian-Americans to root their sense of work in broader identity—and to take their proportionate share of what America has to offer. The dream denied their immigrant grandparents, sacrificed by their culture-conflicted parents, can be realized by them. It can be achieved by adding consciousness, knowledge and imagination to the legacy of courage, work and fortitude inherited from past generations.

45. RALPH ELLISON

I am not protesting, nor pleading, my humanity

The author of *The Invisible Man* has written of the facelessness of all men in our modern impersonal society. In his major novel, Ralph Ellison has attained the distinction of writing on a universal theme as seen through the experience of his Negro protagonist. Rejecting the racial mysticism of Ras the Exhorter, a character patterned on one of Marcus Garvey's Black nationalist successors, Ellison's hero rejects, also, the idea of a significant kinship between American Negroes and Africans. Singularly immune from the fashions of the 1950s and 1960s, Ellison has written and spoken with wisdom and depth of the basic problems of culture and identity for all Americans, including his fellow Negroes. Unlike other Black writers, he has rejected African consciousness as a fecund source of identity between American Negroes and Africans.

The following interview appeared in French translation in the May, 1958, *Preuves*. It appeared in the original English for the first time in *Shadow and Act*, Ellison's collected essays. In the course of the interview, Ellison repeats the final discovery of the Negro hero in *The Invisible Man*: All men must free themselves of their pasts if they are to share in a new world of "infinite possibilities."

Ralph Ellison, "Some Questions and Some Answers," *Shadow and Act* (New York: Random House, 1964), pp. 261–72. Copyright © 1958 by Ralph Ellison. Reprinted by permission of William Morris Agency, Inc., on behalf of author. From the original manuscript, 1958.

What do you understand today *by "Negro culture"?*

What I understand by the term "Negro culture" is so vague as to be meaningless. Indeed, I find the term "Negro" vague even in its racial connotations, for in Africa there are several non-white racial strains and one suspects that the term came into usage as a means of obliterating cultural differences between the various African peoples. In this way the ruthless disruption of highly developed cultures raised no troubling moral questions. The term, used mainly by whites, represented a "trained incapacity" to make or feel moral distinctions where black men were concerned.

As for the term "culture," used in this connection, I know of no valid demonstration that culture is transmitted through the genes.

In Africa the blacks identify themselves by their tribal names; thus it is significant that it is only in the United States that the term "Negro" has acquired specific cultural content. Spelled with a capital "N" by most publications (one of the important early victories of my own people in their fight for self-definition), the term describes a people whose origin began with the introduction of African slaves to the American colonies in 1619, and which today represents the fusing with the original African strains of many racial blood lines—among them English, Irish, Scotch, French, Spanish and American Indian. Although the American Civil War brought an end to the importation of African peoples into the United States, this mixture of bloods has by no means ceased—not even in the South where the whites are obsessed with racial purity—so that today the anthropologists tell us that very few American Negroes are of pure African blood. It occurs to me that in the light of this, even if culture were transmitted through the blood stream we would encounter quite a problem in explaining just how the genes bearing "Negro" culture could so overpower those bearing French or English culture, which in all other ways are assumed to be superior.

But to continue, the American Negro people is North American in origin and has evolved under specifically American conditions: climatic, nutritional, historical, political and social. It takes its character from the experience of American slavery and the struggle for, and the achievement of, emancipation; from the dynamics of American race and caste discrimination, and from living in a highly industrialized and highly mobile society possessing a relatively high standard of living and an explicitly stated equalitarian concept of freedom. Its spiritual outlook is basically Protestant, its system of kinship is Western, its time and historical sense are American (United States), and its secular values are those professed, ideally at least, by all of the people of the United States.

Culturally this people represents one of the many subcultures which make up that great amalgam of European and native American cultures which is the culture of the United States. This "American Negro culture" is expressed in a body of folklore, in the musical forms of the spirituals, the blues and jazz; an idiomatic version of American speech (especially in the Southern United States); a cuisine; a body of dance forms and even a dramaturgy which is generally unrecognized as such because still tied to the more folkish Negro churches. Some Negro preachers are great showmen.

It must, however, be pointed out that due to the close links which Negro Americans have with the rest of the nation these cultural expressions are constantly influencing the larger body of American culture and are in turn influenced by them. Nor should the existence of a specifically "Negro" idiom in any way be confused with the vague, racist terms "white culture" or "black culture"; rather it is a matter of diversity within unity. One could indeed go further and say that, in this sense, there is no other "Negro" culture. Haitians, for instance, are an "American" people and predominantly dark but their culture is an expression of Haitian conditions: it reflects the influence of French culture and the fusion of Catholic and native Haitian religious outlooks. Thus, since most so-called "Negro cultures" outside Africa are necessarily amalgams, it would seem more profitable to stress the term "culture" and leave the term "Negro" out of the discussion. It is not culture which binds the peoples who are of partially African origin now scattered throughout the world, but an identity of passions. We share a hatred for the alienation forced upon us by

Europeans during the process of colonization and empire and we are bound by our common suffering more than by our pigmentation. But even this identification is shared by most non-white peoples, and while it has political value of great potency, its cultural value is almost nil.

In your opinion was there before the arrival of Europeans a single Negro culture that all Negroes shared, or was it the case, as among the whites, that there had been many different cultures, such as Judeo–Christianity, Brahmanism, etc. . . . ?

Before the arrival of Europeans there were many African cultures.

What is the role of modern industrial evolution on the spiritual crisis of the Negro people of our times? Does industrial progress (capitalist or socialist) endanger the future of a genuine Negro culture?

The role of modern industrial evolution in the spiritual crisis of those whom you refer to as "Negro" peoples seems to me to be as ambiguous as its role in the lives of peoples of any racial identity: it depends upon how much human suffering must go into the achievement of industrialization, upon who operates the industries, upon how the products and profits are shared and upon the wisdom used in imposing technology upon the institutions and traditions of each particular society. Ironically, black men with the status of slaves contributed much of the brute labor which helped get the industrial revolution under way; in this process they were exploited, their natural resources were ravaged and their institutions and their cultures were devastated, and in most instances they were denied anything like participation in the European cultures which flowered as a result of the transformation of civilization under the growth of technology. But now it is precisely technology which promises them release from the brutalizing effects of over three hundred years of racism and European domination. Men cannot unmake history, thus it is not a question of reincarnating those cultural traditions which were destroyed, but a matter of using industrialization, modern medicine, modern science generally, to work in the interest of these peoples rather than against them. Nor is the disruption of continuity with the past necessarily a totally negative phenomenon; sometimes it makes possible a modulation of a people's way of life which allows for a more creative use of its energies. The United States is ample proof of this, and though we suffer much from the rupture of tradition, great good has come to the world through those achievements which were made possible. One thing seems clear, certain possibilities of culture are achievable only through the presence of industrial techniques.

It is not industrial progress per se which damages peoples or cultures, it is the exploitation of peoples in order to keep the machines fed with raw materials. It seems to me that the whole world is moving toward some new cultural synthesis, and partially through the discipline imposed by technology. There is, I believe, a threat when industrialism is linked to a political doctrine which has as its goal the subjugation of the world.

Is the birth of various religions in the present Negro societies progressive or regressive as far as culture is concerned?

I am unacquainted with the religious movements in the societies to which you refer. If the Mau Mau is one of these, then I must say that for all my disgust for those who provoked the natives to such obscene extremes, I feel it to be regressive indeed.

Several Negro poets from Africa explain that they write in French or English because the ancient languages are not adequate to express their feeling any longer. What do you think about this?

When it comes to the poet the vagueness of the term "Negro" becomes truly appalling, for if there is a "Negro" language I am unacquainted with it. Are these people Bantu, Sudanese, Nigerian, Watusi or what? As for the poets in question, it seems to me that in a general way they are faced by the problem confronted by the Irish who for all their efforts to keep their language vital have had nevertheless their greatest poets expressing themselves in

English, as in the case of Shaw, Yeats, Joyce and O'Casey. Perhaps the poet's true language is that in which he dreams. At any rate, it is true that for some time now poets throughout the world have drawn freely from all the world's tongues in order to create their vocabularies. One uses whatever one needs, to best express one's vision of the human predicament.

Another way of approaching the matter is to view the poem as a medium of communication—to whom do these poets wish to speak? Each poet creates his own language from that which he finds around him. Thus if these poets find the language of Shakespeare or Racine inadequate to reach their own peoples, then the other choice is to re-create their original language to the point where they may express their complex emotions. This is the manner in which the poet makes his contribution to literature, and the greatest literary creation of any culture is its language. Further, language is most alive when it is capable of dealing with the realities in which it operates. In the myth, God gave man the task of naming the objects of the world, thus one of the functions of the poet is to insist upon a correspondence between words and ever-changing reality, between ideals and actualities. The domain of the unstated, the undefined is his to conquer.

In my own case, having inherited the language of Shakespeare and Melville, Mark Twain and Lincoln and no other, I try to do my part in keeping the American language alive and rich by using in my work the music and idiom of American Negro speech, and by insisting that the words of that language correspond with the reality of American life as seen by my own people. Perhaps if I were a member of a bilingual society I would approach my task differently, but my work is addressed primarily to those who have my immediate group experience, for I am not protesting, nor pleading, my humanity; I am trying to communicate, to articulate and define a group experience.

What do you think of the present level of Negro sculpture? What future do you see for it?

I know little of current work in sculpture by Africans, but that which I have seen appears to possess little of that high artistic excellence characteristic of ancient African art. American Negro sculpture is, of course, simply American sculpture done by Negroes. Some is good, some bad. I don't see any possibility of work by these artists being created in a vacuum outside of those influences, national and international, individual and abstract, which influence any other American artist. When African sculpture is one influence it comes to them through the Cubists just as it did to most contemporary artists. That phenomenon which Malraux calls the "Imaginary Museum" draws no color line.

As for the future of African sculpture, it depends upon the future role which art will play in African societies which are now struggling into being. I doubt, however, that sculpture will ever play the same role that the so-called primitive art played, because the tribal societies which called this art into being have either been shattered or are being rapidly transformed. And if the influence of the primitive sculptures are to be seen in European art wherever one turns, so have the influences of modern Western art found their way into Africa. This process is more likely to increase rather than lessen. To the extent that art is an expression of transcendent values, the role of sculpture in these societies will depend upon the values of those societies.

What do you think of the future of "Negro music"?

I know only American Negro music, in this sense of the term. This music consists of jazz and the spirituals, but as with all things cultural in the United States these forms have been and are still being subjected to a constant process of assimilation. Thus, although it was the specific experience of Negroes which gave rise to these forms, they expressed and gave significance to feelings and sounds so characteristically American that both spirituals and jazz have been absorbed into the musical language of the culture as a whole. On the other hand, American Negro music was never created in a vacuum; it was the shaping of musical elements found in the culture—European, American Indian, the Afro-American rhythmical sense, the sound of the Negro voice—to the needs of a particular group. Today jazz is a national art form, but for me personally the source of the purist stream of this music is the Negro community, wherein the commercial motive in popular music is weaker, and where jazz remains vital because it is still linked with the Saturday night or the Sunday morning breakfast dance, which are still among the living social forms functioning within the Negro community.

Nor does this in any way contradict the fact that some of the leaders in the modern jazz movement are Negroes; we still move from the folk community to a highly conscious acquaintance with the twelve-tone composers and their methods in less time than it takes to complete a course in counterpoint, and these modern methods are quickly absorbed into the body of classical jazz. A man like Duke Ellington remains a vital and imaginative composer precisely because he has never severed his tie with the Negro dance and because his approach to the world's musical speech is eclectic.

Nevertheless there is the danger that the rapid absorption of Negro American musical forms by the commercial interests and their rapid vulgarization and dissemination through the mass media will corrupt the Negro's own taste, just as in Mexico the demand for modern designs in silver jewelry for export is leading to a dying away of native design. Thus I say that so much of the future depends upon the self-acceptance of the Negro composer and his integrity toward his musical tradition. Nor do I exclude the so-called serious composer; all are faced with the humanist American necessity of finding the balance between progress and continuity; between tradition and experimentation. For the jazz artist there is some insurance in continuing to play for dance audiences, for here the criticism is unspoiled by status-directed theories; Negroes simply won't accept shoddy dance music, thus the artist has a vital criticism danced out in the ritual of the dance.

Since the spirituals are religious music it would seem that their future is assured by the revitalization of the Negro American churches as is demonstrated in the leadership which these churches are giving in the struggle for civil rights. The old songs play quite a part in this and they in turn throb with new emotion flowing from the black American's revaluation of his experience. Negroes are no longer ashamed of their slave past but see in it sources of strength, and it is now generally recognized that the spirituals bespoke their birth as a people and asserted and defined their humanity. The desegregation struggle is only the socio-political manifestation of this process. Commercial rock-and-roll music is a brutalization of one stream of contemporary Negro church music, but I do not believe that even this obscene looting of a cultural expression can permanently damage the vital source—not for racial reasons but because for some time to come Negroes will live close to their traditional cultural patterns. Nor do I believe that as we win our struggle for full participation in American life we will abandon our group expression. Too much living and aspiration have gone into it, so that drained of its elements of defensiveness and alienation it will become even more precious to us, for we will see it ever clearer as a transcendent value. What we have counterpoised against the necessary rage for progress in American life (and which we share with other Americans) will have been proved to be at least as valuable as all our triumphs of technology. In spilling out his heart's blood in his contest with the machine, John Henry was asserting a national value as well as a Negro value.

What do you think of the attempt of Brazilian and American Negroes to adopt "White values" in place of "Negro values"? Is this only an illusion on their part, or will it be a source of creative development?

I am unqualified to speak of Brazil, but in the United States, the values of my own people are neither "white" nor "black," they are American. Nor can I see how they could be anything else, since we are a people who are involved in the texture of the American experience. And indeed, today the most dramatic fight for American ideals is being sparked by black Americans. Significantly, we are the only black peoples who are not fighting for separation from the "whites," but for a fuller participation in the society which we share with "whites." And it is of further significance that we pursue our goals precisely in terms of American Constitutionalism. If there is anything in this which points to "black values" it must lie in the circumstance that we really believe that all men are created equal and that they should be given a chance to achieve their highest potentialities, regardless of race, creed, color or past condition of servitude.

The terms in which the question is couched serve to obscure the cultural fact that the dynamism of American life is as much a part of the Negro American's personality as it is of the white American's. We differ from certain white Americans in that we have no reason to assume that race has a positive value, and in that we reject race thinking wherever we find it. And even this attitude is shared by millions of whites. Nor are we interested in being anything other than *Negro* Americans. One's racial identity is, after all, accidental, but the United States is an international country and its conscious character makes it possible for us to abandon the mistakes of the past. The point of our struggle is to be both Negro and American and to bring about that condition in American society in which this would be possible. In brief, there is an American Negro idiom, a style and a way of life, but none of this is inseparable from the conditions of American society, nor from its general modes or culture—mass distribution, race and intra-national conflicts, the radio, television, its system of education, its politics. If general American values influence us; we in turn influence them—speech, concept of liberty, justice, economic distribution, international outlook, our current attitude toward colonialism, our national image of ourselves as a nation. And this despite the fact that nothing which black Americans have won as a people has been won without struggle. For *no* group within the United States achieves anything without asserting its claims against the counterclaims of other groups. Thus as Americans we have accepted this conscious and ceaseless struggle as a condition of our freedom, and we are aware that each of our victories increases the area of freedom for all Americans, regardless of color. When we finally achieve the right of full participation in American life, what we make of it will depend upon our sense of cultural values, and our creative use of freedom, not upon our racial identification. I see no reason why the heritage of world culture—which represents a continuum—should be confused with the notion of race. Japan erected a highly efficient modern technology upon a religious culture which viewed the Emperor as a god. The Germany which produced Beethoven and Hegel and Mann turned its science and technology to the monstrous task of genocide; one hopes that when what are known as the "Negro" societies are in full possession of the world's knowledge and in control of their destinies, they will bring to an end all those savageries which for centuries have been committed in the name of race. From what we are witnessing in certain parts of the world today, however, there is no guarantee that simply being non-white offers any guarantee of this. The demands of state policy are apt to be more influential than morality. I would like to see a qualified Negro as President of the United States. But I suspect that even if this were today possible, the necessities of the office would shape his actions far more than his racial identity.

Would that we could but put the correct questions in these matters, perhaps then great worlds of human energy could be saved—especially by those of us who would be free.

46. ROMAN C. PUCINSKI AND OTHERS

A cultural Bill of Rights

The spotlight that beamed on minorities of non-European origin in the 1960s was extended to those of European origin as well. Particularly stirred by this great concern were white ethnics of southern and eastern European origin. For many, their long-time housing, economic, and social patterns had become most vulnerable to challenge and displacement as a result of the social transformation of the great cities. Trapped between higher status older Americans in the suburbs and the rising militant

From U.S., Congress, House, *Congressional Record*, Hearings Before the General Subcommittee on Education, of the Committee on Education and Labor, on H.R. 14910. . . . 91st Cong., 2nd Sess., Feb. 17–18, 1970, pp. 51–54, 56, 76–79.

non-white minorities, the white ethnics experienced a sense of malaise and cultural deprivation. They were part of a society that made no provision for the perpetuation of their group memories and no reinforcement to their sense of identity.

In November 1969, Congressman Roman C. Pucinski of Illinois, chairman of the General Subcommittee on Education of the Committee on Education and Labor, introduced the Ethnic Heritage Studies Centers bill, intended to support institutions and programs that would formally recognize and legitimize the claim of the invisible white ethnics to a share in the nation's cultural heritage. In 1973, the bill passed both houses of Congress; in 1974 federal funds were appropriated for the first time to support educational and cultural programs at the school level that would introduce white ethnic cultural resources into the curriculum.

The testimony of Pucinski and his committee's invited guests, printed below, suggests the dilemmas of a nation uncertain of the implications of its pluralistic cultural heritage for its present needs.

Mr. PUCINSKI. . . . Dr. Ramirez, I was wondering if you could perhaps . . . tak[e] a particular group and giv[e] us some idea how you envision the group in the context of the ethnic studies centers? . . .

Dr. [MANUEL] RAMIREZ.[1] I think one of the things to which I would give the highest priority is to take those people in the Mexican-American community who have felt the most alienated and yet who possess resources and information that can be used in the curriculum that these centers are developing. I would bring these people in, and have them give us the information, hire them as consultants, hire them as curriculum writers, to give us the information for this curriculum. . . .

Of course, training teachers, I would . . . make . . . the second item on my list of priorities, and emphasiz[e] contact between the community people and the potential trainee. I think this would be very important. . . .

The third one would be to make sure that these curriculum materials get to the schools, that we provide consultant services to them in those cases where teachers want help in teaching them, or have certain questions about the materials. . . .

1. Manuel Ramirez, Associate Professor and Director, Bicultural-Bilingual Project, Claremont College.

Mr. RADCLIFFE. How do you account for the—the only word I can use is "blindness"—the blindness of the educators over the years? Is there some peculiarity of educators that makes them unaware of obvious needs which any citizen ought to be aware of?

Dr. RAMIREZ. I guess it is just the philosophy of the times, and the philosophy of the times said, "the melting pot. . . ."

Mr. PUCINSKI. We had drummed into us in this country for a hundred years this totally fallacious concept that we are a melting pot. We are not a melting pot. You don't take human beings and melt them into a single monolith.

You might do it with machines, and you might be able to take silver and melt it and recoin it, and you might even take some beef and make a stew out of it. But I don't think you can take people.

The fact that a lot of people happen to be born on a piece of real estate identified with the United States does not really remove from them a certain inheritance and culture that they have inherited from their forebears, and I think we are now paying the price for this neglect in this country. . . .

I think to a great extent we have been dominated in this country by the Puritan ethos which . . . viewed everything with great suspicion and scorn, and viewed everything as "foreign," and as a result the extent to which they did this . . . is perhaps demonstrated best in the Latin-American, and the treatment we give the Latin-American in the United States, or the Indian, or the Oriental, or the Negro, or the Slavic groups.

You either were willing to accept the melting pot, permit yourself to be melted into the Puritan ethos, or else you were un-American. You were rejected as a foreigner. . . .

I think we are now paying the price for this. I think it is no accident that you have young people going through all sorts of aberrations, commonly described as the hippie and the yippie and what-not, simply because they are looking for an identity that has been denied to them in their classroom.

We have been on this 100-year binge of trying to deny human beings the identity of their own cultural background, and we have tried to mold them, . . . homogenize them, as if they were apples and pears or a pound of butter, instead of recognizing that they are human beings with their own cultural values, and cultural standards.

I honestly feel that this legislation is 30 years behind its time, 40 or 50 years behind its time. . . .

Dr. JAIPAUL.[2]

I want to provide empirical evidence that proves what we are saying here is practical. It has been practiced on a small scale in Philadelphia. We have developed three experiments—one at high school level, one for elementary school, and one for ethnic leaders.

In the first case, we have taken four different cultures to make a comparative study. We have identified eight or nine values to be compared. We bring in the indigenous resources to do this.

The common values we have identified are geography, history, politics, external relations and science and technology, and so forth. It is not that the 10th graders involved study one culture and go over to the next. They study one value at a time and compare and relate and find out commonalities and differences about this in other cultures. We find indigenous resources for this, because the traditional resources are not there.

Suppose we are talking about religion such as Taoism, Hinduism, Christianity and Islam. We bring persons who practice these religions, and can tell about them.

Sensitivity training sessions are also part of this study. We have added another facet to it. That is, we have combined two schools. One is William Penn public school and the other is Hallahan Catholic Girls parochial school. To the difference between cultural values, we have added different values of public and parochial schools.

We have found after 5 or 6 months' experience that this experiment works and the 10th graders are relating to each other very well. They come from various nationality and racial groups.

At the fifth grade level, we approached Sacred Heart (parochial) School and Abigail Vare (public) School, and developed a

---

2. Dr. Jaipaul, director, National Community Race Relations, National Service Center.

program of teaching ethnic history of the groups involved as part of American history.

It was interesting when we asked fifth graders, "What is your nationality?" and some said Polish, some Irish and so on. There were others who said both Polish and German, because the parents were of different backgrounds.

Suppose the students are talking about the Polish contribution to the Philadelphia area. The parents bring story books, cultural things, they cook meals for them and so on. It has given the fifth graders of the two schools their identity and pride and they are relating to each other so well.

Then we have a group of different nationality leaders: the Ukrainian, Polish, Scottish, Welsh, black, Indian, and Scandinavian. They are creating a consortium to develop ethnic histories. Clearly, the group would be developing its resources for this undertaking.

Here, what we are showing is that it can be done cooperatively, and if there is anyone who feels it can be used for polarization, I think otherwise.

If our larger goal is to develop a complete history of the United States, my suggestion here would be to establish regional centers based on the cooperation between educational institutions and several ethnic groups that are predominant in that particular area. Both will supplement and complement each other and also serve as balances and checks. One will provide the know-how, and the other provides the content. This way no one group can capitalize and use it for some kind of political ends. . . .

Mr. PUCINSKI. How are you financing it?

Dr. JAIPAUL. We are financing it by passing a hat. This is the main problem. We are going to various foundations, individuals, wherever we can find money. Now we have been flooded with requests from suburban schools to pair the schools for next year.

We don't have money for next year to even keep the present staff. . . .

Mr. PUCINSKI. What is the reaction of the students participating in this experimental program?

Dr. JAIPAUL. When we had the first sensitivity training for the

10th graders, we took them to a synagogue. They said this course was what they could not imagine. "Why did you not start it earlier?" summarizes their feelings. Among the fifth graders, there were some Puerto Ricans and black students who were withdrawn from the schools. Now they are equal partners.

To give you an illustration, one of the mothers, who is Jewish, was actually opposed to her children going to join the Catholic school-children. She was called into the principal's office and explained. You will not believe that she was the first one to bring her resources and tell students what is Hanukkah and how it is celebrated. She cooked potato pancakes for 90 students and others that day.

Mr. PUCINSKI. Do you anticipate expanding this program to more youngsters as you move along?

Dr. JAIPAUL. We have been requested by 10 pairs of schools. We don't have resources for next year to commit ourselves. . . .

Dr. VECOLI. The rationale for this bill, as I see it, is both in terms of providing for children of different ethnic backgrounds a sense of positive identification with the American past and also providing them with an intellectual understanding of the nature of the American society as a pluralistic society.

I do think as we proceed with this bill, there will be opposition from critics who will say this will promote group consciousness, that this will simply exacerbate the differences in American society. I don't find this a persuasive argument, because I think we have for decades suffered under the delusion of "melting pot," in which we refused to recognize the reality and the legitimacy of the existence of ethnic groups. The effects of this, as I suggested before, have been that the assimilationist approach has affected generations of children in a very negative way.

I suggest perhaps we need a cultural bill of rights in which the rights of all ethnic groups to pursue their distinctive ways of life and perpetuate their heritages would be explicitly recognized and protected.

The enactment of H.R. 14910 would, in my opinion, put the Government of the United States on record as endorsing the view that ethnicity and diversity are sources of national strength and well-being and enrichment rather than negative forces in our society. . . .

Now, I think that is right down to the guts of the issue. What we are trying to do in this bill is to help Americans know each other better and understand each other better. I have said at the opening of these hearings that we are now paying a heavy price because, for the last century or two, we have tried to homogenize 200 million human beings instead of recognizing . . . [that] Americans are a beautiful mosaic of many people, many races, many religions, many cultural backgrounds, and as we learn more about each other's strengths as human beings, we dissipate many of the needless fears and apprehensions and suspicions about each other and start looking upon each other as a mosaic of people who make up the whole of the Nation. I think that your statement has been developed beautifully. Mr. Brademas. . . .

Mr. [JOHN] BRADEMAS.[3] . . . To what extent are efforts being made in universities of the United States, especially universities located in communities where there are substantial ethnic minorities, to work with the schools in that particular community to afford them teaching materials in respect of the heritage of that particular ethnic group?

I think, for instance, of the University of Notre Dame—our home city of South Bend; we have, Mr. Chairman, some substantial Polish-American community, as the chairman knows, and Hungarian-Americans, to cite two; and does the University of Notre Dame work with the local school system in any way to develop curriculum materials that can be used in the schools where there are large numbers of children or the entire city, for that matter, because it is important that the white Anglo-Saxon Protestant schoolchildren and the black schoolchildren be aware, in my view, of the contributions of the Polish and Hungarian past in view of the fact that there are so many citizens of those two backgrounds in that community, and do I make myself clear?

Dr. [WILLIAM T.] LIU.[4] Yes. I think at this time there has been

3. Congressman John Brademas, Indiana.
4. William T. Liu, Director, Social Science Training Laboratory, University of Notre Dame.

no evidence that the University of Notre Dame or even other universities in the area have engaged in this kind of educational endeavors to either help the schools in disseminating or collecting or teaching the material of ethnic groups. . . . We do have very large Polish and Hungarian ethnic groups in South Bend. Therefore, these two cultural groups are relevant insofar as school curriculum and interests of the pupils are concerned.

I suspect that Spanish-speaking Americans would be more interested in the kinds of teaching material that pertains to the Spanish-speaking culture or heritage in the Southwest United States and perhaps in large cities like New York and Chicago, this whole urban complex.

So, therefore, I think it is important to think about certain single or regional cultural centers because of the geographic distribution of our ethnic population in the United States instead of dispersing them throughout the country, which probably would not be very fruitful at this time.

Mr. BRADEMAS. Thank you.

Mr. LEVINE. Perhaps I can respond, Congressman. Dr. Vecoli has outlined brilliantly in many other places the fact that practically nothing is being done. There is a sudden surge of interest; it has become fashionable, of course, in the black studies field, but in terms of other groups in American life, it took the American Jewish Committee and other Jewish organizations years and years of indigenous fund-raising, and much of this kind of effort is of course quite admirable, to set up chairs in Jewish learning in a number of universities. The nature of these programs was quite specialized, with very few Jewish students except those scholarly concerned, getting involved. I am sure other ethnic groups have had the same kind of experience.

One of the reasons we are so impressed with your effort is because we think you are hitting at the nerve center of American society. You are asking for a modest amount of money; I assume this is only the beginning. It is quite accurate to define significant parts of American history in categories such as group conflict, group interests, and group identity. It probably defines American history more adequately than any other way. Yet in a recent study done by the American Jewish Committee called "Short-changed Children of Suburbia," we show in great detail the fact that these issues of social concern and these issues of ethnic background have been almost totally absent from our suburban schools.

There has been some change in the last two years with some increased interest, but inadequate source materials exist to touch base with historical reality and there is still great confusion as to how one teaches about American group life.

Mr. PUCINSKI. . . . We have totally ignored in this country, the fact that we are unique as a nation. In Poland, 95 percent of the people are Polish; and in Italy, 92 percent of the people are Italian; and in Denmark, I presume 97 percent are Danes, and so on down the line. But here is a unique institution, a polyglot nation, a heterogeneous nation, and yet as we look at the history books of this country, as we look at all of the various textbooks, nowhere do you find any acknowledgement of the fact that America is a mosaic of many people.

Mr. [IRVING M.] LEVINE.[5] We are paying a tremendous price, Congressmen. I don't think we quite realize the pathology that exists in our cities and, overall, the deep disillusionment of youth. The new movements that people are critical of—"groupiness" and "hippiedom," the desire to establish community—is really nothing more than a deep need on the part of people to identify with something smaller than the kind of cancerous anonymous society that has been developed.

5. Irving M. Levine, Director, Urban Project, American Jewish Committee.

PART ELEVEN

The President
The Symbolic American

47. WILLIAM ALLEN WHITE

Al Smith, city feller

The disarmingly sophisticated editor of *The Emporia Gazette* assessed the whole direction of American life in the mid-twenties from the clear perspective of Kansas. In an article that anticipated the presidential candidacy of Alfred Emanuel Smith, William Allen White identified Smith as the most vital symbol of a problematic America whose axis had shifted from country to city. In Smith, White saw "our first urbanite" in national affairs, "city-born, city-bred, 'city-broke,' and city-hearted"; a potential back-alley successor to the backwoods statesmen of the nineteenth century; one of those men with rough edges and tough minds who rode the popular groundswell and seized upon the central issues and dilemmas of their time. But Smith was also the symbol of "the struggle . . . between the hard, ascetic moralities of Puritanism and the lighter, brighter, happier philosophy of Catholicism."

Observe a man—stocky but not pudgy—five feet seven, who looks five feet nine or ten sitting down, for he has a long, sturdy body. He is a blond, well kept, with clear, fine, healthy skin (pink and white, in fact), blue eyes and fair hair that may have been red, possibly even tow, in childhood. He is smooth-shaven, oval-faced, mean-jawed, with a pugnacious set to his head—a head which wags with fine self-assertion.

It is a self-assertion that is never quite vanity. As he talks, one begins to realize that he is merely gesticulating with his long neck above sloping shoulders, over a broad chest, set upon a competent though not distinguished accouterment of intestinal equipment, and all built upon a scaffolding of nimble legs. He is articulate in every inch of his body.

William Allen White, "Al Smith, City Feller," *Collier's*, LXXVIII, August 21, 1926, pp. 8–9. Reprinted by permission of William L. White and *The Emporia Gazette*.

Now let's dress him, for Alfred Emanuel Smith, governor of New York, is a dresser, which fact brands him a city chap, as do the smart clothes he wears. Behold a pink hair-striped collar on top of a dark, wine-colored bow tie, set above a V of shirt front which shows small brownish-crimson figures in a white background, with a slight pink thread running through.

Protruding from the top pocket of a dark, well-tailored coat are the scarlet tips of a handkerchief. Tan shoes, with appropriate silk socks, set off his properly creased gray trousers. He is a tailored man who gives thought to wherewithal he should be clad; again the habit of a city chap.

His blue eyes, looking casually at a man or a scene, remained curtained, bright, flickering specks under dark lashes. Only when his emotions begin to appear do his eyelids open. Then his eyes glow with some incandescence which reveals a deeply earnest nature. His laughter is casual and incidental, but purpose glows in those wide, scathing eyes.

Turn some inner switch in his heart, and affection can burn there as well as purpose, for he is a man of passions, with a capacity for feeling almost as strong as his ability to reason. One gets, therefore, from his spirit, as it is revealed in a well-knit yet nervous body, beautifully controlled, the impression of balance— this kind of balance: a big heart and a clear brain; a balance that makes a man capable of loyalties based upon qualities of both heart and mind.

He can be loyal to a friend, but he can go to the stake for an idea over the body of his friend. Sometimes nice persons, and over-well-bred, come into his office and are shocked at his manner. They who place manner above the inner gifts of heart and mind have revolted at a number of our Presidents; indeed, at a number of our great Presidents. Alfred Emanuel Smith, beloved of his fellow urbanites as Al Smith, as deeply offends the ultra-mannerly of his generation as any other of our statesmen might offend these nice people. They see on him, these most conventional people, the same horns and hoofs which have frightened men from the beginning of time: horns and hoofs of manners growing out of environmental habits; horns and hoofs which every strong man wears as he comes struggling out of his past into leadership.

The background of Al Smith's childhood was the old Brooklyn Bridge. As a boy he played ball under the arches of the old bridge that run in from the river into the water front—cool, deep, shady arches. Here he heroized the policeman on the beat. Here he hopped proudly on the fire wagon. Here he picked up balls on the streets and in alleys back of the saloons, to sell for spending money. Here he led the bridge gang in his early teens. And the Brooklyn Bridge was to him what the woods must have been to the boy of two generations before him in interior America—the great bridge that was suspended like a steel dream across two worlds. Men said, "Ah, it's a great bridge, and it will hold up under the feet of men, but, wait until Jumbo, the elephant, comes across!" And the bridge gang under the arches waited, and Jumbo came, and the bridge stood, and Al Smith learned to hoot at the skeptic.

Jackson, Lincoln—and Al Smith

He learned from the bridge what backwoods boys learned from the trees and the creatures of the forest, from the Indian and the frontiersman. But now, in a new day, the backwoods boy and the backwoodsman, indeed the backwoods themselves are passing from American life.

The backwoodsmen of the last century, of whom Andrew Jackson and Andrew Johnson were types and Lincoln not far out of the picture, seem to be threatened now by the city type. For a hundred years the self-made farmer boy has been proud of the rough edges which he has been too busy to smooth off. American politics has produced thousands of local leaders with sixth-grade education—leaders who came out of the backwoods. Now from the back alley under Brooklyn Bridge comes Al Smith, the new type.

There is no reason why the back alley cannot produce as good moral, spiritual, mental and physical timber for politics as the backwoods. The historical equation reads something like this: as Andrew Jackson was to Clay and Webster, so is Al Smith to

Coolidge and Lowden. Let us therefore consider the back alley from which Al Smith sprang.

Certainly it was, in the seventies, as clean and wholesome a place as the backwoods from which Andrew Jackson sprang in Revolutionary times. Here was a three-story, wooden, New York City tenement facing the river front, cobblestones running down past the old fish market to the tide; square riggers coming in with cargoes and drunken sailors running up over the cobbles eager for the river-front saloon and for the fat prostitute, sitting in her window bare-armed and as alluring as sin in adipose can be.

On the third floor of the tenement where Al Smith was born his father, a dock workman, teamster, day laborer, ready for any job, maintained his little family. The real head of that family was Catherine Mulvehill, his wife, a girl whose father and mother were born in America, but who was, nevertheless, of the good old Irish stock, energetic, faithful, full of visions and dreams, and never afraid of humble work. She was widowed in her twenties and held her brood together by keeping store and doing such honest work as came to her hands: a strong, vigorous character, Roman Catholic in religion and no bigot. . . .

Up the Escalator to Freedom

Al Smith, a young Tammany leader, who had worked his way up through the precinct into the ward—and so to the district in the moving stairway which takes forward and upward men who are industrious, honest and intelligent—found himself in his early thirties a member of the New York Assembly. The escalator also took him from the river front.

He maintained a decent Christian home. He had married Katherine Dunn. Their children were appearing with proper regularity, and Al Smith was a coming man in the district—something better than a leader. He was going to school in politics, in Albany politics, under Barnes, Platt, Bill Ward and Lou Payn, Republican leaders, and under the tutelage of men who had their political education from Croker, Bill Devery, Tom Foley, Judge Van Wyck, and later Mayor Gaynor, who thrust a certain practical idealism into the situation.

But idealism in politics has never greatly affected Al Smith. It was a part of his political education to learn the routine of the public business: how taxes are levied, collected and disbursed; how political appointments are made; what wires hold what men and what ambitions govern others. Thus his education was not unlike that of the good gambler.

Smith was quick to learn the rules. He became party leader and Speaker of the House. His legislative career was curiously typical of the coming new order that he was to represent. Loyalty is a major virtue in an urban organization.

Smith took orders from Tammany until he was able to give orders. In his first legislative years his record was classed as bad by the nonpartisan organization which was trying to promote the rather rural program of welfare legislation which occupied the hearts of the political altruists of the hour.

Smith voted with the Tammany group against the direct primary, for instance, and certain welfare legislation which reformers were seeking. But Tammany thought Smith's record was good. When he took leadership in the Assembly and when he went to the New York State Constitutional Convention he was fairly free.

Elihu Root, chairman of the convention, declared that Smith knew the government of New York State more intelligently than any other delegate. It was then that he began to command attention from his political opponents. He was the tough-brained, hard-headed, fact-seeking, ever-ready, hard-working realist that is called "able." Naturally Senator Elihu Root took a liking to him. The Republican New York *Tribune* spoke well of Smith. He grew in power and stature politically. . . .

Symbol of a Mighty Challenge

We may be facing new issues in our politics, based for the first time upon the conflicting interests, the conflicting morals, the conflicting aspirations of a rural civilization as those interests, morals, and aspirations clash in a nation which is rapidly becoming industrialized and urban. Hence Al Smith—with his pink and white skin, his pink and crimson tie and the scarlet

border of his handkerchief, his silk socks and conventional gray
trousers—becomes something more than a sporadic figure in our
politics. He becomes the symbol of a mighty challenge to our
American traditions, a challenge which, if it wins in the struggle
which may ensue, will bring deep changes into our American life.

In early July, 1924, after the National Democratic Convention
had wrangled through the longest session ever held by a major
party in America and nominated a compromise candidate for the
Presidency on the 103d ballot, Al Smith appeared after the
nomination of John W. Davis had been made. During the long,
bitter session of the convention Smith had appeared as a
Presidential candidate, for days a formidable candidate, always
the candidate of a militant minority in the convention. His
following had come from the Atlantic seaboard and from the
states where the Democratic organization is dominated by large
cities.

The apparent issue upon which Smith rallied his strength was a
distaste for the law prohibiting the sale and manufacture of liquor.
And certainly the opposition to Smith rallied around the presumption that Smith is a "Wet."

As a corollary to his wetness came the fact that he is a Catholic,
and that fact gained and lost delegates for him in the convention.
His strongest opponent, Mr. McAdoo, typified the opposing view
of life. . . .

What changes have come into American life which give this
new kind of statesman the power of a hero? In two words: blood
and iron, but the blood in this instance is the changing blood of
the American nation, the iron is the vast framework of wires and
tubes and beams and stringers, girders, and re-enforcing upon
which the new urban structure of the material life of America is
rising—new blood and new iron.

Perhaps it wasn't the old blood of New England and the
colonial blood of the South, now slowly mixing with new blood, so
much as tradition and environment. But, at any rate, the America
of the last quarter of the nineteenth century was essentially an
agricultural nation. Our cities beyond the seaboard were agricultural towns. The English blood, or Teutonic blood if you will,

naturally takes to agriculture, and we were of one blood as we were of one tongue. The farmer ruled us either actually by his votes, which made powerful minorities, or by his interests and traditions.

Our national leaders thought rurally. Our national policies were such policies as an intelligent, upright, altruistic American farmer might formulate in an eminently respectable world in which each man earned all he got and in which every man got all he earned by the grace of God and by such amendments to the Constitution as were necessary to establish the grace of God. . . .

A Town-Lot Sir Galahad

He recognizes the folly of cramping public opinion—even treasonable public opinion—in a democracy, and by pardoning political prisoners convicted in wartime hysteria, and by vetoing repressive measures he has made a democratic record for free speech which might be more than a local record if there was much real sentiment in America in favor of justice when it threatens the basswood gods of reactionary fear.

Governor Smith's chief victory probably was the law providing for better housing in the larger cities, his only failure his attempt to put the state electric power under state regulation.

Al Smith, like most of the statesmen and probably a considerable majority of the people east of the Alleghenies and north of the Mason-Dixon line, has opposed prohibition because it has never come to the East as it has come to the rest of the country after a slow process of education, experiment, trial and failure, theory and practice. West—beyond the Alleghenies—prohibition was an accomplished fact from ten to forty years before national prohibition.

So, even as an antiprohibition leader, while he picks up some followers in the larger cities of the hinterland, Al Smith still is a local leader dealing in local issues—urban issues all: prohibition, electric power, housing, the centralization of Democratic power, improvement of conditions for defectives.

Governor Al Smith could go to the United States Senate if he chose. His reasons for not going are excuses. Probably deep down in his under-consciousness he halts before tackling the larger economic issues of America in the Senate.

There is not, in American public life to-day, a clearer, stronger, more accurately working brain in any man's head than Al Smith's brain. His processes of thought are logical, and he has the courage to defend them. But he cannot think clearly about matters of which he knows little.

To educate himself on these matters would take ten years. He would blunder in the Senate while he was learning that lesson. Hence he backs off from a senatorial career.

If Republican blundering should shunt Smith into the White House in '28 or '32, he would know where to get advisers on whom to call for expert and administrative wisdom. He would furnish the administrative talent and courage, but in the Senate one must act quickly on one's own immediate resources—which must come from experience or education. Smith has no such resources.

He is a most human, affectionate, wise and brave man whose sincerity is never seriously questioned, whose courage is proverbial, whose humanity holds friends with steel rods. Yet he is at this moment a provincial statesman not because he has no national qualities of leadership. He has striking qualities of leadership. No other statesman in America has such powers of leadership as he, and yet he is provincial, not geographically but because he has not projected himself into the wider range of American issues, and unless the one issue in which he is national—that is, prohibition— should become more widely acute than it is now, Smith's greater qualities of leadership would languish. And he might remain in history, for all his high qualities, a town-lot Sir Galahad who never fared afield.

48.   CHARLES C. MARSHALL

An open letter
to the Honorable Alfred E. Smith

In the 1920s, Alfred E. Smith, governor of the nation's greatest state, was the most available Democrat for the presidential nomination. For the first time in the nation's history, a Catholic, a "wet," a favorite of the new immigrant America, and a graduate of Tammany Hall, was among the front runners. In 1924, the New York governor's chance for the nomination evaporated when the Democratic convention meeting in New York's Madison Square Garden—in the urban immigrant heartland —failed to register a majority vote for a resolution denouncing the Ku Klux Klan, which had become the dominant issue. In the next few years, Smith gained in stature and in visibility.

In 1927, the editor of the *Atlantic Monthly*, a Smith admirer, was convinced that there was "no social poison comparable to the venom of religious prejudice." Therefore, Ellery Sedgwick decided to give form to the anticipated religious debate, in any case inevitable, by placing it on a high intellectual plane. Knowing that Smith would ignore such an invitation, the editor decided on an indirect route. "There lived in New York," he recalled many years later, "a certain highly qualified lawyer, one Charles Marshall, an expert on ecclesiastical polity. This gentleman, being a High Church Anglican, loved Rome as the devil loves Holy Water." Although Sedgwick knew that anything that Marshall would write would be wholly beyond the interest and understanding of many *Atlantic* readers, he also realized that it was exactly the sort of article that was needed. He therefore invited Marshall to write a public letter addressed to the potential presidential candidate, inquiring about the perils of dual loyalty and "to invest the article with all the pomp of legal logic, of precedent, and of ecclesiastical theory." Marshall did.

I

SIR:—

The American people take pride in viewing the progress of an

From Charles C. Marshall, "An Open Letter to the Honorable Alfred E. Smith," *Atlantic Monthly*, April, 1927, pp. 540–49. Reprinted by permission of the publisher.

American citizen from the humble estate in which his life began toward the highest office within the gift of the nation. It is for this reason that your candidacy for the Presidential nomination has stirred the enthusiasm of a great body of your fellow citizens. They know and rejoice in the hardship and the struggle which have fashioned you as a leader of men. They know your fidelity to the morality you have advocated in public and private life and to the religion you have revered; your great record of public trusts successfully and honestly discharged; your spirit of fair play, and justice even to your political opponents. Partisanship bids fair to quail before the challenge of your personality, and men who vote habitually against your party are pondering your candidacy with sincere respect; and yet—through all this tribute there is a note of doubt, a sinister accent of interrogation, not as to intentional rectitude and moral purpose, but as to certain conceptions which your fellow citizens attribute to you as a loyal and conscientious Roman Catholic, which in their minds are irreconcilable with that Constitution which as President you must support and defend, and with the principles of civil and religious liberty on which American institutions are based.

To this consideration no word of yours, or on your behalf, has yet been addressed. Its discussion in the interests of the public weal is obviously necessary, and yet a strange reticence avoids it, often with the unjust and withering attribution of bigotry or prejudice as the unworthy motive of its introduction. Undoubtedly a large part of the public would gladly avoid a subject the discussion of which is so unhappily associated with rancor and malevolence, and yet to avoid the subject is to neglect the profoundest interests in our national welfare.

American life has developed into a variety of religious beliefs and ethical systems, religious and nonreligious, whose claims press more and more upon public attention. None of these presents a more definite philosophy or makes a more positive demand upon the attention and reason of mankind than your venerable Church, which recently at Chicago, in the greatest religious demonstration that the world has ever seen, declared her presence and her power in American life. Is not the time ripe and the occasion opportune for a declaration, if it can be made, that shall clear away all doubt as to the reconcilability of her status and her claims with American constitutional principles? With such a statement the only question as to your proud eligibility to the Presidential office would disappear, and the doubts of your fellow citizens not of the Roman Catholic Church would be instantly resolved in your favor.

The conceptions to which we refer are not superficial. They are of the very life and being of that Church, determining its status and its relation to the State, and to the great masses of men whose convictions deny them the privilege of membership in that Church. Surely the more conscientious the Roman Catholic, and the more loyal to his Church, the more sincere and unqualified should be his acceptance of such conceptions.

These conceptions have been recognized before by Roman Catholics as a potential obstacle to their participation in public office, Pope Leo XIII himself declaring, in one of his encyclical letters, that 'it may in some places be true that for most urgent and just reasons it is by no means expedient for (Roman) Catholics to engage in public affairs or to take an active part in politics.'

It is indeed true that a loyal and conscientious Roman Catholic could and would discharge his oath of office with absolute fidelity to his moral standards. As to that in general, and as to you in particular, your fellow citizens entertain no doubt. But those moral standards differ essentially from the moral standards of all men not Roman Catholics. They are derived from the basic political doctrine of the Roman Catholic Church, asserted against repeated challenges for fifteen hundred years, that God has divided all power over men between the secular State and that Church. Thus Pope Leo XIII, in 1885, in his encyclical letter on *The Christian Constitution of States*, says: 'The Almighty has appointed the charge of the human race between two powers, the ecclesiastical and the civil, the one being set over divine, and the other over human things.'

The deduction is inevitable that, as all power over human affairs, not given to the State by God, is given by God to the Roman Catholic Church, no other churches or religious or ethical societies have in theory any direct power from God and are without direct divine sanction, and therefore without natural right to function on the same basis as the Roman Catholic Church in the religious and moral affairs of the State. The result is that that Church, if true to her basic political doctrine, is hopelessly committed to that intolerance that has disfigured so much of her history. This is frankly admitted by Roman Catholic authorities.

Pope Pius IX in the famous Syllabus (1864) said: 'To hold that national churches, withdrawn from the authority of the Roman Pontiff and altogether separated, can be established, is error.'

That great compendium of Roman Catholic teaching, the *Catholic Encyclopedia*, declares that the Roman Catholic Church 'regards dogmatic intolerance, not alone as her incontestable right, but as her sacred duty.' It is obvious that such convictions leave nothing in theory of the religious and moral rights of those who are not Roman Catholics. And, indeed, that *is* Roman Catholic teaching and the inevitable deduction from Roman Catholic claims, if we use the word 'rights' strictly. Other churches, other religious societies, are tolerated in the State, not by right, but by favor.

Pope Leo XIII is explicit on this point: 'The (Roman Catholic) Church, indeed, deems it unlawful to place the various forms of divine worship on the same footing as the true religion, but does not, on that account, condemn those rulers who, for the sake of securing some great good or of hindering some great evil, allow patiently custom or usage to be a kind of sanction for each kind of religion having its place in the State.'

That is, there is not a lawful equality of other religions with that of the Roman Catholic Church, but that Church will allow state authorities for politic reasons—that is, by favor, but not by right—to tolerate other religious societies. We would ask, sir, whether such favors can be accepted in place of rights by those owning the name of freemen?

II

Furthermore, the doctrine of the Two Powers, in effect and theory, inevitably makes the Roman Catholic Church at times sovereign and paramount over the State. It is true that in theory the doctrine assigns to the secular State jurisdiction over secular matters and to the Roman Catholic Church jurisdiction over matters of faith and morals, each jurisdiction being exclusive of the other within undisputed lines. But the universal experience of mankind has demonstrated, and reason teaches, that many questions must arise between the State and the Roman Catholic Church in respect to which it is impossible to determine to the satisfaction of both in which jurisdiction the matter at issue lies.

Here arises the irrepressible conflict. Shall the State or the Roman Catholic Church determine? The Constitution of the United States clearly ordains that the State shall determine the question. The Roman Catholic Church demands for itself the sole right to determine it, and holds that within the limits of that claim it is superior to and supreme over the State. The *Catholic Encyclopedia* clearly so declares: 'In case of direct contradiction, making it impossible for both jurisdictions to be exercised, the jurisdiction of the Church prevails and that of the State is excluded.' And Pope Pius IX in the Syllabus asserted: 'To say in the case of conflicting laws enacted by the Two Powers, the civil law prevails, is error.'

Extreme as such a conclusion may appear, it is inevitable in Roman Catholic philosophy. That Church by the very theory of her existence cannot yield, because what she claims as her right and her truth she claims is hers by the 'direct act of God'; in her theory, God himself directly forbids. The State cannot yield because of a great mass of citizens who are not Roman Catholics. By its constitutional law and in the nature of things, practices of religion in its opinion inconsistent with its peace and safety are unlawful; the law of its being—the law of necessity—forbids. If we could all concede the 'divine and exclusive' claims of the Roman Catholic Church, conflict would be eliminated; but, as it is, there is a wide consensus of opinion that those claims are false in fact and in flat conflict with the very being and order of the State.

In our constitutional order this consensus is bulwarked on the doctrine of the Supreme Court of the United States that our religious liberty and our constitutional guaranties thereof are subject to the supreme qualification that religious 'practices inconsistent with the peace and safety of the State shall not be justified.' (*Watson* v. *Jones* 13 Wall. p. 579)

The Roman Catholic Church, of course, makes no claim, and never has made any claim, to jurisdiction over matters that *in her opinion* are solely secular and civil. She makes the claim obviously only when the matter in question is not, *in her opinion*, solely secular and civil. But as determination of jurisdiction, in a conflict with the State, rests solely in her sovereign discretion, no argument is needed to show that she may in theory and effect annihilate the rights of all who are not Roman Catholics, sweeping into the jurisdiction of a single religious society the most important interests of human well-being. The education of youth, the institution of marriage, the international relations of the State, and its domestic peace, as we shall proceed to show, are, in certain exigencies, wrested from the jurisdiction of the State, in which all citizens share, and confided to the jurisdiction of a single religious society in which all citizens cannot share, great numbers being excluded by the barriers of religious belief. Do you, sir, regard such claims as tolerable in a republic that calls itself free?

And, in addition to all this, the exclusive powers of the Roman Catholic Church are claimed by her to be vested in and exercised by a sovereignty that is not only created therefor by the special act of God, but is foreign and extraterritorial to these United States and to all secular states. This sovereignty, by the highest Roman Catholic authority, that of Pope Leo XIII, is not only superior in theory to the sovereignty of the secular State, but is substituted upon earth in place of the authority of God himself.

We quote Pope Leo in his encyclical letter on *The Christian Constitution of States*: 'Over the mighty multitude of mankind, God has set rulers with power to govern, and He has willed that one of them (the Pope) should be the head of all.' We quote Pope Leo in his encyclical letter on *The Reunion of Christendom*: 'We who hold upon this earth the place of God Almighty.'

It follows naturally on all this that there is a conflict between authoritative Roman Catholic claims on the one side and our constitutional law and principles on the other. Pope Leo XIII says: 'It is not lawful for the State, any more than for the individual, either to disregard all religious duties or to hold in equal favor different kinds of religion.' But the Constitution of the United States declares otherwise: 'Congress shall make no law respecting an establishment of religion or prohibiting the free exercise thereof.'

Thus the Constitution declares the United States shall hold in equal favor different kinds of religion or no religion and the Pope declares it is not lawful to hold them in equal favor. Is there not here a quandary for that man who is at once a loyal churchman and a loyal citizen?

Pope Leo says that the Roman Catholic Church 'deems it unlawful to place the various forms of divine worship on the same footing as the true religion.' But the Supreme Court of the United States says that our 'law knows no heresy and is committed to the support of no dogma, the establishment of no sect.' (*Watson* v. *Jones* 13 Wall. p. 728)

Americans indulge themselves in the felicitation that they have achieved an ideal religious situation in the United States. But Pope Leo, in his encyclical letter on *Catholicity in the United States*, asserts: 'It would be very erroneous to draw the conclusion that in America is to be sought the type of the most desirable status of the Church.' The modern world reposes in the comfortable reflection that the severance of Church and State has ended a long and unhappy conflict, when the same Pope calls our attention to the error of supposing 'that it would be universally lawful or expedient for State and Church to be, as in America, dissevered and divorced.'

Is our law, then, in papal theory, no law? Is it contrary to natural right? Is it in conflict with the will and fiat of Almighty God? Clearly the Supreme Court and Pope Leo are profoundly at variance. Is it not obvious that such a difference of opinion, concerning the fundamental rights between two sovereignties operating within the same territory, may, even with the best intentions and the most sensitive consciences, be fruitful of political offenses that are odious among men?

Citizens who waver in your support would ask whether, as a
Roman Catholic, you accept as authoritative the teaching of the
Roman Catholic Church that in case of contradiction, making it
impossible for the jurisdiction of that Church and the jurisdiction
of the State to agree, the jurisdiction of the Church shall prevail;
whether, as statesman, you accept the teaching of the Supreme
Court of the United States that, in matters of religious practices
which in the opinion of the State are inconsistent with its peace
and safety, the jurisdiction of the State shall prevail; and, if you
accept both teachings, how you will reconcile them.

III

At the present time no question assumes greater importance
than the education of youth. The legislatures of Tennessee, of
Oregon, and of Nebraska have of late laid impious hands upon it
and the judiciary has sternly curbed them. From what has been
said above, it is clear that the claims of the Roman Catholic
Church touching this point, more than those of any other
institution, may conflict with the authority of the State.

It is true that in the famous Oregon School cases the Supreme
Court of the United States held a state law unconstitutional that
forbade parents to educate their children at church schools of
every denomination. But there was no assertion in the law that the
church schools in question gave instruction inconsistent with the
peace and safety of the State and there was no allegation of that
tenor in the pleadings. On the record the church schools were
void of offense. But, had that feature existed in the cases, it would
necessarily have led to a reversal of the decision. There would
have been a conflict between Church and State as to whether the
instruction was inconsistent with the peace and safety of the
State. The Roman Catholic Church, if true to her doctrine and
dogma, would have had to assert exclusive jurisdiction over the
determination of this point. Equally the State, in self-preservation,
would have had to assert exclusive jurisdiction. The conflict would
have been irreconcilable. What would have been the results and
what the test of a sincere and conscientious Roman Catholic in
executive office or on the bench?

Nothing can be clearer to the American mind than that the plain political teaching of Pope Pius IX and of Pope Leo XIII, as set forth in their encyclical letters, is inconsistent with the peace and safety of the State within the meaning of those words as used by the Supreme Court of the United States in its great decision. That it is 'not lawful for the State to hold in equal favor different kinds of religion'; that it is not universally lawful for the State and the Roman Catholic Church to be dissevered and divorced; that the various kinds of religion in theory have their place in the State, not by natural right, but by favor; that dogmatic intolerance is not alone the incontestable right of the Roman Catholic Church, but her sacred duty; that in the case of conflicting laws of the State and the Roman Catholic Church the law of that Church shall prevail, are propositions that would make up a strange textbook for the instruction of American youth.

IV

A direct conflict between the Roman Catholic Church and the State arises on the institution of marriage, through the claim of that Church that in theory in the case of all baptized persons, quite irrespective of specific consent, Protestants and Roman Catholics alike, jurisdiction touching marriage is wrested from the State and appropriated to the Roman Catholic Church, its exercise reposing ultimately in the Pope. In Roman Catholic theory the civil contract over which the State claims jurisdiction merges in the religious sacrament of marriage, which is, as to baptized persons, exclusively within the jurisdiction of the Roman Catholic Church. Pope Pius IX in 1864 proclaimed in the famous Syllabus: 'It is error to hold that the sacrament of marriage is only a something accessory to the contract and separate from it.'

It would be generally conceded that the Roman Catholic Church—and indeed any religious society—has the natural right, in case of a question as to the validity of the marriage of a member, to determine as to whether that member may receive its sacramental ministrations and on what terms. Action by the Church would obviously relate only to the religious incidents of the civil contract and would leave untouched the civil contract over which the State claims jurisdiction. But the doctrine expressed by Pope Pius IX and the nature of the claims of his Church forbid such reasonable action. The Church proceeds in disregard of the law and sovereignty of the State, and claims, at its discretion, the right to annul and destroy the bond of the civil contract. The practical result of such claims in the conflict of Church and State appears in the light of the recent and notorious annulment of the Marlborough marriage.

The essential facts are few. It was the case of a marriage between two 'Protestants,' solemnized within the sovereignty of the State of New York, by ecclesiastics of the Episcopal Church duly authorized in the matter by the commission of that sovereignty. The parties took up their residence within the sovereignty of England. Twenty-five years after the marriage, and after the birth of two children, the wife, disregarding the remedy of annulment that existed in the law of England and in the law of New York, as well as in the Roman Catholic Church (and, if she were entitled to it at all, could have been had for the asking in either jurisdiction), sued the husband for divorce in the English courts, on the grounds of his gross misconduct. The divorce was granted. After the divorce both parties contracted civil marriages with new partners, religious marriages being difficult for them for obvious reasons. The wife's second marriage was contracted with a Roman Catholic. An annulment of the first marriage became manifestly desirable.

In the courts of New York and of England, several matters barred the way. New York had solemnized the contract under the due and usual safeguards as to the freedom of the contracting parties, and, in her sovereign right, recognized the contract as valid. England, at the request of the wife, had recognized the New York contract as valid and had taken jurisdiction over it so as to base the civil decree of divorce upon it. The parties for twenty-five years had proceeded in a course of life based on the assumption that the marriage was valid, and the wife, by her own election under the advice of able counsel, had waived all claim to annulment and had sought divorce. In the jurisprudence of every civilized country the wife was estopped from claiming annulment, by her own acts, by the lapse of time, and by the conclusive presumptions of secular law established in the interest of social morality and the sanctity of contracts. But the wife applied to the Roman Catholic authorities, who granted the annulment upon the theory that she had been under fear and duress at the time of the marriage thirty-one years before, and had not known in all that time that such fear, if it existed, established her right in the Roman Catholic court to an annulment. Disregarding facts in the case which might reflect upon the ingenuousness of the ecclesiastical court of the Sacred Rota at Rome, we would point solely to the fact that in the proceeding before that court the sovereignties of New York State and of England, and all that they had done in the matter, were ignored. The evidence at the time on the record of the English court, and conclusively against the claims of the wife, was not even produced. The decree was granted on an *ex parte* hearing, on the testimony of interested witnesses only. It would be difficult to find a more utter disregard of the sovereignty of States than this by the sovereignty of Rome, touching that comity which, in good morals and public decency, is supposed to exist between sovereign powers.

In your opinion, sir, are such proceedings consistent with the peace and safety of States? . . .

VI

We have no desire to impute to the Roman Catholic Church aught but high and sincere motives in the assertion of her claims as one of the Two Powers. Her members believe in those claims, and, so believing, it is their conscientious duty to stand for them. We are satisfied if they will but concede that those claims, unless modified and historically redressed, precipitate an inevitable conflict between the Roman Catholic Church and the American State irreconcilable with domestic peace. With two illustrations— and those relating to English Christianity—we have done.

In the sixteenth century the decree of Pope Pius V in terms deposed Elizabeth, Queen of England, from the English throne and absolved her subjects from their allegiance. The result is well known. Much that pertained to the venerable forms of religion in the preceding centuries became associated in the popular mind of England with treason—even the Mass itself when celebrated in the Roman form. Roman Catholics were oppressed in their rights and privileges. Roman Catholic priests were forbidden within the realm. The mills of God turned slowly, but they turned. The Roman Catholics of England endured the penalties of hostile legislation with heroic fortitude and resignation. Public opinion slowly changed and gradually Roman Catholic disabilities were removed, and in 1850, under Cardinal Wiseman, the Roman Catholic Hierarchy was restored in England, with no other condition than that its sees should not use the ancient titles that the Hierarchy of the Church of England had retained. Peace and amity reigned within the realm, irrespective of different religions, and domestic repose marked a happy epoch. But the toleration and magnanimity of England bore strange fruit. Scarcely was the Roman Hierarchy restored to its ancient privileges when the astounding *Apostolic Letter* of Pope Leo XIII appeared (1896), declaring to the world that the orders of the Church of England were void, her priests not priests, her bishops not bishops, and her sacraments so many empty forms.

But this was not all. Reaching hands back through three centuries, the Roman Pontiff drew from obscurity the case of John Felton, an English citizen who in 1570, contrary to the law of treason at that time on the statute book of England, posted on the walls of London the decree of Pope Pius V already referred to, deposing the English Queen. Felton was beatified in 1886 by the act of Pope Leo XIII.

The honors paid him were rendered three hundred years after his treasonable act. There lies their sinister import. They are no part of the mediæval milieu; they belong to the modern world and must have judgment not by mediæval but by modern standards. One would have supposed, in view of the critical situation in modern States in relation to the respect for authority of government and the obedience of citizens to the law, that the beatification might have been omitted. One would have supposed that the changes in political thought and theory through three hundred years would have dictated the wisdom of letting the dead past bury its dead, and the memory of blessed John Felton rest in peace with those abandoned political doctrines that inspired his heroic but unhappy deed.

Is the record of the Roman Catholic Church in England consistent, sir, in your opinion, with the peace and safety of the State?

Nothing will be of greater satisfaction to those of your fellow citizens who hesitate in their endorsement of your candidacy because of the religious issues involved than such a disclaimer by you of the convictions here imputed, or such an exposition by others of the questions here presented, as may justly turn public opinion in your favor.

Yours with great respect,
Charles C. Marshall

49. ALFRED E. SMITH

Catholic and patriot

Upon receiving Marshall's "unreadably intelligent paper," Sedgwick sent the galleys to a fellow Grotonian and Harvardian who had nominated "the Happy Warrior" for the presidency in 1924. The editor urged Franklin D. Roosevelt to reply, arguing that the governor had a choice between a street fight and a gentleman's debate worthy of a candidate for the highest office in the land. Smith bridled at even considering the "religious issue" as real, regarding its mere suggestion as a slur upon his Americanism and beyond his comprehension. Indeed, if not for the prompting of the editor of the *Atlantic Monthly*, Smith's supporters would have ignored the "religious issue" as long as possible. But once it had been made explicit, Smith's advisors agreed to reply despite Smith's protests. They wrote and rewrote the reply for him to the accompaniment of his repeated plea, "I've been a devout Catholic all my life and I never heard of these bulls and encyclicals and books."

The New York governor's article with the touches added that made it

From Alfred E. Smith, "Catholic and Patriot: Governor Smith Replies," *Atlantic Monthly*, May, 1927, pp. 721–28. Reprinted by permission of the publisher.

his own was reprinted in almost every daily paper in the country. Over a year later, Smith reminded reporters, "Gentlemen, you think all of you together nominated me. It wasn't you. It was this High Hat from Boston." During the presidential campaign, except for his New Year's message to the Jews reiterating his dedication to the separation of church and state, Smith broke his silence on the "religious issue" only twice. On September 20, 1928, no longer able to hold back, he chose Oklahoma City, a center of Klan strength, to denounce his detractors. There he attacked those who had made much of his associations with Tammany Hall and who had charged him with sabotaging the public school system and appointing only Roman Catholics to office. Smith's vice-presidential running mate, Senator Joseph T. Robinson of Arkansas, promptly called religion the chief issue in the campaign. For the next ten days, the "religious issue" overshadowed all others in the daily press.

> This is an historic incident, historic for the country and for the Church. Now for the first time in the republic's history, under a constitution which forever forbids religious tests as qualifications for office, a candidate for the Presidency has been subjected to public questioning as to how he can give undivided allegiance to his country when his church restricts the freedom of his choice; and the candidate has answered—answered not deviously and with indirection, but straightforwardly, bravely, with the clear ring of candor.
>
> It is an issue of infinite possibilities. Is the principle of religious tolerance, universal and complete, which every schoolboy has repeated for one hundred and fifty years, mere platitudinous vaporing? Can men worshiping God in their differing ways believe without reservation of conscience in a common political ideal? Is the United States of America based on a delusion? Can the vast experiment of the Republic, Protestant and Catholic, churched and unchurched, succeed?
>
> And this is the converse of the question: Will the churches suffer their members to be really free? 'Thou shalt have none other gods but me,' thundered the Jewish Jehovah from Sinai, and ever since the gods of the churches have demanded that their control be not abridged nor diminished. But as the creeds clash about us, we remember that not in political programmes only may religion have its place separate and apart from politics, from public discussion, and from the laws of society. Quite elsewhere is it written, 'Render therefore unto Cæsar the things that are Cæsar's; and unto God the things that are God's.'

✦

The discussion has served its purpose. Not in this campaign will whispering and innuendoes, shruggings and hunchings, usurp the place of reason and of argument. The thoughts rising almost unbidden in the minds of the least bigoted of us when we watch a Roman Catholic aspire to the Presidency of the United States have become matters of high, serious, and eloquent debate.

THE EDITOR [*Atlantic Monthly*]

DEAR SIR:—

In your open letter to me in the April *Atlantic Monthly* you 'impute' to American Catholics views which, if held by them, would leave open to question the loyalty and devotion to this country and its Constitution of more than twenty million American Catholic citizens. I am grateful to you for defining this issue in the open and for your courteous expression of the satisfaction it will bring to my fellow citizens for me to give 'a disclaimer of the convictions' thus imputed. Without mental reservation I can and do make that disclaimer. These convictions are held neither by me nor by any other American Catholic, as far as I know. Before answering the argument of your letter, however, I must dispose of one of its implications. You put your questions to me in connection with my candidacy for the office of President of the United States. My attitude with respect to that candidacy was fully stated in my last inaugural address as Governor when, on January 1, 1927, I said:—

'I have no idea what the future has in store for me. Everyone else in the United States has some notion about it except myself. No man could stand before this intelligent gathering and say that he was not receptive to the greatest position the world has to give anyone. But I can say this, that I will do nothing to achieve it except to give to the people of the State the kind and character of service that will make me deserve it.'

I should be a poor American and a poor Catholic alike if I injected religious discussion into a political campaign. Therefore I would ask you to accept this answer from me not as a candidate for any public office but as an American citizen, honored with high elective office, meeting a challenge to his patriotism and his intellectual integrity. Moreover, I call your attention to the fact that I am only a layman. The *Atlantic Monthly* describes you as 'an experienced attorney' who 'has made himself an authority upon canon law.' I am neither a lawyer nor a theologian. What knowledge of law I have was gained in the course of my long experience in the Legislature and as Chief Executive of New York State. I had no such opportunity to study theology.

My first thought was to answer you with just the faith that is in me. But I knew instinctively that your conclusions could be logically proved false. It seemed right, therefore, to take counsel with someone schooled in the Church law, from whom I learned whatever is hereafter set forth in definite answer to the theological questions you raise. I selected one whose patriotism neither you nor any other man will question. He wears upon his breast the Distinguished Service Cross of our country, its Distinguished Service Medal, the Ribbon of the Legion of Honor, and the Croix de Guerre with Palm of the French Republic. He was the Catholic Chaplain of the almost wholly Catholic 165th Regiment in the World War—Father Francis P. Duffy, now in the military service of my own State.

Taking your letter as a whole and reducing it to commonplace English, you imply that there is conflict between religious loyalty to the Catholic faith and patriotic loyalty to the United States. Everything that has actually happened to me during my long public career leads me to know that no such thing as that is true. I have taken an oath of office in this State nineteen times. Each time I swore to defend and maintain the Constitution of the United States. All of this represents a period of public service in elective office almost continuous since 1903. I have never known any conflict between my official duties and my religious belief. No such conflict could exist. Certainly the people of this State recognize no such conflict. They have testified to my devotion to public duty by electing me to the highest office within their gift four times. You yourself do me the honor, in addressing me, to refer to 'your fidelity to the morality you have advocated in public and private life and to the religion you have revered; your great record of public trusts successfully and honestly discharged.'

During the years I have discharged these trusts I have been a communicant of the Roman Catholic Church. If there were conflict, I, of all men, could not have escaped it, because I have not been a silent man, but a battler for social and political reform. These battles would in their very nature disclose this conflict if there were any.

I regard public education as one of the foremost functions of government and I have supported to the last degree the State Department of Education in every effort to promote our public-school system. The largest single item of increased appropriations under my administration appears in the educational group for the support of common schools. Since 1919, when I first became Governor, this item has grown from $9,000,000 to $82,500,000. My aim—and I may say I have succeeded in achieving it—has been legislation for child welfare, the protection of working men, women, and children, the modernization of the State's institutions for the care of helpless or unfortunate wards, the preservation of freedom of speech and opinion against the attack of war-time hysteria, and the complete reorganization of the structure of the government of the State.

I did not struggle for these things for any single element, but in the interest of all of the eleven million people who make up the State. In all of this work I had the support of churches of all denominations. I probably know as many ecclesiastics of my Church as any other layman. During my long and active public career I never received from any of them anything except co-operation and encouragement in the full and complete discharge of my duty to the State. Moreover, I am unable to understand how anything that I was taught to believe as a Catholic could possibly be in conflict with what is good citizenship. The essence of my faith is built upon the Commandments of God. The law of the land is built upon the Commandments of God. There can be no conflict between them.

Instead of quarreling among ourselves over dogmatic principles, it would be infinitely better if we joined together in inculcating obedience to these Commandments in the hearts and minds of the youth of the country as the surest and best road to happiness on this earth and to peace in the world to come. This is the common ideal of all religions. What we need is more religion for our young people, not less; and the way to get more religion is to stop the bickering among our sects which can only have for its effect the creation of doubt in the minds of our youth as to whether or not it is necessary to pay attention to religion at all.

Then I know your imputations are false when I recall the long list of other public servants of my faith who have loyally served the State. You as a lawyer will probably agree that the office of Chief Justice of the United States is second not even to that of the President in its influence on the national development and policy. That court by its interpretation of the Federal Constitution is a check not only upon the President himself but upon Congress as well. During one fourth of its history it has been presided over by two Catholics, Roger Brooke Taney and Edward Douglass White. No one has suggested that the official conduct of either of these men was affected by any unwarranted religious influence or that religion played with them any part other than it should play in the life of every God-fearing man.

And I know your imputations are false when I recall the tens of thousands of young Catholics who have risked and sacrificed their lives in defense of our country. These fundamentals of life could not be true unless your imputations were false.

But, wishing to meet you on your own ground, I address myself to your definite questions, against which I have thus far made only general statements. I must first call attention to the fact that you often divorce sentences from their context in such a way as to give them something other than their real meaning. I will specify. You refer to the Apostolic Letter of Pope Leo XIII as 'declaring to the world that the orders of the Church of England were void, her priests not priests,' and so forth. You say that this was the 'strange fruit' of the toleration of England to the Catholics. You imply that the Pope gratuitously issued an affront to the Anglican Church. In fact, this Apostolic Letter was an answer to a request made at the instance of priests of the Anglican Church for recognition by the Roman Catholic Church of the validity of their priestly orders. The request was based on the ground that they had been ordained in succession from the Roman Catholic priests who became the first priests of the Anglican Church. The Apostolic Letter was a mere adverse answer to this request, ruling that Anglican priests were not Roman Catholic priests, and was in no sense the gratuitous insult which you suggest it to be. It was not directed against England or citizens of that Empire.

Again, you quote from the *Catholic Encyclopedia* that my Church 'regards dogmatic intolerance, not alone as her incontestable right, but as her sacred duty.' And you say that these words show that Catholics are taught to be politically, socially, and intellectually intolerant of all other people. If you had read the whole of that article in the *Catholic Encyclopedia*, you would know that the real meaning of these words is that for Catholics alone the Church recognizes no deviation from complete acceptance of its dogma. These words are used in a chapter dealing with that subject only. The very same article in another chapter dealing with toleration toward non-Catholics contains these words: 'The intolerant man is avoided as much as possible by every high-minded person. . . . The man who is tolerant in every emergency is alone lovable.' The phrase 'dogmatic intolerance' does not mean that Catholics are to be dogmatically intolerant of other people, but merely that inside the Catholic Church they are to be intolerant of any variance from the dogma of the Church.

Similar criticism can be made of many of your quotations. But, beyond this, by what right do you ask me to assume responsibility for every statement that may be made in any encyclical letter? As you will find in the *Catholic Encyclopedia* (Vol. V, p. 414), these encyclicals are not articles of our faith. The Syllabus of Pope Pius IX, which you quote on the possible conflict between Church and State, is declared by Cardinal Newman to have 'no dogmatic force.' You seem to think that Catholics must be all alike in mind and in heart, as though they had been poured into and taken out of the same mould. You have no more right to ask me to defend as part of my faith every statement coming from a prelate than I should have to ask you to accept as an article of your religious faith every statement of an Episcopal bishop, or of your political faith every statement of a President of the United States. So little

are these matters of the essence of my faith that I, a devout
Catholic since childhood, never heard of them until I read your
letter. Nor can you quote from the canons of our faith a syllable
that would make us less good citizens than non-Catholics. In fact
and in truth, I have been taught the spirit of tolerance, and when
you, Mr. Marshall, as a Protestant Episcopalian, join with me in
saying the Lord's Prayer, we both pray, not to 'My Father,' but to
'Our Father.'

But I go further to demonstrate that the true construction of
your quotations by the leaders of Catholic thought is diametrically
the opposite of what you suggest it to be.

I

Your first proposition is that Catholics believe that other
religions should, in the United States, be tolerated only as a matter
of favor and that there should be an established church. You may
find some dream of an ideal of a Catholic State, having no relation
whatever to actuality, somewhere described. But, voicing the best
Catholic thought on this subject, Dr. John A. Ryan, Professor of
Moral Theology at the Catholic University of America, writes in
The State and the Church of the encyclical of Pope Leo XIII,
quoted by you:—

'In practice, however, the foregoing propositions have full
application only to the completely Catholic State. . . . The
propositions of Pope Pius IX condemning the toleration of
non-Catholic sects do not now, says Father Pohle, "apply even to
Spain or the South American republics, to say nothing of countries
possessing a greatly mixed population." He lays down the
following general rule: "When several religions have firmly
established themselves and taken root in the same territory,
nothing else remains for the State than to exercise tolerance
towards them all, or, as conditions exist to-day, to make complete
religious liberty for individual and religious bodies a principle of
government." '

That is good Americanism and good Catholicism. And Father
Pohle, one of the great writers of the Catholic Church, says
further:—

'If religious freedom has been accepted and sworn to as a fundamental law in a constitution, the obligation to show this tolerance is binding in conscience.'

The American prelates of our Church stoutly defend our constitutional declaration of equality of all religions before the law. Cardinal O'Connell has said: 'Thus to every American citizen has come the blessed inheritance of civil, political, and religious liberty safe-guarded by the American Constitution . . . the right to worship God according to the dictates of his conscience.'

Archbishop Ireland has said: 'The Constitution of the United States reads: "Congress shall make no laws respecting an establishment of religion, or prohibiting the free exercise thereof." It was a great leap forward on the part of the new nation towards personal liberty and the consecration of the rights of conscience.'

Archbishop Dowling, referring to any conceivable union of Church and State, says: 'So many conditions for its accomplishment are lacking in every government of the world that the thesis may well be relegated to the limbo of defunct controversies.'

I think you have taken your thesis from this limbo of defunct controversies.

Archbishop Ireland again said: 'Religious freedom is the basic life of America, the cement running through all its walls and battlements, the safeguard of its peace and prosperity. Violate religious freedom against Catholics, our swords are at once unsheathed. Violate it in favor of Catholics, against non-Catholics, no less readily do they leap from the scabbard.'

Cardinal Gibbons has said: 'American Catholics rejoice in our separation of Church and State, and I can conceive no combination of circumstances likely to arise which would make a union desirable to either Church or State. . . . For ourselves we thank God that we live in America, "in this happy country of ours," to quote Mr. Roosevelt, where "religion and liberty are natural allies." '

And referring particularly to your quotation from Pope Pius IX, Dr. Ryan, in *The State and the Church*, says: 'Pope Pius IX did not intend to declare that separation is always unadvisable, for he had more than once expressed his satisfaction with the arrangement obtaining in the United States.'

With these great Catholics I stand squarely in support of the provisions of the Constitution which guarantee religious freedom and equality.

II

I come now to the speculation with which theorists have played for generations as to the respective functions of Church and State. You claim that the Roman Catholic Church holds that, if conflict arises, the Church must prevail over the State. You write as though there were some Catholic authority or tribunal to decide with respect to such conflict. Of course there is no such thing. As Dr. Ryan writes: 'The Catholic doctrine concedes, nay, maintains, that the State is coördinate with the Church and equally independent and supreme in its own distinct sphere.'

What is the Protestant position? The Articles of Religion of your Protestant Episcopal Church (XXXVII) declare: 'The Power of the Civil Magistrate extendeth to all men, as well Clergy as Laity, in all things temporal; but hath no authority in things purely spiritual.'

Your Church, just as mine, is voicing the injunction of our common Saviour to render unto Cæsar the things that are Cæsar's, and unto God the things that are God's.

What is this conflict about which you talk? It may exist in some lands which do not guarantee religious freedom. But in the wildest dreams of your imagination you cannot conjure up a possible conflict between religious principle and political duty in the United States, except on the unthinkable hypothesis that some law were to be passed which violated the common morality of all God-fearing men. And if you can conjure up such a conflict, how would a Protestant resolve it? Obviously by the dictates of his conscience. That is exactly what a Catholic would do. There is no ecclesiastical tribunal which would have the slightest claim upon the obedience of Catholic communicants in the resolution of such a conflict. As Cardinal Gibbons said of the supposition that 'the Pope were to issue commands in purely civil matters':—

'He would be offending not only against civil society, but against God, and violating an authority as truly from God as his own. Any Catholic who clearly recognized this would not be bound to obey the Pope; or rather his conscience would bind him absolutely to disobey, because with Catholics conscience is the supreme law which under no circumstances can we ever lawfully disobey.'

Archbishop Ireland said: 'To priest, to Bishop, or to Pope (I am willing to consider the hypothesis) who should attempt to rule in matters civil and political, to influence the citizen beyond the range of their own orbit of jurisdiction that are the things of God, the answer is quickly made: "Back to your own sphere of rights and duties, back to the things of God." '

Bishop England, referring to our Constitution, said: 'Let the Pope and the Cardinals and all the powers of the Catholic world united make the least encroachment on that Constitution, we will protect it with our lives. Summon a General Council—let that Council interfere in the mode of our electing but an assistant to a turnkey of a prison—we deny the right, we reject the usurpation.'

Our Supreme Court has marked out the spheres of influence of Church and State in a case from which you quote copiously, *Watson* v. *Jones,* 13 Wall. 729; but you refrain from quoting this statement:—

'The right to organize voluntary religious associations, to assist in the expression and dissemination of any religious doctrine, and to create tribunals for the decision of controverted questions of faith within the association, and for the ecclesiastical government of all of the individual members, the congregation and officers within the general association, is unquestioned. . . . It is of the essence of these religious unions and of their right to establish tribunals for the decision of questions arising among themselves that those decisions could be binding in all cases of ecclesiastical cognizance, subject only to such appeal as the organism itself provides for.'

That is the State's attitude toward the Church. Archbishop Ireland thus puts the Church's attitude toward the State:—

'To the Catholic obedience to law is a religious obligation, binding in God's name the conscience of the citizen. . . . Both Americanism and Catholicism bow to the sway of personal conscience.'

Under our system of government the electorate entrusts to its officers of every faith the solemn duty of action according to the dictates of conscience. I may fairly refer once more to my own record to support these truths. No man, cleric or lay, has ever directly or indirectly attempted to exercise Church influence on my administration of any office I have ever held, nor asked me to show special favor to Catholics or exercise discrimination against non-Catholics.

It is a well-known fact that I have made all of my appointments to public office on the basis of merit and have never asked any man about his religious belief. In the first month of this year there gathered in the Capitol at Albany the first Governor's cabinet that ever sat in this State. It was composed, under my appointment, of two Catholics, thirteen Protestants, and one Jew. The man closest to me in the administration of the government of the State of New York is he who bears the title of Assistant to the Governor. He had been connected with the Governor's office for thirty years, in subordinate capacities, until I promoted him to the position which makes him the sharer with me of my every thought and hope and ambition in the administration of the State. He is a Protestant, a Republican, and a thirty-second-degree Mason. In my public life I have exemplified that complete separation of Church from State which is the faith of American Catholics to-day.

III

I next come to education. You admit that the Supreme Court guaranteed to Catholics the right to maintain their parochial schools; and you ask me whether they would have so ruled if it had been shown that children in parochial schools were taught that the State should show discrimination between religions, that Protestants should be recognized only as a matter of favor, that they should be intolerant to non-Catholics, and that the laws of the State could be flouted on the ground of the imaginary conflict. My summary answer is: I and all my children went to a parochial school. I never heard of any such stuff being taught or of anybody who claimed that it was. That any group of Catholics would teach it is unthinkable.

IV

You next challenge the action of the Rota in annulling the Marlborough marriage. You suggest that the Rota by annulling the marriage (where the civil courts recognized it, but granted only a divorce) is interfering with the civil jurisdiction. That might be so if anybody claimed that the decree of the Rota had any effect under the laws of America, or any other nation of the world. But you must know that it has no such effect and that nobody claims it has. The decree merely defined the status of the parties as communicants of the Church. Your Church refuses to recognize the ecclesiastical validity of divorces granted by the civil tribunals. Your Church has its tribunals to administer its laws for the government of its members as communicants of your Church. But their decrees have no bearing upon the status of the members as citizens of the United States. There is no difference in that respect between your tribunals and the Rota. . . .

VI

I summarize my creed as an American Catholic. I believe in the worship of God according to the faith and practice of the Roman Catholic Church. I recognize no power in the institutions of my Church to interfere with the operations of the Constitution of the United States or the enforcement of the law of the land. I believe in absolute freedom of conscience for all men and in equality of all churches, all sects, and all beliefs before the law as a matter of right and not as a matter of favor. I believe in the absolute separation of Church and State and in the strict enforcement of the provisions of the Constitution that Congress shall make no law respecting an establishment of religion or prohibiting the free exercise thereof. I believe that no tribunal of any church has any power to make any decree of any force in the law of the land, other than to establish the status of its own communicants within its own church. I believe in the support of the public school as one

of the corner stones of American liberty. I believe in the right of
every parent to choose whether his child shall be educated in the
public school or in a religious school supported by those of his
own faith. I believe in the principle of noninterference by this
country in the internal affairs of other nations and that we should
stand steadfastly against any such interference by whomsoever it
may be urged. And I believe in the common brotherhood of man
under the common fatherhood of God.

In this spirit I join with fellow Americans of all creeds in a
fervent prayer that never again in this land will any public servant
be challenged because of the faith in which he has tried to walk
humbly with his God.

> Very truly yours,
> *Alfred E. Smith*

50. The Religious Issues

The Roman Catholic church will go to the polls almost as one man and vote for Mr. Smith

Unlike fundamentalists, respectable Protestant spokesmen chose to
remain silent on the religious issue until a few weeks before the election.
Then the liberal Protestant interdenominational weekly, *The Christian
Century*, made it quite clear that all Protestants, not merely Southern
fundamentalists, found legitimate sanction for voting against Smith.

The church is in politics. It has a right to be in politics. Always
and everywhere it has been in politics. Both the Roman Catholic
church and the Protestant churches are in politics. In countries
where public sentiment is overwhelmingly Roman Catholic, the

From "The Religious Issues," *The Christian Century*, October 18, 1928, vol. 45,
pp. 1251–53. Copyright © 1928, Christian Century Foundation. Reprinted by
permission of Christian Century Foundation.

church is the dominant factor in politics. In countries where that church is strong but not dominant, it frequently takes part in politics through a party of its own—a clerical party. In the United States and Great Britain, where Catholicism is a fractional minority and where Protestant opinion is overwhelming, the Roman church has exercised great circumspection in its political activity, but it has never yielded its right to influence political events. In the present campaign, where for the first time in American history a Roman Catholic has aspired to the presidency, the church affects a remote indifference. But this apparent detachment is a strategic pose, for a political purpose, and no enlightened citizens, whether Protestant or Catholic, are in doubt as to its meaning.

The Protestant churches are in politics. From the beginning of our history they have been in politics. As they become increasingly ethical in their aims and increasingly social in their ethics, they are bound to accept the political implications of their gospel. They cannot function in a vacuum. They will not be content with pious abstractions. They are compelled to take the secular consequences of their social convictions, which means that they must bear their testimony in practical and concrete ways so that their social convictions may be incorporated in the policies and institutions of the state. There is no need of being squeamish about this, no reason to apologize for it, nor to be ashamed of it, nor to be furtive in acting upon it. It should be set down as the bold major premise of social-minded Christianity.

Having stated the major premise in unqualified terms, it is important to guard it against unwarranted inferences. It does not follow that the church should therefore make of itself a political party or ally itself in a partisan spirit with some political party. Catholicism in other countries has frequently done so. Protestantism in the United States has never done so, and there is not the slightest indication that it is in danger of doing so.

Nor does it follow that the church in politics endangers the American principle of the complete separation of church and state. Whether that principle is endangered or not by a church's assumption of the secular responsibility for its social convictions will depend wholly upon the kind of church it is. The Roman Catholic church makes certain claims as to its preeminence over the state. Protestantism has not only never made any such claims, but has positively repudiated them. Our American principle of the absolute separation of church and state is a Protestant principle, conceived and enacted into law by a Protestant-minded democracy. Its surest defense and the best guarantee of its perpetuation lies in the free Protestant conscience more than in any other agency in our political system.

A third erroneous inference would be that the church, being in politics and rightly so, would inevitably use and would be justified in using some sort of ecclesiastical coercion or other pressure upon her members to assure their voting as she directs. In the case of the Protestant churches, such an abuse of democracy is unthinkable—and for the simple reason that all those churches are themselves thoroughly democratic. Protestant churches are self-corrective at this point. They carry in their constitution the principle of their own reform in case they are tempted to exercise such tyranny. Not only so, but they are amenable to all the influences of the democratic social order in which they live. The democratic principle, both inside the churches and in the social order by which the churches are environed, may be trusted in the long run to maintain the freedom of the ballot against its abuse by ecclesiastical tyranny, just as this principle is trusted in the sphere of industrial organization or labor union organization or any other sphere. With the Roman Catholic church, the case is different, because that church is not democratically conditioned. It is not directly amenable to the influences of a democratic social order. Its authority is vested in a hierarchy which, transcending all democratic control, is derived from an oligarchy of rulers whose seat is in a foreign country. But waiving these differences, our point at present is simply to deny that because the church has a legitimate political responsibility it therefore is empowered to override the free action of its members in the exercise of their citizenship.

And finally, it would be erroneous to infer that because the church is and by right must be in politics, it must therefore take sides on all political issues and at every election. The church has no testimony to bear on the technique of farm relief, or the tariff, or government ownership of water power, or a score of other problems which disturb the electorate. And many an election is held in which the church has no substantial stake at all.

How, then, is the church to decide that a specific issue or a particular election demands and justifies its participation? The answer is that it need never decide. It will never be in doubt. Its participation in politics cannot be determined by rule. It is not based upon an arbitrary choice. If there is doubt about it, that in itself is a sure sign that the church's hour has not yet come. The church will be legitimately active in politics only when some principle which has been woven into its own moral character is at stake. The issue and the church's character will then coalesce. The church's activity in that election will not rest upon specific choice. It will be inevitable. In such a situation no power in heaven or on earth can keep the church out of politics. It will go in because it is already in.

It is not often in the history of the United States that the orbit of a national political contest has swung so wide as to involve conditions which are integral to the moral character of the church, although in local contests this has more frequently occurred. The struggle over slavery was, of course, an outstanding historic instance. The churches of the north had taken to their bosom, as a veritable part of themselves, the conviction that slavery was inherently evil and an absolute contradiction of the purposes of Christianity. It is inconceivable that they could have been restrained from political action on behalf of their convictions. You might as well have tried to dam Niagara.

In our time we are able to see actually going on this process of a moral conviction being woven into the texture of the church's character. For example, the conviction that war is the world's chief collective sin is becoming an article in the living creed of the churches. . . .

We do not criticize the Roman church for being in politics. Her activity is humanly inevitable. It does not take the form of overt and strident demand. That would be the worst kind of politics under present conditions. But the Roman Catholic church will go to the polls almost as one man and vote for Mr. Smith. The chief public expression of its activity is Mr. Smith's characterization of his opponents as bigots. The candidate himself declares that the prohibition question and other questions are but screens to hide the anti-Catholic motives of his opponents. This sentiment is echoed in the Catholic press and the Catholic-controlled press. Even Protestant writers and preachers aid its currency and, thus browbeaten, it is becoming quite the thing for men otherwise quite intelligent to assert that they are going to vote for Al Smith, if only to prove their liberality, their tolerance!

For Protestants and non-Catholics generally, the candidacy of Mr. Smith has raised the same issue as for Catholics, but in its obverse form. The reasons why Catholics wish to elect Smith are the reasons why Protestant-minded Americans do not wish him elected. They cannot look with unconcern upon the seating of a representative of an alien culture, of a medieval Latin mentality, of an undemocratic hierarchy and of a foreign potentate, in the great office of President of the United States. This is no casual issue on the part of Protestants. In historic origin and in organic character their churches are a corporate protest against the system which such a President would represent. The issue is of the very texture of their corporate conviction. This being so, how unrealistic it is to hope to suppress it! How preposterous to call him a "bigot" who is intelligent enough to let his vote be determined by so deep-going a cleavage in social idealism! And what a mere tin toy democracy must be if it is unpatriotic for one candidly to face an issue like this in the exercise of his suffrage!

The other issue is prohibition. The Protestant churches are drawn by this issue into the orbit of the political struggle because this too involves an organic conviction on their part. For two generations the churches underwent a process of education with respect to the drink traffic, until at last the conviction was formed as a part of the living creed of the churches that the traffic in liquor for beverage purposes was inherently and unqualifiedly evil. It is in no prudential or expedient terms that this conviction is held. It is a profound and intense moral conviction, a more vital article in the real creed of effective American Protestantism than the belief in the virgin birth of Christ. It was the church's legitimate activity in politics that brought the prohibition principle up to the level where industry and commerce united with religion to enact it into law.

Therefore when Mrs. Willebrandt appears before a Methodist or Presbyterian conference and exhorts ministers and laymen to go back to their churches and work for the election of the man who is pledged to carry on the moral reform whose essential principle is part of their own organic conviction, she is no more guilty of trespassing upon the proprieties either of religion or of democracy than if she had told them to go home and hold a revival meeting. Prohibition has come to be a part of the orthodoxy of the churches. When Governor Smith made it an issue by defying his party platform, he widened the orbit of the political contest so that the churches were inevitably brought into its sweep.

Thus the election canvass baffles the politicians. They do not know what the issue is. They talk of farm relief, of power control, of prosperity, of economy, of tariff. But the people take only an academic interest in the insubstantial distinctions between the two major parties on these questions. The thing the politician does not see is the most conspicuous and significant thing in the campaign. It is this: the great issues are the religious issues. Politicians have had no experience since 1860 in dealing with the church in national politics. The daily press, even that part of it which is Protestant-minded, is inhibited by its Catholic patronage from discussing the deeper issues that are in everybody's mind. Thus embarrassed, it joins in the hue and cry against bigotry, following the lead of the Catholic press and politicians.

But the people, denied a candid and vital discussion of the issues that interest them most deeply, are making up their minds without much aid from leaders. It is quite probable that the politicians will not know what the real issues are until the returns are in on the night of November 6. It is also probable that our most intense discussion of the issues of the campaign will come after the campaign is over.

51. JOHN F. KENNEDY

It is my job to face it
frankly and fully

In 1960 John F. Kennedy chose to address himself formally to the "religious issue" on three occasions: in a talk on April 21 in Washington, D.C., before the Society of American Newspaper Editors; on July 15 in Los Angeles in his acceptance speech following his nomination; and on September 12 in a televised interview before the Greater Houston Ministerial Association.

The following selection is drawn from his Washington address.

I have decided, in view of current press reports, that it would be appropriate to speak with you today about what has widely been called "the religious issue" in American politics.

The phrase covers a multitude of meanings. There is no religious issue in the sense that any of the major candidates differ on the role of religion in our political life. Every Presidential contender, I am certain, is dedicated to the separation of church and state, to the preservation of religious liberty, to an end to religious bigotry, and to the total independence of the officeholder from any form of ecclesiastical dictation.

Nor is there any real issue in the sense that any candidate is exploiting his religious affiliation. No one's candidacy, by itself, raises a religious issue. And I believe it is inaccurate to state that my "candidacy created the issue."

Nor am I appealing, as is too often claimed, to a so-called Catholic vote. Even if such a vote exists—which I doubt—I want to make one thing clear again: I want no votes solely on account of my religion. Any voter, Catholic or otherwise, who feels another candidate would be a superior President should support that candidate. I do not want any vote cast for me for such illogical and irrelevant reasons.

Neither do I want anyone to support my candidacy merely to

Published in the *New York Times*, April 22, 1960, p. 16.

prove that this nation is not bigoted—and that a Catholic can be elected President. I have never suggested that those opposed to me are thereby anti-Catholic. There are ample legitimate grounds for supporting other candidates (though I will not, of course, detail them here).

Nor have I ever suggested that the Democratic party is required to nominate me or face a Catholic revolt in November. I do not believe that to be true—I cannot believe our convention would act on such a premise—and I do believe that a majority of Americans of every faith will support the Democratic nominee, whoever he is.

What, then, is the so-called religious issue in American politics today? It is not, it seems to me, my actual religious convictions—but a misunderstanding of what those convictions actually are.

I know the press did not create this religious issue. My religious affiliation is a fact—religious intolerance is a fact. And the proper role of the press is to report all facts that are a matter of public interest.

But the press has a responsibility, I think you will agree, which goes far beyond a reporting of the facts. It goes beyond lofty editorials deploring intolerance. For my religion is hardly, in this critical year of 1960, the dominant issue of our time.

The members of the press should report the facts as they find them. But they should beware, it seems to me, of either magnifying this issue or over-simplifying it.

I spoke in Wisconsin, for example, on farm legislation, foreign policy, defense, civil rights and several dozen other issues. But I rarely found them reported in the press—except when they were occasionally sandwiched in between descriptions of my hand-shaking, my theme-song, family, haircut and, inevitably, my religion.

At almost every stop in Wisconsin I invited questions and the questions came—on price supports, labor unions, disengagement, taxes and inflation. But these sessions were rarely reported in the press except when one topic was discussed: religion.

One article, in a news magazine for example, supposedly summing the primary up in advance, mentioned the word

Catholic twenty times in fifteen paragraphs—not mentioning even once dairy farms, disarmament, labor legislation or any other issue. And on the Sunday before the primary, The Milwaukee *Journal* featured a map of the state, listing county by county the relative strength of three types of voters—Democrats, Republicans and Catholics.

Now we are in West Virginia. As reported to today's Washington *Post*, the great bulk of West Virginians paid very little attention to my religion—until they read repeatedly in the nation's press that this was the decisive issue in West Virginia. There are many serious problems in that state—problems big enough to dominate any campaign—but religion is not one of them.

I do not think that religion is the decisive issue in any state. I do not think it should be, and recognizing my own responsibilities in that regard, I am hopeful that you will recognize yours also.

For the past month and years I have answered almost daily inquiries from the press about the religious issue. I want to take this opportunity to turn the tables—and to raise some questions for your thoughtful consideration.

First: Is the religious issue a legislative issue in this campaign?

There is only one legitimate question underlying all the rest: Would you, as President of the United States, be responsive in any way to ecclesiastical pressures or obligations of any kind that might in any fashion influence or interfere with your conduct of that office in the national interest? I have answered that question many times. My answer was—and is—"No."

Once that question is answered, there is no legitimate issue of my religion, but there are, I think, legitimate questions of public policy—of concern to religious groups which no one should feel bigoted about raising, and to which I do not object answering. But I do object to being the only candidate required to answer those questions.

Federal assistance to parochial schools, for example, is a very legitimate issue actually before the Congress. I am opposed to it. I believe it is clearly unconstitutional. I. voted against it on the Senate floor this year, when offered by Senator Morse. But interestingly enough, I was the only announced candidate in the Senate who did so. Nevertheless, I have not yet charged my opponents with taking orders from Rome.

An Ambassador to the Vatican could conceivably become a real issue again. I am opposed to it, and said so long ago. But even though it was last proposed by a Baptist President, I know of no other candidate who has been even asked about this matter.

The prospects of any President ever receiving for his signature a bill providing foreign aid funds for birth control are very remote indeed. It is hardly the major issue some have suggested. Nevertheless, I have made it clear that I would neither veto nor sign such a bill on any basis except what I considered to be the public interest, without regard to my private religious views. I have said the same about bills dealing with censorship, divorce, our relations with Spain or any other subject.

These are legitimate inquiries about real questions which the next President may conceivably have to face. But these inquiries ought to be directed equally to all candidates.

Secondly, can we justify analyzing voters as well as candidates strictly in terms of their religion? I think the voters of Wisconsin objected to being categorized simply as either Catholics or Protestants in analyzing their political choices. I think they objected to being accosted by reporters outside of political meetings and asked one question only—their religion—not their occupation or education or philosophy or income—only their religion.

The flood of post-primary analyses on the so-called "Catholic vote" and "Protestant vote"—carefully shaped to conform with their author's pre-primary predictions—would never be published in any competent statistical journal.

Only this week, I received a very careful analysis of the Wisconsin results. It conclusively shows two significant patterns of bloc voting: I ran strongest in those areas where the average temperature in January was 20 degrees or higher, and poorest in those areas where it was 14 degrees or lower—and that I ran well in the beech tree and basswood counties and not so well among the hemlock and pine.

It has been suggested that to offset my apparent political handicaps I may have to pick a running-mate from Maine or, preferably, Alaska.

The facts of the matter are that this analysis stands up statistically much better than all the so-called analyses of the religious vote. And so do analyses of each county based on their distance from the Minnesota border, the length of their Democratic tradition and their inclusion in my campaign itinerary. I carried some areas with large proportions of voters who are Catholics—and I lost some. I carried some areas where Protestants predominate—and I lost some.

It is true that I ran well in cities—and large numbers of Catholics live in cities. But so do union members and older voters and veterans and chess fans and basswood lovers. To say my support in the cities is due only to the religion of the voters is incapable of proof.

Of those Catholics who voted for me, how many did so on grounds of my religion—how many because they felt my opponent was too radical—how many because they resented the attacks on my record—how many because they were union members—how many for some other reason? I do not know. And the facts are that no one knows.

The voters are more than Catholics, Protestants or Jews. They make up their minds for many diverse reasons, good and bad. To submit the candidates to a religious test is unfair—to apply it to the voters themselves is divisive, degrading and wholly unwarranted.

Third and finally: Is there any justification for applying special religious tests to one office only? The Presidency? Little or no attention was paid to my religion when I took the oath as Senator in 1953—as a Congressman in 1947—or as a naval officer in 1941. Members of my faith abound in public office at every level except the White House. What is there about the Presidency that justifies this constant emphasis upon a candidate's religion and that of his supporters?

The Presidency is not, after all, the British crown, serving a dual capacity in both church and state. The President is not elected to be protector of the faith—or guardian of the public morals. His attendance at church on Sunday should be his business alone, not a showcase for the nation.

On the other hand, we are in no danger of a one-man Constitutional upheaval. The President, however intent he may be on subverting our institutions, cannot ignore the Congress—or the voters—or the courts. And our highest court, incidentally, has a long history of Catholic justices, none of whom, as far as I know, was ever challenged on the fairness of his ruling on sensitive church-state issues.

Some may say we treat the Presidency differently because we have had only one previous Catholic candidate for President. But I am growing weary of that term. I am not the Catholic candidate for President. I do not speak for the Catholic church on issues of public policy—and no one in that church speaks for me. My record on aid to education, aid to Tito, the Conant nomination and other issues has displeased some prominent Catholic clergymen and organizations; and it has been approved by others. The fact is that the Catholic church is not a monolith—it is committed in this country to the principles of individual liberty—and it has no claim over my conduct as a public officer sworn to do the public interest.

So I hope we can see the beginning of the end of references to me as "the Catholic candidate" for President. Do not expect me to explain or defend every act or statement of every Pope or priest, in this country or some other, in this century or the last—and that includes the Mayor of Dijon.

I have tried to examine with you today the press' responsibility in meeting this religious issue. The question remains: What is my responsibility? I am a candidate. The issue is here. Two alternatives have been suggested:

1. The first suggestion is that I withdraw to avoid a "dangerous religious controversy"; and accept the Vice-Presidential nomination in order to placate the so-called Catholic vote.

I find that suggestion highly distasteful. It assumes the worst about a country which prides itself on being more tolerant and better educated than it was in 1928. It assumes that Catholics are a pawn on the political chess-board, moved hither and yon, and somehow "bought off" by the party putting in the second-spot a Catholic whom the party barred from the top for reasons of religion. And it forgets, finally, that such a performance would have an effect on our image abroad as well as our self-respect here at home.

Are we going to admit to the world that a Jew can be elected Mayor of Dublin, a Protestant can be chosen Foreign Minister of France, a Moslem can serve for the Israeli Parliament—but a Catholic cannot be President of the United States? Are we to tell Chancellor Adenauer, for example, that we want him risking his all on our front lines; but that—if he were an American—we would never entrust him with our Presidency—nor would we accept our distinguished guest, General de Gaulle? Are we to admit to the world—worse still, are we to admit to ourselves— that one-third of our population is forever barred from the White House?

So I am not impressed by those pleas that I settle for the Vice Presidency in order to avert a religious spectacle. Surely those who believe it dangerous to elect a Catholic as President will not want him to serve as Vice President, a heart-beat away from the office.

2. The alternative is to proceed with the primaries, the convention and the election. If there is bigotry in the country, then so be it—there is bigotry. If that bigotry is too great to permit the fair consideration of a Catholic who has made clear his complete independence and his complete dedication to separation of church and state, then we ought to know it.

But I do not believe this is the case. I believe the American people are more concerned with a man's views and abilities than with the church to which he belongs. I believe that the founding fathers meant it when they provided in Article VI of the Constitution that there should be no religious test for public office—a provision that brought not one dissenting vote, only the comment of Roger Sherman that it was surely unnecessary—"the prevailing liberality being a sufficient security against such tests."

And I believe that the American people mean to adhere to those principles today.

But regardless of the political outcome, this issue is here to be faced. It is my job to face it frankly and fully. And it is your job to face it fairly, in perspective and in proportion.

I am confident that the press and other media of this country will recognize their responsibilities in this area—to refute falsehood, to inform the ignorant, and to concentrate on the issues, the real issues in this hour of the nation's peril.

The Supreme Court has written that as public officials "we are neither Jew nor gentile, neither Catholic nor agnostic. We owe equal attachment to the Constitution and are equally bound by our obligation, whether we derive our citizenship from the earliest or latest immigrants to these shores . . . (for) religion is outside the sphere of political government."

We must all—candidates, press, and voters alike—dedicate ourselves to these principles, for they are the key to a free society.

52.   Reformation and Election

The equilibrium between private judgment and churchly authority is not likely to be disturbed

On the eve of the 1960 election, a *Christian Century* editorial made it clear that Protestant theologians would no longer impugn the integrity of a candidate for the presidency on the grounds that his Catholic religious affiliation and his attitude toward the separation of church and state disqualified him for the highest office in the land. This statement was in vivid contrast to *The Christian Century* editorial exactly thirty-two years earlier.

"Reformation and Election," *The Christian Century*, October 26, 1960, vol. 77, pp. 1235–36. Copyright © 1960, Christian Century Foundation. Reprinted by permission of Christian Century Foundation.

In all the discussions concerning the religious issue in the presidential campaign, the most important fact concerning this issue has received little attention. It is the fact that we have in the United States a state of equilibrium between two religious principles which are polar opposites. The two principles which are held in balance in our society are private judgment and churchly authority. These principles are basically irreconcilable, yet people holding one or the other coexist peacefully and maintain a country which is stronger because this tension has been successfully contained in one political and social order.

I

The "religion issue" in the 1960 election began to subside as the major center of attention only when a large number of people became convinced that the equilibrium between private judgment and churchly authority is not likely to be disturbed no matter what the outcome of the election. Statements by Senator John F. Kennedy that he would not allow his exercise of private judgment to be interfered with by his church, which is authoritarian, were necessary and they were given without equivocation. The principle of separation of church and state, which allows a Catholic to exercise private judgment in civic affairs, was affirmed. A public statement by 150 leading Catholic laymen backed up the senator's assertion that most American Catholics espouse the freedoms he espouses.

These statements showed that as far as the great majority of Catholics are concerned, the right of private judgment is not challenged in the domain of politics. In theology they allow the authoritarian principle to prevail; in politics they insist on using private judgment. Ecclesiastically they are Catholics; politically they are Protestants.

The gulf between the responsible individual who says "Here I stand" and the conformist who says "The church has spoken; therefore I must bow" has not been bridged, and will not be. Compromise is impossible, but agreement to differ is possible. That this is a fact of great importance becomes apparent with a glance at the situation which prevailed in medieval times.

Agreement to differ was not possible then, any more than it is possible today in communist countries. Authoritarianism ruled. It was a crime for a man to differ publicly with authority. For him to differ persistently was a capital offense. The inquisition—which in Spain is still regarded as an institution of official repute—hunted down nonconformists and destroyed or drove underground those who differed from the prevailing orthodoxy. This orthodoxy was political as well as ecclesiastical, since church-state separation had not yet been thought of. Thought control in forms not basically different from those enforced by modern totalitarianisms was the prevailing rule.

The Reformation broke through the hard crust of authoritarianism by its assertion of the responsibility of the individual to exercise his private judgment. The action came in relation to the Bible. Luther and his associates held that the Bible is to be interpreted by the individual for the sake of his immortal soul and in fulfillment of his duty to society. The Roman Catholic Church asserted that the Bible must be interpreted by the church for the benefit of the individual, the corporate order and the church. It also held that tradition, again only as interpreted by the church, must be given equal weight with the Bible. The decision as to whether the Scriptures or tradition is to prevail must be made by the same authority—the church. It took the long agony of the subsequent wars of religion to create even a tacit agreement between Catholicism and Reformation Christianity peacefully to differ.

In Europe Catholicism was finally forced to negotiate with Protestants on somewhat equal terms, thus sharply curtailing the arena in which churchly authority prevailed and destroying the reality behind the medieval idea of the church. In time the church was compelled to recognize, however reluctantly, that in public life the principle of private judgment had to be accepted. Since the lure of America brought to these shores so many who had suffered persecution for their faith, one of their greatest concerns was to establish here an order of freedom. This was not accomplished overnight, and the struggle to complete it continues to this day.

II

But there is no question in anybody's mind concerning the nature of the American political order. Here an order exists in which all that civilized men hold dear depends for its security on the providence of God and the intelligence, the religious conviction, the political wisdom and the common sense of the individual citizen, acting singly and in concert with others.

This order exists, but it is the nature of such an order that its existence is always precarious. It holds in tension freedom and authority. It does so within a context in which freedom must limit itself and authority must recognize ground rules. We are reminded of the danger in which the civic exercise of private judgment always stands by periodic outbreaks of political or ecclesiastical mccarthyism, or by churchly attempts to censor, to suppress discussion or to control education. The dangers are not all found in one area. Efforts of men in church or government to suppress the flow of information needed for the effective use of private judgment, efforts to abridge individual freedom of speech, assembly, press and the right of petition constantly recur and must be valiantly resisted. The peril in which freedom stands even finds echoes in the efforts of political candidates to inhibit discussion of vital issues because the communists may be listening or because our allies may take offense.

III

Protestantism has suffered damage in this fall's presidential election campaign in being assailed by the shallow but persistent criticism which equates any mention of religion with bigotry. The religion of any candidate who belongs to a church which is or claims to be a political as well as an ecclesiastical power is a legitimate subject for discussion. Protestants who consider this question in perspective, along with other issues, have no reason to apologize for assessing it. Such action is nothing more than a responsible exercise of their right and duty of private judgment.

The damage received by the Roman Catholic Church in this election is of a different character. The doctrine of the church has been held up to the country as an ideological liability of the candidate who holds membership in it. He and other Catholic laymen have had to dissociate themselves from the practices of their church in Spain and other places where its authority is great. They have felt they must specifically repudiate the authority of the church in civil affairs in the United States. Nobody expects that this repudiation will produce a formal change in church polity; the opinions of the laity do not carry that much weight. But their declaration of independence, their exercise of private judgment, is nevertheless significant. It is irreversible. And it is likely to spread.

In conclusion, it would be deeply regrettable if Reformation Sunday were to be diverted this year into a gigantic anti-Catholic rally, as some fundamentalist groups urge should be done. Such political misuse of Protestant churches would tend to discredit among Catholics their growing practice of using private judgment in widening fields of political and personal decision. Also, such action would spread among Protestants the authoritarianism, the use of the church as an instrument of political power, against which the Reformation protested. The complicated issues of the presidential campaign, including that of the religious affiliation of the candidates, must be decided on their merits. These merits are not all on one side. Protestants and Catholics should reaffirm and exercise their basic right of private judgment in deciding between these merits.

PART TWELVE

Beyond Race
An Ecumenical Law

53. Edward Kennedy

Favoritism based on nationality will disappear

The Immigration Act of 1965, like the civil rights legislation of the previous year, was not revolutionary. Rather, it was a reassertion and return to the American liberal tradition. It peremptorily rejected the racist assumptions of an earlier era, amended those sections of the Immigration and Nationality Act of 1952 incorporating the original national origins quota system, and set up individual rather than group criteria for the admission of immigrants. The debate in the United States Senate before the passage of the bill reflected the full gamut of hopes and fears that had molded American public opinion for well over a century.

Edward Kennedy of Massachusetts voiced the sentiments of all Americans aggrieved by the un-American national origins quota system. Sam J. Ervin of North Carolina expressed the views of a dwindling Anglo-Saxon Southern minority still committed to the national origins quota system. Hiram Fong of Hawaii spoke for the nonwhite immigrants whose claim to equality the new bill was to legitimize for the first time. Their varying perspectives underlined the critical nature of the legislation as an earnest of the nation's high sense of fair play as it looked inward to itself and outward to world public opinion. A major negative feature of the bill, however, which the Democratic administration was forced to accept as the price for Southern votes, was a limit on immigration from the Western hemisphere, hitherto immune from any quota controls.

Mr. [Edward] Kennedy [of Massachusetts]. Mr. President, the bill we are considering today accomplishes major reforms in our

From U.S., Congress, Senate, *Congressional Record*, 89th Cong., 1st Sess., 111, September 17, 20, 21, 22, 1965, pp. 24225–29 passim, 24231–33 passim, 24446–51 passim, 24467–68 passim.

immigration policy. This bill is not concerned with increasing immigration to this country, nor will it lower any of the high standards we apply in selection of immigrants. The basic change it makes is the elimination of the national origins quota system in line with the recommendations of the last four Presidents of the United States and Members of Congress from both parties.

For forty-one years the immigration policy of our country has been crippled by this system. Because of it we have never been able to achieve the annual quota use authorized by law. We have discriminated in favor of some people over others, contrary to our basic principles as a nation, simply on the basis of birth. We have separated families needlessly. We have been forced to forgo the talents of many professionals whose skills were needed to cure, to teach, and to enhance the lives of Americans.

The present law has caused thousands of instances of personal hardship, of which every senator is aware. Several times Congress has tried to correct the twisted results of the national origins system through emergency legislation. Six times between 1948 and 1962 laws were passed for the admission of refugees. Four times between 1957 and 1962 we have made special provisions for relatives of American citizens or orphans. In addition, each year we are called upon to consider thousands of private bills to accommodate persons caught in the backwash of this origins system.

These efforts at circumvention are further proof that the national origins system is in disrepute. We cannot continue to respect a law we constantly seek to circumvent. To continue with such a law brings discredit upon ourselves as legislators. The national origins system has even failed in the purpose for which it was intended: to keep the ethnic balance of our country forever as it was in 1920. In 1920, 79 percent of our white population was of northern and western European origin. During the first 30 years of the national origins system, only 39 percent of our total immigration came from such areas. Since 1952, some 3.5 million persons have been admitted to this country as immigrants. Two-thirds of them came outside the national origins quota. Since 1952, we have authorized 2.1 million national origins quota numbers. Only one-half of these numbers were used.

From these figures it was obvious to the Judiciary Committee that the current system is as much a failure as a device as it is an embarrassment as a doctrine. The bill now before the Senate abolishes it altogether.

The new policy in the bill before us was developed under the administration of President Kennedy by experts both in Congress and the executive branch. Extensive hearings were held both last year and this, in the Senate and the House. The Senate Immigration Subcommittee has sat regularly since last February. We have heard over fifty witnesses. I can report, Mr. President, that opposition to this measure is minimal. Many of the private organizations who differed with us in the past now agree the national origins system must be eliminated.

The current bill phases out the national origins system over a three-year period. Beginning July 1, 1968, our immigration policy will be based on the concept of "first come, first served." We no longer will ask a man where he was born. Instead we will ask if he seeks to join his family, or if he can help meet the economic and social needs of the Nation. Favoritism based on nationality will disappear. Favoritism based on individual worth and qualifications will take its place. . . .

There have been, however, certain questions raised in the course of our hearings that indicated certain fears or concerns in the minds of some interested people. I would like to set them straight.

First was the fear that this legislation would result in a significant increase in overall immigration. As I have previously stated, the number of quotas authorized each year will not be substantially increased. The world total—exclusive of Western Hemisphere—will be 170,000, an increase of approximately 11,500 over current authorization. But 10,200 of that increase is accounted for by the inclusion of refugees in our general law for the first time.

There will be some increase in total immigration to the United States—about 50,000 to 60,000 per year. This results from changing the law from an individual country quota system to a worldwide system. These are the numbers that go unused each year because quota numbers given to a country that are not utilized are wasted. By removing that obstacle to use, all numbers authorized will now be used, thus the increase in immigration will be about the same as the number of quotas now wasted. More specifically, the future use of numbers can be estimated as follows. Under this bill, we will use the 170,000 numbers given to the world, exclusive of the Western Hemisphere, and about 60,000 more for immediate relatives. Over the past 10 years we have averaged 110,000 per year from the Western Hemisphere. This should continue, along with approximately 15,000 immediate relatives. Thus we will admit an estimated total of 355,000. This is but a 60,000 increase in total immigration over our average total for the last decade.

We are talking about 60,000 people, in a population nearing 200 million, that is growing, without immigration, at a rate of 3 million per year. The percentage increase that immigration will represent is infinitesimally small. This legislation opens no "floodgate." Rather it admits about the same number of immigrants that current law would allow, but for the national origins restriction.

Another fear is that immigrants from nations other than those in northern Europe will not assimilate into our society. The difficulty with this argument is that it comes 40 years too late. Hundreds of thousands of such immigrants have come here in recent years, and their adjustment has been notable. At my request, many voluntary agencies that assist new immigrants conducted lengthy surveys covering people who have arrived since the late 1940's. The results would be most gratifying to any American. I have only found five cases of criminal complaints involving immigrants in our studies of many thousands. Unemployment rates among these people are much lower than the national average; business ownership between 10 percent and 15 percent higher; home ownership as high as 80 percent in one city and averaging about 30 percent elsewhere. Economic self-sufficiency after approximately 4½ months from the date of arrival. By every standard of assimilation these immigrants have adjusted faster than any previous group.

In whatever other definition we wish to give to assimilate, we would find our new residents doing well. Family stability is found to be excellent; cases of immigrants on public welfare are difficult to find; 85 to 95 percent of those eligible have become naturalized citizens, and so forth.

The fact is, Mr. President, that the people who comprise the new immigration—the type which this bill would give preference to—are relatively well educated and well to do. They are familiar with American ways. They share our ideals. Our merchandise, our styles, our patterns of living are an integral part of their own countries. Many of them learn English as a second language in their schools. In an age of global television and the universality of American culture, their assimilation, in a real sense, begins before they come here.

Finally, the fear is raised that under this bill immigrants will be taking jobs away from Americans at a time we find it difficult to lower our unemployment rate below 4 percent. Mr. President, I have already described the more stringent controls that this bill gives to the Secretary of Labor to insure against any adverse effects of immigration on American labor. I would also point out that this measure has the complete support of the AFL–CIO; support that would not be forthcoming if the fear of job loss for Americans were real.

The fact is that most immigrants do not enter the labor market at all—they are consumers and create demands for additional labor. Since 1947, only 47 percent of our total immigration entered the labor force, while 53 percent became consumers only, providing a net increase in the demand for goods and services. Of our total immigrant work force since 1947, approximately one-third entered professional and technical occupations—a ratio higher than that for our own domestic labor force. Last year alone, some 20,000 immigrants entered jobs defined as critical occupations by the Selective Service System. These are the people whose creativity makes more jobs, not fewer. . . .

Mr. [Sam] Ervin [of North Carolina]. Mr. President, I have

been involved, as a member of the Subcommittee on Immigration and Naturalization since February, with the processes which have led to the presentation to the Senate of the pending bill. I believe I can truthfully say that the bill in its present form is a result of the legislative process working in its finest fashion. The bill represents the combined efforts of many men who entertain divergent views upon many aspects of the legislation, and it represents a compromise of those divergent positions of interested members of the subcommittee on various features of the bill. In its present form, it is a bill which I can support with good grace. . . .

I disagree with the view that the national origins quota system devised by those two great American legislators, Senator Pat McCarran and Representative Francis Walter, is discriminatory either in purpose or in effect. To be sure, the national origins quota system prescribed by the act which bears the names of those two eminent Americans gave larger quotas to certain of the countries of western and northern Europe than to countries elsewhere in the Eastern Hemisphere. It did so for what I conceive to have been a very good reason, that is, because the people who originally came to the United States from those countries and their descendants constituted the major portion of the population and thus had made the greatest contributions to the culture and development of America. . . .

The purpose of the national origins quota system under the McCarran-Walter Act was to receive for permanent residence in America and for eventual citizenship, immigrants who had cultural backgrounds similar to those of the people already here, and who for that reason were most readily assimilable into our way of life. . . .

There was one serious defect in the bill before us, and in the McCarran-Walter Act; and that defect arose out of the fact that while existing immigration laws placed a limitation upon the number of immigrants receivable from countries of the Eastern Hemisphere, they placed no limitation whatever upon the number of immigrants admissible from the Western Hemisphere.

I know of no one in Congress at the present moment who favors unrestricted immigration. I am satisfied, from my work with them, that all of the other members of the Subcommittee on Immigration and Naturalization of the Senate Committee on the Judiciary favor reasonable restrictions on immigration, and that such disagreements that may have existed in the past in respect to this point were concerned only with ways in which that objective could be best attained.

I felt that it was unjust to all the people of the Western Hemisphere for the United States to say, "We are willing to have all of you move into the United States," and at that same time place in the immigration laws provisions which would deny them admission, after such a broad invitation had been extended, because of their failure to meet certain labor requirements of the laws. To my mind, there was a certain amount of hypocrisy in the immigration laws which made that proclamation and had that effect. It seemed to me that it was like inviting a man to dinner, and then digging a pit for him to fall into before he could get to the dinner table.

Accordingly, I thought that, in order to abolish the hypocrisy which our existing immigration laws practice, telling the people of the Western Hemisphere that they are all welcome to move into the United States immediately, we should place a reasonable limitation upon immigration from the countries of the Western Hemisphere, as we did in the case of immigration from the countries of the Eastern Hemisphere.

I felt that in addition to there being something in the nature of legislative hypocrisy in the existing immigration laws in this respect, it was also a gross discrimination against all the people of the Eastern Hemisphere for us to have immigration laws which specified that only a limited number could come in from the Eastern Hemisphere but that, on the contrary, unlimited numbers could move into the United States from the Western Hemisphere.

For that reason, I submitted an amendment to provide a limitation on immigration from the Western Hemisphere. As the distinguished Senator from Massachusetts has stated, the pending bill, with that amendment, would place a limitation on immigrants from the Western Hemisphere of 120,000 annually, plus the spouses and the children of American citizens who may come from those countries outside and above the limitation.

To enable the immigration authorities to adjust their action to this new limitation, the bill would provide that it would not become effective until the 1st day of July 1968.

To me, it is vitally important for the amendment to be retained in the Senate and for the Senate conferees to insist upon its retention, in the event it should become necessary to have a conference with the House upon the bill.

Those who disagree with the wisdom of my amendment contend that special privileges are warranted by the special relationship which exists between us and our hemispheric neighbors.

I submit that there is no relationship which is closer or more special than that which our country bears to England, our great ally, which gave us our language, our law, and much of our literature. Yet, under the pending bill, those who disagree with me express no shock that Britain, in the future, can send us 10,000 fewer immigrants than she has sent on an annual average in the past. They are only shocked that British Guiana cannot send us every single citizen of that country who wishes to come.

Those who disagree with me on this point say that there is nothing invidious in the discrimination in favor of the Western Hemisphere, because the discrimination "is not based on race, religion, or ethnic origin." They fail to note that every witness at the hearings agreed with me that there was also no discrimination based on race, religion, or ethnic origin in the national origins quota system of the McCarran-Walter Act. Yet, those who disagree with me never failed to take the opportunity to castigate that system as discriminatory.

Mr. President, a man born in England, be he Catholic, Jew, or Protestant, is charged to the British quota. The system allows immigration according to place of birth, just as the present bill does. Under it, a person born in the Western Hemisphere would be charged to the Western Hemisphere ceiling. A man born in the

Eastern Hemisphere would be charged to the Eastern Hemisphere ceiling.

This bill creates a commission to study the Western Hemisphere problem, among others. I suggest the possibility that this commission might find that the ceiling which the bill establishes for immigration from the Western Hemisphere is still too discriminatory, since it allows 45 percent of immigrants to come from only 15 percent of the world's population.

I have also heard it said that the ceiling will somehow adversely affect the Alliance for Progress. This is a perverse argument, indeed, since under the labor restrictions imposed, we will take only the best of those we are helping to train. I hope that those in charge of administering the Alliance for Progress will understand the necessity of keeping the best qualified where they are most needed, which is in the Latin American countries.

The substance of my amendment has been endorsed by the *New York Times*, the *Christian Science Monitor*, the *Minneapolis Tribune*, the *St. Paul Pioneer Press*, and the distinguished columnist Charles Bartlett.

On July 17, 1965, the *New York Times* published an editorial entitled "Progress on Immigration." I wish to read this portion:

> Secretary Rusk urges that Latin-American nations remain outside any ceiling, as they are now outside of the quota system. But this well-intentioned position could lead to trouble and ill will in the not so distant future if immigration from Latin America and the Caribbean should grow sharply—as there are signs that it will—and pressure were then built up to limit a sudden flood of immigrants for which the country was unprepared. While the entire law is being overhauled, it would be better to place all the nations of the world, including those to the south of the United States, on exactly the same footing.

Ideal of Brotherhood, Equality

[HIRAM FONG—HAWAII] We live in brotherhood; we believe in it, for we know it has real prospect for success nationally and internationally, and it has the force of logic.

Believing in this ideal and constantly working to achieve it, we cannot but write from our books the discriminatory quota provisions of the Immigration and Nationality Act, which give offense to many peoples of the world.

During my tour of the Far East and southeast Asia, I was asked many questions about our immigration policies. I was pressed again and again to explain the small quotas we allot inhabitants of those nations. These people feel greatly the sting of discriminatory treatment.

America's role of leadership in the free world is one of great sensitivity, and our position is hardly enhanced by an immigration policy which implies that some nationalities and some ethnic groups are less desirable members of the American family.

Many countries of Asia and the Pacific have traditionally sought more than a token of immigration to the United States. These are the countries that will play a large and vital role in determining the future course of world events. Their friendship is crucial to all those who are fighting to preserve freedom.

The problem of immigration is no longer merely a domestic issue; on the contrary, it has great international significance. . . .

America's struggle with totalitarianism is a struggle to vindicate democracy's belief in the individual worth of human beings, as opposed to the totalitarian concept that individuals have no identity except as components in the political and economic structure of society.

Until the racial incongruities of our present basic immigration laws which discriminate against certain national and ethnic groups are eliminated, our laws needlessly impede our struggle for global peace.

Our forebears, coming to America from all corners of the world, have worked together to transform a vast continent of wilderness and desert into a powerful bastion of freedom and opportunity.

Mr. President, our Nation is the great pilot demonstration of the most influential principles and ideals in history. Our tenets of equality irrespective of race, creed, or color have inspired freedom-loving people everywhere to look to America as a beacon in their struggle to win freedom and independence. Our opportunity is to live up to these ideals.

Since 1924 we have come a long way in our immigration laws. Let us go the final mile in writing a fair and just law. We will then be demonstrating to the world that we practice what we preach, and that all men are equal under law.

54. THE IMMIGRATION AND NATIONALITY ACT

No person shall be discriminated against

The Immigration Act of 1965 repealed the national origins quota system that had governed American immigration policy since 1924. It did not, however, return the United States to its nineteenth-century policy of unrestricted immigration, a policy now without advocates. The law did eliminate all vestiges of racism progressively grafted on American immigration policy. The new law of the land no longer distinguished among immigrants on the basis of race or national origins. But it did establish new quotas that favored immigrants with family ties or with skills that were much in demand in the United States. The new law set an annual limit of 170,000 immigrants from outside the Western hemisphere, with a maximum of 20,000 for any individual country, exclusive of any "immediate relatives" of American citizens. Immigration from the Western hemisphere was set at 120,000 annually.

AN ACT TO AMEND THE IMMIGRATION AND NATIONALITY ACT, AND FOR OTHER PURPOSES.

[H. R. 2580] October 3, 1965

Public Law 89–236

Be it enacted by the Senate and House of Representatives of the United States of America in Congress assembled, That section 201 of the Immigration and Nationality Act (66 Stat. 175; 8 U.S.C. 1151) be amended to read as follows:

From U.S., *Statutes at Large*, 89th Cong., 1st Sess., LXXIX, October 3, 1965, pp. 911–21.

SEC. 201. (a) Exclusive of special immigrants defined in section 101(a) (27), and of the immediate relatives of United States citizens specified in subsection (b) of this section, the number of aliens who may be issued immigrant visas or who may otherwise acquire the status of an alien lawfully admitted to the United States for permanent residence, or who may, pursuant to section 203(a) (7) enter conditionally, (i) shall not in any of the first three quarters of any fiscal year exceed a total of 45,000 and (ii) shall not in any fiscal year exceed a total of 170,000.

(b) The 'immediate relatives' referred to in subsection (a) of this section shall mean the children, spouses, and parents of a citizen of the United States: *Provided,* That in the case of parents, such citizen must be at least twenty-one years of age. The immediate relatives specified in this subsection who are otherwise qualified for admission as immigrants shall be admitted as such, without regard to the numerical limitations in this Act. . . .

SEC. 2. Section 202 of the Immigration and Nationality Act (66 Stat. 175; 8 U.S.C. 1152) is amended to read as follows:

(a) No person shall receive any preference or priority or be discriminated against in the issuance of an immigrant visa because of his race, sex, nationality, place of birth, or place of residence, except as specifically provided in section 101(a) (27), section 201(b), and section 203: *Provided,* That the total number of immigrant visas and the number of conditional entries made available to natives of any single foreign state under paragraphs (1) through (8) of section 203(a) shall not exceed 20,000 in any fiscal year: *Provided further,* That the foregoing proviso shall not operate to reduce the number of immigrants who may be admitted under the quota of any quota area before June 30, 1968.

(b) Each independent country, self-governing dominion, mandated territory, and territory under the international trusteeship system of the United Nations, other than the United States and its outlying possessions shall be treated as a separate foreign state for the purposes of the numerical limitation set forth in the proviso to subsection (a) of this section when approved by the Secretary of State. All other inhabited lands shall be attributed to a foreign state specified by the Secretary of State. For the purposes of this Act the foreign state to which an immigrant is chargeable shall be determined by birth within such foreign state except that (1) an alien child, when accompanied by his alien parent or parents, may be charged to the same foreign state as the accompanying parent or of either accompanying parent if such parent has received or would be qualified for an immigrant visa, if necessary to prevent the separation of the child from the accompanying parent or parents, and if the foreign state to which such parent has been or would be chargeable has not exceeded the numerical limitation set forth in the proviso to subsection (a) of this section for that fiscal year; (2) if an alien is chargeable to a different foreign state from that of his accompanying spouse, the foreign state to which such alien is chargeable may, if necessary to prevent the separation of husband and wife, be determined by the foreign state of the accompanying spouse, if such spouse has received or would be qualified for an immigrant visa and if the foreign state to which such spouse has been or would be chargeable has not exceeded the numerical limitation set forth in the proviso to subsection (a) of this section for that fiscal year; (3) an alien born in the United States shall be considered as having been born in the country of which he is a citizen or subject, or if he is not a citizen or subject of any country then in the last foreign country in which he had his residence as determined by the consular officer; (4) an alien born within any foreign state in which neither of his parents was born and in which neither of his parents had a residence at the time of such alien's birth may be charged to the foreign state of either parent.

(c) Any immigrant born in a colony or other component or dependent area of a foreign state unless a special immigrant as provided in section 101(a) (27) or an immediate relative of a United States citizen as specified in section 201(b), shall be chargeable, for the purpose of limitation set forth in section 202(a), to the foreign state, except that the number of persons born in any such colony or other component or dependent area overseas from the foreign state chargeable to the foreign state in any one fiscal year shall not exceed 1 per centum of the maximum number of immigrant visas available to such foreign state.

(d) In the case of any change in the territorial limits of foreign states, the Secretary of State shall, upon recognition of such change, issue appropriate instructions to all diplomatic and consular offices.

SEC. 3. Section 203 of the Immigration and Nationality Act (66 Stat. 175; 8 U.S.C. 1153) is amended to read as follows:

Sec. 203. (a) Aliens who are subject to the numerical limitations specified in section 201(a) shall be allotted visas or their conditional entry authorized, as the case may be, as follows:

(1) Visas shall be first made available, in a number not to exceed 20 per centum of the number specified in section 201(a) (ii), to qualified immigrants who are the unmarried sons or daughters of citizens of the United States.

(2) Visas shall next be made available, in a number not to exceed 20 per centum of the number specified in section 201(a) (ii), plus any visas not required for the classes specified in paragraph (1), to qualified immigrants who are the spouses, unmarried sons or unmarried daughters of an alien lawfully admitted for permanent residence.

(3) Visas shall next be made available, in a number not to exceed 10 per centum of the number specified in section 201(a) (ii), to qualified immigrants who are members of the professions, or who because of their exceptional ability in the sciences or the arts will substantially benefit prospectively the national economy, cultural interests, or welfare of the United States.

(4) Visas shall next be made available, in a number not to exceed 10 per centum of the number specified in section 201(a) (ii), plus any visas not required for the classes specified in paragraphs (1) through (3), to qualified immigrants who are the married sons or the married daughters of citizens of the United States.

(5) Visas shall next be made available, in a number not to exceed 24 per centum of the number specified in section 201(a) (ii), plus any visas not required for the classes specified in paragraphs (1) through (4), to qualified immigrants who are the brothers or sisters of citizens of the United States.

(6) Visas shall next be made available, in a number not to exceed 10 per centum of the number specified in section 201(a) (ii), to qualified immigrants who are capable of performing specified skilled or unskilled labor, not of a temporary or seasonal nature, for which a shortage of employable and willing persons exists in the United States.

(7) Conditional entries shall next be made available by the Attorney General, pursuant to such regulations as he may prescribe and in a number not to exceed 6 per centum of the number specified in section 201(a) (ii), to aliens who satisfy an Immigration and Naturalization Service officer at an examination in any non-Commu-

nist or non-Communist-dominated country, (A) that (i) because of persecution or fear of persecution on account of race, religion, or political opinion they have fled (I) from any Communist or Communist-dominated country or area, or (II) from any country within the general area of the Middle East, and (ii) are unable or unwilling to return to such country or area on account of race, religion, or political opinion, and (iii) are not nationals of the countries or areas in which their application for conditional entry is made; or (B) that they are persons uprooted by catastrophic natural calamity as defined by the President who are unable to return to their usual place of abode. For the purpose of the foregoing the term 'general area of the Middle East' means the area between and including (1) Libya on the west, (2) Turkey on the north, (3) Pakistan on the east, and (4) Saudi Arabia and Ethiopia on the south: *Provided,* That immigrant visas in a number not exceeding one-half the number specified in this paragraph may be made available, in lieu of conditional entries of a like number, to such aliens who have been continuously physically present in the United States for a period of at least two years prior to application for adjustment of status.

(8) Visas authorized in any fiscal year, less those required for issuance to the classes specified in paragraphs (1) through (6) and less the number of conditional entries and visas made available pursuant to paragraph (7), shall be made available to other qualified immigrants strictly in the chronological order in which they qualify. Waiting lists of applicants shall be maintained in accordance with regulations prescribed by the Secretary of State. No immigrant visa shall be issued to a nonpreference immigrant under this paragraph, or to an immigrant with a preference under paragraph (3) or (6) of this subsection, until the consular officer is in receipt of a determination made by the Secretary of Labor pursuant to the provisions of section 212(a) (14).

(9) (a) A spouse or child as defined in section 101(b) (1) (A), (B), (C), (D), or (E) shall, if not otherwise entitled to an immigrant status and the immediate issuance of a visa or to conditional entry under paragraphs (1) through (8), be entitled to the same status, and the same order of consideration provided in subsection (b), if accompanying, or following to join, his spouse or parent.

(b) In considering applications for immigrant visas under subsection (a) consideration shall be given to applicants in the order in which the classes of which they are members are listed in subsection (a).

(c) Immigrant visas issued pursuant to paragraphs (1) through (6) of subsection (a) shall be issued to eligible immigrants in the order in which a petition in behalf of each such immigrant is filed with the Attorney General as provided in section 204.

(d) Every immigrant shall be presumed to be a nonpreference immigrant until he establishes to the satisfaction of the consular officer and the immigration officer that he is entitled to a preference status under paragraphs (1) through (7) of subsection (a), or to a special immigrant status under section 101(a) (27), or that he is an immediate relative of a United States citizen as specified in section 201(b). In the case of any alien claiming in his application for an immigrant visa to be an immediate relative of a United States citizen as specified in section 201(b) or to be entitled to preference immigrant status under paragraphs (1) through (6) of subsection (a), the consular officer shall not grant such status until he has been authorized to do so as provided by section 204.

(e) For the purposes of carrying out his responsibilities in the orderly administration of this section, the Secretary of State is authorized to make reasonable estimates of the anticipated numbers of visas to be issued during any quarter of any fiscal year within each of the categories of subsection (a), and to rely upon such estimates in authorizing the issuance of such visas. The Secretary of State, in his discretion, may terminate the registration on a waiting list of any alien who fails to evidence his continued intention to apply for a visa in such manner as may be by regulation prescribed.

(f) The Attorney General shall submit to the Congress a report containing complete and detailed statement of facts in the case of each alien who conditionally entered the United States pursuant to subsection (a) (7) of this section. Such reports shall be submitted on or before January 15 and June 15 of each year.

(g) Any alien who conditionally entered the United States as a refugee, pursuant to subsection (a) (7) of this section, whose conditional entry has not been terminated by the Attorney General pursuant to such regulations as he may prescribe, who has been in the United States for at least two years, and who has not acquired permanent residence, shall forthwith return or be returned to the custody of the Immigration and Naturalization Service and shall thereupon be inspected and examined for admission into the United

States, and his case dealt with in accordance with the provisions of sections 235, 236, and 237 of this Act.

(h) Any alien who, pursuant to subsection (g) of this section, is found, upon inspection by the immigration officer or after hearing before a special inquiry officer, to be admissible as an immigrant under this Act at the time of his inspection and examination, except for the fact that he was not and is not in possession of the documents required by section 212(a) (20), shall be regarded as lawfully admitted to the United States for permanent residence as of the date of his arrival.

SEC. 4. Section 204 of the Immigration and Nationality Act (66 Stat. 176; 8 U.S.C. 1154) is amended to read as follows:

SEC. 204. (a) Any citizen of the United States claiming that an alien is entitled to a preference status by reason of the relationships described in paragraphs (1), (4), or (5) of section 203(a), or to an immediate relative status under section 201(b), or any alien lawfully admitted for permanent residence claiming that an alien is entitled to a preference status by reason of the relationship described in section 203(a) (2), or any alien desiring to be classified as a preference immigrant under section 203(a) (3) (or any person on behalf of such an alien), or any person desiring and intending to employ within the United States an alien entitled to classification as a preference immigrant under section 203(a) (6), may file a petition with the Attorney General for such classification. The petition shall be in such form as the Attorney General may by regulations prescribe and shall contain such information and be supported by such documentary evidence as the Attorney General may require. The petition shall be made under oath administered by any individual having authority to administer oaths, if executed in the United States, but, if executed outside the United States, administered by a consular officer or an immigration officer.

(b) After an investigation of the facts in each case, and after consultation with the Secretary of Labor with respect to petitions to accord a status under section 203(a) (3) or (6), the Attorney General shall, if he determines that the facts stated in the petition are true and that the alien in behalf of whom the petition is made is an immediate relative specified in section 201(b) or is eligible for a preference status under section 203(a), approve the petition and forward one copy thereof to the Department of State. The Secretary of State shall then authorize the consular officer concerned to grant the preference status.

(c) Notwithstanding the provisions of subsection (b) no more than two petitions may be approved for one petitioner in behalf of a child as defined in section 101(b) (1) (E) or (F) unless necessary to prevent the separation of brothers and sisters and no petition shall be approved if the alien has previously been accorded a nonquota or preference status as the spouse of a citizen of the United States or the spouse of an alien lawfully admitted for permanent residence, by reason of a marriage determined by the Attorney General to have been entered into for the purpose of evading the immigration laws.

(d) The Attorney General shall forward to the Congress a report on each approved petition for immigrant status under sections 203(a) (3) or 203(a) (6) stating the basis for his approval and such facts as were by him deemed to be pertinent in establishing the beneficiary's qualifications for the preferential status. Such reports shall be submitted to the Congress on the first and fifteenth day of each calendar month in which the Congress is in session.

(e) Nothing in this section shall be construed to entitle an immigrant, in behalf of whom a petition under this section is approved, to enter the United States as a preference immigrant under section 203(a) or as an immediate relative under section 201(b) if upon his arrival at a port of entry in the United States he is found not to be entitled to such classification. . . .

Sec. 21. (a) There is hereby established a Select Commission on Western Hemisphere Immigration (hereinafter referred to as the "Commission") to be composed of fifteen members. The President shall appoint the Chairman of the Commission and four other members thereof. The President of the Senate, with the approval of the majority and minority leaders of the Senate, shall appoint five members from the membership of the Senate. The Speaker of the House of Representatives, with the approval of the majority and minority leaders of the House, shall appoint five members from the membership of the House. Not more than three members appointed by the President of the Senate and the Speaker of the House of Representatives, respectively, shall be members of the same political party. A vacancy in the membership of the

Commission shall be filled in the same manner as the original designation and appointment.

(b) The Commission shall study the following matters:

(1) Prevailing and projected demographic, technological, and economic trends, particularly as they pertain to Western Hemisphere nations;

(2) Present and projected unemployment in the United States, by occupations, industries, geographic areas and other factors, in relation to immigration from the Western Hemisphere;

(3) The interrelationships between immigration, present and future, and existing and contemplated national and international programs and projects of Western Hemisphere nations, including programs and projects for economic and social development;

(4) The operation of the immigration laws of the United States as they pertain to Western Hemisphere nations, including the adjustment of status for Cuban refugees, with emphasis on the adequacy of such laws from the standpoint of fairness and from the standpoint of the impact of such laws on employment and working conditions within the United States;

(5) The implications of the foregoing with respect to the security and international relations of Western Hemisphere nations; and

(6) Any other matters which the Commission believes to be germane to the purposes for which it was established.

(c) On or before July 1, 1967, the Commission shall make a first report to the President and the Congress, and on or before January 15, 1968, the Commission shall make a final report to the President and the Congress. Such reports shall include the recommendations of the Commission as to what changes, if any, are needed in the immigration laws in the light of its study. The Commission's recommendations shall include, but shall not be limited to, recommendations as to whether, and if so how, numerical limitations should be imposed upon immigration to the United States from the nations of the Western Hemisphere. In formulating its recommendations on the latter subject, the

Commission shall give particular attention to the impact of such immigration on employment and working conditions within the United States and to the necessity of preserving the special relationship of the United States with its sister Republics of the Western Hemisphere.

(d) The life of the Commission shall expire upon the filing of its final report, except that the Commission may continue to function for up to sixty days thereafter for the purpose of winding up its affairs. . . .

55. LYNDON B. JOHNSON

This grand old lady is brighter today

On October 3, 1965, in front of the Statue of Liberty in New York harbor, President Lyndon B. Johnson signed into law HR 2580 which enunciated the new criteria for the admission of immigrants.

The main passages in the text of President Johnson's address communicate the spirit of this historic occasion.

. . . This bill that we sign today is not a revolutionary bill. It does not affect the lives of millions. It will not reshape the structure of our daily lives, or really add importantly to either our wealth or our power. Yet it is still one of the most important acts of this Congress and of this Administration. For it does repair a very deep and painful flaw in the fabric of American justice. It corrects a cruel and enduring wrong in the conduct of the American nation.

Speaker McCormack and Congressman Celler more than almost forty years ago first pointed that out in their maiden speeches in the Congress. And this measure that we will sign

Lyndon Johnson, remarks on immigration law, *Congressional Quarterly* 23 (October 1965); 2063–64.

today will really make us truer to ourselves both as a country and as a people. It will strengthen us in a hundred unseen ways. . . .

This bill says simply that from this day forth those wishing to emigrate to America shall be admitted on the basis of their skills and their close relationship to those already here.

This is a simple test, and it is a fair test. Those who can contribute most to this country—to its growth, to its strength, to its spirit—will be the first that are admitted to this land.

The fairness of this standard is so self evident that we may well wonder that it has not always been applied. Yet the fact is that for over four decades the immigration policy of the United States has been twisted and has been distorted by the harsh injustice of the National Origins Quota System.

Under that system the ability of new immigrants to come to America depended upon the country of their birth. Only three countries were allowed to supply seventy percent of all the immigrants. Families were kept apart because a husband or a wife or a child had been born in the wrong place. Men of needed skill and talent were denied entrance because they came from southern or eastern Europe or from one of the developing continents. This system violated the basic principle of American democracy—the principle that values and rewards each man on the basis of his merit as a man. It has been un-American in the highest sense because it has been untrue to the faith that brought thousands to these shores even before we were a country.

Today, with my signature, this system is abolished.

We can now believe that it will never again shadow the gate to the American nation with the twin barriers of prejudice and privilege.

Our beautiful America was built by a nation of strangers. From a hundred different places or more, they have poured forth into an empty land—joining and blending in one mighty and irresistible tide.

The land flourished because it was fed from so many sources— because it was nourished by so many cultures and traditions and peoples.

And from this experience, almost unique in the history of nations, has come America's attitude toward the rest of the world. We, because of what we are, feel safer and stronger in a world as varied as the people who make it up—a world where no country rules another and all countries can deal with the basic problems of human dignity and deal with those problems in their own way.

Now, under the monument which has welcomed so many to our shores, the American nation returns to the finest of its traditions today. The days of unlimited immigration are past. But those who do come will come because of what they are, and not because of the land from which they sprang.

When the earliest settlers poured into a wild continent there was no one to ask them where they came from. The only question was: Were they sturdy enough to make the journey, were they strong enough to clear the land, were they enduring enough to make a home for freedom, and were they brave enough to die for liberty if it became necessary to do so.

And so it has been through all the great and testing moments of American history. This year we see in Vietnam men dying—men named Fernandez and Zajac and Zelinko and Mariano and McCormick.

Neither the enemy who killed them nor the people whose independence they have fought to save ever asked them where they or their parents came from. They were all Americans. It was for free men and for America that they gave their all, they gave their lives and selves.

By eliminating that same question as a test for immigration the Congress proves ourselves worthy of those men and worthy of our own traditions as a nation. . . .

Over my shoulder here you can see Ellis Island, whose vacant corridors echo today the joyous sounds of long-ago voices.

And today we can all believe that the lamp of this grand old lady is brighter today—and the golden door that she guards gleams more brilliantly in the light of an increased liberty for the people from all the countries of the globe.

Thank you very much.

Index